US & Comparative Government & Politics

Anthony J. Bennett

Philip Allan Updates
Market Place
Deddington
Oxfordshire
OX15 0SE

tel: 01869 338652
fax: 01869 337590
e-mail: sales@philipallan.co.uk
www.philipallan.co.uk

Design and illustrations by Neil Fozzard
Printed by Raithby, Lawrence & Co Ltd, Leicester

P00298

Contents

Section B

US/UK Comparative Government & Politics

Introduction

US & Comparative Government & Politics is a textbook written for students of the A2 specifications offered by Edexcel, OCR and AQA; it covers both parts of these A2 courses. The first nine chapters of this 14-chapter book take you through your course in US Government and Politics. The last five chapters deal with the comparative/synoptic element of the course; this is the first textbook to devote specific chapters to this important part of the A2 specification. Other textbooks have offered only 'add-ons' to the chapters on US politics, or some 'boxes' inserted within them, dealing with some comparative issues.

Using this textbook

You may choose to go through the book in the order in which it is set out, studying US politics first and then moving on to the comparative material. Alternatively, you may prefer to study the comparative material as you complete each chapter of US politics. If you choose the latter, then you would use the book in the following order:

Chapter	1	The Constitution
Chapter	*10A*	*Constitutions*
Chapter	2	Presidential elections
Chapter	*11*	*Elections*
Chapter	3	Political parties
Chapter	*12A*	*Political parties*
Chapter	4	Pressure groups
Chapter	*12B*	*Pressure groups*
Chapter	5	Congress
Chapter	*13*	*Congress and Parliament*
Chapter	6	The presidency
Chapter	7	The federal bureaucracy

Each chapter begins with a short introduction and a series of questions which will be answered during that chapter. Chapters are divided into short sections, each one concluding with a brief 'boxed' summary. 'Key terms' appear in bold in the text and are explained in a separate box nearby. At the end of each chapter, you will find the following:

➢ **Exercises** — provided to help you with note making. If you work through all the exercises at the end of a chapter, you will extract the main points of that chapter. Some of these 'exercise' questions may be used for short-answer essay practice too.

➢ **Exam focus** — essay questions in the style of the long-answer essay papers of the awarding bodies. You can use them either as homework exercises or as in-class essays under examination conditions.

➢ **References** — the details of authors and books quoted during the chapter.

➢ **Further reading** — a few suggestions of up-to-date books on the topic covered in the chapter.

How to improve your performance

What other ways are there to improve your performance? Here are a few suggestions:

➢ **Note making.** Make thorough, well-organised notes both of what you read and of what you are taught in your classes. All your notes should be clearly headed with the area you are studying: Congress, the presidency, the Supreme Court etc.

➢ **Ask questions.** This is an important activity — the learning process is not a spectator sport.

➢ **Keep up to date.** This is especially important in a subject such as government and politics because examiners differentiate the merely competent answers from the really good by rewarding the use of relevant, up-to-date examples. On pages x–xii there are some suggestions of sources — both printed and electronic — which will help you with this.

➢ **Essay writing.** Get as much practice as you can at writing essays under examination conditions. Your teacher/lecturer will doubtless give you practice in classes, but you can do this at home, too, using the 'Exam focus' questions at the end of each chapter. Learn the work and then set yourself to write the answer in whatever time you will be permitted in your final exam. Always plan your essays before starting to write. An essay plan is basically a list of the subjects to be covered in each paragraph. Always ensure that your essay answers the question that has been asked.

Assessment objectives

When writing your essays, always keep in mind that your answers will be marked according to two main assessment objectives (AO):

➢ AO1 — knowledge and understanding
➢ AO2 — analysis and evaluation

AO1 concerns facts. AO2 concerns argument. All your essays must include both ingredients. You must find out from your teacher/lecturer how the marks are allocated between these two main assessment objectives. Whereas at AS there tended to be more marks for AO1 than for AO2, at A2 the mark allocation for AO2 is likely to be as great as, or greater than, that for AO1. In other words, at A2 your essays need to include more in the way of argument and analysis. Therefore it is important that in every essay you focus on the question asked and answer it.

Exam preparation

Exam preparation comes in a number of different forms at different times during your course. First, it will consist of reading through notes of work you did some weeks or months ago, to keep the material fresh in your mind. Second, the time will come when you need to start committing material to memory. Start early. Test yourself often and do not mistake instant recall — being able to say something back to yourself within minutes (or seconds) of looking at it — for *real* learning. You will find it much easier to concentrate if you write things down. Don't try to commit things to memory by just staring at a book. Third, there will be the practice essays that need to be written under a strict time limit.

As the exam season approaches, learn to pace yourself. Plan your work and your time carefully. Take regular breaks. Remove all distractions — you know what they are! Get to bed in good time the night before an examination.

On the day of your exam, ensure that you have all you need before leaving for the examination venue. Arrive in good time.

Once the exam begins, read *all* the questions. Decide which ones you are going to do. Plan each one quickly but carefully. The better you know your material, the less you will have to write as a plan. Watch the time. Don't spend too much time on any one question.

Other sources

It is my hope that American politics is a subject in which you will become genuinely interested. This textbook will give you grounding in the subject, but there are a number of other printed sources which you should try to make use of. Philip Allan Updates, which publishes this textbook, also publishes *Politics Review*, a magazine written exclusively for students of A-level Government and Politics. Issues are published four times each academic year and include articles on US and comparative politics as well as on UK politics.

Philip Allan Updates also publishes the *US Government & Politics Annual Survey*, which updates you on what has happened in Washington over the previous 12 months. It is full of up-to-date examples, tables and anecdotes for you to use in your essays, and is written exclusively for A-level students. As you move towards preparing for your final examinations, yet another Philip Allan Updates resource will prove useful — *US Government & Politics: Exam Revision Notes*. This is a mainly bullet-point guide, which will help you with your revision.

The Economist magazine, published every Friday and available either through your local newsagent or by subscription, contains an invaluable 'American Survey', a collection of around six short, highly readable articles on matters of topical interest in American politics and society. The main UK broadsheet newspapers — *The Times*, *Guardian*, *Independent* and *Daily Telegraph* — include articles on US politics too.

Electronic sources

In this internet age, students of US politics have unrivalled opportunities to access and read a wealth of material which just a decade ago would have been unimaginable. You are strongly urged, as much as your own and your school's resources permit, to use this opportunity. If I could make just one recommendation, it would be to get into the habit of logging on daily to the website of the *Washington Post*, www.washingtonpost.com, one of the best, frequently updated and freely accessible sites. Click on the 'On Politics' button and the world of US politics is there for you to read and browse. True, the *Washington Post* has a clearly liberal perspective on politics, as does the *New York Times* at www.nytimes.com. If you want to see things discussed from a conservative perspective, go to the website of the *Washington Times* at www.washtimes.com and you will get a different slant on events and people.

Other media sites worth looking at include the CNN/*Time* site at www.allpolitics.com as well as that of the Public Broadcasting Service (PBS) at www.pbs.org. On this latter site, click on the 'A–Z of programmes', go to 'N' for 'News Hour with Jim Lehrer', then 'Videos' and, if your computer has the right software, you will be able to watch extracts from the most recent edition and a wealth of archive material that goes back some 4 years. There is even a facility to read the text of the programme.

Here are some websites set out by chapters, which you might find useful.

1 Constitution
www.constitutioncenter.org
www.stateline.org
www.nga.org
www.census.gov

2 Presidential elections
www.politics1.com
www.allpolitics.com
www.uselectionatlas.org
www.gallup.com

3 Political parties
www.democrats.org
www.rnc.org
www.greens.org
www.politics1.com

4 Pressure groups
www.politics1.com
www.policy.com

5 Congress
www.senate.gov
www.house.gov
http://thomas.loc.gov
www.c-span.org

6 The presidency
www.whitehouse.gov

7 The federal bureaucracy
www.whitehouse.gov

8 The Supreme Court
www.fjc.gov
www.uscourts.gov
www.law.cornell.edu

9 Civil rights and liberties
www.law.cornell.edu
www.doj.gov
www.aclu.org

Now it's over to you. I hope you will find these suggestions helpful and that the chapters which follow will help you to understand the way government and politics work in Washington. If you have the chance, get on a plane and go there, if only for a few days. It's a most beautiful city, and those days will bring to life both the text and the photographs in this book. But if you can't see Washington in reality, just make sure you see it electronically. The internet will be your route. It's quicker — and less expensive.

US Government
& Politics

Chapter 1

The Constitution

Most people think they know quite a lot about the USA. Some might have visited part, or parts, of the country, but, for many, their knowledge and experience of the USA will be limited mainly to McDonald's, Coca-Cola, Hollywood, MTV and the Walt Disney Corporation. Of course, they also know something about US politics — they could name the president of the USA.

Students of US politics need to go beyond these superficial images and mere knowledge of names and need to understand more about US society than just what Americans eat and drink and who runs their entertainment industry. They need to realise that US society is still influenced by the principles that led to its establishment over 200 years ago. This will involve learning about some new concepts, such as the separation of powers, federalism and checks and balances. This is not a course in US history; rather, it is a course in contemporary US government and politics. However, it is impossible to appreciate the intricacies of what goes on in Washington today without knowing something about George Washington and the men around him who set up the Republic in 1787.

Questions to be answered in this chapter
➢ What are the important characteristics of the USA?
➢ How did the US Constitution come to be written?
➢ What are the key features of the US Constitution?
➢ How are amendments to the US Constitution made?
➢ What is the doctrine of the separation of powers?
➢ How do the 'checks and balances' of the Constitution work?
➢ What is federalism and how has it changed?

The size and diversity of the USA

The USA is a vast country. The entire UK would fit into the state of Oregon. From coast to coast is over 3,000 miles (4,800 kilometres) and in covering that distance — from, say, New York to San Francisco — the traveller would encounter four different time zones (see Figure 1.1). At midday in London, it is 7 a.m. in New York but still 4 a.m. on the west coast. A non-stop jet takes 6–7 hours to travel across the country — only slightly less than the time to travel across the Atlantic from London to Boston. A train journey from Washington DC to Chicago, across the northern plains of North Dakota and Montana, through the Rockies and on to Portland, Oregon would take $2\frac{1}{2}$ days. These are sizes and distances unthinkable within the UK.

Figure 1.1 Time zones of the 48 contiguous states of the USA

The USA is also a very diverse country. There is the tropical landscape of Florida but also the frozen Arctic wastes of Alaska. There are the flat prairies of Kansas but also the Rockies of Wyoming and Colorado. There are the deserts of Arizona but also the forests of New Hampshire and Maine. It is diverse in its landscape, its climate, its economy and its people. The USA is also 'the hyphenated society', in which people think of themselves as African-Americans, Irish-Americans, Polish-Americans, Japanese-Americans or even Native-Americans. American society has been described as a 'melting pot' — a great cauldron filled with people from diverse lands, cultures, languages and religions.

This diversity gives rise to Americans' need for symbols of unity — most notably in their attachment to the American flag. While flag waving is regarded as something of an oddity in the UK — generally associated with football supporters or the Last Night of the Proms — countless families in rural and suburban America go through the daily

Figure 1.2 Regions of the 48 contiguous states of the USA

ritual of raising and lowering the flag each morning and evening. Public buildings in the USA display the flag as a matter of course. On 4 July in Washington DC, even the city's buses sport a flag. Each day begins in most American schools with children standing to face the flag at the front of the classroom and reciting the Pledge of Allegiance (see Box 1.1). There is even a day each year designated as 'Flag Day'.

Box 1.1 Pledge of Allegiance

'I pledge allegiance to the flag of the United States of America and to the Republic for which it stands, one nation, under God, indivisible, with liberty and justice for all.'

These characteristics of size and diversity have important political implications too. Size brings with it the need for decentralisation — for the federal system of government established by the country's Founding Fathers in 1787. Diversity comes in the form of laws which differ between states about such matters as elections, crime and punishment. Different regions of the country (see Figure 1.2) have discernibly different ideological characteristics. The 'conservative' South — the 'Bible Belt' — stretches from Texas to Virginia. The 'liberal' Northeast includes such states as Massachusetts and Rhode Island. The west coast, too, is liberal-leaning, especially in the Californian cities of Los Angeles and San Francisco. This has implications for political parties. As we shall see, California Democrats are very different from Texas Democrats. And South Carolina Republicans are equally different from Massachusetts Republicans.

Summary

The size and diversity of the USA

The size and diversity of the USA leads to:

➢ the need for symbols of unity ➢ decentralisation ➢ regional differences

The events leading to the Philadelphia Convention

How did it all start? Students of US government and politics need to know something of the origins of the country. The 13 original British colonies were strung out along the eastern seaboard of America from Maine in the north to Georgia in the south (see Figure 1.3). Some were the creations of commercial interests, others of religious groups. All had written charters setting out their form of government and the rights of the colonists. Democracy was limited. Although each colony had a governor, a legislature and a judiciary, each also had a property qualification for voting from which women and blacks were excluded. And then, of course, there was slavery. Yet, despite their short-comings, the colonies provided a blueprint of what was to come.

Figure 1.3 The original 13 colonies

In the view of the British government, the American colonies existed principally for the economic benefit of the mother country. The colonists were obliged to pay tax to Britain, but they had no representation in the British Parliament. This led to a growing resentment. Bostonian patriot James Otis declared: 'Taxation without representation is tyranny!' As Britain tried to tighten its grip of the colonies' economic affairs in the 1770s, revolution became inevitable. The War of Independence began in April 1775.

On 4 July 1776, the colonies issued the Declaration of Independence, declaring themselves 'free and independent states'. The liberties that the colonists were fighting to protect were based not on the generosity of the king, but on a 'higher law' embodying 'natural rights' that were ordained by God and essential to the progress of human society. Thomas Jefferson's glowing words in the opening sentence of the Declaration of Independence (see Box 1.2) became the touchstone of the American colonists' ambitions.

Box 1.2 The Declaration of Independence

'We hold these truths to be self-evident, that all men are created equal, that they are endowed by their Creator with certain unalienable Rights, that among these are Life, Liberty and the pursuit of Happiness.'

At the same time as Jefferson was announcing high principles, the less well-remembered Richard H. Lee was offering his 'plan of confederation' for post-colonial government. The **Articles of Confederation** were eventually ratified by the 13 independent states by March 1781, although the hostilities with Great Britain were not formally concluded until the Treaty of Paris in 1783. These Articles set up a **confederacy** — a 'league of friendship', a loose collection of independent states — rather than a national government. Having just fought for — and won — their independence from Great Britain, the Virginians, New Yorkers and the rest were not going to give it away again to some new centralised government. Virginians wanted to govern Virginia. New Yorkers wanted to govern New York. The national government was a feeble affair with no executive branch, no judiciary and a legislature that was little more than a talking shop. The most significant fact about the government created by the Articles of Confederation was that it was weak. Thus, the ex-colonists had succeeded in gaining their independence but had failed to form a nation, and by this failure they almost turned their victory into defeat. What ensued was a shambles.

Key terms

➤ **Articles of Confederation.** The compact made between the 13 original states that formed the basis of their government from 1781 until it was replaced by the US Constitution in 1789.

➤ **Confederacy.** A league of independent states in which the central government lacks significant powers and resembles more an international organisation — such as the United Nations — than a traditional national government.

Many of the leaders of the Revolutionary War, such as George Washington and Alexander Hamilton, believed that a strong national government was essential. As the states squabbled over currency, commerce and much else, they began to fear the reappearance of the British and the loss of all they had so remarkably achieved. A small group of men with such fears met at Annapolis, Maryland, in September 1786. Attendance was poor, so another meeting was called in Philadelphia in May 1787 with the declared purpose of strengthening the Articles of Confederation. That might have been their purpose, but 4 months later the attendees had scrapped the Articles, written an entirely new Constitution and become the Founding Fathers of the United States of America.

George Washington, 1732–99

Summary

The events leading to the Philadelphia Convention
➤ The American colonies fought a War of Independence against Britain.
➤ The 13 newly independent states then set up a confederacy.
➤ This posed problems because of the lack of a strong national government.

The writing of the federal Constitution

The **Philadelphia Convention** was made up of 55 delegates representing 12 of the 13 states. (Rhode Island, suspicious of what was planned, refused to send any delegates.) In those four stifling hot months of the summer of 1787 they wrote a new form of government. They quickly concluded that a confederacy was structurally flawed and hopelessly weak, but they saw from political history that stronger forms of government led to the trampling underfoot of the citizens' rights and liberties. Thus they would have to create an entirely new form of government — one that had a strong centre while still preserving states' rights and individual liberties. The answer was a federal constitution, a bill of rights and an intricate set of checks and balances between the different levels and branches of government.

Key term
➤ **Philadelphia Convention.** The convention held in Philadelphia from 25 May to 18 September 1787, presided over by George Washington, which framed the Constitution. Its original purpose was merely to revise the Articles of Confederation, but the delegates instead decided to draft an entirely new document.

The convention initially considered two plans: one put forward by New Jersey, the other by Virginia. The New Jersey Plan — favoured by the states with smaller populations — was designed merely to strengthen the Articles of Confederation. The Virginia Plan — favoured by the states with larger populations — was much more radical. But with support equally divided, the Convention was deadlocked.

Box 1.3 The Preamble to the Constitution of the United States of America

'We the People of the United States, in Order to form a more perfect Union, establish Justice, insure domestic Tranquility, provide for the common defence, promote the general Welfare, and secure the Blessings of Liberty to ourselves and our Posterity, do ordain and establish this Constitution for the United States of America.'

The impasse was broken with what became known as the Connecticut Compromise. The stroke of genius came in the plan's recommendation that the new national legislature should be made up of two chambers. In the lower house (the House of Representatives) the states would be represented proportionally to their population, but in the upper house (the Senate) the states would be represented equally, regardless of population. Other compromises followed, concerning such matters as the method of electing the president.

On 17 September 1787, the task was complete. When the delegates emerged from their self-imposed silence in Independence Hall, it is said that a woman approached delegate Benjamin Franklin and asked: 'Well, Doctor, what have we got — a republic or a monarchy?' Replied Franklin: 'A republic, if you can keep it.'

Independence Hall, Philadelphia

Box 1.4 What the Constitution provided

Article I   'All legislative Powers herein granted shall be vested in a Congress of the United States, which shall consist of a Senate and House of Representatives.'

Article II   'The executive Power shall be vested in a President of the United States of America.'

Article III   'The judicial Power of the United States shall be vested in one Supreme Court and in such inferior Courts as the Congress may from time to time ordain and establish.'

Article IV   Federal–state and state–state relationships

Article V   Amendment procedures

Article VI   Miscellaneous provisions, including the 'supremacy clause'

Article VII   Ratification procedure of the Constitution

Article I of the new Constitution established Congress as the national legislature, defining its membership, the qualifications and method of election of its members as well as its powers. Under Article I, Section 8, Congress was given specific powers such as those to 'lay and collect taxes', 'coin money' and 'declare war'. It was also given much less specific powers such as those to 'provide for the common defence and general welfare of the United States' and to make all 'necessary and proper laws' — the latter often called the 'elastic clause' of the Constitution.

Article II decided — somewhat surprisingly — on a singular, rather than a plural, executive by vesting all executive power in the hands of 'a President'. The president would be chosen indirectly by an Electoral College.

Article III established the United States Supreme Court, though Congress quickly added trial and appeal courts. Although not explicitly granted, the Court was to have the role of umpire of the Constitution, implied in the 'supremacy clause' of Article VI and the provision in Article III itself that the Court's judicial power applies to 'all Cases...arising under this Constitution'. The Court would make this more explicit in its landmark decision of *Marbury v. Madison* in 1803.

Summary

The writing of the federal Constitution

➤ The Philadelphia Convention rejected the Articles of Confederation and wrote a new Constitution.

➤ The new Constitution established a strong central government made up of a legislature, an executive and a judiciary.

The amendment process

The Founding Fathers, while realising the likely need to amend the Constitution, wanted to make doing so a difficult process. Thus, it was to be a two-stage process requiring super-majorities of more than 50%, such as a two-thirds or a three-fifths majority (see Table 1.1). Stage 1 is the proposal and stage 2 is the ratification. Constitutional

Table 1.1 The amendment process

Amendments proposed by:	Amendments ratified by:
Either: **Congress**: two-thirds majority in both houses required	Either: **State legislatures**: three-quarters of the state legislatures must vote to ratify
Or: **National constitutional convention**: called by at least two-thirds of the states (never used)	Or: **State constitutional convention**: three-quarters of the states must hold conventions and vote to ratify

amendments can be proposed either by Congress or by a national constitutional convention called by Congress at the request of two thirds of the state legislatures. All constitutional amendments thus far have been proposed by Congress. No national constitutional convention has ever been called, although by 1992, 32 state legislatures had petitioned Congress for a convention to propose a balanced budget amendment — just two states short of the required two thirds.

In the 6 years when the Republicans controlled both houses of Congress — January 1995 to December 2000 — there were 17 votes on proposed constitutional amendments, an unusually high number (see Table 1.2). A proposal to amend the Constitution requires a two-thirds majority in both houses to be successful. During this period, the House of Representatives agreed to a Balanced Budget Amendment (1995) and a Flag Desecration Amendment (1995, 1997 and 1999). However, the Senate agreed to none of these, although it was only one vote short of the required two-thirds majority to pass the Balanced Budget Amendment in 1997 and four votes short of passing a Flag Desecration Amendment in 2000. Of the hundreds of amendments debated, Congress has passed only 33.

Once the amendment has been successfully proposed, it is sent to the states for ratification. An amendment can be ratified either by three-quarters of the state

Table 1.2 Attempts to propose constitutional amendments in Congress, 1995–2000

Date	Chamber	Subject	Vote	Two-thirds majority?
1995				
28 January	House	Balanced budget	300–132	Yes
2 March	Senate	Balanced budget	65–35	No
29 March	House	Term limits	227–204	No
28 June	House	Flag desecration	312–120	Yes
12 December	Senate	Flag desecration	62–36	No
1996				
15 April	House	Tax limitation	243–177	No
6 June	Senate	Balanced budget	64–35	No
1997				
12 February	House	Term limits	217–211	No
4 March	Senate	Balanced budget	66–34	No
15 April	House	Tax limitation	233–190	No
12 June	House	Flag desecration	310–114	Yes
1998				
22 April	House	Tax limitation	238–186	No
4 June	House	School prayers	224–203	No
1999				
15 April	House	Tax limitation	229–199	No
24 June	House	Flag desecration	305–124	Yes
2000				
29 March	Senate	Flag desecration	63–37	No
12 April	House	Tax limitation	234–192	No

legislatures or by state constitutional conventions in three-quarters of the states. Of the 27 amendments added to the Constitution, only one has been ratified by state constitutional conventions — the 21st Amendment, which repealed the 18th Amendment and thus ended the prohibition of alcohol. Of the 33 amendments passed to them for ratification by Congress, the states have ratified 27. Thus, once an amendment has been successfully proposed by Congress, it stands a good chance of finding its way into the Constitution. Only six amendments have failed at the ratification stage in over 210 years. The most recent was the amendment designed to guarantee equal rights for women. Proposed by Congress in 1972, only 35 state legislatures ratified it — three short of the required three-quarters.

Summary

The amendment process

➢ The Founding Fathers made the amendment process deliberately difficult.

➢ The process involves Congress and the states.

➢ Amendments need super-majorities to be both proposed and ratified.

➢ Only 27 amendments have been ratified so far.

The Bill of Rights and later amendments

Of the 27 amendments to the Constitution, the first ten must be considered together. They were proposed together by Congress in September 1789 and were ratified together by three-quarters of the states by December 1791. Collectively, they are known as the Bill of Rights. Many states had somewhat reluctantly signed up to the new federal Constitution with its potentially powerful centralised government. The Bill of Rights was designed to sugar the constitutional pill by protecting Americans against an over-powerful federal government.

Of the ten amendments in the Bill of Rights, the 1st, 2nd, 5th, 8th and 10th are perhaps the most important today. The 1st Amendment guarantees basic rights: freedom of religion; freedom of speech; freedom of the press; freedom of assembly. Debates such as those concerning prayers in public (i.e. state) schools, pornography on the internet, flag burning and press censorship all centre upon 1st Amendment rights. The 2nd Amendment guarantees that 'the right of the people to keep and bear arms shall not be infringed'. It is on this amendment that the debate about gun control focuses. You might well have heard of Americans 'pleading the 5th Amendment' — the right of silence, protecting the individual from self-incrimination. The 8th Amendment, which states that 'cruel and unusual punishments' shall not be inflicted, is the focus of the death penalty debate. The 10th Amendment has become an article of faith of the modern Republican Party in standing up for states' rights over the increasing power of the federal government in Washington DC.

Box 1.5 **Amendments to the Constitution**

Amendments I–X: the Bill of Rights (1791)

    I .... Freedom of religion, speech, press and assembly
   II .... Right to bear arms
  III .... No quartering of troops in private homes
  IV .... Unreasonable searches and seizures prohibited
   V .... Rights of accused persons
  VI .... Rights when on trial
 VII .... Common-law suits
VIII .... Excessive bail and cruel and unusual punishments prohibited
  IX .... Unenumerated rights protected
   X .... Powers reserved to the states and to the people

Some later amendments

  XII (1804) .... Electoral College process revised for electing president and vice-president
 XIII (1865) .... Slavery prohibited
 XIV (1868) .... Ex-slaves made citizens
  XV (1870) .... Blacks given the right to vote
 XVI (1913) .... Federal government authorised to impose income tax
XVII (1913) .... Direct election of the Senate
XXII (1951) .... Two-term limit for the president
XXV (1967) .... Presidential disability and succession procedures
XXVI (1971) .... Voting age lowered to 18

Seventeen further amendments have been passed since the Bill of Rights, of which we shall come across only around half. The 12th Amendment (1804) revised the process for electing the president and vice-president. The 13th (1865), 14th (1868) and 15th (1870) Amendments were proposed and ratified immediately after the Civil War to end slavery and guarantee rights to the former slaves. The 16th Amendment (1913) is of crucial importance in understanding how the federal government's power increased during the twentieth century. It allowed the federal government to impose an income tax. The 17th Amendment (also 1913) provided for the direct election of the Senate. Previously, Senators were appointed by their state legislatures. The 22nd Amendment (1951) limited the president to a maximum of two terms in office. The 25th Amendment (1967) dealt with issues of presidential disability and succession, which had come to the fore following the assassination 4 years earlier of President Kennedy. The 26th Amendment (1971) lowered the voting age to 18.

Why the Constitution has been amended so rarely

With only 27 amendments passed, and only 17 of those in the last 210 years, the question is raised as to why so few amendments have been passed. There are four significant reasons.

> The Founding Fathers created a deliberately difficult process. The need for both Congress and the states to agree, and the need for super-majorities, make the amendment process difficult. Hundreds of amendments have been initiated, but very few have made it successfully through the process.

> The Founding Fathers created a document that was, at least in parts, deliberately unspecific. Congress is given the power, for example, 'to provide for the common defence and general welfare' of the United States. This has allowed the document to evolve without the need for formal amendment.

> The most important reason, the Supreme Court's power of judicial review, is considered in Chapters 8 and 9. Suffice it to say here that this power allows the Court to interpret the Constitution and thereby, in effect, change the meaning of words written over two centuries ago — to make what one might call 'interpretative amendments' rather than formal amendments. Thus, for example, the Court can state what the phrase in Amendment VIII which forbids 'cruel and unusual punishments' means today.

> Americans have become cautious of tampering with their Constitution. They hold it in some degree of veneration. In the early decades of the twentieth century, they got themselves into difficulties by amending the Constitution to prohibit the manufacture, sale and importation of alcohol. Fourteen years later, 'prohibition' was discredited and the offending amendment was repealed. This experience proved to be an important lesson for subsequent generations.

Summary

The Bill of Rights and later amendments
> The first ten amendments are called 'the Bill of Rights'.
> Seventeen further amendments have been ratified.
> There are important reasons why the Constitution has been so rarely amended.

Separation of powers

The Constitution drawn up at the Philadelphia Convention in 1787 divided the national government into three branches based on what is known as the doctrine of the **separation of powers**. This is a theory of government whereby political power is distributed among three branches of government — the legislature, the executive and the judiciary — acting both independently and interdependently (see Figure 1.4).

This framework of government was put in place by the Founding Fathers because of their fear of tyranny. The framers were influenced by the writings of the French political philosopher Baron de Montesquieu (1689–1755). In his book *L'Esprit des Lois* (*The Spirit of the Laws*), published in 1748, Montesquieu argued for a separation of powers into

Key term

> **Separation of powers.** A theory of government whereby political power is distributed among three branches of government — the legislature, the executive and the judiciary — acting both independently and interdependently. As applied to the United States government, the theory is better understood as one of 'shared powers'. It is the institutions of government that are separate, while the powers are shared through an elaborate series of checks and balances.

legislative, executive and judicial branches in order to avoid tyranny. 'When the legislative and executive powers are united in the same person...there can be no liberty,' wrote Montesquieu.

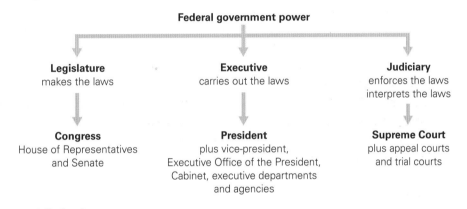

Federal government power

Legislature	Executive	Judiciary
makes the laws	carries out the laws	enforces the laws interprets the laws
Congress	**President**	**Supreme Court**
House of Representatives and Senate	plus vice-president, Executive Office of the President, Cabinet, executive departments and agencies	plus appeal courts and trial courts

Figure 1.4 Federal government power

The Founding Fathers had the idea that each of these three independent yet co-equal branches should check the power of the others. The framers wanted 'limited government', whereby government would do only what was essential, leaving the citizens' fundamental rights and freedoms as untouched as is possible in an organised and orderly society. James Madison, writing later in *The Federalist Papers*, put it this way:

> If men were angels, no government would be necessary. If angels were to govern men, neither external nor internal controls on government would be necessary. In framing a government which is to be administered by men over men, the great difficulty lies in this: you must first enable the government to control the governed; and in the next place oblige it to control itself.

Thus, the three branches were to be separate in terms of their personnel. No person can be in more than one branch of the federal government at the same time — what we might call 'the separation of personnel'. When Senator John F. Kennedy was elected president in 1960, he had to resign from the Senate (the legislative branch) in order to become president (head of the executive branch). When in 1992, Senator Al Gore was elected vice-president, he likewise had to resign from the Senate. In this sense the three branches — the institutions of government — are entirely separate.

However, the term 'separation of powers' is misleading, for it is the *institutions* that are separate, not the *powers*. Professor Richard Neustadt was the most helpful in clearing up this potential confusion. Neustadt (1960) wrote: 'The Constitutional Convention of 1787 is supposed to have created a government of "separated powers". It did nothing of the sort. Rather, it created a government of separated institutions *sharing* powers.'

Quite right. So the concept is best thought of as the doctrine of 'shared powers'. And those 'shared powers' are what 'checks and balances' are all about, for the Founding Fathers set up an intricate system whereby each branch of the federal government would check and balance the other two. This is especially important in terms of the legislature and the executive, which Professor S. E. Finer (1970) has described as being 'like two halves of a bank note — each useless without the other'.

Summary

Separation of powers

The doctrine of the separation of powers embodies three fundamental principles:

➤ separation of personnel
➤ limited government
➤ checks and balances

Checks and balances

The checks exercised by each branch of the federal government — the legislature, the executive and the judiciary — on the other two branches are detailed in Table 1.3. We shall look at each of these in turn.

Checks by the executive on the legislature

The president is given the power to recommend legislation to the Congress. He (or she, though no female president has yet been elected) does this formally in January of each year in what is known as the **State of the Union Address**. Presidents use this set-piece speech, delivered to a joint session of the House of Representatives and the Senate — as well as cabinet members and the nine justices of the Supreme Court — on primetime television before a nationwide audience. It is the president's main opportunity to lay out his legislative agenda: in effect saying to Congress, 'this is what I want you to debate and pass into law'. President George W. Bush used his State of the Union Address in January 2002 to try to get Congress to focus on his 'war on terrorism' and budget priorities.

In addition, the president has the power to veto bills passed by Congress. During his 8 years in office, President Clinton used the veto power on 36 occasions, including his veto of the 1999 Republican tax cut.

Table 1.3 Checks and balances

Checks on → Checks by ↓	The legislature	The executive	The judiciary
The legislature		• amend/delay/reject legislation • override president's veto • power of the purse • declare war • ratify treaties (Senate) • confirm appointments (Senate) • investigation • impeachment, trial, conviction and removal from office	• impeachment, trial, conviction and removal from office • propose constitutional amendments
The executive	• recommend legislation • veto legislation		• appointment of judges • pardon
The judiciary	• judicial review	• judicial review	

Key term

> **State of the Union Address.** An annual speech made by the president — usually in late January — to a joint session of Congress meeting in the chamber of the House of Representatives, in which he lays out his proposed legislative programme for the coming year. The name comes from the phrase in Article II, Section 3 of the Constitution that states that the president 'shall from time to time give to the Congress information on the state of the Union, and recommend to their consideration such measures as he shall judge necessary and expedient'.

Checks by the executive on the judiciary

Here the president has two significant checks. First, he nominates all federal judges — to the trial court, appeal court and Supreme Court. It is the latter that are the most important. President Clinton was able to make two appointments to the Supreme Court — Ruth Bader Ginsburg (1993) and Stephen Breyer (1994). By choosing justices whose judicial philosophy matches their own, presidents can hope to mould the outlook of the Court for years to come.

Second, the president has the power of pardon. This has become something of a controversy in recent times. In 1974, President Ford pardoned his predecessor — President Nixon — for any crimes that Nixon might have committed in the so-called **Watergate affair**. On the final day of his presidency, President Clinton pardoned 140 people, including Mark Rich, a notorious tax fugitive. Incoming President George W. Bush pointedly made no use of the power in the first 2 years of his administration.

Key term

> **Watergate affair.** A term used to refer to a collection of illegal activities conducted by senior members of the Nixon administration and the subsequent attempted cover-up. The name was drawn from the Watergate building in downtown Washington DC, where the Democratic National Committee had its headquarters during the 1972 presidential election. The building was broken into by people working on behalf of President Nixon's re-election committee. These illegal activities, which included illegal use of the CIA and other government agencies, bugging and bribery, led to Nixon's resignation in August 1974.

Checks by the legislature on the executive

Because the Founding Fathers were most anxious about the possible power of the singular executive they had created — the president — they hedged this branch of government with the most checks. Congress exercises eight significant checks on the president.

> Congress can amend, block or even reject items of legislation recommended by the president. In 2001, it passed — but in a significantly amended form — President Bush's Education Reform Bill. In 1993–94, President Clinton found his flagship health care reforms blocked by Congress. In 1999, Congress rejected Clinton's request for an increase in the minimum wage.

> Congress can override the president's veto. To do this, it needs to gain a two-thirds majority in both houses of Congress. During President Clinton's two terms, Congress overrode two of his vetoes, including the one on the 1995 Securities Bill.

> Congress has the significant power that is referred to as 'the power of the purse'. All the money that the president wants to spend on his policies must be voted for by Congress. Its refusal to vote for this money will significantly curtail what the president can do — be it in domestic or foreign policy.

> In the field of foreign policy, Congress has two further checks on the president. Although the Constitution confers on the president the power to be 'commander-in-chief' of the armed forces, it confers on Congress the power to declare war. Although this power seems to have fallen into disuse — the last time Congress declared war was on Japan in 1941 — Congress has successfully forced presidents since then to seek specific authorisation before committing troops to situations in which hostilities are likely or inevitable. In January 1991, President George Bush gained specific authorisation from Congress to launch his Desert Storm campaign to free Kuwait from Iraqi invasion.

> The Senate has the power to ratify treaties negotiated by the president. This requires a two-thirds majority. In 1997, the Senate ratified the Chemical Weapons Ban Treaty. Negotiated by President Bush and backed by Clinton, the treaty was ratified by the Senate by 74 votes to 26. However, 2 years later, the Senate rejected the Comprehensive Test Ban Treaty by 48 votes to 51 — 14 votes short of the 66 votes

required to ratify it. This was the first major treaty to be rejected by the Senate since the rejection of the Versailles Treaty in 1920. Five minor treaties have been rejected in between.

- The check exercised by Congress over the president is an important power held by the Senate alone — the power to confirm many of the appointments that the president makes to the executive branch and all the appointments he makes to the federal judiciary. Executive appointments subject to Senate confirmation include such high-profile posts as cabinet members, ambassadors and heads of important agencies such as the CIA and the FBI. Only a simple majority is required for confirmation. Rejections are unusual, but only because presidents usually consult informally with key Senators before announcing such appointments, naming only those for whom confirmation is a fair certainty. In 1987, the Senate rejected (42–58) President Reagan's nominee, Robert Bork, for a place on the Supreme Court (see Chapter 8). In 1989, the Senate rejected (47–53) John Tower as secretary of defense. In 1997, it refused to confirm William Weld — President Clinton's choice as ambassador to Mexico. In 1999, it rejected (45–54) Ronnie White — President Clinton's nominee to a vacancy on the United States District (trial) Court.

- Two further important checks on the president are given to Congress. The first is the power of investigation: Congress — usually through its committees — may investigate the actions or policies of any member of the executive branch, including the president. President George W. Bush's handling of national security issues both before and after the events of 11 September 2001 was investigated by Congress.

- Finally, in the most serious circumstances, investigation may lead to **impeachment** — the ultimate check that Congress holds over the executive. Congress may impeach (formally accuse) any member of the executive branch, including the president. Two presidents — Andrew Johnson (1868) and Bill Clinton (1998) — have been impeached by Congress. It is the House of Representatives which has the power of impeachment.

In 1998, it passed two articles of impeachment against President Clinton — for perjury (228–206) and obstruction of justice (221–212). Just a simple majority is required. Once the House has impeached, the Senate then conducts the trial. If found guilty by a two-thirds majority, the accused person is removed from office. In President Clinton's case, the Senate found him not guilty on both articles of impeachment — the votes being 45–55 on perjury and 50–50 on obstruction of justice, respectively 22 and 17 votes short of the required two-thirds majority. In the 1860s, President Johnson escaped conviction by the Senate by just one vote. In 1974, President Nixon resigned rather than face near certain impeachment

President Clinton's apology to the nation on 11 December 1998 was followed by impeachment

by the House and conviction by the Senate. Thus, through impeachment — what someone has described as 'the political equivalent of the death penalty' — Congress can remove the president. This is the ultimate check. The president holds no similar power — he cannot remove Congress.

Key term

> **Impeachment.** A formal accusation of a federal official by a simple majority vote of the House of Representatives. Impeachment is the first step in a two-stage process: it is followed by a trial by the Senate in which a two-thirds majority is required for conviction. If convicted, the federal official is removed from office.

Checks by the legislature on the judiciary

Congress has two important checks on the courts. First, there is the power of impeachment, trial and — if found guilty by a two-thirds majority — removal from office. In the space of 3 years (1986–89), Congress removed three federal judges from office — Harry Claiborne for tax evasion, Alcee Hastings for bribery and Walter Nixon for perjury.

A more subtle but still significant check is that Congress can propose constitutional amendments to — in effect — overturn a decision of the Supreme Court. When in 1896 the Supreme Court declared federal income tax to be unconstitutional, Congress proposed the 16th Amendment granting Congress the power to levy income tax. It was ratified and became operative in 1913. Congress has more recently attempted unsuccessfully to reverse Supreme Court decisions on such issues as flag burning and prayer in public schools.

Checks by the judiciary on the legislature

The judiciary — headed by the Supreme Court — possesses one very significant power over the Congress: the power of judicial review. This is the power of the court to declare Acts of Congress to be unconstitutional and therefore null and void. In the 1997 case of *Reno v. American Civil Liberties Union*, the Supreme Court declared the Communications Decency Act unconstitutional. In 1998, in *Clinton v. New York City*, it declared the Line Item Veto Act unconstitutional.

Checks by the judiciary on the executive

The courts have the same power of judicial review over the executive branch. Here the power of judicial review is the ability to declare actions of any member of the executive branch to be unconstitutional. In *Youngstown Sheet & Tube Company v. Sawyer* (1952), the Supreme Court ordered President Truman's commerce secretary, Charles Sawyer, to remove federal troops whom he had sent into steel mills to break an industry-wide strike. In *United States v. Richard Nixon* (1974), the Court ordered President Nixon to hand over the so-called White House tapes and thereby stop impeding investigation of the Watergate affair. Nixon obeyed, handed over the tapes and resigned within days once the tapes showed his involvement in an intricate cover-up.

The political importance of checks and balances

The checks and balances between the three branches of the federal government — especially those between the legislature and the executive — have important consequences for US politics. They encourage a spirit of **bipartisanship** and compromise between the president and Congress. Laws are passed, treaties ratified, appointments confirmed and budgets fixed only when both branches work together rather than pursue a partisan approach. President George W. Bush managed to achieve his education reforms in 2001–02 because he worked with leading congressional Democrats such as Senator Edward Kennedy. President Bill Clinton failed to get his healthcare reform passed by Congress in 1993–94 because he adopted a partisan approach in which the views of even moderate Republicans in Congress were ignored.

Key term

> **Bipartisanship.** Close cooperation between the two major parties. In the US system of government, where it is possible to have a president of one party and a Congress controlled by the other party, bipartisanship is thought to be crucial to political success.

The trouble is that gridlock can result. Most recent presidents have accused the Senate of either rejecting or blocking their judicial nominations for partisan reasons. As a consequence, a large number of posts in both the federal trial and appeal courts remain unfilled for months, even years, slowing down the work of the courts. In 1995, such a serious impasse developed between the Republican-controlled Congress and Democrat President Clinton over the passage of the federal budget that parts of the federal government had to close when they ran out of money.

This raises the issue of 'divided government'. In US politics, this term is used to refer to the situation in which one political party controls the presidency and another controls one or both houses of Congress. Of late, this has indeed become the norm. The 34 years between 1969 and 2003 have seen $27\frac{1}{2}$ years of divided government. For only $6\frac{1}{2}$ years of this period did one party control the presidency and both houses of Congress: 1977–81 (President Carter) and 1993–95 (President Clinton) for the Democrats, and January–June 2001 (President George W. Bush) for the Republicans. It is worth noting, too, that divided government has not always been the norm. In the previous 34 years — from 1935 to 1969 — there was divided government for only 8 years.

Does divided government make the checks and balances between Congress and the president more or less effective? There are arguments on both sides. Some think that divided government leads to *more* effective government. Bills are scrutinised more closely, treaties checked more carefully and nominees questioned more rigorously in the confirmation process. There is some evidence that when Congress and the president are of the same party, legislation, nominations, budgets, treaties and the like are nodded through without as much careful scrutiny as there should be. Not since 1935 has the Senate rejected a treaty of a president of its own party. Only twice in the last 50 years has Congress overridden a veto of a president of its party. In 1964, Democrat President Johnson managed to persuade a Congress with Democrat majorities in both houses to pass the Tonkin Gulf Resolution which authorised the President to take whatever action was deemed appropriate in south Vietnam.

Others, however, think that divided government leads to *less* effective government. Examples such as the treatment of Republican Supreme Court nominees Robert Bork (1987) and Clarence Thomas (1991) by a Democrat-controlled Senate, and the impeachment proceedings conducted against Democrat President Bill Clinton by a Republican-controlled Congress (1998–99), seem poor advertisements for effective checks and balances.

There are specific checks and balances that have proved problematic in modern times. Congress's power to declare war is one obvious example. Modern presidents have managed to conduct overt wars in Korea, Vietnam and the Persian Gulf, to name but three, with no congressional declarations of war. Impeachment used against Presidents Andrew Johnson and Bill Clinton seems to have become overtly political. Analysts suggest, with considerable evidence, that the confirmation process of federal judges has become overly politicised. 'Innocent until nominated' is how one US political figure has described the situation.

That having been said, the checks and balances of the Constitution have stood the test of time remarkably well. The Founding Fathers would be pleased with how well their creation has survived. Few back wholesale constitutional reform — and certainly those who do are likely to be disappointed.

Summary

Checks and balances

➢ The US Constitution includes a series of checks and balances between all three branches of government.

➢ The most important are those which the legislature has on the executive, reflecting the Founding Fathers' fear of tyranny.

➢ These checks and balances can help promote bipartisanship, but often result in gridlock.

Federalism and the changing federal–state relationship

Federalism and the Constitution

'We the People of the United States, *in order to form a more perfect Union...*' So began the preamble to the new Constitution. Certainly, the first attempt at union was weak and almost disastrous. The Articles of Confederation showed just about how far the newly independent peoples of America were prepared to go in the formation of a national government — not very far; but the experience of confederacy had been educative. The compromise between a strong central government and states' rights was to be **federalism**. It was what James Madison called 'a middle ground'.

Key term

> **Federalism.** A theory of government by which political power is divided between a national government and state governments, each having their own area of substantive jurisdiction.

Federalism involves a degree of decentralisation, which has proved suitable for a country as large and diverse as the USA has become. As Benjamin Franklin knew at the signing of the Declaration of Independence, a certain level of national unity was vital: 'We must all hang together, or, most assuredly, we shall all hang separately.' Thus, out of the disunity of the Articles of Confederation came the *United* States of America — *e pluribus unum* — 'out of many, one'.

Nowhere is the word 'federal' or 'federalism' mentioned in the Constitution. How, then, was it written into the document? First, it was written into the enumerated powers of the three branches of the federal government — Congress was 'to coin money', the president was to 'be commander-in-chief' and so on. Second, it was included in the implied powers of the federal government. These are the powers that flow from, for example, the 'elastic clause' of the Constitution — Congress's power to 'make all laws necessary and proper for carrying into execution the foregoing powers'. Third, the federal government and the states were given certain concurrent powers: for example, the power to tax. Fourth, the 10th Amendment reserved all remaining powers 'to the states and to the people'. Finally, the Supreme Court was to be the umpire of all disagreements between the federal and state governments. As Chief Justice Charles Evans Hughes wrote in 1907: 'We are under a Constitution, but the Constitution is what the judges say it is.'

The changing federal–state relationship

Federalism is not, however, a fixed concept. It is ever changing. As America has changed, so has the concept of federalism.

During the latter part of the nineteenth century and the first two thirds of the twentieth century, a number of factors led to an increased role for the federal government.

> **Westward expansion.** From 13 colonies clustered up and down the Atlantic coast, settlement spread westwards across the Appalachian mountains, over the plains of the Midwest, across the Rockies and all the way to the Pacific coast.
> **The growth of population.** Simultaneously, the population grew from just under 4 million in 1790 to 76 million by 1900 and 275 million by 2000. A growing nation required management by a growing government.
> **Industrialisation.** This brought the need for government regulation — federal executive departments of Commerce and Labor were formed in 1903.
> **Improvements in communication.** While the nation grew in size, it shrank in terms

of accessibility as modern methods of communication gradually developed. Journeys that took weeks eventually took only days or hours as roads, railways and aircraft opened up the nation. Radio, followed by television, brought instant communication and a feeling of national identity. People could communicate with others thousands of miles away, first by telephone and then by fax and e-mail.

> **The Great Depression.** Events influenced the federal–state relationship, too. When the Great Depression hit the USA in 1929, the states looked to the federal government to cure their ills. The state governments did not possess the necessary resources to reverse the huge levels of unemployment, launch vast public works schemes or rescue agriculture from the effects of the dust bowl conditions. It was Franklin Roosevelt's 'New Deal', with its ambitious schemes to build roads and schools and provide hydroelectric power, that helped get the USA back to work.

> **Foreign policy.** With the onset of the Second World War, the USA stepped out as a world superpower and the federal government — with exclusive jurisdiction over foreign policy — found its role enhanced significantly.

> **Supreme Court decisions.** Political changes occurred to alter the federal–state relationship. Decisions made by the Supreme Court — especially between 1937 and the 1970s — further enhanced the power of the federal government through their interpretation of the implied powers of the Constitution.

> **Constitutional amendments.** Equally importantly, the passage of the 16th Amendment (1913) allowed the federal government to impose an income tax. This gave the federal government the means to launch all the grand programmes that would flourish from Roosevelt's New Deal through the presidencies of Truman, Kennedy and Johnson to the late 1960s.

Phases of federalism

These changes in the federal–state relationship are distinguished by different phases through which this relationship has passed: dual federalism, cooperative federalism and new federalism.

> 'Dual federalism' is the term associated with approximately the first 150 years of the nation's history — from the 1780s to the 1920s. During this era, the state governments exercised most political power. The role of the federal government was limited mainly to matters concerning money, war and peace. In President Washington's day, there were only three federal executive departments — the Department of the Treasury, the Department of War and the Department of State. The relatively minor role played by the federal government can best be seen by listing some of the little-known presidents of this era: James Polk, Millard Fillmore, Ulysses Grant and Chester Arthur. The federal and state governments each guarded their own powers jealously. Morton Grodzins (1966) called this 'layer-cake' federalism, in which the federal and state governments had distinct areas of responsibility.

> The effects of the Wall Street Crash and the Great Depression changed all that. The term 'cooperative federalism' is used to refer to an era, from the 1930s to the 1960s, in which the federal and state governments cooperated to solve the problems facing US society — such as those relating to poverty, health, education, transport and national security. This era coincides with the administrations of four Democrat presidents — Franklin Roosevelt, Harry Truman, John Kennedy and Lyndon Johnson. It was during this era that the role of the federal government increased significantly. New federal executive departments were created to cope with new policy areas: Defense (1949); Health, Education and Welfare (1953); Housing and Urban Development (1965); and Transportation (1966). The federal government administered categorical grants — schemes by which it was able to stipulate how federal tax dollars were used by the states. By the Clinton era, the federal government was giving over $200 billion to the states, over 90% of which went in the form of categorical grants. So by now the federal government was involved in a number of policy areas where previously only the state governments had operated — such as education, transport and welfare. The two levels of Grodzins' cake had become mixed in what he would now describe as 'marble-cake' federalism.

> During the final three decades of the twentieth century, however, there was a discernible movement towards decentralisation — what President Nixon called 'new federalism'. This era saw the rise of block grants — money given to states by the federal government to be used at their discretion within broad policy areas. This change in the federal–state relationship coincides with the administrations of four Republican presidents: Richard Nixon, Gerald Ford, Ronald Reagan and George Bush. Ronald Reagan, speaking in his first Inaugural Address in January 1981, had this to say:

> It is my intention to curb the size and influence of the Federal establishment and to demand recognition of the distinction between the powers granted to the Federal Government and those reserved to the States or to the people. All of us need to be reminded that the Federal Government did not create the States; the States created the Federal Government.

Even Democrat President Bill Clinton recognised that Americans' view of the federal–state relationship had changed, when he stated in his 1996 State of the Union Address: 'The era of big government is over.'

There are a number of reasons for the shift back towards state government power.

> First, a perception had grown that the great federal government programmes of FDR's 'New Deal' or Johnson's 'Great Society' had not been as successful as first thought. Too much money had been wasted on bureaucracy.

> Second, there was a belief that the federal government had simply failed to tackle some pressing social problems, such as gun crime, drugs, abortion, welfare and poverty. As a result, scepticism about the federal government's effectiveness had developed.

> Third, there was a growing distrust of 'Washington politicians'. The Watergate affair and the débâcle in Vietnam both lowered trust in the federal government. Between 1976 and 2000, America elected five presidents — four were former state governors, while only one, George Bush (1988), was a Washington politician. The unsuccessful movement to impose term limits on members of Congress, which became very vocal in the early 1990s, was a manifestation of this distrust of Washington politics.

> Fourth, decisions by the mainly Republican-appointed Supreme Court began to limit the scope of federal government power. 'New federalism' was strongly associated with the Republican Party.

> Finally, the frequent election of Republican presidents during this era, the election of a Republican-controlled Congress in 1994 and the election of Republican state governors allowed the party to put its policies into effect.

Summary

Federalism and the changing federal–state relationship

> Federalism is a fundamental principle of the US Constitution.

> For some fundamental reasons, the relationship between the federal government and the states has changed significantly since the 1780s.

Consequences of federalism

Federalism has consequences throughout US government and politics.

> **Legal consequences.** There is tremendous variety in state laws on such matters as the age at which people can marry, drive a car or have to attend school. Laws vary on drugs and whether the death penalty is used. Oregon allows doctor-assisted suicide. There are both federal and state courts.

> **Political consequences**. All elections in the United States are state-based and run under state law. Even the presidential election is really 50 separate state-based elections with the outcome decided by a state-based Electoral College. Each state decides such matters as: how candidates will be chosen for elections in their state; the procedures for getting a candidate's name on the ballot paper; what mechanisms are used in polling stations — punch cards or touch-screen computers. Arizona has experimented with on-line voting and Montana with an entirely postal ballot.

It is important to realise that political parties in America are essentially de-centralised, state-based parties. Texas Democrats are more conservative than

Massachusetts Democrats; Vermont Republicans more liberal than South Carolina Republicans. One can see the effects of federalism in the United States Congress with its state-based representation.

➤ **Economic consequences.** These are seen not only in the huge federal grants going to the states, but also in the complexity of the tax system in America. Income tax is levied by both the federal government and some state governments, different property taxes are levied by the state governments, and sales taxes vary between cities.

➤ **Regionalism.** The regions of the South, the Midwest, the Northeast and the West have distinct cultures and accents, as well as racial, religious and ideological differences. There is a distinct difference between the conservatism of the Deep South and the liberalism of the Northeast. What plays well in 'the Bible Belt' may not be popular in 'New England'.

When all is said and done, federalism has proved to be an appropriate system of government for the United States. It has adapted itself to the ever-changing nation. Despite its frustrations, there are few who question its future. Some Americans may think the federal–state relationship has at times got out of kilter, but most believe that its strengths far outweigh its weaknesses.

Box 1.6 Federalism: pros and cons

Pros

➤ permits diversity

➤ creates more access points in government

➤ better protection of individual rights

➤ states become 'policy laboratories', experimenting with new solutions to old problems

➤ well suited to a geographically large nation

Cons

➤ can mask economic and racial inequalities

➤ frustrates the 'national will', making solving problems more complex

➤ the federal–state government relationship is a continual source of conflict and controversy

➤ overly bureaucratic — therefore costly to run and resistant to change

Summary

The consequences of federalism

➤ Federalism has legal, political and economic consequences for America.

➤ Federalism also leads to 'regionalism'.

➤ Federalism has both merits and demerits for America.

Exercises

1 What significant events occurred before 1787 which had an effect on what occurred at the Philadelphia Convention?
2 What are the principal provisions of the original seven Articles of the Constitution?
3 What is the process for amending the Constitution?
4 What is the 'Bill of Rights'?
5 Give some examples of constitutional amendments passed successfully during the nineteenth and twentieth centuries.
6 Give some examples of constitutional amendments that failed to be passed during the 1990s.
7 Explain what Richard Neustadt meant when he described US government as one of 'separated institutions, sharing powers.'
8 What checks (with examples, if possible) does the executive exercise on the legislature and on the judiciary?
9 What checks (with examples, if possible) does the legislature exercise on the executive and on the judiciary?
10 What checks (with examples, if possible) does the judiciary have on the legislature and on the executive?
11 What is meant by 'divided government' and how often has it occurred since 1969?
12 Explain what is meant by 'federalism'.
13 How is federalism included in the Constitution?
14 Explain what is meant by the terms (a) dual federalism; (b) cooperative federalism; (c) new federalism.
15 Why has power tended to shift back to the state governments in recent decades?
16 What are the main consequences of federalism for US government and politics?

Exam focus

1 How effective are the checks and balances of the Constitution today?
2 Which is the most accurate description of US government: 'separated powers' or 'shared powers'?
3 How and why has the relationship between the federal and state governments changed since the 1960s?
4 What are the merits and demerits of federalism for US government and politics?

References

Finer, S. E., *Comparative Government* (Penguin, 1970).

Grodzins, M., *The American System* (Rand McNally & Co, 1966).

Neustadt, R. E., *Presidential Power* (John Wiley, 1960).

Further reading

Ashbee, E., *American Society Today* (Manchester University Press, 2002).

Fletcher, R., 'Developments in American federalism since 1972', *Politics Review*, vol. 12, no. 4, April 2003.

Chapter 2

Presidential elections

The aspect of US politics that is most thoroughly covered by the British media is presidential elections. Maybe because the election of the US president is seen as the election of the leader of the world's only superpower, this event is deemed to be of significance even 3,000 miles (5,000 kilometres) from Washington DC. Yet the presidential election is much more than what happens on election day. It is a more than year-long event in which ordinary voters are given a chance to say whom they would like to see as the major parties' candidates. Important issues concerning democracy, campaign finance and the role of the media are raised. There is also the question of how an electoral system devised more than two centuries ago as an indirect election has been adapted to become a direct election. Finally, there are issues concerning voting behaviour: who votes for whom, and why? It is easy to criticise a process that lasts so long, costs so much, seems at times to be more about style than substance, and sometimes, as in 2000, allows into the White House the candidate with fewer votes than his major rival.

Questions to be answered in this chapter
➢ When do presidential elections occur?
➢ What are the requirements for presidential candidates?
➢ How are presidential candidates selected?
➢ What roles do money and the media play?
➢ What factors explain voting behaviour?
➢ How does the Electoral College system work?

When presidential elections occur

America has fixed-term elections that occur every 4 years. The first presidential election was held in 1788. Since then, a presidential election has been held every 4 years, even during wartime. If the president dies in office, there is still no special election. When President Kennedy was assassinated in November 1963, Vice-President Lyndon Johnson automatically became president and completed the remaining months of Kennedy's term. The next presidential election was not until 1964.

The fact that these elections occur every 4 years is laid down in Article II of the Constitution. But federal law goes even further, stating that the election shall be held on the Tuesday after the first Monday in November of every fourth year. In practice, that means that the election occurs between 2 and 8 November.

Presidential elections can best be thought of as occurring in four distinct stages (see Table 2.1). The first two are concerned with choosing the candidates. The second two are concerned with electing the president.

Table 2.1 Presidential elections: a four-stage process

Stage	Functions	Occurs
(1) Primaries and caucuses	Show popular support for candidates Choose delegates to attend National Party Conventions	Late January–early June
(2) National Party Conventions	Choose presidential candidate Choose vice-presidential candidate Decide on party platform	July/August (each lasts about 4 days)
(3) General election campaign	The campaign between the candidates of various parties	September, October, first week of November
(4) Election day and Electoral College	Elect the president and vice-president	November/December

Summary

When presidential elections occur

Presidential elections:

➢ are fixed-term elections ➢ occur every 4 years
➢ are held on the Tuesday after the first Monday in November

Requirements for a presidential candidate

What does a person need to become a candidate for the presidency? In answering such a question, consider carefully the word 'need'. There are two possible meanings: first, what is *absolutely essential* — the constitutional requirements; and second, what is *very helpful* — things without which your candidacy either won't be taken very seriously or won't get very far.

Constitutional requirements

Several constitutional qualifications are necessary in order to be president.

➢ One must be a natural-born American citizen.

➢ One must be at least 35 years old. The youngest ever president was Theodore Roosevelt, who was just 42 when he became president following the assassination of President William McKinley in 1901. The youngest ever *elected* president was John Kennedy, who was 43.

➢ There is a residency qualification — 14 years.

➢ In 1951, the Constitution was amended to limit presidents to two terms in office. The first president to feel the effect of this two-term limit was Dwight Eisenhower in 1960. Subsequently, two more presidents have been term limited: Ronald Reagan (elected 1980; re-elected 1984) and Bill Clinton (elected 1992; re-elected 1996). So a fourth constitutional requirement could be added — not to have already served two terms as president.

Extra-constitutional requirements

In addition to the constitutional requirements, there are a number of other elements which candidates need to stand a chance of making a serious bid for the presidency. They are not mentioned in the Constitution, hence they are 'extra-constitutional' requirements. They fall into seven areas.

Political experience

Probably the most important of these extra-constitutional requirements is political experience. Three groups of politicians are good pools of recruitment for the presidency: vice-presidents, state governors and Senators. One could add a fourth — members of the House of Representatives. However, very few serving members of the House manage to get themselves regarded as leading presidential candidates. The most recent political office of six of the 10 candidates for the presidential nomination of the Democratic party in 2004 was state governor or Senator (see Table 2.2).

Of the 16 politicians who were nominated as presidential candidates in the last 11 elections to 2004, seven were or had been vice-president, four were Senators and five were governors. The last time either the Democrats or the Republicans nominated someone for the presidency who did not have this political background was 1952, when the Republicans nominated the former Second World War general, Dwight Eisenhower. The only two people who have recently been mentioned as serious presidential candidates without such political experience are ex-army generals, Colin Powell and Wesley Clark.

Table 2.2 Most recent political office of Democratic candidates, 2004

Candidate	Most recent political office
Wesley Clark	None
Howard Dean	Governor
John Edwards	Senator
Dick Gephardt	Congressman
Bob Graham	Senator
John Kerry	Senator
Dennis Kucinich	Congressman
Joseph Lieberman	Senator
Carol Moseley Braun	Senator
Al Sharpton	None

Table 2.3 Winning and losing candidates in presidential elections, 1960–2000

Year	Winning candidate	Losing candidate
1960	John Kennedy (D)	Richard Nixon (R)
1964	Lyndon Johnson (D)	Barry Goldwater (R)
1968	Richard Nixon (R)	Hubert Humphrey (D)
1972	Richard Nixon (R)	George McGovern (D)
1976	Jimmy Carter (D)	Gerald Ford (R)
1980	Ronald Reagan (R)	Jimmy Carter (D)
1984	Ronald Reagan (R)	Walter Mondale (D)
1988	George Bush (R)	Michael Dukakis (D)
1992	Bill Clinton (D)	George Bush (R)
1996	Bill Clinton (D)	Bob Dole (R)
2000	George W. Bush (R)	Al Gore (D)

Major party endorsement

If someone is serious about becoming president, it is vital to be chosen as the candidate for one of the two major parties. Even Eisenhower in 1952 had to become a Republican. The political endeavours of George Wallace (1968), John Anderson (1980), Ross Perot (1992 and 1996) and Pat Buchanan (2000) show that third party or independent candidacies do not lead to the White House.

Personal characteristics

All presidential candidates for major parties have been white males. Given the pools of recruitment — the vice-presidency, state governors and US Senators — this is hardly surprising. All vice-presidents have been white males. In 2004 there were only 14 women out of 100 members in the US Senate — and no African-Americans.

It is an advantage to be married. There has been no bachelor president since the nineteenth century. Until 1992, it was said that scandal involving marital infidelity could rule out a possible candidate. Senator Edward Kennedy's chances of the presidency were ended by the Chappaquiddick affair, in which a young female acquaintance drowned in his car after a late-night party. Senator Gary Hart pulled out of the 1988 nomination race after the press revealed photographs of him with a scantily-clad model named Donna Rice on a yacht called *Monkey Business*. But Bill Clinton managed to secure the Democratic Party's nomination in 1992 despite allegations surrounding Gennifer Flowers, which surfaced early in the campaign. In 1980 Ronald Reagan proved that divorce was not an insuperable problem — Nancy Reagan was his second wife.

Ability to raise large sums of money

The ability to raise money is crucial to a successful bid for the presidency. Campaigns are so expensive that very few candidates can afford to finance their own campaigns. Only billionaire candidates such as Ross Perot (1992) and Steve Forbes (1996 and 2000) have been able to finance their campaigns from their own pockets. & GEORGE BUSH

Effective organisation

During the candidate selection process, the major parties cannot endorse specific candidates. A candidate is running to *become* the Republican or Democratic presidential candidate, so candidates cannot use the party's organisational structure, either nationally or in each state. They must therefore create their own organisation. This is time-consuming, expensive and demanding. But candidates who fail to put together an effective organisation will stumble badly during the campaign. It is not coincidental that candidates such as Michael Dukakis (1988) and Bob Dole (1996), who had significant weaknesses in their campaign organisations, went on to lose the general election.

Oratorical skills and being telegenic

In the media age, the abilities to speak well and look good on television are crucial. It would be interesting to see whether candidates such as Abraham Lincoln — lampooned for his long, gangling physique — or wheelchair-bound Franklin Roosevelt could have made it to the White House in the television age. 'I'm no good at television,' Democratic candidate Walter Mondale complained in 1984. Republican Senator Phil Gramm went even further in 1996, declaring: 'I'm too ugly to be president.'

But Mondale's 1984 opponent, President Reagan, watching a recording of himself on television, joked: 'Am I really that good?' Reagan had been a Hollywood actor before going into politics. Bill Clinton's oratorical skills and his telegenic looks were advantages that contributed significantly to his victories in 1992 and 1996.

Sound and relevant policies

There is a danger that presidential elections are portrayed as all style and no substance. Style is important, but voters will soon detect a candidate whose campaign turns out to be a 'policy-free zone'. A candidate must have policies that are both practical and relevant. Sometimes candidates will start by majoring on one significant issue. For Democrat candidate Bill Clinton (1992) it was 'the economy, stupid!' For John McCain (2000) it was campaign finance reform. For Howard Dean (2004) it was the war in Iraq.

Summary

Requirements for a presidential candidate

There are two types of requirement for presidential candidates:

➤ constitutional requirements
➤ extra-constitutional requirements

The invisible primary

Unlike many democracies, in which the political parties choose candidates themselves, in the USA the candidates are chosen by ordinary voters. Although presidential elections are held in every fourth year, the manoeuvring in preparation for the elections begins months, if not years, beforehand. Because these events take place before the official first stage — the primaries — and because there is very little to see, this stage is often referred to as the invisible primary.

The invisible primary is played out mainly in the media. A candidate will hope to be 'mentioned' as a possible serious presidential candidate in such newspapers as the *Washington Post* and the *New York Times*. Or there might be a promising article in one of the weeklies, such as *Time*, *Newsweek* or *US News and World Report*. There might be offers of an in-depth interview on such serious political television programmes as *Face the Nation* (CBS), *The News Hour with Jim Lehrer* (PBS) or one of CNN's political talk shows such as *Late Edition*, *Crossfire* or *Inside Politics*.

Support for a candidate at this stage is demonstrated principally by opinion polls. Some of these polls, reported regularly by the press, may be based on a certain state while others are regional. From time to time, some polling organisations may conduct a nationwide poll. They may run head-to-head match-ups to see how candidates of one party might fair against fancied contenders from the other party.

Not all of the 'invisible' primary is invisible. Some relatively formal events do occur. There may be an opportunity for would-be candidates to address the party faithful. As early as July 2002, the Democratic Leadership Council staged such an event in New York at which such presidential hopefuls as Senators John Kerry, John Edwards and Joseph Lieberman addressed the audience. State parties sometimes organise similar events.

Then there are visits to certain key states, especially Iowa and New Hampshire, which traditionally hold the first presidential caucuses and primary, respectively. Senator Bob Dole spent so much time in Iowa in the run-up to his 1996 presidential bid that he joked he was the 'President of Iowa'.

Some candidates publish a book. Before the 2000 election we had autobiographies such as John McCain's *Faith of my Fathers* and George W. Bush's *A Charge to Keep*. Others write on a policy about which they feel strongly.

The invisible primary is also the period when money raising has to occur in earnest to accumulate a large enough 'war chest' to be taken seriously. In preparation for his 1996 presidential bid, Republican Senator Phil Gramm of Texas said he would have to raise at least $10 million before the end of 1995. Only then, said Gramm, would he be taken seriously: 'because I have the best friend in American politics — ready money.' In 1999, Elizabeth Dole ended her presidential bid during the invisible primary season, claiming that she simply could not raise enough money to be regarded as a viable candidate, while Al Gore's successful raising of huge amounts of money during 1999 deterred would-be challengers for the 2000 Democratic nomination, such as Dick Gephardt and Bob Kerrey. In 2003, Howard Dean's strong fund raising helped to propel him to the front-runner position in the Democrats' invisible primary.

Summary

The invisible primary
- occurs in the year before the election
- is played out mainly in the media
- is important for fundraising and gaining both credibility and name recognition
- eliminates a number of candidates before the first primaries and caucuses occur

Primaries and caucuses

A **primary** is an election to choose a party's candidate for an elective office, in this case the presidency. A few states hold **caucuses** instead. A caucus is a meeting for the selection of a party's candidate for an elective office. States that hold caucuses are usually geographically large but thinly populated, such as Iowa, North Dakota and Nevada.

Key terms

- **Presidential primary.** A state-based election to choose a party's candidate for the presidency. A presidential primary shows support for a candidate among ordinary voters and chooses delegates committed to vote for that candidate at the National Party Convention.
- **Presidential caucuses.** A state-based series of meetings for the selection of a party's candidate for the presidency. Held in a few geographically large but thinly populated states, caucuses attract unrepresentative and very low turnout. They fulfil the same functions as presidential primaries.

Primaries have two specific functions: to show the popularity of presidential candidates; and to choose delegates to go to the National Party Conventions. They are run under state law, which means that a great number of variations exist. The main rules of thumb are outlined below.

Timing of primaries

States must decide when to hold their primary or caucuses. The national parties usually lay down the earliest and latest possible dates — often mid-January to the beginning of June — but within that period each state can decide its own date. Some states, such as New Hampshire, schedule their contest on a day when no other primaries are being held, thereby hoping to give their state primary a prominence that it would not otherwise have. Other states deliberately arrange their primaries to coincide with other, often neighbouring, states, thereby creating a regional primary. A Tuesday early in March when a number of states arrange their primaries together has come to be known as **Super Tuesday**.

Key term

➤ **Super Tuesday.** A Tuesday in early March when a number of states coincide their presidential primaries in order to try to gain influence for their region in the selection of major party presidential candidates.

An increasing number of states like to schedule their primary early in election year, believing that the earlier primaries have more influence over candidate selection. This recent move to early scheduling is called **front loading**. The number of states holding their primaries or caucuses before the end of March increased from just 11 in 1980 to 36 in 2004, and those 36 states included seven of the eight largest states — New York, Texas, California, Florida, Illinois, Michigan and Ohio. California, for example, moved from early June to early March; New York moved from mid-April to early March. By the end of March 2004, almost 80% of the delegates to the Democratic Convention had already been chosen.

Key term

➤ **Front loading.** The phenomenon by which an increasing number of states schedule their presidential primaries or caucuses earlier in the cycle, in an attempt to increase the importance of their state in choosing major party presidential candidates.

Types of primary

There are a number of different ways of classifying primaries by type. Let us consider two. First, primaries can be divided into 'closed primaries' and 'open primaries'. It is important to understand that any registered voter can vote in a primary. But in some states, when you register, you are asked to declare your party affiliation — whether you consider yourself to be a Democrat or a Republican. In a 'closed primary', only registered Democrats can vote in the Democrat primary and only registered Republicans can vote in the Republican primary. In an 'open primary', any registered voter can vote in either primary. You decide on the day of the primary. In some states, even those who describe themselves as 'independents' are allowed to participate.

Open primaries allow what is called 'cross-over voting' which means that Democrat voters can opt to participate in the Republican primary and vice versa. This became an important issue in the Republican primaries in 2000 when, in open primary states, large numbers of independents and Democrats opted to vote in the Republican primary and voted for Senator John McCain. Take Michigan, for example. According to exit polls, only 48% of voters in the Republican primary were registered Republicans; 35% were Independents and 17% were Democrats. Among those who were actually Republicans, George W. Bush beat John McCain by 66% to 29%. But among Independents, McCain led by 67% to 26%; and among registered Democrats, McCain beat Bush by a huge 82% to 10%.

Table 2.4 A proportional primary: the California Democratic primary, 2000

Candidate	Votes	Percentage	Delegates
Al Gore	1,965,716	81.3	304
Bill Bradley	438,010	18.1	63

Table 2.5 A winner-takes-all primary: the California Republican primary, 2000

Candidate	Votes	Percentage	Delegates
George W. Bush	1,542,447	60.6	162
John McCain	885,438	34.8	0
Alan Keyes	100,195	4.0	0

Primaries can also be classified according to how delegates to the National Party Conventions are won in them. In most primaries, candidates are awarded delegates in proportion to the votes they get. These are known as 'proportional primaries' (see Table 2.4). Most states set a threshold — a minimum percentage of votes that a candidate must receive to get any of that state's delegates, usually around 10% of the vote. All Democrat and most Republican primaries are proportional primaries; but some Republican primaries are 'winner-takes-all primaries', in which whoever gets the most votes wins *all* that state's delegates (see Table 2.5).

In 2000, Arizona Democrats held the first ever presidential primary that allowed participation using the internet. Some 60,000 Arizona Democrats applied for a special password in order to vote electronically. Meanwhile, other states, such as Oregon, experimented with postal voting.

The early primaries and caucuses

For many decades now, the early primaries and caucuses have come to be regarded as crucial. Iowa traditionally holds the first caucus. But because caucuses usually attract low turnout — the 2000 Democratic caucus in Kansas attracted just 566 voters — this is usually not regarded as important as the first primary. However, the 2004 Iowa caucuses proved to be very important in the Democratic race.

For many years it was said that a candidate could not win the White House without first winning the New Hampshire primary. However, this has been proved wrong in some recent elections. Neither Bill Clinton (1992) nor George W. Bush (2000) won his party's New Hampshire primary. Indeed, as New Hampshire holds an open primary, a good deal of cross-over voting occurs, allowing unlikely challengers to do well.

In five of the last six election cycles, New Hampshire primary voters have delivered a rebuff to the front-runner of the challenging party (see Table 2.6). In the same five elections, the New Hampshire primary confirmed the front-runner of the incumbent party on every occasion (see Table 2.7).

Table 2.6 Challenging party New Hampshire primary, 1984–2004

Year	Challenging party	Front-runner	New Hampshire primary winner
1984	Democrat	Walter Mondale	Gary Hart
1988	Democrat	Michael Dukakis	Michael Dukakis
1992	Democrat	Bill Clinton	Paul Tsongas
1996	Republican	Bob Dole	Pat Buchanan
2000	Republican	George W. Bush	John McCain
2004	Democrat	Howard Dean	John Kerry

Table 2.7 Incumbent party New Hampshire primary, 1984–2004

Year	Incumbent party	Front-runner	New Hampshire primary winner
1984	Republican	Ronald Reagan	Ronald Reagan
1988	Republican	George Bush	George Bush
1992	Republican	George Bush	George Bush
1996	Democrat	Bill Clinton	Bill Clinton
2000	Democrat	Al Gore	Al Gore
2004	Republican	George W. Bush	George W. Bush

What is really important at this early stage is matching expectations. Take 1992, for example. The numerical winners of the Democratic and Republican New Hampshire primaries were, respectively, Senator Paul Tsongas and President George Bush. But the moral victors were Bill Clinton and Pat Buchanan. Beset by serious allegations of womanising, drug taking and draft dodging in the Vietnam War, Clinton was not expected to do well. So when he came a respectable second with 25% of the vote, Clinton was able to claim that he was 'the comeback kid'. Although Pat Buchanan finished second in the Republican primary, the fact that he managed to gain 37% of the vote against an incumbent president was an impressive performance, and far better than had been expected.

Victory in New Hampshire or simply exceeding expectations — or in John McCain's case in 2000, both — brings three big bonuses: media coverage, money and a boost in the opinion polls. Following his New Hampshire victory in 2000, John McCain enjoyed pages of favourable stories in such weeklies as *Time* and *Newsweek*. And in the 48 hours after his New Hampshire win, the McCain campaign raised $810,000 through its internet site alone. An opinion poll in South Carolina, which held its primary just 18 days later, showed McCain going from trailing Bush by 20 percentage points to leading Bush by 5 percentage points. Likewise, failing to live up to expectations can be devastating. The day after gaining just 1% in the Republican Iowa caucuses in 2000, Senator Orrin Hatch withdrew from the race. In 2004, John Kerry's strong showing in both Iowa and New Hampshire was critical in his winning the nomination.

The increased importance of primaries

Nowadays, presidential primaries play an important role in the process of choosing presidential candidates. They really are the only route to becoming the presidential nominee of a major party. However, that was not always the case.

In the 1950s and 1960s, most states did not hold presidential primaries. The parties preferred to control candidate selection through a series of State Party Conventions. Whereas any registered voter can vote in a primary or caucus, only certain selected party members could participate in these state conventions. Here, in the so-called 'smoke-filled rooms', decisions were made largely by the 'party bosses' — powerful state party leaders such as city mayors. It was they, and not the ordinary voters, who decided who would become the party's presidential candidate. The few primaries that were held were not decisive. In 1968, in neither party did the overall winner of the primaries get his party's presidential nomination (see Table 2.8).

Table 2.8 Presidential primary results, 1968

Candidate	Total popular vote in primaries (%)
Democratic Party	
Senator Eugene McCarthy	38.7
Senator Robert Kennedy	30.6
President Lyndon Johnson	5.1
Vice-President Hubert Humphrey*	2.2
Republican Party	
Governor Ronald Reagan	37.9
Vice-President Richard Nixon*	37.5
Governor Nelson Rockefeller	3.7

*Eventual nominees

This system was deemed undemocratic, elitist, non-participatory and potentially corrupt. It was reformed significantly at the instigation of the Democratic Party following the events at its 1968 National Party Convention. That convention chose Vice-President Humphrey as the party's presidential candidate despite the fact that he had not entered any primaries at all. The few votes he got were gained by voters writing in his name on the ballot paper — so-called 'write-in' votes.

Following Humphrey's loss to Richard Nixon in the general election that November, the Democrats established the **McGovern–Fraser Commission** to recommend reforms of the presidential nomination process. It was this commission that led to the significant increase in the number of states holding presidential primaries from 1972 onwards. Thus, the nomination process has changed dramatically over the past 30 years.

Strengths of the new nomination process

The new nomination system is certainly an improvement on what went before.

➤ There is an increased level of participation by ordinary voters. In 1968, the last year

Key term

> **McGovern–Fraser Commission.** The commission established by the Democratic Party following the 1968 presidential election to recommend reforms to the presidential nomination process. The commission was largely responsible for the significant reforms that democratised the presidential candidate selection system, starting with the 1972 election cycle.

of the unreformed system, only 11.7 million Americans took part in the nomination process, or 11% of the voting-age population. By 1988, the figure was 35 million, or 21% of the voting-age population.

> There is a significant increase in the choice of candidates. In 1968, there were just five presidential candidates to choose from — three Democrats and two Republicans. In 2000, there were 14 candidates — 12 Republicans and two Democrats.

> The process is opened up to outsiders — politicians who do not initially have a national reputation, such as Jimmy Carter (1976), Bill Clinton (1992) and Howard Dean (2004).

> The power of the party bosses is done away with, thus lessening opportunities for corruption and making the process more democratic.

> The gruelling race through the primaries is seen by many as an appropriately demanding test for a demanding job. In 1992, Senator Paul Tsongas, who had fought back from cancer to run for the presidency, was seen to have a lighter schedule than his rivals. Although many admired Tsongas as a person and liked his policies, they saw in the primaries that he might not have the physical resilience to be president.

Criticisms of the new nominating process

Writing in the *Washington Post* at the end of March 1996, David Broder commented on the presidential nominating process: 'Any way you look at it, this is madness.' Meanwhile, the *New York Times* editorial of 3 March described it as 'a crazy process'. Academics, too, have criticisms. Professor Robert Loevy (1995) wrote:

> More voters, to be sure, take part in [presidential] primary elections than in [the old system of] caucuses and [state] conventions. But what of the *quality* of that partici-pation? Primary voters often know little about the many candidates listed on the ballot. They may drop in at the primary election booth between a trip to the drug store and the local supermarket and give little more thought to choosing candidates than to choosing among brands of toothpaste or canned vegetables.

There is widespread voter apathy and boredom

More people do participate in the nominating process than was the case 30 years ago. However, the 36 million people who voted in presidential primaries and caucuses in 2000 represented just 15% of the voting-age population.

Primary voters are unrepresentative of the voting-age population

Low turnout would not matter too much if those who did vote were a representative cross-section of the voting-age population — but they are not. Primary voters tend to be older, better educated, wealthier and more ideological than the voting-age population as a whole. As a result, certain types of candidate — especially more ideological candidates — tend to do better in primaries than they should do. In 1996, Pat Buchanan — a conservative Republican — won at least 20% of the vote in 26 primaries, and in six of those primaries his vote exceeded 30%. Buchanan would never reach anything like those percentages in a general election.

The process is far too long

In 1960, Senator John Kennedy announced his candidacy for the presidency just 66 days before the first primary. In readiness for the 2004 campaign, Senator John Kerry announced his candidacy 423 days before the first primary. Table 2.9 shows the significant effect of the McGovern–Fraser reforms in the early 1970s in this respect.

Table 2.9 **Number of days before the first primary that the eventual nominee of the challenging party announced candidacy, 1960–2004**

Year	Challenging party	Presidential candidate	Days before first primary
1960	Democrat	John Kennedy	66
1964	Republican	Barry Goldwater	67
1968	Republican	Richard Nixon	40
1972	Democrat	George McGovern	414
1976	Democrat	Jimmy Carter	449
1980	Republican	Ronald Reagan	105
1984	Democrat	Walter Mondale	372
1988	Democrat	Michael Dukakis	293
1992	Democrat	Bill Clinton	138
1996	Republican	Bob Dole	252
2000	Republican	George W. Bush	253
2004	Democrat	John Kerry	423

The process is very expensive

This is something of a circular argument. Candidates need to raise a large amount of money, so they need to start their campaigns early. Campaigns are therefore much longer and much more expensive. With the onset of 'front loading', there is now little time to raise money once the primaries have started. It has to be done before they begin, so candidates start early. In the 2000 primaries, Al Gore raised $33.8 million and received a further $15.3 million in matching funds. George W. Bush raised $91.3 million. When Elizabeth Dole pulled out of the 2000 Republican race before the primaries had even started, she complained that 'the money has become the message'.

The process is too dominated by the media, especially television

In the pre-reform era, decisions about candidates were made by a small group of professional politicians. They were people who knew the candidates. The role for the media was small. But in today's process, the decision-makers — ordinary voters — must rely on the media for information about the candidates. Some think the media ill-suited for this role. The media become the new 'king makers', the replacements of the latter-day 'party bosses'. Loevy (1995) is critical of this. He writes:

> Our present nominating process has become a televised horse race focusing more on rival media consultants and advertising executives than on competing ideas, programmes, or even the character of the candidates.... Popularity polls, slick spot ads and television coverage of the early primaries offer episodes and spectacles and the average citizen is hard pressed to distinguish significance from entertainment.

Primaries can all too easily develop into bitter personal battles ·

In the 2000 Republican primaries, a McCain television commercial accused George W. Bush of not telling the truth, likening Bush to President Clinton. 'That's about as low as you can get,' shot back an angry Governor Bush. Other campaigns that have become notoriously bad-tempered were those between George Bush and Pat Buchanan in 1992, between George Bush and Bob Dole in 1988, and between Jimmy Carter and Ted Kennedy in 1980. It is no coincidence that all three of the eventual nominees in these contests went on to lose in the general election.

There is a lack of 'peer review', leading to a failure to test presidential qualities

Back in the pre-reform era, presidential candidates were selected largely by other professional politicians. This constituted what is known as 'peer review' — the judgment of one's colleagues or equals. They had a good idea as to what qualities were required to be a successful president. Nowadays, however, candidates are chosen by ordinary voters who cannot be expected to know much about presidential qualities, let alone whether this governor or that Senator possesses any of them. As a result, primaries tend to test *campaigning* qualities rather than *presidential* qualities. Professors Cronin and Genovese (1998) draw attention to this state of affairs:

> What it takes to become president may not be what is needed to govern the nation. To win a presidential election takes ambition, money, luck and masterful public relations strategies. To govern a democracy requires much more. It requires the formation of a governing coalition and the ability to compromise and bargain. 'People who win primaries may become good presidents, but it ain't necessarily so,' wrote columnist David Broder.

Professor Jeane Kirkpatrick has spoken of how professional politicians are 'uniquely qualified' to choose presidential candidates because 'they know the nature of the political job'. Professor Austin Ranney bemoans the fact that the parties are now 'the prizes, not the judges' in the nomination process.

How to improve the nomination process further

No one is suggesting that the reforms introduced in the early 1970s have been completely useless, or that there should be a return to the era before the reforms were adopted, with party bosses in smoke-filled rooms, but there are a number of suggested reforms which some think would further improve the nomination process. The reforms are mostly concerned with the timing of primaries and attempts to increase the role of professional politicians without losing the democratic elements of the current system. Three possible reforms are detailed below.

Regional primaries

The country would be divided into four regions: Northeast, South, Midwest and West. Four days would be set aside for these regional primaries: the first Tuesdays of March, April, May and June. The order of the regions would change every 4 years, with the region that went last in the previous election going first in the next one. Iowa and New Hampshire would probably be allowed to opt out of this scheme and hold their contests in February. The three main advantages would be: the end of front loading; cutting down the amount of travelling required by candidates; and allowing a more measured decision with a chance for second thoughts by the voters in later primaries.

Another variation of this plan is to divide the states into four groups according to population size, with the smallest states voting first and the largest states voting last. This would certainly get rid of front loading. This plan was put before the 2000 Republican National Convention but was defeated when Governor George W. Bush let it be known that he was not in favour of it.

Weighting votes for elected politicians at the National Party Conventions

The second proposal would require the parties to devise a mechanism for weighting the votes of elected politicians — members of Congress, state governors, city mayors and the like — at their National Party Conventions. This would clearly increase both the opportunities for 'peer review' and the role of the parties themselves. Professor Thomas Cronin has called for putting 'the party back into presidential picking'. This proposal would move in that direction.

A pre-primary mini-convention

This proposal is the most radical of the three. It involves the introduction by each party of a pre-primary mini-convention: 'pre-primary' because these conventions would be held before the primaries; 'mini' because these conventions would be significantly smaller and shorter than the traditional National Conventions. The delegates attending the mini-conventions would be all the major elected office holders of the party, numbering maybe 500 or 600 for each party.

The sole function of the mini-convention would be to approve a list of up to three possible presidential candidates, who would then run in the primaries. To be nominated at the mini-convention, a would-be candidate would need to present a petition signed by at least 10% of the mini-convention delegates. Having presented the petition, any would-be candidate would be allowed an hour of the convention's time: 30 minutes to have someone of their choice make a nominating speech on their behalf; 30 minutes to deliver their own speech. Once all the speeches had been made, delegates would vote, with each delegate having one vote. The top three candidates in this ballot would then enter the primaries. The others would be eliminated.

But are primaries really that important?

One final thought on presidential primaries. Are they really important? Do they really choose the presidential candidates of the major parties, or do they merely confirm the frontrunners who emerged during the 'invisible primary'? Between 1960 and 2004 there were 12 presidential elections and therefore 24 major party presidential candidates chosen. On 20 of those 24 occasions, the candidate who was finally chosen was the same as the candidate who was the frontrunner before a single vote was cast in any primary or caucus. In the Republican Party during this period, all 12 front-runners were confirmed as presidential candidates. Only in the Democratic Party — in 1968, 1972, 1988 and 2004 — did the primaries truly play a significant role and choose a candidate who was not the frontrunner before the start of the formal nominating process. In that sense, the nomination of Senator John Kerry rather than Governor Howard Dean by the Democrats in 2004 was unusual. Dean had been the frontrunner throughout the invisible primary, yet collapsed in the first set of caucuses and primaries.

Summary

Primaries and caucuses

➢ Primaries show the level of popularity for presidential candidates.
➢ They choose delegates to go to the National Party Conventions.
➢ They are more important than they used to be.
➢ They have a number of merits and demerits.
➢ They may become the subject of further reforms.

National Party Conventions

The Democrats and Republicans — and some third parties — hold a **National Party Convention** during July or August of election year which usually lasts for 4 days. It is traditional for the challenging party to hold its convention first. In 2004, the Democrats met in Boston while the Republicans went to New York. The venue is decided at least a year in advance by each party's National Committee. Conventions are attended by delegates, most of them chosen in the primaries and caucuses. The US — and the world's — media also turn up.

Key term

➢ **National Party Convention.** The meeting held once every 4 years by each of the major — and some minor — parties to select their presidential and vice-presidential candidates and write a party platform.

Formal functions

The National Party Conventions are said to perform three formal functions.

Choosing the party's presidential candidate

In theory, the conventions choose the party's presidential candidate in a roll-call vote, in which each state's delegates announce which candidate they wish to vote for. In the pre-reform days, delegates came to the convention and made up their minds in the convention hall, but these days, the vast majority of delegates arrive at the convention as 'committed delegates' — committed, that is, to vote for a particular candidate in the first ballot if that candidate is still in the race. As the number of committed delegates is known beforehand — because it is decided in each state primary or caucus — the result of the convention ballot to choose the presidential candidate is, these days, a foregone conclusion.

To win the presidential nomination, a candidate must receive an absolute majority of the delegate votes. In 2004, the number of delegates attending the Democratic National Convention was 4,322. John Kerry therefore required 2,162 delegate votes to win the nomination, but by late March — 4 months before the convention — it was known that Senator Kerry had over 2,000 committed delegates.

It would be more accurate, therefore, to say that the convention confirms — rather than chooses — the party's presidential candidate. Not since the Republican convention of 1976 has the choice of the presidential candidate really been in any doubt at the opening of either party's convention. In that year, President Gerald Ford defeated the former Governor of California, Ronald Reagan, by 1,187 votes to 1,070 votes. Had 60 delegates switched from Ford to Reagan, Reagan would have won.

If no candidate gains an absolute majority on the first ballot, balloting continues until one candidate does. During these ballots, delegates become free agents, no longer committed to vote for a certain candidate. Furthermore, new candidates could enter at this stage. The first 13 elections of the twentieth century — between 1900 and 1948 — saw seven occasions when either one or both parties required more than one ballot to choose

Republican delegates at the 2000 National Party Convention

Table 2.10 National Party Conventions, 1952–2004: venues, candidates, ballots

	Republican Party			Democratic Party		
Year	Venue	Candidate	Ballots	Venue	Candidate	Ballots
1952	Chicago	Dwight Eisenhower	1	Chicago	Adlai Stevenson	3
1956	San Francisco	Dwight Eisenhower	1	Chicago	Adlai Stevenson	1
1960	Chicago	Richard Nixon	1	Los Angeles	John Kennedy	1
1964	San Francisco	Barry Goldwater	1	Atlantic City	Lyndon Johnson	1
1968	Miami Beach	Richard Nixon	1	Chicago	Hubert Humphrey	1
1972	Miami Beach	Richard Nixon	1	Miami Beach	George McGovern	1
1976	Kansas City	Gerald Ford	1	New York	Jimmy Carter	1
1980	Detroit	Ronald Reagan	1	New York	Jimmy Carter	1
1984	Dallas	Ronald Reagan	1	San Francisco	Walter Mondale	1
1988	New Orleans	George Bush	1	Atlanta	Michael Dukakis	1
1992	Houston	George Bush	1	New York	Bill Clinton	1
1996	San Diego	Bob Dole	1	Chicago	Bill Clinton	1
2000	Philadelphia	George W. Bush	1	Los Angeles	Al Gore	1
2004	New York	George W. Bush	1	Boston	John Kerry	1

their presidential candidate. In the next 14 elections — between 1952 and 2004 — there was only one such occasion, in 1952. There has not been a second ballot at a major party convention for over 50 years (see Table 2.10).

Choosing the vice-presidential candidate

Formally, the National Party Convention chooses the vice-presidential candidate, but, again, this function has been lost. Not since 1956 has a convention chosen the vice-presidential candidate — or 'running mate', as they are called. Nowadays, the running mate is chosen by the presidential candidate and merely confirmed by the convention. Indeed, in 2000, both George W. Bush and Al Gore announced their running mates — Dick Cheney and Joseph Lieberman — a week *before* their respective conventions.

Deciding the party platform

The **party platform** is a document containing policies that the candidate intends to pursue if elected president (see Box 2.1). It is put together by the Platform Committee under the direction of the party's National Committee. The Platform Committee holds hearings around the country during the first 6 months of the election year. A draft platform is then presented to delegates at the National Party Convention. There may be debates at the convention on various parts of the platform — known as 'planks'. More recently, however, parties have sought to avoid heated debates on policy issues at their conventions. The media often portray such debates as evidence of a divided party.

Key term

> **Party platform.** A statement of a party's policies for an upcoming presidential election that is used during the campaign to win support from voters. It contains the policies that the party's candidate intends to pursue if elected president.

In 1992, the Republican platform stated that 'we believe the unborn child has a fundamental individual right to life that cannot be infringed', ruling out abortion under any circumstances, and went on to call for 'a human life amendment to the Constitution'. A *CBS News* poll found that only 7% of delegates supported the plank. Much of what is in party platforms is little more than support for motherhood, the American Dream and apple pie (see Box 2.1).

Box 2.1 Party platforms

'We share a common dream and common goals:
A strong America that protects its citizens and champions their democratic ideals;
An America with a vibrant and growing economy that improves the standard of living for all;
An America where people feel safe and secure in their homes, on their streets and in their communities;
An America where our children receive the best education in the world.'

Republican Party platform, 1996

'We need a smaller, more effective, more efficient, less bureaucratic government that reflects our time-honoured values. The American people do not want big government solutions and they do not want empty promises. They want a government that is for them, not against them; that doesn't interfere with their lives but enhances their quality of life. They want a course that is reasonable, help that is realistic, and solutions that can be delivered — a moderate, achievable, common-sense agenda that will improve people's daily lives and not increase the size of government.'

Democratic Party platform, 1996

Informal functions

Given that all three of the formal functions of the National Party Conventions are now questionable, it might appear that there is little point in holding them. The importance of the conventions is in their informal, or hidden, functions.

Promoting party unity

This may be the most important function of all. The primaries can turn into bitter personal battles, and it is vital that internal party wounds are healed before the general election campaign begins. Divided parties are rarely winning parties. The convention gives a golden opportunity to heal the wounds.

In the 2000 Republican Convention, it was important that George W. Bush and John McCain portrayed a united front. Twice in his convention speech, Senator McCain referred to 'my friend Governor Bush'. He then went on: 'I support him, I am grateful to him and I am proud of him.'

There are, however, examples of conventions at which party unity was not rebuilt: the 1992 Republican Convention, where President George Bush remained at loggerheads with his primary election rival, Pat Buchanan; and the 1980 Democrat Convention, where President Carter and Senator Edward Kennedy continued their unfriendly rivalry. It is no coincidence that Bush and Carter were both defeated later in the year.

Enthusing the party faithful

In the general election campaign there is a lot of hard work to do. It is vital that the party faithful in all the 50 states feel enthusiastic and committed as they head home to fight for their party and candidate during the 9-week campaign. There will be meetings to organise, phone calls to make, literature to distribute and voters to transport to and from the polls, and they will be at the forefront of the organisation.

Enthusing the ordinary voters

It is equally important to enthuse the ordinary voters. As they are not present in the convention hall, this must be done through television. There is one golden opportunity to gain the attention of the ordinary voters during the convention and that is when the newly adopted presidential candidate delivers his **acceptance speech** — traditionally on the convention's final night (see Box 2.2).

Key term
> **Acceptance speech.** The nationally televised speech delivered by a party's presidential candidate in prime time on the final night of the National Party Convention.

Most voters will have paid little, if any, attention to the primaries. Now that the candidates have been selected and the policies finalised, voters may well tune in and take their first serious look at the party, its candidate and its policies. First impressions can be important, especially if the candidate is running for national office for the first time — as Governor Bush was doing in 2000. Indeed, Bush was the first politician to win the presidential nomination of his party at the first attempt since Senator Barry Goldwater in 1964. This meant that Bush had to introduce himself more thoroughly to the US voters in his convention speech.

In his acceptance speech, Governor Bush made subtle but telling references to President Clinton's problems concerning the Monica Lewinsky scandal. Vice-President Al Gore used his speech to try to make sure that voters saw him, not in the shadow of Bill Clinton, but as his 'own man'.

Opinion polls register the immediate effect of the acceptance speeches, with instant polls showing what, if any, increase the candidate has enjoyed as a result of the speech. The increase in a candidate's poll rating as compared with the last pre-convention poll is referred to as 'bounce'. In the elections between 1960 and 2000, the average 'bounce'

Box 2.2 **Acceptance speeches at the 2000 National Party Conventions**

Governor George W. Bush

➤ 'They have not led. We will.'

➤ 'Our current president [Clinton] embodied the potential of a generation. So many talents. So much charm. Such great skill. But in the end, to what end? So much promise, to no great purpose.'

➤ 'And so when [at the Inauguration] I put my hand on the Bible, I will swear to not only uphold the laws of our land, I will swear to uphold the honour and dignity of the Office to which I have been elected, so help me God.'

Vice-President Al Gore

➤ 'Millions of Americans will live better lives for a long time to come because of the job that's been done by President Bill Clinton.'

➤ 'I stand before you tonight as my own man, and I want you to know me for who I truly am.'

➤ 'This election is not an award for past performance. I'm not asking you to vote for me on the basis of the economy we have.'

---

for the candidate of the challenging party was between 7 and 8 percentage points, and for the White House party candidate just over 4 percentage points. As Table 2.11 shows, in 2000 George Bush's 'bounce' was just below average, while Al Gore's was well above average.

The importance of modern-day conventions

Many commentators suggest that, in comparison to the conventions of years ago, modern-day National Party Conventions are of little importance. The parties seek to deliver scripted, sanitised conventions, devoid of much political content. No longer are the conventions addressed by an endless line of politicians. Modern-day conventions feature choreographed videos along with stars of stage and screen. In 1996, actor Christopher Reeve appeared at the Democrat Convention. The 2000 Republican Convention featured the professional wrestling star The Rock. Even the traditional 'roll call' — once one of the highlights of the convention — has been shuffled away from prime time lest its predictability encourage viewers to reach for their remote controls.

Television coverage of the conventions has declined significantly in recent years. In 1968, the three terrestrial television companies — ABC, CBS and NBC — put out 46 hours of coverage of that year's Republican Convention. In 2000, the same three companies managed just $10\frac{1}{2}$ hours of coverage of the Republican Convention. The only comprehensive television coverage was to be found on the cable channels — CNN, MSNBC and C-SPAN.

It would be wrong to write off the National Party Conventions as useless: they do still perform important functions. As presidential election scholar Stephen Wayne (2001) put it, the conventions 'may have become less newsworthy, but they are still important'.

Table 2.11 Post-convention 'bounce', 1960–2000

Year	Challenging party candidate	Bounce	White House party candidate	Bounce
1960	John Kennedy (D)	+5	Richard Nixon (R)	+4
1964	Barry Goldwater (R)	+5	Lyndon Johnson (D)	+3
1968	Richard Nixon (R)	+5	Hubert Humphrey (D)	–7
1972	George McGovern (D)	0	Richard Nixon (R)	+7
1976	Jimmy Carter (D)	+9	Gerald Ford (R)	+5
1980	Ronald Reagan (R)	+8	Jimmy Carter (D)	+10
1984	Walter Mondale (D)	+9	Ronald Reagan (R)	+4
1988	Michael Dukakis (D)	+7	George Bush (R)	+6
1992	Bill Clinton (D)	+16	George Bush (R)	+5
1996	Bob Dole (R)	+11	Bill Clinton (D)	+5
2000	George W. Bush (R)	+6	Al Gore (D)	+7

Summary

National Party Conventions

➤ National Party Conventions have both formal and informal functions.

➤ They are regarded as less important than they used to be.

➤ They may still be of more importance than some commentators suggest.

Campaign finance

By the 1970s there were increasing concerns about the amount of money being spent in presidential elections and how it was being spent. In the 1972 presidential election, President Nixon formed his own re-election committee — the Committee for the Re-election of the President (CRP). Through this committee, the Nixon campaign managed to raise vast sums of money, far more than the Democratic contender George McGovern. It was through CRP that the break-in and bugging at the Watergate complex in Washington DC was masterminded. From this developed what came to be known as the Watergate affair, which in the end led to Nixon's resignation from the presidency less than 2 years after the election.

The Watergate affair gave much-needed impetus to reforming the campaign finance system. Congress had begun to pass campaign finance reform legislation in 1971, but the year in which Nixon resigned — 1974 — saw a much more significant set of reforms. The Federal Election Campaign Act of 1974 made a number of significant changes (see Box 2.3), hoping to reduce candidates' reliance on a few, very wealthy donors — known as 'fat cats' — and equalise the amount of money spent by both the major parties.

Box 2.3 Federal Election Campaign Act (1974)

The Federal Election Campaign Act:

➤ limited individual contributions to a candidate to $1,000

➤ limited corporate contributions to a candidate to $5,000

➤ forbade donations from foreign donors

➤ limited candidates' expenditure to $10 million in the primaries and a further $20 million in the general election: these figures were index-linked for inflation, rising to around $34 million and $68 million respectively by 2000

➤ provided 'matching funds' from federal taxpayers on a dollar-for-dollar basis for contributions up to $250

➤ established the Federal Election Commission (FEC) to enforce and regulate the new system

The objectives of these reforms were praiseworthy and they were partly successful. But the law was found to have too many loopholes and was weakened by both the Supreme Court and Congress. In 1976, in *Buckley v. Valeo*, the Supreme Court ruled that limitations on what individuals or Political Action Committees could spend either supporting or opposing a candidate infringed 1st Amendment rights and were therefore unconstitutional. In 1979, Congress further weakened the law by allowing parties to raise money for such aspects as voter registration and get-out-the-vote drives as well as 'party building' activities. This is the so-called 'soft money' that would soon be regarded by most observers to be out of control.

By the 1990s, campaign finance reform was again on the political agenda. The 1996 election saw allegations surrounding President Clinton's re-election campaign, involving foreign donations and a fundraiser at a Buddhist temple in California. There were also stories of White House fundraising through coffee meetings with the president and overnight stays in the White House's Lincoln Bedroom. Four years later, Senator John McCain made campaign finance reform the focal point of his bid for the Republican presidential nomination. These and other unconnected incidents gave increased momentum to attempts both in the House of Representatives and in the Senate to pass a Campaign Finance Reform Bill. Success eventually came in 2002, mainly through the endeavours of Senators John McCain and Russell Feingold (see Box 2.4).

John McCain wanted to stop excessive campaign finance

Box 2.4 McCain–Feingold reforms (2002)

➤ National party committees banned from raising or spending 'soft money'.

➤ Labour unions and corporations forbidden from funding issue advertisements directly.

➤ The use of union and corporate money to broadcast advertisements that mention a federal candidate within 60 days of a general election or 30 days of a primary prohibited.

➤ Fundraising on federal property forbidden.

Summary

Campaign finance

➤ Campaign finance has been subject to two major sets of reforms in the past 30 years.

➤ The reforms have often proved ineffective in curbing abuses.

➤ The courts have often found the reforms to be unconstitutional.

The role of the media

Professor Thomas Patterson (1993) wrote: 'The United States is the only democracy that organises its national election campaign around the news media.' The term 'the media' includes print journalism as well as television, but the latter is by far the more important. It is also important to remember that newspapers, weekly journals and television stations have their own websites. This gives these media a much wider audience than in the pre-electronic age.

Print journalism

What is important about the role of newspapers such as the *Washington Post* and the *New York Times* during the election is not just their reporting of campaign events, but their editorial comment and analysis. The *op-ed* pages — short for 'Opinion-Editorial' — are where the paper may have a national voice. The views expressed in the op-ed pages of papers such as these will often be quoted nationally — by other papers, on television discussion programmes or even by politicians themselves. Nearer to election day, such papers often endorse one or other of the major party candidates.

Another important form of print journalism comes in what are called 'the weeklies'. The two leading weeklies are *Time* and *Newsweek*, which are widely sold at convenience stores, airport shops and the like. Writers such as Joe Klein of *Newsweek* have a national reputation. When Klein wrote of the 2000 Democratic primary challenger Bill Bradley that 'he had the opposite-of-John McCain effect because he is so removed [from the voters]', people sat up and took notice. The election often forms the 'cover story' of these publications.

Television

Television can be divided into two groups: old television, meaning the terrestrial channels — ABC, CBS, NBC and PBS; and new television, meaning the cable channels, such as CNN and MSNBC. Television carries a variety of programmes that contribute to the presidential election.

News, interview and talk show programmes

➤ **News coverage.** This is where most Americans gain their knowledge of the campaign, be it from the 24-hour-a-day style programme of *CNN Headline News* or ABC's *World News Tonight*. These programmes constitute mainly news reporting of the day's events with a small amount of analysis and comment.

➤ **Political comment programmes.** These include the Sunday morning talk shows on the terrestrial channels, such as *Meet the Press*, as well as *The News Hour with Jim Lehrer* each weekday evening on PBS and *The Capital Gang* on CNN. These programmes have in-depth interviews by respected interviewers and attract a more politically aware audience.

➤ **Chat shows.** The most notable show is CNN's *Larry King Live*. The interviews on this programme are less searching and are aimed at a less politically aware audience. After the interview there is a phone-in — a chance for viewers to put their questions to the Republican or Democrat politician. One might go even further and include programmes like *The Arsenio Hall Show*, on which candidate Bill Clinton played his saxophone in 1992. In 2000, both Gore and Bush appeared on *Oprah* with the celebrity talk show host Oprah Winfrey, as well as recording parodies of themselves for a special edition of NBC's satirical show *Saturday Night Live*. In October 2000, George W. Bush appeared in a 13-minute segment of *The Late Show with David Letterman* — longer than the total time he appeared on the evening news of all three networks (ABC, NBC and CBS) during the whole month.

Political commercials

The use candidates can make of the free media is limited. They need to buy time on commercial television to air their political commercials, or 'spots' as they are often called. Political commercials started on television in 1952 when Republican candidate Dwight Eisenhower put out a 30-second biographical spot titled *The Man from Abilene*. There was also a series of policy-based spots called *Eisenhower Answers America*, in which Eisenhower gave short answers to questions put by ordinary Americans.

To the biographical and policy commercials, the 1960s added the negative commercial. In 1964, the campaign of President Johnson came up with what became known as the *Daisy Girl* commercial, in which the image of a little girl counting and pulling out the petals of a daisy suddenly turns into a nuclear countdown and explosion. The spot, aired only once, did not even mention Johnson's political opponent, Senator Barry Goldwater. But viewers made the connection unprompted. This poses an interesting question about political advertising: whether it actually changes people's minds, or merely confirms what they already know about a particular candidate. Goldwater was already known to advocate what some saw as a rather trigger-happy foreign policy. The *Daisy Girl* commercial merely reinforced many voters' fears about a Goldwater presidency.

Negative commercials can backfire too. In 1988, a spot about crime featured the story of Willie Horton, a criminal who had been let out of a jail in Massachusetts — the state of which Bush's opponent, Michael Dukakis, was governor — and had then committed rape and murder. When it later transpired that Horton was black, the Bush campaign was accused of playing on people's fears about blacks and crime.

Box 2.5 Television commercials from the 2000 election

'I think there's a lot of cynicism today in America because of broken promises. I believe most people expect the best of our elected officials, and when elected officials disappoint them, it creates a cynical environment. Secondly, I believe oftentimes campaigns resort to mud throwing and name-calling. And Americans are sick and tired of that kind of campaigning. What they want to hear is what's on people's minds and where the candidates' hearts are. I'm going to run a campaign that is hopeful and optimistic and very positive.'

An early Governor Bush commercial with Bush in casual clothes sitting alone, talking with ordinary people and spending time with his family

'Vietnam veteran. Father of four. Married 30 years. Al Gore will fight for families. Tax cuts for middle-class families, including a $10,000-a-year tax deduction for college tuition. Continued welfare reform with time limits, work requirements. Force deadbeat parents to take responsibility for their children. A crime victim's bill of rights to protect victims, not just criminals. Fight violence and pornography on the internet, helping parents block out what children shouldn't see. Al Gore. He'll put his values to work for us.'

A commercial aired from late September 2000 by the Gore campaign with pictures of Gore in an army uniform in Vietnam, then with his family and finally meeting ordinary people

Perhaps a safer bet is to use humour in negative commercials, attempting to poke fun at political opponents. In 1992, President Bush's campaign created a spot featuring two politicians — both with their faces blanked out to conceal their identity — making opposing speeches on such issues as free trade, drugs and the Persian Gulf War. As, one at a time, the faces of the politicians were revealed, the voice-over said: 'One of these politicians is Bill Clinton. Unfortunately, so is the other!'

Another potential pitfall of television commercials is that the words a candidate uses in one election can be replayed by an opponent 4 years later to draw attention to the fact that promises might have been broken. Some of General Eisenhower's answers from the 1952 *Eisenhower Answers America* spots were re-used in 1956 by the Democrats under the title of *What's that again, General?* In 1992, President Bush found his 1988 'Read my lips — no new taxes' promise replayed by the Clinton campaign.

Televised debates

Televised debates between the major party candidates have now become a traditional part of the campaign. Debates have varied in number and format since they were first used, but a pattern has now developed: three 90-minute debates between the two major parties' presidential candidates and one 90-minute debate between their vice-presidential candidates in differing formats, occurring usually between late September and mid-October.

The first debates were held in 1960, but it was another 16 years before televised debates were held again. Over the years, different debate formats have evolved. Initially, the candidates, standing behind podiums some distance from each other, were asked questions by one 'moderator'. This developed into a panel of up to three members of the press who asked questions. A non-participatory audience was introduced in 1976.

Then, in 1992, what has become known as the 'Town Hall' style of debate was tried for the second of the three debates. The candidates did not stand behind podiums but were seated on bar stools, facing an audience of undecided voters who put questions directly to the candidates. A moderator was there merely to keep order. This format was used for one of the three debates in 1992, 1996 and 2000.

The 2000 debates saw another new format — the round-table discussion in which the candidates talked *with* each other rather than *at* each other or an audience.

The only time a third-party candidate was allowed to participate was in 1992, when independent candidate Ross Perot took part in the three presidential debates and his running mate, James Stockdale, joined the vice-presidential debate.

The rules of televised debates

Four rules of thumb are worth noting about presidential debates.

➤ Style is often more important than substance. What you say is not as important as how you say it and how you look. In the second Bush–Clinton debate in 1992, the camera caught Bush at one moment looking at his watch. He appeared eager to end his discomfort. In the first Gore–Bush debate in 2000, Gore appeared overly made-up. He interrupted Bush frequently and, while Bush was answering, made audible sighs and rolled his eyes. Within days, Gore was being ridiculed on *Saturday Night Live* as a 'smarty pants'. Just after the start of the second — Town Hall style — debate, Gore strode across the stage to stand right next to Bush while the latter was still speaking. Bush merely gave him a quizzical glance.

Al Gore gestures to the audience in a 'Town Hall' style televised presidential debate with George W. Bush, 2000

➤ Verbal gaffes can be costly. When, in 1976, President Ford mistakenly claimed that Poland was not under the control of the Soviet Union, it was an expensive error. When, in 1980, President Carter tried to personalise an answer by mentioning how he and his 10-year old daughter Amy had talked about nuclear weapons, the cartoon artists had a field day at Carter's expense. In 2000, Gore was caught out in the first debate making some exaggerated claims to which the Bush campaign immediately drew attention after the debate.

➤ Good sound bites are helpful. Many voters do not watch the full debate but they do see the sound bite the television networks clip out for their breakfast shows the next morning. In 1992, when President Bush attacked Governor Clinton for protesting against the Vietnam War while a Rhodes Scholar at Oxford, Clinton shot back:

> When [Senator] Joe McCarthy went around this country attacking people's patri-otism, he was wrong. And a Senator from Connecticut stood up to him named Prescott Bush. Your father was right to stand up to Joe McCarthy; you were wrong to attack my patriotism. I was opposed to the war, but I love my country.

Bush looked away from Clinton and down at the podium in front of him, indicating that Clinton's response had hit home. Four years later, debating Senator Dole, President Clinton was asked whether he thought 73-year-old Bob Dole was too old to be president. His answer provided a perfect sound bite: 'I don't think Senator Dole is too old to be president. It's the age of his ideas that I question.'

➤ The fourth 'rule' is that debates are potentially more difficult for incumbents than for challengers. Incumbents have a record to defend and they have words spoken 4 years earlier that can be thrown back at them this time around. In 1980, challenger Ronald Reagan had jauntily dismissed President Carter's attacks with a nod of the head, a smile and the words: 'There you go again.' Four years later Reagan unwisely tried the same phrase on challenger Walter Mondale, who was ready for it:

> Now, Mr President, you said, 'There you go again.' Remember the last time you said that? You said it when President Carter said that you were going to cut Medicare. And what did you do right after the election? You went out and tried to cut $20 billion out of Medicare.

The supposed-to-be-silent audience burst into applause and Reagan looked distinctly uncomfortable.

Do the debates have an impact on the race?

The evidence suggests that, as with televised commercials, debates do more to confirm what the voters already feel about the candidates than to change many voters' minds. They might also help to convert passive supporters — those who will not turn out and vote on election day — into active voters. But the 2000 debates clearly helped Bush and hurt Gore. Gore entered the debates with a reputation as a good debater. Bush, on the other hand, started with low expectations. Yet that might have been to his advantage. The Gallup polling organisation found that Gore led Bush by an average of 47% to 44% in the month before the debates but trailed Bush by an average of 43% to 47% in the fortnight following them (see Table 2.12).

That said, the audience for these debates has declined significantly in the last two election cycles. While an average of 66 million viewers watched the debates of 1984, 1988 and 1992, the debates in 1996 and 2000 were watched by only 40 million viewers.

Table 2.12 Impact of presidential debates on electoral support, 2000 (% support)

Dates	Gore	Bush
1–3 October	49	41
First debate: 3 October		
4–6 October	41	48
7–9 October	44	47
10–12 October	45	45
Second debate: 11 October		
13–15 October	44	47
16–18 October	39	49
Third debate: 17 October		
19–21 October	41	50

Source: **www.gallup.com**

Election day coverage

Election day polling hours are decided by state law, but most states permit polling from 8 a.m. to 7 p.m. Once the polls close, the votes are counted and declared in each state with the television networks announcing 'results' based on exit poll data. This led them into embarrassing problems on the evening of 7 November 2000. Just 35 minutes after most — but not all — of the polls had closed in Florida, CNN proclaimed Gore the winner in that state. The other networks quickly followed suit. But less than 3 hours later, the television networks changed their minds, deciding that Florida was 'too close to call'. Then the networks announced that Bush was the winner of Florida, only to retract that statement 2 hours later. It would take another 35 days and numerous court decisions before the result was finally declared. NBC's Tom Brokaw gave voice to the networks' utter humiliation: 'We don't have egg on our face, we have omelette all over our suits.'

Summary

The role of the media

➤ Television plays a crucial role in modern presidential elections.
➤ This is done principally through the airing of political commercials as well as through the broadcasting of televised debates between the major party candidates.

Factors explaining voting behaviour

For the 50% or so of the American voting-age population who *do* vote, what are the most important factors that help to determine how they vote? There are seven possible factors.

➢ **Party affiliation.** Despite all that is said about the weakness of US political parties, party affiliation seems to be an important determinant of voting behaviour. In 11 out of the 13 presidential elections between 1952 and 2000, the party that managed to gain the highest level of support from its own identifiers was the party that won the election. In 2000, 86% of Democrats voted for Gore, but 91% of Republicans voted for Bush.

➢ **Gender.** In nine out of the ten elections between 1964 and 2000, women were significantly more supportive of the Democrat candidate than men. This is what we call 'the gender gap', meaning that men and women vote in a distinctly different fashion. In 2000, Bush gained the votes of 53% of men but only 43% of women. Gore, on the other hand, gained the votes of only 42% of men but 54% of women. The gap was even wider in 1996, when men split equally between Clinton and Dole but women favoured Clinton by 16 percentage points. Remember too that more women tend to register and turn out to vote. In 2000, 52% of the voters were women.

The reason for the gender gap is often thought to be connected with policy differences between the two parties. In five major policy areas — abortion, defence, law and order, gun control and women's rights — the Democrats tend to take positions that are more favoured by women. Democrats are pro-choice on abortion, tend to favour lower levels of spending on defence, oppose capital punishment and support gun control. It was the Democrats who pushed — albeit unsuccessfully — for an Equal Rights Amendment to the Constitution protecting the civil rights of women.

➢ **Race.** The most significant minority racial groups in the American electorate are African-Americans and Hispanics. Since the 1960s, African-Americans have given solid support to the Democratic Party. Democrat presidents such as Kennedy and Johnson persuaded Congress to pass civil rights laws that protected African-Americans' rights in such areas as housing, employment, education and voting. In the six elections between 1980 and 2000, African-Americans never gave less than 83% support to the Democrats. President Clinton had a particular affinity with African-Americans and they were his most loyal group of supporters, especially during the difficult period of his impeachment and trial.

Hispanics are a growing group. According to the 2000 census, they formed 12% of the population, but because they are a young group and a significant proportion is not yet of voting age, their full political importance is yet to show. The states where Hispanics make up more than 25% of the population include California, Arizona, Texas and New York. Hispanics are a disparate group — from Mexico, Puerto Rico

Americans in Arlington, Virginia, line up to vote in the 2000 elections

and Cuba, as well as other Central American countries. Bush's Republican campaign in 2000 made a significant pitch for the Hispanic vote. Bush himself speaks fluent Spanish. His brother, Governor Jeb Bush of Florida, is married to a Hispanic. The Republican vote among Hispanics increased significantly from 20% in 1996 to 31% in 2000. As Hispanics become a larger cohort within the voting-age population in future decades, they will become an increasingly important racial group for the two parties to attract.

➤ **Religion.** There are certain important trends in voting according to religion. First, Protestant voters tend to vote Republican, giving a majority of their votes to Bush in 1992, Dole in 1996 and George W. Bush in 2000. Second, Catholic voters tend to vote Democrat, giving a majority of their votes to Clinton in both 1992 and 1996, and to Gore in 2000. However, the Democrats' 'pro-choice' stance on abortion can cause problems for Catholic voters, whose church is unmistakably 'pro-life'. Third, Jewish voters vote solidly for Democrats. They gave 78% support to Clinton in both his elections and 79% to Gore in 2000. One might have expected a rather higher percentage in 2000, given that Joseph Lieberman, Gore's running mate, was the first Jew to appear on a major party's national ticket.

The most interesting correlation is between frequency of attendance at religious services and candidate support, shown in Table 2.13. Those 42% of voters who attend religious services weekly or more often, voted 59% to 39% for George W. Bush, whereas the 42% of the voters who seldom or never attend religious services voted 56% to 39% for Al Gore. White Protestants — 56% of the voters — were even more

Table 2.13 Frequency of attendance at religious services and candidate support, 2000

Attend religious services	Proportion of electorate (%)	Voted for Bush (%)	Voted for Gore (%)
More than weekly	14	63	36
Weekly	28	57	40
Monthly	14	46	51
Seldom	28	42	54
Never	14	32	61

Source: Voter News Service exit poll, *New York Times*, 12 November 2000

supportive of Bush, voting for him by 63% to 34%. Even white Catholics — 25% of the voters — supported Bush, by 52% to 45%. One of the hidden stories of the 2000 election was the way in which the Bush campaign targeted traditional Catholics with some obvious success. In the words of political commentator Michael Barone (2002), America is now 'two nations of different faiths'. One is observant of religious practice, tradition-minded and morally conservative. The other is unobservant of religious practice, liberation-minded and morally liberal. You could see these two 'nations' in their starkly different reactions to the impeachment and trial of Bill Clinton. You could see them again in their voting in the 2000 elections.

➤ **Wealth.** About a year before the 2000 election, a number of political scientists in America predicted that Gore would easily win the forthcoming election with around 56% of the two-party vote. They based their forecast on the outcome of previous elections, looking at economic factors: good economy, incumbent party re-elected; poor economy, incumbent party defeated. But, as Michael Barone has commented, 'man does not vote by bread alone', and the economic cycle is not the only determinant of voting in presidential elections.

As is shown in Table 2.14, Gore's support was stronger among the less wealthy sectors of the electorate; Bush was stronger among the more wealthy. But the margins of difference are not all that large. Bush led Gore by only 9 percentage points among those voters earning more than $75,000 (£50,000) per year. This 'wealth gap' is not nearly as big as it was back in the New Deal period; not even as large as when Bush's father was elected in 1988. Then, the Republicans carried the highest income group by 25 percentage points — and the Democrats carried the lowest income group by the same margin. So neither Bush's promise of big tax cuts nor Gore's slogan of 'the people versus the powerful' seemed to pay off in terms of votes.

➤ **Geographic region.** There are two important trends when it comes to voting in relation to geographic region. First, the Northeast has become the new heartland of the Democratic Party. Gone, as we shall see, are the days of the Democrats' 'solid South'. Now it's the 'solid Northeast'. In the five elections from 1984 through to 2000, the Northeast gave the Democratic Party candidate his largest percentage of the vote.

Table 2.14 Who voted for whom, 2000

Category	Proportion of electorate (%)	Voted for Bush (%)	Voted for Gore (%)
All	100	48	48
Democrats	39	11	86
Republicans	35	91	8
Independents	27	47	45
Men	48	53	42
Women	52	43	54
African-American	10	9	90
Hispanic	7	35	62
White men	39	60	36
White women	43	49	48
Black men	4	12	85
Black women	6	6	94
Protestant	54	57	40
Catholic	26	47	49
Jewish	4	19	79
White Protestant	56	63	42
White Catholic	25	52	50
Family income:			
Under $15,000	7	37	57
$15,000–29,999	16	41	54
$30,000–49,999	24	48	49
$50,000–74,999	25	48	48
Over $75,000	28	53	44
East	23	39	56
South	31	55	43
West	21	46	48
Midwest	26	49	48

Source: Voter News Service exit poll, *New York Times*, 12 November 2000

In 2000, the Democrats won every northeastern state bar New Hampshire. But the bad news for the Democrats is that the Northeast is one region that has a declining proportion of the nation's population.

Second, the South has moved from being 'solid' for Democrats to being supportive of Republicans. This was shown most clearly when in 1996 the South was the only region in which the Democratic ticket of Clinton–Gore — both southerners — failed to beat the Republican ticket of Dole–Kemp, neither of whom was from the South. In 2000, the Republicans won every state in the South, including Gore's home state of Tennessee.

➤ **Policies.** Policies can be an important determinant of voting. Which policies they are tends to vary from one election cycle to another. The state of the economy can be critical. Bush's breaking of his 1988 'No New Taxes' pledge was central to his defeat in 1992. 'It's the economy, stupid!' became the Clinton campaign catchphrase. In that election 82% of those who thought the economy was in 'good shape' voted for Bush, while 65% of those who thought it in 'bad shape' voted for Clinton. The trouble for Bush was that the latter group was twice as big as the former group.

In 2000, the four policy issues most frequently mentioned by voters as being important to them were: the economy and jobs; education; social security; and taxes. Voters preferred Gore's policy positions on the first three. Only on taxes were Bush's preferred over Gore's — but it was 80% to 17% (see Table 2.15).

Table 2.15 Policy issues and candidate support, 2000

Which issues mattered most	Proportion of electorate (%)	Voted for Bush (%)	Voted for Gore (%)
Economy/jobs	18	37	59
Education	15	44	52
Social security	14	40	58
Taxes	14	80	17
World affairs	12	54	49
Healthcare	8	33	64
Medicare	7	39	60

Source: Voter News Service exit poll, *New York Times*, 12 November 2000

The parties' typical voter

Who is the typical Democrat voter? She is a woman, probably unmarried, could be white but is equally likely to be an ethnic minority, a Catholic who attends church less than once a week (if at all), earns less than $15,000 (£10,000) per year, belongs to a trade union and thinks of herself as liberal and pro-choice. Typical Democrat voters live in a big city either in the Northeast, the upper Midwest or on the west coast, and left school to get a job. They think the federal government should do 'more' rather than 'less'. In 2000, they thought that issues were more important than personalities and that Bill Clinton was largely responsible for the strong economy.

The typical Republican voter is a white male who is married with children, a Protestant who attends church at least once a week, a white-collar professional who earns at least $50,000 (£35,000) per year, owns shares — and guns — and thinks of himself as conservative and pro-life. Typical Republican voters live in small town, rural America in the South or the Midwest and they are college educated. They usually think that the federal government should do 'less' rather than 'more'. In 2000, they thought 'character' was more important than issues and that the strong economy was largely the product of Federal Reserve Chairman Alan Greenspan and their own hard work.

During the first few years of the twenty-first century, these two groups seem to be pretty evenly matched. The 2000 election produced a result so close that the popular vote was won by Gore by just 539,947 votes out of over 103 million cast. The **Electoral College** vote was 271–266. The Supreme Court decision that finally brought an end to the election was decided by five votes to four. And in Congress, the Republicans had a nine-seat majority in the House while the Senate divided exactly 50–50. At least after those elections, the USA was seen as a 50/50 nation.

Summary

Factors explaining voting behaviour

➢ Numerous factors may affect voting behaviour in US elections.

➢ The importance of each may vary from one election to another.

➢ By 2000, the USA was seen as an evenly divided nation, which made elections competitive.

The Electoral College

How it works

In the **Electoral College**, each state is awarded a certain number of Electoral College votes. This number is equal to that state's representation in Congress — the number of Senators (2 for every state) plus the number of Representatives. Thus in 2004, California had 55 (2 + 53) while Wyoming had just 3 (2 + 1). There are 538 Electoral College votes. To win the presidency, a candidate must win an absolute majority, which is 270.

Key term

➢ **Electoral College.** The institution established by the Founding Fathers to elect the president indirectly. The Electoral College never meets. Instead, the presidential Electors who make up the Electoral College meet in their state capitals to cast ballots for president and vice-president.

The popular votes for each candidate are counted in each state. In all but two states whichever candidate wins the most popular votes receives all the Electoral College votes of that state — the so-called 'winner-takes-all' rule. This 'rule', however, is not in the Constitution. It is purely a convention that developed during the nineteenth century in most states. The exceptions are Maine and Nebraska.

The Electoral College never meets together. Its members — called Electors — meet in their respective state capitals on the Monday after the second Wednesday in December. They then send their results to the vice-president of the United States in Washington DC. The vice-president formally counts the Electoral College votes and announces the result to a joint session of Congress in early January. Thus, on 6 January 2001, Vice-President Al Gore had the dubious privilege of announcing his own defeat at the hands of Governor George W. Bush of Texas by 271 Electoral votes to 266.

What if no candidate wins an absolute majority of Electoral votes? This could happen either if a 269–269 split occurred between two candidates, or if more than two candidates won Electoral votes. The former situation almost occurred in 2000. The latter situation might have occurred in 1968 when third-party candidate George Wallace won five states with 45 Electoral votes.

Under such circumstances, the president would be elected by the House of Representatives from the three presidential candidates with the most Electoral votes. Each state would have one vote. The winner would require an absolute majority — 26 of the 50 votes. Balloting would continue until one candidate emerged as the winner. Meanwhile the vice-president would be elected by the Senate from the two vice-presidential candidates with the most Electoral votes. Each Senator would have a vote. The winner would require an absolute majority — 51 of the 100 votes. Again, balloting would continue until this occurred. Only twice has the Electoral College failed to come up with a winner and the election been thrown to Congress — in 1800 and 1824.

Criticisms of the Electoral College system

An institution devised over 200 years ago still nominally elects the president of the United States. Many critics see it as beset with problems and potential malfunctions. Here are five criticisms made of the Electoral College.

Small states are over-represented

By 2004, California will have 55 Electoral College votes representing its 34 million inhabitants. Wyoming will have 3 Electoral votes representing its half-a-million inhabitants. Thus California receives one Electoral College vote for every 617,000 people. Wyoming receives one Electoral College vote for every 165,000 people. Put another way, if California were to receive Electoral College votes on the same basis as Wyoming, it would have not 55 Electoral votes but 205.

Winner-takes-all system distorts the result

In 1996, Bill Clinton won only 49% of the popular vote, yet he won just over 70% of the Electoral College votes (see Table 2.16). In the 11 elections between 1960 and 2000, the Electoral College could be said to have seriously distorted the result on seven occasions.

It is also possible for the candidate who wins the popular vote to lose the Electoral College vote. This is what occurred in 2000. Al Gore won 48.4% of the popular vote to George W. Bush's 48%. But in the Electoral College, Bush came out the winner by 271 votes to 266. This was the third occasion in the nation's history that this had occurred, the other two occasions being 1876 and 1888 (see Table 2.17). It almost occurred in both 1960 and 1968: in 1960, Nixon was only 0.3% behind Kennedy in the popular vote yet lost in the Electoral College by 303 to 219; in 1968, Humphrey was only 0.5% behind Nixon in the popular vote yet lost in the Electoral College by 301 to 191.

Table 2.16 Distortion of victory by Electoral College votes, 1960–2000

Year	Winner	Party	Popular vote (%)	EC vote (%)	% distortion
1960	John Kennedy	Democrat	49.8	56.6	6.8
1964	Lyndon Johnson	Democrat	61.0	90.3	29.3
1968	Richard Nixon	Republican	43.2	55.9	12.7
1972	Richard Nixon	Republican	60.7	96.6	35.9
1976	Jimmy Carter	Democrat	50.1	55.2	5.1
1980	Ronald Reagan	Republican	50.7	90.9	40.2
1984	Ronald Reagan	Republican	58.8	97.5	38.7
1988	George Bush	Republican	53.4	79.2	25.8
1992	Bill Clinton	Democrat	43.0	68.8	25.8
1996	Bill Clinton	Democrat	49.2	70.4	21.2
2000	George W. Bush	Republican	48.0	50.4	2.4

Table 2.17 Elections in which the popular vote winner lost in the Electoral College

Year	Candidates	Popular vote (%)	Electoral College votes
1876	Samuel Tilden (D)	51.0	184
	Rutherford Hayes (R)	47.9	185
1888	Grover Cleveland (D)	48.6	168
	Benjamin Harrison (R)	47.8	233
2000	Al Gore (D)	48.4	266
	George W. Bush (R)	47.9	271

Unfair to national third parties

In 1980, Congressman John Anderson, running as an independent, won 6.6% of the popular vote. In 1992, another independent candidate, Ross Perot, won 18.9% of the popular vote. In 1996, as the Reform Party candidate, Perot won 8.5% of the popular vote. In 2000, Green Party candidate Ralph Nader won over 3 million votes (2.9%). None of these candidates won a single Electoral College vote. Take Perot in 1992: in only one state — Mississippi — did he fail to gain at least 10% of the popular vote, yet in only one state — Maine — did he succeed in getting over 30% of the popular vote. Regional third-party candidates fare better. In 1968, American Independent Party candidate George Wallace won 13.5% of the popular vote — considerably less than Perot's 1992 figure, yet, because his support was concentrated in the Deep South, he managed to win five states with 45 Electoral College votes.

'Rogue' Electors

Many states have state laws requiring Electors to cast their ballots for the state-wide popular vote winner, but others do not, leaving open the possibility that so-called 'rogue' or 'faithless' Electors will cast their ballots some other way. Six of the 11 presidential elections between 1960 and 2000 have seen this occur (see Table 2.18). In 2000, a Washington DC Elector refused to cast her Electoral College vote for Al Gore in protest at the city's lack of congressional representation. She left her ballot blank.

Table 2.18 Rogue Electors, 1960–2000

Year	State	Number of Electors	Elector should have voted for	Elector voted for
1960	Alabama	8	John Kennedy	Harry Byrd
	Mississippi	6	John Kennedy	Harry Byrd
	Oklahoma	1	Richard Nixon	Harry Byrd
1968	North Carolina	1	Richard Nixon	George Wallace
1972	Virginia	1	Richard Nixon	John Hospers
1976	Washington	1	Gerald Ford	Ronald Reagan
1988	West Virginia	1	Michael Dukakis	Lloyd Bentsen
2000	Washington DC	1	Al Gore	[Abstained]

President and vice-president of different parties

At the beginning of the Republic, when political parties in the way they are understood today did not truly exist, it did not matter if the president and vice-president were of different parties, as a result of the system used in the case of Electoral College deadlock. In 2000, however, it was certainly possible that the House of Representatives could have chosen Republican George W. Bush as president and the Senate could have chosen Democrat Joseph Lieberman as vice-president.

Strengths of the current system

It is not difficult to come up with criticisms of the Electoral College. But the Founding Fathers invented the system because of some presumed strengths, two of which are still thought by some to be relevant today.

It preserves the voice of the small-population states

This has already been touched upon in the first of the criticisms, but what some perceive as a weakness, others see as a strength. The small-population states, as in 1787, still worry that, were the Electoral College to be abolished, the votes of their inhabitants would become almost worthless, swept aside by the size of such states as California, Texas, New York and Florida. If this was a concern in 1787, it should be even more of a concern now. In the first presidential election, held in 1788, of the 13 states that took part, the smallest had 3 Electoral College votes while the largest — Virginia — had 12: that is, four times as many. But in 2000, California had 54 Electoral College votes — 18 times as many as states such as Wyoming and Alaska with just 3.

It tends to promote a two-horse race

This is important in an election for the president, who is both chief executive and head of state — a symbol of national unity. In such a two-horse race, the winner will therefore tend to receive more than 50% of the popular vote, a definite aid to uniting the nation. In 23 of the 35 elections held between 1864 and 2000 — that is, 66% — the winner gained more than 50% of the popular vote. The trouble is that three of the 12 elections in which this did not occur were 1992, 1996 and 2000.

Possible reforms

Because it is so easy to see weaknesses within the Electoral College system, numerous reforms have been suggested. Some, requiring only changes in state or federal law, are relatively minor. Any major reform is likely to require a constitutional amendment, and because these amendments need to be passed by two-thirds majorities in both houses of Congress as well as by three-quarters of the state legislatures, such reforms are unlikely to come about. However, four reforms are possible.

The Maine system

Two states do not use the 'winner-takes-all' system of allocating Electoral College votes. The first state in modern times to adopt a different system was Maine. The so-called 'Maine system' involves awarding one vote to a candidate for each congressional district (the constituencies used to elect members of the House of Representatives) that they win and two votes to the candidate who is the state-wide winner, but, as Table 2.19 shows, this reform would lead to the results being only marginally different. Indeed, in 2000 the Maine system would have produced a *less* proportionate result, with Gore losing in the Electoral College by 38 votes rather than by 4. Neither would it have helped Ross Perot in either 1992 or 1996.

Table 2.19 Winner-takes-all and Maine systems compared, 1984–2000

Year	Candidates	Winner-takes-all system	Maine system
1984	Ronald Reagan (R)	521	472
	Walter Mondale (D)	17	66
1988	George Bush (R)	426	369
	Michael Dukakis (D)	112	169
1992	Bill Clinton (D)	370	322
	George Bush (R)	168	216
	Ross Perot (I)	0	0
1996	Bill Clinton (D)	379	345
	Bob Dole (R)	159	193
	Ross Perot (Reform)	0	0
2000	George W. Bush (R)	271	288
	Al Gore (D)	267	250

Allocation of Electoral College votes in each state in proportion to the popular vote

By allocating Electoral College votes in each state proportional to the popular vote in that state there would be a more equable allocation of Electoral votes. Such a system would be much fairer to national third parties too, but then it would also encourage more voters to vote for such parties, thereby making it more likely that no candidate would gain an absolute majority of Electoral College votes and throwing the election into Congress.

In 1988, for example, such a system — presuming (probably incorrectly) that everyone would have voted the same way — would have given George Bush just 290.14 votes rather than 369 under the Maine system or 426 under winner-takes-all. And that 290 is only 20 over the absolute majority required. In 2000, this system would still have given George W. Bush more Electoral College votes than Al Gore, though depriving him of the required absolute majority of 270. The result would have been: Bush 260.2; Gore 258.4; Others 19.4.

Other reforms would therefore probably need to be made: the setting of a threshold — maybe 10% — for winning Electoral College votes within a state, and the abolition of the requirement for a nationwide absolute majority.

The Automatic Plan

In comparison with the above proposals, this plan is trivial and seeks to deal with only one of the weaknesses of the Electoral College — the 'rogue' or 'faithless' Electors. Sixteen states plus the District of Columbia already have state laws that require their Electors to cast their ballots for the state's popular-vote winner. The trouble is that these laws are probably unenforceable, as was shown in 2000 when a District of Columbia Elector abstained instead of voting for Al Gore. If the laws were adopted nationwide, it would mean getting rid of the Electors, making the allocation of Electoral College votes purely automatic.

The Direct Election Plan

Opinion polls have recently shown that Americans would support a move to a directly elected president. 'Most Americans don't think the Electoral College is as fair as a direct election would be,' states Robert Richie, director of the Maryland-based Center for Voting and Democracy, which is headed by former third-party presidential candidate John Anderson. In a Gallup poll conducted the weekend after the 2000 election, 61% favoured a direct election for president compared with only 35% for keeping the Electoral College.

However opinion polls don't themselves change anything. Only a constitutional amendment could bring about this particular reform. With the small-population states wedded to the current system, the requirement of a two-thirds majority in both houses of Congress, and equal representation of large- and small-population states in the Senate, success is unlikely.

In any case, the Direct Election Plan is not without its drawbacks. Stephen Wayne (2001) points out that, had this system been in place in 2000, America might have been faced with recounts in every state in the nation — what Professor Wayne describes as the nightmare scenario of 'Florida times 50'.

Summary

Electoral College

➤ The Electoral College was set up by the Founding Fathers as a system of indirect election for the president and vice-president.

➤ It has been modified and adapted to serve a direct system of election.

➤ It has both merits and demerits.

➤ A number of reforms have been proposed, but the more substantial ones, which require a constitutional amendment, are unlikely to be carried out.

Exercises

1 What are the constitutional requirements to be president of the USA?
2 What other requirements would be helpful for a presidential candidate?
3 Explain what is meant by the 'invisible primary' and why it is important.
4 What are primaries and caucuses, and what functions do they perform?
5 Explain the terms: (a) Super Tuesday; (b) front loading; (c) the McGovern–Fraser Commission.
6 Explain what is meant by 'peer review' and why some people think it is so important.
7 Explain the following proposed reforms of the presidential primary system: (a) regional primaries; (b) weighted votes at the National Party Conventions; (c) pre-primary mini-convention.
8 What are (a) the formal functions and (b) the informal functions of the National Party Conventions?
9 What is the 'acceptance speech' and why is it thought to be so important?
10 Explain the reforms of campaign finance in both 1974 and 2002.
11 What role do television commercials play in the presidential campaign?
12 Explain the potential importance of the televised presidential debates.
13 What factors explain the way Americans vote in presidential elections?
14 Explain how the Electoral College works.
15 What problems are there concerning the Electoral College?
16 What reforms are suggested to the Electoral College?

Exam focus

1 What are the strengths and weaknesses of the current system for selecting presidential candidates?
2 Do the National Party Conventions still fulfil any significant functions?

3 Does television enhance democracy or merely trivialise the issues in presidential elections?

4 What are the major concerns regarding campaign finance in presidential elections?

5 Should the Electoral College be reformed, abolished or left as it is?

6 Money, policies or personality: which is most important in winning the presidency today?

7 How do Americans decide how to vote in presidential elections?

References

Barone, M., 'The Bush Nation and the Gore Nation', in B. E. Shafer (ed.), *The State of American Politics* (Rowman and Littlefield, 2002).

Cronin, T. E. and Genovese, M. A., *The Paradoxes of the American Presidency* (Oxford University Press, 1998).

Loevy, R. D., *The Flawed Path to the Presidency 1992* (State University of New York, 1995).

Patterson, T. E., *Out of Order* (Alfred Knopf, 1993).

Wayne, S. J., *The Road to the White House* (Bedford-St Martin's, 2001).

Further reading

Ashbee, E., 'The black vote in American politics', *Politics Review*, vol. 11, no. 2, November 2001.

Bennett, A. J., 'The US elections of 2000', *Politics Review*, vol. 10, no. 4, April 2001.

Ceasar, J. W. and Busch, A. E., *The Perfect Tie: The True Story of the 2000 Presidential Election* (Rowman and Littlefield, 2001).

Palmer, N., 'Primaries and caucuses', *Politics Review*, vol. 13, no. 2, November 2003.

Chapter 3

Political parties

Political parties are an essential element of any democracy. So it may come as something of a surprise to find that political parties do not play as important a role in US politics as might at first be expected. A number of the traditional functions played by parties — organisation, fund raising, communication, policy formulation — are not the sole prerogative of parties in the US political system. To some extent, these functions have been usurped by pressure groups, political action committees, candidate-centred organisations and the media. The size of the USA also makes the national political parties weaker than is the case in a small nation-state such as Great Britain, and we must not forget that the US parties are very much state-based organisations.

The USA is nonetheless said to have a two-party system, and, because it has a first-past-the-post electoral system, this might not come as too much of a surprise. In terms of the institutions of government, the Democrats and the Republicans dominate the scene to an extraordinary degree. Third parties seem to have only a minor role to play in US politics. Thus, we have something of a paradox to explain: a political system in which the two major political parties are both relatively unimportant and yet dominate the political scene.

Questions to be answered in this chapter

➤ What is the history of the USA's two major parties?
➤ What is the link between the major parties and ideology?
➤ What is the organisational structure of the major parties?
➤ Does the USA have a two-party system?
➤ What role is played by third parties?
➤ Are the US's parties in a period of decline or renewal?

The history of the USA's two main parties

For almost a century-and-a-half, the USA has had two major political parties: the Democrats and the Republicans. How did they come about and why are they as they are today? We need know only the main outline of their histories, but knowing their 'past' will help us better understand their 'present'.

The six big issues

The history of America's two major parties can best be understood against six watershed issues that helped shape the nation's history.

The form of government

Back in the 1780s, the newly independent states had to decide what form of government they would establish. Chapter 1 showed that there were those who wanted a highly decentralised form of government — a confederacy. They were the initial winners when the Articles of Confederation were agreed upon in 1781, but before the end of the decade, the confederation was a shambles. At the 1787 Philadelphia Convention the question about the form of government had to be asked again. There were essentially two schools of thought: those who wanted to move to a more centralised form of government — the Federalists — and those who did not — the Anti-Federalists. With the signing of the new federal constitution, the Federalists won.

The Federalists were the party of George Washington (President: 1789–97) and of John Adams (President: 1797–1801). They represented the commercial and business interests of the new republic. A more centralised form of government was what traders and merchants wanted. The Anti-Federalists (otherwise known as the Democratic-Republicans) were the party of Thomas Jefferson (President: 1801–09) and James Madison (President: 1809–17). They represented the agricultural and land-owning interests, who yearned for a more decentralised form of government.

With the capital city of Washington DC taking shape on the banks of the Potomac river on the border between Maryland and Virginia, Great Britain (again) defeated — in the War of 1812 — and the federal republic on a surer footing, the issue of the form of government seemed settled. Party issues became blurred. What followed is what American historians refer to as 'the era of good feelings'.

Democracy

The second issue shaping America's history was democracy. The Founding Fathers had established a form of democracy that for the late eighteenth century was quite advanced. One of the two houses of Congress was to be directly elected by the people. The Senate and the president were to be indirectly elected. In the 1828 election, Andrew Jackson stood for a more radical view of democracy — for more popular participation in politics. Jackson (President: 1829–37) renamed the Democratic-Republicans the Democratic Party, seeking thereby to emphasise their *democratic* credentials. Like its current namesake, the Democratic Party became the party of the poor, immigrants and minority groups — the 'have-nots'.

Slavery

The third issue was slavery. The Democratic Party was becoming increasingly the party of the South and preached the continuing virtues of slavery. Democrats Franklin Pierce (President: 1853–57) and James Buchanan (President: 1857–61) followed policies that spelled a poor future for the business and commercial interests of the North. For most of this period, slavery was contained to the states south of what was known as the Mason–Dixon Line. To preserve the balance of the Union, 'slave states' and 'free states' were admitted to the Union in equal numbers. But in the 1857 *Dred Scott v. Sandford* decision, the Supreme Court effectively ruled that slavery could not be limited to the southern states. The Republican Party, often called the Grand Old Party (GOP), was reputedly born in 1854 as an anti-slavery party of the North. The 1860 election pitted Democrat William Douglas against Republican Abraham Lincoln.

Lincoln won, and the defeated southern states — 11 states from Texas to Virginia — announced they were leaving the Union and forming their own confederacy. The Civil War (1861–65) was fought by Lincoln's federal army of the North against the confederate army of the South. The defeat of the South in the Civil War was a political humiliation for the Democratic Party. Of the 12 presidential elections held between 1864 and 1908, the Democrats won only twice — in 1884 and 1892 with Grover Cleveland. For over 50 years — from Abraham Lincoln (President: 1861–65) to William Howard Taft (President: 1909–13) — the Republicans reigned supreme in Washington. As America became industrialised, expanded westwards and grew hugely

Abraham Lincoln, 1809–65

through immigration, the Republicans became the party of the North: of big business and industrialists, of free enterprise and the Protestant work ethic. The Democrats survived as the party of small farmers, urban workers, immigrants and Catholics. For 100 years the 'solid South' was 'solid' for the Democrats. It was a case of 'vote as you shot'. The South had 'shot' for the Democrats in the Civil War; now they voted for them.

The economy

The Great Depression of the 1920s did for the Republicans what the Civil War had done for the Democrats. It sent them out into the political wilderness for 40 years. The Republicans — the party of big business — presided over the federal government with Presidents Harding (1921–23), Coolidge (1923–29) and Hoover (1929–33) at the time when 'boom' turned into 'bust'. The desperately squalid camps of the unemployed on the

1780s
The Anti-Federalists
(Democratic-Republicans)
The Articles of Confederation (1781)

1780s
The Federalists

The Philadelphia Convention (1787)
The 1788 election
George Washington
John Adams

The 1800 election
Thomas Jefferson
James Madison

1820s
The Democratic Party
The 1828 election
Andrew Jackson

1850s
The Republican Party
The 1860 election
Abraham Lincoln
The Civil War

1920s
The Great Depression
The 1932 election
Franklin D. Roosevelt (1933–45)
Harry Truman (1945–53)

Dwight Eisenhower (1953–61)

The 1960 election
John Kennedy (1961–63)
Lyndon Johnson (1963–69)

Richard Nixon (1969–74)
Gerald Ford (1974–77)

Jimmy Carter (1977–81)

The 1980 election
Ronald Reagan (1981–89)
George Bush (1989–93)

Bill Clinton (1993–2001)

George W. Bush (2001–)

Figure 3.1 The development of America's two major parties

outskirts of many of the USA's big cities were sardonically called 'Hoovervilles', named after President Herbert Hoover.

The 1932 election saw the resurrection of the Democratic Party with its candidate Franklin Delano Roosevelt (FDR) and his promise of a 'new deal for the American people'. The Democrats — the party that had for so long championed the doctrine of decentralised government — now became the party of big federal government. Of the nine presidential elections held between 1932 and 1964, the Republicans won only twice — in 1952 and 1956 with Dwight Eisenhower. For 36 years — from FDR (President: 1933–45) to Lyndon Johnson (President: 1963–69) — the Democrats ruled in Washington. They became the party of an extraordinary coalition — the 'New Deal

A 'Hooverville' on the edge of Chicago in the Great Depression of the early 1930s

coalition' — of southern white conservatives and northern black liberals, of city-dwellers, blue-collar workers, Catholics, Jews and ethnic minorities. The Republicans garnered their support from a more homogeneous group made up principally of those living in the more rural Midwest and Plain states, of WASPS (white, Anglo-Saxon Protestants) and white-collar workers.

Civil rights

The fifth issue that has crucially shaped America's political parties is that of black civil rights. In the 1950s and 1960s there are strange echoes of circumstances exactly a century before. Again, there was a Supreme Court decision, this time the 1954 decision in *Brown v. Board of Education of Topeka*. Just as the *Dred Scott* decision of 1857 had spawned the dispute over slavery, so the 1954 *Brown* decision spawned the dispute over black civil rights. In this decision, the Court declared that segregated schooling — a way of life in the South — was unconstitutional and that states should desegregate their schools 'with all deliberate speed'. It was essentially this decision that both ended the 100-year manifestation of the 'solid South' and blew apart the 'New Deal coalition'. In crude political terms, it was bad news for the Democrats and a great political opportunity for the Republicans.

In 1960, 100 years after the start of the Civil War, the 'solid South' was still intact: whether you were black, white, liberal or conservative, you voted for the Democrats. Southerners would sometimes describe themselves as 'yellow dog Democrats', meaning that, even if the Democrats put up a yellow dog as an election candidate, they would still vote Democrat. As a result of the 1960 election, of the 106 members of the House of Representatives from the South, 99 were Democrats. All 22 southern Senators and all 11 southern state governors were Democrats. That was the extent of the 'solid South'. In the presidential election of that year, the Democrat candidate John Kennedy won eight of the 11 southern states. There was little to suggest that the 'solid South' was about to disintegrate, but in the ten subsequent presidential elections (1964–2000), the Democrats won a majority of the South on only one occasion — in 1976, with southerner Jimmy Carter. By 1992 and 1996, they could not even win the South with a presidential ticket made up of two southerners — Bill Clinton of Arkansas and Al Gore of Tennessee. What happened and why?

Table 3.1 Votes for Democratic presidential candidates in selected southern states, 1960–72

States	1960 vote for Kennedy (D)	1964 vote for Johnson (D)	1968 vote for Humphrey (D)	1972 vote for McGovern (D)
Alabama	56.8% won	0% lost	18.8% lost	25.5% lost
Arkansas	50.2% won	56.1% won	30.4% lost	30.7% lost
Georgia	62.5% won	45.9% lost	26.8% lost	24.7% lost
Louisiana	50.4% won	43.2% lost	28.2% lost	28.6% lost
Mississippi	36.3% lost	12.9% lost	23.0% lost	19.6% lost
South Carolina	51.2% won	41.1% lost	29.6% lost	27.7% lost

In 1964, the South made a break from the Democrat fold to support the conservative Republican candidate, Senator Barry Goldwater of Arizona. Goldwater won Alabama, Georgia, Louisiana, Mississippi and South Carolina (see Figure 3.2). Four years later, five southern states — Alabama, Arkansas, Georgia, Louisiana and Mississippi — voted for the ultra-conservative Democrat Governor of Alabama George Wallace running as a third-party candidate (see Figure 3.3), rather than for the Democrats' official candidate, the liberal Hubert Humphrey.

The breakaway from the Democrats by conservative southerners in both 1964 and 1968 prompted Republican Richard Nixon to launch his 'southern strategy' during his first term as president. By 1972, he had wooed ex-Wallace voters over to the Republican Party with the promise of policies and appointments more to their liking. Nixon persuaded significant numbers of white southerners that the Republicans had more to offer them than did a Democratic Party dominated by northeastern liberals such as John Kennedy, Hubert Humphrey and George McGovern. In 12 years, Nixon doubled the Republican vote in Georgia and Louisiana and more than tripled it in Mississippi (see Table 3.2). In 1972, Nixon made a clean sweep of all 11 southern states.

Figure 3.2 Presidential election, 1964 — win for Lyndon Johnson (D)

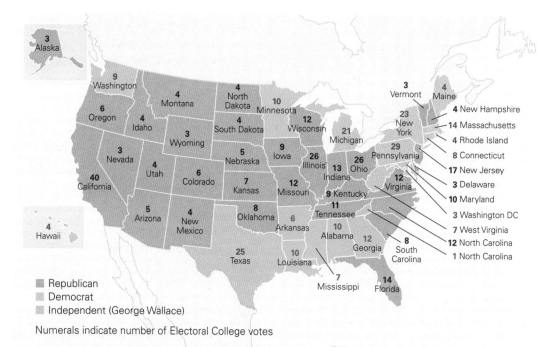

Figure 3.3 Presidential election, 1968 — win for Richard Nixon (R)

Table 3.2 Votes for Nixon in selected southern states: 1960 and 1972 compared

States	Vote for Nixon (R) 1960	Vote for Nixon (R) 1972
Alabama	42.1% lost	72.4% won
Arkansas	43.1% lost	68.9% won
Georgia	37.4% lost	75.3% won
Louisiana	28.6% lost	66.0% won
Mississippi	24.7% lost	78.2% won
South Carolina	48.8% lost	70.8% won

The role of the federal government

What Nixon began in the early 1970s, conservative Republican Ronald Reagan cemented in the early 1980s. And he cemented it with the sixth and final issue we need to consider: the role of the federal government. History had turned full circle as the issue that divided the parties in the 1780s replayed in the 1980s. For half-a-century, the Democrats had stood for big federal government programmes — Roosevelt's 'New Deal', Truman's 'Fair Deal', Kennedy's 'New Frontiers' and Johnson's 'Great Society'. Now Reagan planned to hand back power to the states and to curb the power of the federal government. Speaking in his inaugural address in January 1981, President Reagan announced:

> Government is not the solution to our problem. We are a nation that has a govern-
> ment — not the other way around. It is my intention to curb the size and influence of
> the federal establishment and to demand recognition of the distinction between the
> powers granted to the federal government and those reserved to the states or to the
> people. The federal government did not create the states; the states created the federal
> government.

Running against an incumbent president who was himself a southerner — Jimmy Carter — Reagan had swept 10 of the 11 southern states for the Republicans. In 20 years, the Republicans had increased their southern representation in the House from 7 seats to 39, in the Senate from 0 to 10 and in the governors' mansions from 0 to 5.

The 1990s brought the final seismic shift. In 1992 there was the extraordinary spectacle of the all-southern Democrat ticket of Clinton–Gore losing 7 of the 11 southern states to a New England-Midwestern Republican ticket of Bush–Quayle. Two years later, the Republicans shot to majority status in the House, Senate and state governors in the South. They now controlled 64 House seats to the Democrats' 61, 13 Senate seats to the Democrats' 9, and 6 state governorships to the Democrats' 5 (see Table 3.3).

Thus, we arrive at the typical Republican and Democrat voters (see Chapter 2). The reason why these socioeconomic groups vote as they do is largely the product of these six issues, which have been played out over 200 years: the form of government; democracy; slavery; the economy; race; and the role of the federal government. The

Table 3.3 The break-up of the 'solid South', 1960–2002

Year	House: Democrats– Republicans	Senate: Democrats– Republicans	Governors: Democrats– Republicans
1960	99–7	22–0	11–0
1962	95–11	21–1	11–0
1964	89–17	21–1	11–0
1966	83–23	19–3	9–2
1968	80–26	18–4	9–2
1970	79–27	16–5	9–2
1972	77–31	14–7	8–3
1974	81–27	15–6	8–3
1976	80–28	16–5	9–2
1978	78–30	15–6	8–3
1980	69–39	11–10	6–5
1982	82–34	11–11	9–2
1984	80–36	12–10	8–3
1986	78–38	16–6	6–5
1988	77–39	15–7	6–5
1990	77–39	15–7	8–3
1992	77–48	13–9	8–3
1994	61–64	9–13	5–6
1996	54–71	7–15	5–6
1998	54–71	8–14	4–7
2000	53–71	9–13	5–6
2002	55–76	9–13	4–7

stands that the parties have taken on these issues have shaped the two parties into what they are today and have given them their ideological colours.

Summary

The history of the USA's two main parties

➤ The USA's two major parties have been shaped by six big political issues over the past 200 years.

➤ Both major parties have experienced periods of strength and weakness.

➤ In the past 50 years, the South has changed from a region that voted solidly Democrat to one that now favours Republicans.

➤ This change has had a profound effect on modern US politics.

Major parties and ideology

The names of the two major parties immediately suggest that they are not ideologically exclusive parties, for 'democracy' and 'republicanism' are two all-embracing ideologies, if ideologies they are. An ideology is a collectively held set of ideas and beliefs. Some ideologies, such as fascism and socialism, are narrow in their compass, but this is not so with the two being considered here. Indeed, John Kerry, who is a Democrat (i.e. a member of the Democratic Party), is also a republican, in that he believes in the principles of republican government. Likewise, George W. Bush, who is a Republican (i.e. a member of the Republican Party), is also a democrat, in that he believes in the principles of democratic government.

Because the parties' names do not necessarily suggest an ideological colour, we find that commentators, and even politicians themselves, attach ideological labels ahead of the party names. Thus, there are 'conservative Democrats' and 'liberal Democrats'; 'conservative Republicans' and 'moderate Republicans'. George W. Bush ran his 2000 election campaign calling himself a 'compassionate conservative'. As we have already seen, in the USA ideology and region are often linked. The South tends to be more conservative; the Northeast and the west coast tend to be more liberal or libertarian. Thus, for both parties to be viable in all regions of the country, they need to take on the ideological colours of the region. Southern Democrats such as Senator John Breaux of Louisiana are more conservative than New England Democrats such as Senator Ted Kennedy of Massachusetts. Similarly, New England Republicans such as Senator Olympia Snowe of Maine are more liberal than southern Republicans such as Senator Trent Lott of Mississippi.

That said, it is still possible to discern some clear ideological differences between the two major parties. This can be done most easily by looking at the stands the parties tend

Table 3.4 Differences between Democrat and Republican positions on ten key policy areas

Key issue	Democrat position	Republican position
Cut taxes	Oppose	Support
Increased spending on social welfare programmes	Support	Oppose
A 'get tough' attitude to criminals and crime	Oppose	Support
Death penalty	Oppose	Support
Gun control	Support	Oppose
A woman's right to an abortion	Support	Oppose
Increased defence spending	Oppose	Support
Rights for gays and lesbians	Support	Oppose
'The federal government should do less'	Oppose	Support
Prayer in public (i.e. state) schools	Oppose	Support

to adopt on certain high-profile political issues. Table 3.4 shows the parties' stands on ten key policy issues. All these issues will be debated in any modern-day, national political campaign. We are not, of course, suggesting that *all* Democrats oppose the death penalty or *all* Republicans support tax cuts, but we can say that, in general, *most* Democrats tend to oppose the death penalty and *most* Republicans tend to support tax cuts. This can be seen in the positions taken by presidential candidates as well as in the voting patterns on these issues in Congress.

It is possible to suggest that the ideological pattern of Democrats — support for abortion and gay rights, opposition to prayer in public schools — is one that could be described as 'liberal'. Equally, one could suggest that the ideological pattern of Republicans — support for cutting taxes, the death penalty and opposing abortion rights — is one that could be described as 'conservative'. Such ideological leanings can be clearly seen in the way Americans vote for the two major parties (see Table 3.5).

Table 3.5 Ideological voting in the 2000 election

Position		% of all voters	Voted for Gore (%)	Voted for Bush (%)
Liberal		20	80	13
Conservative		29	17	81
White religious right?	Yes	14	18	80
	No	83	54	42

Source: Voter News Service exit poll, *New York Times*, 12 November 2000

Both major parties have experienced internal ideological debates during the past two decades. Within the Democratic Party this has been between what might be described as old-fashioned, liberal Democrats and New Democrats. Many within the party saw the defeats in the 1968 and 1972 presidential elections, and again in the 1984 and 1988 presidential elections, as a repudiation of old-style Democrat ideology. The candidates in those four elections were all old-style liberals from the North — Hubert Humphrey of Minnesota (1968), George McGovern of South Dakota (1972), Walter Mondale also of Minnesota (1984) and Michael Dukakis of Massachusetts (1988). The Democrats' only victory during this period was with a southerner — Jimmy Carter of Georgia in 1976.

Out of the ashes of these defeats was born the Democratic Leadership Council (DLC). The DLC sought to reposition the Democratic Party further to the centre of US politics. It was their candidate, Governor Bill Clinton of Arkansas, who finally broke the succession of defeats and became the first Democrat since Franklin Roosevelt to serve two full terms as president. The old-style Democrats, with their roots still in unionised labour, are still around, finding a voice in such politicians as Senator Ted Kennedy of Massachusetts, Congressman Dick Gephardt of Missouri and the late Senator Paul Wellstone of Minnesota.

The Republican Party has for decades been engaged in an ideological debate within the party. In the 1960s this was seen in the fight between conservatives led by Senator Barry Goldwater of Arizona — the party's defeated 1964 presidential candidate — and the moderate Governor Nelson Rockefeller of New York. Indeed, the term 'Rockefeller Republican' was used by those on the conservative wing of the party as one of scorn. The battle between these two ideological wings was evident in almost every presidential election cycle. In 1976, the moderates had the upper hand, as Gerald Ford won a close nomination contest against Governor Ronald Reagan of California. But following Ford's defeat in that election, Reagan returned triumphant in 1980, winning re-election by a landslide in 1984.

The 'succession' of Reagan's vice-president, George H. W. Bush, in the 1988 election was seen as putting the moderates back in charge. The first President Bush represented the 'eastern establishment' wing of the party and gave key jobs to those of a similar ideological perspective, such as Secretary of State James Baker. The second President Bush sought partly to blur these ideological issues within the Republican Party with his 'compassionate conservative' label. 'Compassionate' has overtones of 'Rockefeller Republicanism', while 'conservative' speaks of 'Reagan Republicanism'. But the ideological battle is still there. In domestic policy it was seen in the inclusion in Bush's first cabinet of people as diverse as conservative John Ashcroft (Attorney General) and moderate Christine Todd Whitman (Administrator of the Environmental Protection Agency). In foreign policy it was seen in the inclusion of conservative Donald Rumsfeld (Secretary of Defense) and moderate Colin Powell (Secretary of State).

The break-up of the 'solid South' may have led to the two major parties becoming more ideologically distinct. A significant group of conservative voters have crossed from the Democratic Party and joined the Republicans. The result is to make the Republican Party more conservative and the Democratic Party more homogeneous as a left-of-centre party. Remember that it is not just voters who have moved — some politicians have too. Such noted conservative luminaries of the Republican Party as the late Strom Thurmond of South Carolina and the former Senator Phil Gramm of Texas were once Democrats but switched to the Republican Party, believing that they would find more of an ideological home there.

Summary

Major parties and ideology

➤ The names of the two major parties are ideologically inclusive.
➤ Both major parties include a broad ideological spectrum.
➤ Democrats tend to be the more liberal party; Republicans the more conservative.
➤ Ideology is closely connected with region.

Organisational structure of the two major parties

As we saw in Chapter 1, the USA has a decentralised form of government based on the principle of federalism. If government is decentralised, political parties are likely to be decentralised too. This can best be seen by asking the questions: 'Who is the leader of the Democratic Party?' and 'Who is the leader of the Republican Party?' The latter question might elicit the answer of 'President Bush', but that is questionable. As Chapter 6 explains, the president may be able to exercise very little leadership in Congress, even among those members of his own party. President Bush was, after all, elected as *president* in a national election, not as party leader in an internal party election. Contrast that with the position of the British prime minister.

National committees

The only manifestation of party structure at the national level is the national committees — the Democratic National Committee (DNC) and the Republican National Committee (RNC). Both have offices in Washington DC. Each has a chair elected by fellow committee members. Currently, the DNC chair is Terry McAuliffe; the RNC chair is Ed Gillespie, yet few ordinary voters will have heard of them. The DNC and RNC organise the parties' respective National Conventions (see Chapter 2) — the most public manifestation of the parties. However, it is difficult to think of conventions made up of between 2,000 and 4,000 people, meeting for only 4 days every 4 years, being responsible for very much.

Congressional committees

Each party has a series of committees in both houses of Congress overseeing policy and campaigning. The then chair of the National Republican Senatorial Committee, Senator Bill Frist of Tennessee, was given much of the credit for the Republicans' successful 2002 mid-term election campaign, which resulted in the party regaining control of the Senate.

State-level organisation

Everything else to do with political parties in America is at the state level, where there is a bewildering variety of organisation, laws and customs and considerable power is vested in the state governors and mayors of big cities. Indeed, it is worth remembering that the so-called *National* Party Conventions are merely the coming together of the delegates from the *state* parties, chosen in *state-run* primaries. There are State Party Committees (headed by the State Party chair) and State Party Conventions. Below that exist party committees at county, city and ward levels. Although big-city 'machine' politics still exists in some regions, the picture of the cigar-chomping, fedora-hatted political 'boss' is now somewhat outdated. Mayor Richard Daley, often thought of as the last of the big-city party bosses, died in 1976.

Increasingly, the state and local parties are dominated by two new kinds of party activist. First, there are the 'issue activists' — people committed to a particular political issue, such as civil rights or women's rights — and, second, there are what might be called 'candidate activists' — people who have come into politics through working on the campaign of a particular candidate.

Summary

Organisational structure of the two major parties

➢ US parties have very little in the way of national organisation.

➢ Parties are principally state-based organisations.

The two-party system

A **two-party system** might be defined as one in which two major parties regularly win at least 80% of the popular vote in general elections, regularly win at least 90% of the seats in the legislature and alternately control the executive branch of government. If these criteria are used in the USA, then US politics is clearly a two-party system.

As Table 3.6 shows, in the nine presidential elections between 1968 and 2000, the Democrats and Republicans accounted for more than 80% of the popular vote on every occasion. Indeed, in five of these nine elections, their combined vote exceeded 95%. This is the case in terms of Electoral College votes too. In only one of these nine elections — 1968 — did the Democrats and

Table 3.6 Combined Democrat and Republican vote in presidential elections, 1968–2000

Year	Combined Democrat and Republican vote (%)
1968	86
1972	98
1976	98
1980	92
1984	99
1988	99
1992	81
1996	91
2000	97

Republicans fail to win all the Electoral College votes — rogue Electors apart.

When it comes to seats in Congress, the picture is clearly that of a two-party system. Following the 2002 mid-term elections, only one member of the House of Representatives (Bernie Sanders of Vermont) and one member of the Senate (James Jeffords, also of Vermont) were not sitting as either Democrats or Republicans. Sanders, although elected under the banner of the Socialist Party, is opposed only by a Republican candidate at each election. The Democrats, with whom he invariably votes, allow him a free run. Jeffords has been elected to the Senate three times (1988, 1994 and 2000) as a Republican, defecting from the party in June 2001 to sit as an independent. Even in terms of state government, the picture is the same. By January 2003, all 50 state governors were either Democrats or Republicans.

Every president since 1853 has been either a Democrat or a Republican. That is 37 straight presidential elections won by the two major parties over a 150-year period.

The reasons for the US two-party system

> The first-past-the-post electoral system makes life difficult for national third parties. As we shall see in greater detail later on in this chapter, their support is usually widespread but shallow. They pick up a fraction of the vote in almost every state but under a winner-takes-all system they receive no reward at all. A national third-party candidate on the ticket merely lowers the percentage of the vote needed by the major-party candidate to win the election.

> When two parties encompass such a wide ideological spectrum — from Jesse Jackson and the late Senator Paul Wellstone on the left to Republican Congressman Ron Paul and former Ambassador Alan Keyes on the right — there is not much room left for any other parties to attract substantial support. The two major parties are all-embracing.

> The phenomenon of primary elections helps to make the major parties more responsive to the electorate, minimising the need for protest voting. Protest votes often go to third parties.

Some analysts challenge the simple assumption that the USA has a two-party system and come up with other theses. Some argue that the two major parties have become so ideologically indistinct that it is meaningless to talk of a two-party system. Democrats in the 1990s were stealing such Republican issues as welfare reform and deficit reduction. A *Democrat* president — Bill Clinton — was declaring that 'the era of big government is over'. The current decade has seen a *Republican* president adding a new Executive Department to Washington's bureaucratic labyrinth. This is US parties as Tweedledum and Tweedledee — the two identical characters from *Alice through the Looking Glass* who spend their time arguing about their apparent differences. Writing in the *Washington Post* in 1997, political commentator Mark Shields stated: 'As of today, the country has two Republican parties, separated by the issue of abortion.' But this verdict seems at variance with observations earlier in this chapter.

A more convincing argument is to suggest that the USA has not a two-party system, but a 50-party system. The term 'two-party system' seems to convey the idea of two disciplined, centralised national parties with national leaders and national policy programmes. Nothing could be further from the truth as far as US political parties are concerned, for these parties are undisciplined, decentralised, state-based parties with no national 'leader' in the accepted sense and no national policy programme — except maybe for 4 months of every fourth year when these state-based parties must unite in a presidential campaign. The idea of a 50-party system reminds us that the Texas Republican Party is a very different creature from the Massachusetts Republican Party; that the California Democratic Party is a very different animal from the Georgia Democratic Party. This is the natural consequence of federalism and a country in which every election — even the presidential one — is a state-based election run largely under state laws by state officials. We have only to remember the events in Florida following the 2000 presidential election to see that even the presidential election is nothing like a national election in the accepted sense.

Summary

The two-party system

➤ America can be said to have a two-party system for reasons connected with the electoral system, the all-embracing nature of the two major parties and the holding of primary elections.

➤ Equally, one could claim that the decentralised nature of the parties gives the USA a '50-party system'.

Third parties

Despite the domination of US politics by the Democrats and Republicans, third parties do exist. There are different types: national, regional and state-based; permanent and temporary; issues-based and ideological. The best-known third parties are national: the Reform Party, the Libertarian Party and the Green Party; these three had candidates on the ballot in all 50 states in the 2000 presidential election. Regional third parties are those such as Strom Thurmond's States Rights Party (founded 1948) and George Wallace's American Independent Party (founded 1968). The Green Party and the Libertarian Party are examples of permanent third parties, while the Reform Party and the American Independent Party are examples of temporary third parties. The Green Party and the Prohibition Party are both examples of issue-based third parties, while the Socialist Party and the Libertarian Party are examples of ideological third parties.

What the USA does not have are national, permanent third parties that regularly win a sizeable proportion of the votes in general elections. There are reasons for this. The status of third parties in US politics is something of a paradox: they are both unimportant and important. Their unimportance is shown in Table 3.7 — their combined popular vote

Table 3.7 Third party support in the 2000 presidential election

Candidate	Party	Popular votes	Popular vote (%)	Electoral College votes
Ralph Nader	Green	2,831,066	2.7	0
Patrick Buchanan	Reform	447,798	0.4	0
Harry Browne	Libertarian	385,515	0.3	0
Howard Phillips	Constitution	96,907	0.0	0
John Hagelin	Natural Law	83,134	0.0	0
James Harris	Socialist Workers	7,408	0.0	0
Neil Smith	Libertarian	5,775	0.0	0
Monica Moorehead	Workers' World	5,335	0.0	0
David McReynolds	Socialist	4,233	0.0	0
Denny Lane	Grass Roots	1,044	0.0	0
Earl Dodge	Prohibition	208	0.0	0

Table 3.8 Effect of third parties in recent presidential elections

Year	Candidate	Party	Vote (%)	Effect
1968	George Wallace	American Independent Party	13.5	Split Democrat vote, leading to Republican victory
1980	John Anderson	National Unity Party	7.0	Took votes mainly from Democrats
1992	Ross Perot	–	19.0	Took votes mainly from Republicans, leading to Democrat victory
1996	Ross Perot	Reform Party	9.0	Took votes mainly from Republicans
2000	Ralph Nader	Green Party	2.7	Took votes almost exclusively from Democrats, leading to Republican victory

in 2000 was less than 4%. But their potential importance is shown in the fact that in five of the nine presidential elections between 1968 and 2000, a third party played a significant role (see Table 3.8). On three of those occasions — in 1968, 1992 and 2000 — it could be argued that a third party decided the outcome.

Third-party difficulties

Third parties face eight difficulties in their attempts to win votes in elections.

➢ The electoral system is a first-past-the-post, winner-takes-all system. All elections — whether for president, Congress or state or local office — use this system, which makes life difficult for national third parties. Regional third parties can do well. In 1968 George Wallace won 45 Electoral College votes with 13% of the vote, but his votes were concentrated in a small number of southern states. In 1992, Ross Perot won no Electoral College votes with 19% of the vote. Perot's votes, by contrast, were spread throughout the entire USA.

➢ Third parties are disadvantaged by the way they qualify for 'matching funds' in presidential elections. Major party candidates qualify by raising at least $5,000 in contributions of $250 or less in at least 20 states — not a difficult requirement. But third-party candidates qualify only by winning at least 5% of the popular vote in the previous election. There are two problems with this. First, very few third parties achieve this. In the last 50 years, only three third-party candidates — Wallace (1968), Anderson (1980) and Perot (1992 and 1996) — have managed it. Second, as many third parties are temporary parties, they often contest only one election as, for example, John Anderson did. This rule accounts for the oddity that Perot did not qualify for 'matching funds' in 1992 when he was attracting almost one-fifth of the votes, but Reform Party candidate Patrick Buchanan did qualify in 2000 when he was attracting less than one-hundredth of the votes.

➢ They are disadvantaged by the states' ballot access laws. Laws in each state regulate how third-party candidates can qualify to get their name on the ballot. Some, such as those in Tennessee, are straightforward. Tennessee requires just 25 signatures on a petition. Little wonder that there were six third-party candidates on the ballot for the Senate seat in Tennessee in 2002 (see Table 3.9). Other states, such as New York and California, are much more demanding. In New York, a third-party candidate must gain a certain number of signatures in every county in the state. In California, the number of signatures required is equal to 1% of the electorate in the state. In 1980, John Anderson estimated he had to gather around 1.2 million signatures nationwide to get on the ballot in all 50 states. He had to spend around $3 million doing just that.

Table 3.9 Candidates for the US Senate seat in Tennessee, 2002

Candidate	Votes
Lamar Alexander (R)	891,498
Bob Clement (D)	728,232
John Jay Hooker (I)	6,401
Wesley M. Baker (I)	6,106
Connie Gammon (I)	5,349
Karl Stanley Davidson (I)	2,217
Basil J. Marceaux (I)	1,170
H. Gary Keplinger (I)	1,103

Source: Congressional Quarterly

➤ Third parties' lack of resources is, to some extent, exacerbated by the two previous points. It is hard for third parties to qualify for 'matching funds'. They must spend much of their hard-earned cash on ballot access petitions rather than on real campaigning. People are understandably reluctant to give money to parties that they know are going to lose: this creates something of a 'catch 22' situation.

➤ Third parties suffer from a lack of media coverage. News programmes do not think them sufficiently newsworthy. The parties can rarely afford the cost of making — let alone of airing — television commercials. Their candidates are usually barred from appearing on both state and national televised debates. In 2000, only Bush and Gore appeared in the three presidential debates. Nader was excluded. In the razor-close 2002 Minnesota Senate race, only Democrat Walter Mondale and Republican Norm Coleman took part in an election eve state-wide televised debate. Independence Party candidate Tim Penny was excluded, much to the annoyance of the state Governor, Jesse Ventura, himself a member of the Independence Party.

➤ The sixth problem for third parties is that they tend to suffer from a lack of well-known and well-qualified candidates. Consider the difficulties experienced by John Anderson (1980) and Ross Perot (1992 and 1996) in trying to attract suitable running mates. Anderson had to settle for a former Governor of Wisconsin, Patrick Lucey. In 1992, Perot, despite talk of such big names as Colin Powell, had to settle for Admiral James Stockdale. In 1996, it was the equally odd Orson Swindle. Lucey, Stockdale and Swindle might pass as a likely name for a Washington law firm, but in terms of elective politics they were no-hopers.

➤ The two major parties often have little difficulty in portraying third-party candidates as ideological extremists. Many of them are. If they weren't, they would be running under the umbrella of either the Democrats or Republicans. Republicans smeared pro-segregationist George Wallace with the slogan: 'If you liked Hitler, you'll love Wallace.' Candidates from the Constitution Party, the Libertarian Party or the Socialist Party are not difficult to paint as ideologues. Americans have a deep-seated fear of political extremism, especially that of the left. The 'red scares' after both world wars and the McCarthy witch-hunts of the 1950s are examples of this.

> What if a third party, against all the odds, does well in pre-election opinion polls and even wins a significant number of votes on election day? Wallace did in 1968, as did Perot in 1992. This success brings with it a final problem for a third party: the adoption of its key policies by one or both of the major parties. It happened to Wallace when Republican President Richard Nixon launched his 'southern strategy' to woo Wallace voters in the run-up to the 1972 election. It happened to Perot when both Democrat President Bill Clinton and the congressional Republicans adopted policies to deal with Perot's flagship policy — the federal budget deficit. By 2000 the federal budget was in surplus and the Reform Party's vote had fallen from 19% in 1992 to 0.4% in 2000. Political scientists call this 'co-optation'.

It is, however, important to ask: what are the aims of third parties? For in the cases of Wallace and Perot, one could argue that it was not to win the presidency, but to have a significant effect on the policy debate. In this, Wallace and Perot scored a significant victory. Nader's ability to affect the outcome of the 2000 election is another case in point. It would there-fore not be true to write off all third-party candi-dates as 'failures'. Although third parties often fail in electoral terms — they get few votes — they may, as in 2000, affect both the outcome of the election in certain states, and possibly nationally, as well as the policy agendas of one or both of the two major parties.

Ralph Nader, candidate for the Green Party, probably contributed to Al Gore's defeat in 2000

Summary

Third parties

> While the USA has third parties, it does not have any national, permanent third parties of any significance.
> Third parties tend to be temporary, regional and/or insignificant.
> Third parties face considerable difficulties.
> Although electoral failures, they may occasionally wield political power in affecting both electoral outcomes and policy agendas.

Theories of party decline

It was David Broder who popularised the idea that US political parties were in serious decline. In 1972, he published a book with the ominous title *The Party's Over: The Failure of Politics in America*. The first three words of that title caught on as being shorthand for the demise of America's two major political parties. Earlier, Denis Brogan remarked that America's two major parties were 'like two bottles with different labels, both empty'. Then came Ruth Scott's volume *Parties in Crisis* (1979), followed 5 years later by Martin Wattenberg's *The Decline of American Political Parties*.

Broder's title has often been taken out of context, however. What he wrote was:

> It is called *The Party's Over* not in prophecy but in alarm. I am not predicting the demise of the Republicans or the Democrats. Party loyalties have been seriously eroded, the Democrat and Republican organisations weakened by years of neglect. But our parties are not yet dead.... Whatever the fate of our political parties, for America the party *is* over.

There are four factors to consider regarding theories of party decline.

- The parties have lost control over presidential candidate selection (see Chapter 2). Whereas until the late 1960s, presidential candidates were largely selected by 'party bosses' in 'smoke-filled rooms', now they are chosen largely by ordinary voters in presidential primaries. This is a significant loss of clout for the parties.
- Parties have lost their traditional function as the communicator between politicians and the voters, and vice versa. Politicians who wished to communicate with the voters would do so through a party rally. The same party-organised function gave the voters a chance to communicate with politicians, either through a formal question-and-answer session, or by heckling. Today, politicians communicate their message largely through television, while voters 'speak back' to the politicians through opinion polls. The role of the party is cut out.
- Campaigns in the television era have become less party-centred and more candidate- or issue-centred. Voters tend to cast their ballots, not for a party, but because they feel strongly attracted either to a candidate or to an issue that he or she is espousing.
- The effect of such candidate- or issue-centred voting is **split-ticket voting**. Split-ticket voting refers to voting for candidates of different parties for different offices at the same election. One might, at the same election, vote for a Republican President but a Democrat Senator, for example. Back in 1952, only 13% of voters split their ticket between the candidates for president and the House of Representatives. By 1980, that figure was 28%. In 1952, only 9% of voters split their ticket between the candidates for the Senate and the House of Representatives. By 1980, that figure was 31%. There was a further effect, the rise of 'independent' voters — those who do not identify with either of the two major parties (see Table 3.10). Both split-ticket voting and the number of independent voters have fuelled theories of party decline.

Key term

- **Split-ticket voting.** Voting for candidates of two or more parties for different offices in the same election.

Table 3.10 Rise of 'independent' voters, 1960–2000

Identification	1960	1964	1968	1972	1976	1980	1984	1988	1992	1996	2000
Democrat	45	52	45	41	40	41	37	35	36	37	32
Independent	23	23	30	34	37	34	34	36	38	35	34
Republican	30	25	25	23	23	23	27	28	25	27	33

Summary

Theories of party decline

➤ A number of commentators suggest a theory of party decline.

➤ They stress changes in presidential selection, the increased role of the media and the rise in candidate-centred and issue-centred campaigns as causes.

➤ Split-ticket voting and independent voters increased in number.

Theories of party renewal

Theories of party decline were popular in the 1970s and 1980s. More recently, however, many commentators have been arguing that US political parties are undergoing renewal. How can these theories of party renewal be supported?

Reasons for theories of party renewal

➤ First, it is probably the case that the theories of party decline were exaggerated. Parties might be less important than they used to be, but they still play a significant role in US politics. Both parties could echo the words of Mark Twain: 'The report of my death was an exaggeration.' The death of the Republican Party was reported following the Watergate affair and Nixon's resignation; its candidate was back in the White House in just over 6 years. The death of the Democratic Party was reported following the leftward shift of the party in the 1960s, 1970s and 1980s, but the party was resurrected by the New Democrat model of the Clinton–Gore ticket in 1992. And when all is said and done, the two major parties controlled the White House, Congress and the vast majority of state governorships throughout the entire twentieth century. As that century closed, only two seats in Congress and only two state governorships were not controlled by the two major parties.

➤ The parties have fought back and regained some control over the presidential nomination process. In the mid-1980s, the Democratic Party introduced 'super delegates' — elected office holders who are given *ex officio* seats at the Democratic National Convention as uncommitted delegates. By 2000, these super delegates accounted for almost 20% of the delegate votes at the Democratic National Convention. In the same year, it was possible to see how the choice of the Republican Party 'establishment', Governor George W. Bush, triumphed over the preferred choice of a significant number of rank-and-file Republican voters, Senator John McCain. The fact that Governor Bush enjoyed the almost unanimous support of the Republican Party hierarchy still counted for a lot, even in a system dominated by presidential primaries. Much the same could be said of the choice by the Democrats of John Kerry over Howard Dean in 2004.

➢ The parties have made significant strides in modernising their national party structures and networks. For the Republicans, the Brock reforms — initiated by then Republican National Committee chair Bill Brock — significantly strengthened the standing of the Republican National Committee over the past two decades. In the 1990s, Democratic National Committee chair Charles Manatt did much the same for the Democrats, developing computerised direct-mail facilities and a permanent headquarters in Washington DC.

➢ Another factor that led to the renewal of parties was the phenomenon of 'soft money' in the 1980s and 1990s. In an attempt to overcome the negative effects of matching funds going directly to the candidates rather than the parties, both major parties utilised the fact that funds for 'party building' and get-out-the-vote activities remained largely unregulated. This soft money provided a useful way for the national parties to enhance their role significantly in national campaigns. This could change again following the passage of further campaign finance reform legislation in 2002.

➢ Party renewal has been seen in moves towards the nationalising of electoral campaigns. This was especially true of the Republican Party in the mid-term elections of 1994 and 2002. In 1994, the Republicans campaigned around a ten-point policy programme called the **Contract with America**. The brainchild of Congressman Newt Gingrich, this national policy document was supported by nearly all Republican House candidates in that election. It promised that, under a Republican-controlled Congress, votes would be held within the first 100 days of such a Congress on ten policy issues of interest to conservative voters, such as a constitutional amendment providing for a balanced budget and congressional term limits. Then, in 2002, the Republicans launched another successful nationalised mid-term election, resulting in the White House gaining seats in both houses of Congress in a mid-term election for the first time since 1934.

Key term

➢ **Contract with America.** The Republican Party policy document that was behind the party's campaign to win control of the House of Representatives in the 1994 mid-term elections. It was the brainchild of Newt Gingrich, who became Speaker of the House following the Republicans' successes in those elections. It laid out ten policies that Republicans promised to bring to a vote on the House floor during the first 100 days of the new Congress, including a balanced budget constitutional amendment, an anti-crime package, welfare reform and congressional term limits.

➤ A final pointer to party renewal came in the 1990s with increased levels of partisanship in Congress. If parties were declining in importance, a decline in partisanship could be anticipated. After all, if parties no longer matter, why should their members continually disagree? But in 1995, recorded votes in the Senate showed the highest levels of partisanship since 1922 and in the House of Representatives the highest levels of partisanship since 1910. Partisanship reached a crescendo during the impeachment and trial of President Clinton in 1998 and early 1999. The votes in the House of Representatives on the Articles of Impeachment were largely along party lines. Increased levels of partisanship have also been seen clearly in both the reaction to the Supreme Court's ruling in *Bush v. Gore* (2000) and a prolonged stand-off between presidents — both Clinton and George W. Bush — and the Senate on their nominations to the federal courts. Partisanship is a significant pointer to party renewal.

Summary

Theories of party renewal

➤ More recently, theories of party renewal have become popular.
➤ A fightback by the parties, modernisation and soft money are among the causes suggested.

Exercises

1 Briefly explain how the USA's two major parties came about.
2 Explain the following terms: (a) the 'solid South'; (b) the New Deal coalition.
3 Using Table 3.3 as well as the text, explain when and how the 'solid South' was broken up.
4 How can one distinguish Democrats from Republicans in terms of policies?
5 Explain the following terms: (a) New Democrat; (b) Rockefeller Republican; (c) compassionate conservative.
6 Explain the organisational structure of the two major parties.
7 What evidence exists to suggest that the USA does have a two-party system?
8 What three factors are suggested that contribute towards the USA having a two-party system?
9 What is meant by the suggestion that the USA has a '50-party system'?
10 Give examples of different types of third party that exist in the USA.
11 Explain the difficulties faced by the USA's third parties.
12 Explain why some commentators think that US parties have declined.
13 Explain why others talk of 'party renewal' in the USA.

Exam focus

1 Does the USA still have a two-party system?
2 Examine the claim that the USA's two parties are 'decentralised, non-ideological and undisciplined'.
3 Why do third parties in the USA always fail?
4 'For America, the party's over.' Discuss.

Further reading

Ashbee, E., 'Minor parties in the US', *Politics Review*, vol. 13, no. 2, November 2003.
Bibby, J. F. and Maisel, L. S., *Two Parties — Or More?* (Westview, 1998).

Chapter 4

Pressure groups

Pressure groups are regarded as having important implications for a modern democracy. Through them, citizens can participate in the political process between elections. They can also use their membership of them to pressurise all three branches of the federal government — the legislature (Congress), the executive (the president and the bureaucracy) and the judiciary (headed by the Supreme Court). In a country like the United States, with a participatory tradition and an open form of government, pressure groups seem to take on added importance. They benefit from numerous 'access points' within the political system. They also benefit from a weak and fragmented party system and from election campaigns that are often issue-based rather than merely party-based.

Questions to be answered in this chapter
> What types of pressure group exist in the USA?
> What are their traditional functions?
> What methods do pressure groups use?
> What impact do they have?
> How effectively are pressure groups regulated?
> What are their merits and demerits?

Types of pressure group

Pressure groups are quite different from political parties. Whereas political parties seek to win control of government, pressure groups seek to influence those who have control of government.

Key term

> **Pressure group.** An organised interest group in which members hold similar beliefs and actively pursue ways to influence government. Unlike political parties, which seek to win control of government, pressure groups are principally interested in influencing those who determine policy.

Pressure groups vary considerably in size, wealth and influence. Pressure groups in the United States operate at all levels of government — federal, state and local — and seek to bring their influence to bear on all three branches of government. As a result there are numerous typologies of pressure groups. First of all, one can divide pressure groups into two broad categories: institutional groups and membership groups (see Table 4.1).

Table 4.1 Categorisation of pressure groups into institutional and membership groups

Institutional groups	Membership groups
Business/trade groups	Single-issue groups
Labour unions and agricultural groups	Ideological groups
Professional groups	Group rights groups
Intergovernmental groups	Public interest groups
	Think-tanks

Institutional pressure groups

Institutional pressure groups seek to represent other organisations and groups. In this first category, therefore, come business and trade groups such as the American Business Conference, the National Association of Manufacturers and the National Automobile Dealers Association. Of great important are the US Chamber of Commerce, which represents thousands of different businesses across the nation, and the labour unions, most of which represent a particular trade, such as the United Auto Workers or the Teamsters representing truck drivers. The American Federation of Labor–Congress of Industrial Organizations (AFL–CIO) is the US equivalent of the British Trades Union Congress. Not only industry has such groups: there are institutional groups representing the interests of America's agriculture, such as the American Farm Bureau Federation, the National Farmers' Union and Associated Milk Producers Incorporated.

Institutional groups include professional pressure groups, such as the American Medical Association, the National Education Association and the American Bar Association. Then there are intergovernmental pressure groups — those that lobby one level of government on behalf of another, such as the National Governors' Conference.

Membership pressure groups

Membership pressure groups seek to represent individual Americans rather than organisations and groups. Americans like to join groups, but they are selective. They are more likely than, for example, their European counterparts to join social, charitable, civic, political and religious groups, although they are less likely to join trade unions. On the whole, however, Americans join, subscribe, write, phone, petition, protest and march more than the citizens of most nation-states.

The membership groups they join may be single-issue groups, such as the National Rifle Association (NRA), Mothers Against Drunk Driving (MADD), or the National Abortion and Reproductive Rights Action League. Equally, they might join an ideological group, such as the American Conservative Union, People for the American Way, or the American Civil Liberties Union (ACLU).

Alternatively, they might join a group that represents individuals with a common gender, ethnic, religious or social characteristic, such as the National Organization for Women (NOW), the National Association for the Advancement of Colored People (NAACP), the Christian Coalition, or the American Association of Retired Persons (AARP). They might, on the other hand, join a public interest group: for instance, Common Cause, Friends of the Earth, or the Sierra Club.

Think-tanks are a particularly important type of public interest group and they are especially numerous in the United States. Think-tanks conduct research, write reports, write articles for publication in leading broadsheet newspapers, publish journals and books, organise conferences and give evidence to congressional committees. Most have a particular ideological slant. On the liberal side come the Institute for Policy Studies and the Brookings Institution. On the conservative side are the Heritage Foundation and the American Enterprise Institute.

Summary

Types of pressure group

➤ There are two main types of pressure group: institutional groups and membership groups.

Functions of pressure groups

Pressure groups perform five basic functions, although not all pressure groups perform all these functions.

➤ Pressure groups may perform a representative function. They are a means whereby US citizens can have their views represented and their grievances articulated.

➤ Pressure groups aid citizen participation. They increase the opportunities for ordinary citizens to participate in the decision-making process between elections.

➤ Pressure groups may enhance public education. They attempt to educate public opinion, warning people of the possible dangers if issues are not addressed, as well as the likely effects of decisions made by the government.

➤ Pressure groups may perform the function of agenda building. In so doing they attempt to influence the agendas of political parties, legislators and bureaucrats to give priority to their members' interests. They may attempt to bring together different parts of US society — for example, business groups, religious groups, state governments and professional organisations — to work together to achieve a common interest.

➤ Pressure groups may perform the function of programme monitoring. They may scrutinise and hold government to account in the implementation of policies, to try to ensure that promises are fulfilled, policies delivered and regulations enforced.

How does all this work in practice? Let us consider a few current key policy areas and the functions being performed by pressure groups associated with them. Take the issue of prescription drug provision, especially for senior citizens. The American Association of Retired Persons (AARP) boasts more than 35 million members over the age of 50. Even politicians who do not agree with the AARP's policy positions cannot ignore its political clout. The Pharmaceutical Research and Manufacturers of America, representing more than 100 American drug companies, is lobbying hard for legislation that would give the private sector — not the federal government — the management role in administering any prescription drug programme for senior citizens. Add to those two groups the United Seniors Association — a conservative grassroots group with some 1.5 million members — and the 13 million-member AFL–CIO, which claims that proposed legislation too often favours drug company profits rather than the wallets of senior citizens, and you have an extraordinary amount of lobbying going on.

Alternatively, take the area of the environment and, specifically, clean air. There is lobbying from industrial groups such as the Alliance of Automobile Manufacturers, whose former boss Andrew Card is now White House chief of staff, and environmental groups such as the Sierra Club and Environmental Defense.

The provision of broadband technology is of concern to phone companies and cable television companies as well as to the representatives of high-tech industry, such as Silicon Valley's TechNet association and the Consumer Electronics Association, and the Hollywood film and music industry — the Motion Pictures Association of America and the Recording Industry Association of America. Not only providers but also consumers have pressure groups. The Consumer Federation of America and the Centre for Digital Democracy want curbs on the provider companies to prevent them acting as broadband gatekeepers and thereby hindering consumers' easy access to news and information.

Between them, such organisations fulfil the functions of pressure groups within these policy areas.

Summary

Functions of pressure groups

➤ Pressure groups can be said to fulfil five principal functions within the US political system: representation, participation, education, agenda building and programme monitoring.

Methods used by pressure groups

Pressure groups use five principal methods in fulfilling their functions.

Electioneering

Since the campaign finance reforms of the 1970s, considerable changes have taken place in the role of pressure groups and political fundraising. The reforms limited the amount that any pressure group could give to a candidate in a federal election. What the reforms encouraged, therefore, was the setting up of **political action committees** (PACs) that could make such donations. A PAC is an organisation whose purpose is to raise and then give campaign funds to candidates for political office. The vast majority of PAC money is spent on behalf of incumbents. In the 2002 mid-term elections, incumbent House members received $176 million, while House challengers received a mere $29 million (see Table 4.2). It was much the same picture in the Senate, with $43 million going to incumbents and only $15 million going to challengers (see Table 4.3). In that election

Table 4.2 House of Representatives top ten PAC recipients: 2002 election cycle

House member	District	Party	PAC receipts ($)	Result
John Dingell	Michigan	D	1,735,646	Won 72%
Nancy Johnson	Connecticut	R	1,676,167	Won 54%
Richard Gephardt	Missouri	D	1,463,704	Won 59%
Billy Tauzin	Louisiana	R	1,462,005	Won 87%
Dennis Hastert	Illinois	R	1,318,855	Won 74%
Karen Thurman	Florida	R	1,299,271	Lost 46%
Earl Pomeroy	North Dakota	D	1,297,426	Won 52%
Shelley Moore Capito	West Virginia	D	1,273,171	Won 60%
Roy Blunt	Missouri	R	1,249,671	Won 75%
Charles Pickering	Mississippi	R	1,206,049	Won 64%

Table 4.3 Senate top ten PAC recipients: 2002 election cycle

Senator	State	Party	PAC receipts ($)	Result
Max Baucus	Montana	D	2,620,108	Won 63%
Tim Johnson	South Dakota	D	2,065,663	Won 50%
Mary Landrieu	Louisiana	D	1,972,062	Won 51%
Wayne Allard	Colorado	R	1,940,956	Won 51%
Max Cleland	Georgia	D	1,827,709	Lost 46%
James Talent	Missouri	R	1,774,818	Won 50%
Norm Coleman	Minnesota	R	1,735,858	Won 49%
Tim Hutchinson	Arkansas	R	1,693,422	Lost 46%
Lindsey Graham	South Carolina	R	1,637,951	Won 54%
John Cornyn	Texas	R	1,627,531	Won 55%

cycle, the National Association of Realtors — representing America's estate agents — gave $3.8 million, the Association of Trial Lawyers gave $3.4, but both were topped by the American Federation of Teachers, which gave $4 million.

Key term

> **Political action committees.** Pressure groups that collect money from their members and then give it to candidates and political parties who support their interests.

However, what pressure groups get for this money is open to question. Research has yet to prove any clear link between PAC contributions and the way members of Congress cast their votes on the floor of the House or Senate. Members of Congress are more likely to be influenced by direct lobbying than by donations to their campaigns.

Lobbying

Perhaps the most effective method of lobbying is the provision of accurate, detailed, up-to-date information to those who need it. Legislators and bureaucrats are busy people who have many demands made upon their limited time and resources. Legislators, in particular, must appear knowledgeable about and take positions on a bewildering number of policy issues. Pressure groups are often the only source of information.

In order to facilitate this method of operation, pressure groups maintain offices in Washington DC, state capitals and in other major cities. This allows them to be on hand to lobby members of federal, state and local government. The presence of lobbyists in Washington DC itself is almost overwhelming and is often referred to as the 'K Street corridor', named after the street in the capital where the offices of many lobbyists are located (see Table 4.4).

Pressure groups also provide legislators with voting cues. Liberal Democrats look to such groups as the AFL–CIO, the NAACP and Americans for Democratic Action (ADA) to provide reassurance that they are taking the right stand on a particular issue.

Table 4.4 Examples of 'K Street corridor' lobbyists

Lobbyist	Washington DC address
Alliance for Aging Research	2021 K Street, NW
The American Legion	1608 K Street, NW
American Psychiatric Association	1400 K Street, NW
American Public Transportation Association	1666 K Street, NW
Association of Flight Attendants	1275 K Street, NW
The Education Trust	1725 K Street, NW
Institute for Mental Health Initiatives	2175 K Street, NW
Leadership Conference on Civil Rights	1629 K Street, NW
Media Access Project	1625 K Street, NW
National Legal Center for the Public Interest	1600 K Street, NW

Conservative Republicans find the Christian Coalition, the American Conservative Union (ACU), Americans for Constitutional Action (ACA) and the US Chamber of Commerce equally helpful. Pressure groups such as ADA, the AFL–CIO and the ACU publish regular ratings of legislators, showing how often — or how rarely — a particular legislator has supported the policy positions in line with the views of that particular group. However, although being ranked as 'very liberal' or 'very conservative' may help legislators among those respective groups of voters, it may also make them a target for the other side. Within 4 years of the ACU giving Republican Senators John Ashcroft, Lauch Faircloth, Jesse Helms, Tim Hutchinson and Bob Smith a 100% rating, four of the five had been defeated, and the fifth — Helms — had retired.

Every 2 years, the League of Conservation Voters (LCV) publishes its 'dirty dozen' list — the 12 federal and state politicians with the worst voting record on environmental conservation. Its 'dirty dozen' list for the year 2000 included nine members of Congress, of whom six were defeated that year (see Table 4.5).

Table 4.5 Members of Congress on the 'dirty dozen' list, 2000

Member of Congress	Party	State	Election outcome
Rep. Anne Northrup	R	Kentucky	Won (53%)
Rep. Bill McCollum	R	Florida	Defeated for Senate
Rep. James Rogan	R	California	Defeated
Rep. Jim Traficant	D	Ohio	Won (49%)
Rep. Steve Kykendall	R	California	Defeated
Sen. Rod Grams	R	Minnesota	Defeated
Sen. Spencer Abraham	R	Michigan	Defeated
Sen. Conrad Burns	R	Montana	Won (50.5%)
Sen. Slade Gorton	R	Washington	Defeated

Source: www.lev.org

Publicity

Pressure groups frequently launch public relations campaigns in order to educate the people at large. Such publicity takes a number of different forms. It might involve television advertising — often known as 'issue advertising'. The role that insurance companies played in killing off President Clinton's healthcare reforms in 1993–94 was certainly decisive. A pressure group called US Term Limits conducted a high-profile publicity campaign to defeat long-serving members of the House of Representatives in the 1994 mid-term elections. Its successes even included the defeat of the then Speaker of the House, Democrat Tom Foley. The AFL–CIO has launched numerous negative publicity campaigns aimed at Republican legislators opposed to increases in the minimum wage.

When the Food and Drug Administration announced plans to ban saccharin due to possible links with cancer, the Calorie Control Council — which has close links with the Coca-Cola Company — ran an advertisement campaign denouncing the proposal.

Public policy journals — whose circulation includes almost all members of Congress, senior staff at the White House and executive departments and agencies — are also used for the placement of advertisements. The 7 December 2002 edition of *National Journal* — a low-circulation but high-reputation Washington weekly — carried advertisements from the Religious Coalition for Reproductive Choice and the American Medical Association.

Roadside hoardings, bumper stickers and badges are among other methods used for pressure group publicity. Pressure groups send some publicity directly to law-makers in the form of informative or promotional videos. A campaign to encourage Congress to tighten laws on the production of veal meat bombarded members with a video entitled *Murder on the Menu*.

Organising grassroots activities

Grassroots activities by members are often thought to be the most effective of pressure groups' methods, especially when these activities are aimed directly at legislators or policy-makers. Such grassroots activities may include the organisation of a postal 'blitz' on Congress, the White House or a government department. However, knowing that members of Congress pay little attention to the arrival of sack loads of identical letters or postcards, pressure groups encourage their members to frame their own communications. There are even firms that exist to orchestrate mail and telephone blitzes. Now that a wide range of more sophisticated electronic media is available, faxes and e-mails may be used too.

Marches and demonstrations are sometimes aimed at state and federal court houses, where other forms of lobbying are inappropriate. Whenever the United States Supreme Court delivers a judgment on a controversial issue such as abortion, school prayers, capital punishment or minority rights, the pavement outside the Supreme Court building in Washington DC is filled with people from pressure groups representing the opposing sides of the argument.

Some groups may go further and resort to violence and disorder. The bombing of the federal government building in Oklahoma City in 1995 was linked to militia groups on the extreme right of US politics. Some of the more extreme anti-abortion groups have set fire to and bombed abortion clinics, intimidating staff who work in them and women who visit them, and even shooting doctors who carry out abortions.

The devastating effects of the bombing of the Alfred P. Murrah building in Oklahoma City, 19 April 1995

Litigation in the courts

As Chapter 8 explains, the courts play an important role in interpreting the laws and the Constitution of both the state and federal governments. The courtroom therefore provides pressure groups with another place to pursue their goals. The historic civil rights case in 1954 — *Brown v. Board of Education of Topeka* — was brought by the National Association for the Advancement of Colored People (NAACP), which saw it as a way of effecting changes in the educational rights of blacks that could not be done through Congress or the state governments. In 1989, in *Allegheny County v. American Civil Liberties Union*, the ACLU brought a case to the Supreme Court which resulted in the banning of religious Christmas displays in publicly owned shopping malls. The same pressure group brought another case in 1997 — *Reno v. ACLU* — which resulted in the Court declaring that the 1996 Communications Decency Act was unconstitutional, thereby overturning Congress's attempt to ban pornography on the internet.

Summary

Methods used by pressure groups
- Pressure groups use a number of different methods.
- The role of PACs in electioneering has become increasingly important.
- There is a close relationship in Washington between lobbyists and legislators.

The impact of pressure groups

In recent decades, pressure groups have had a significant impact in a number of policy areas.

Civil rights for African-Americans

The NAACP was the force behind not only the landmark 1954 Supreme Court decision of *Brown v. Board of Education of Topeka*, but also the subsequent passage of much civil rights legislation. The NAACP used its money and professional expertise to bring cases to court for people who could not otherwise afford it. These were cases that the NAACP believed it could win and which would benefit the interests of African-Americans. The NAACP has continued to be at the centre of political debate in America over affirmative action programmes.

Environmental protection

Towards the end of the nineteenth century, when both industrialisation and 'westward expansion' were well under way, the matter of environmental conservation became important. This is when the Sierra Club was formed. It was followed in the early twentieth century by the Wilderness Society and the National Wildlife Federation. Such groups have been behind the push towards stricter laws for environmental protection.

WE CAN BREATHE EASY NOW! AN INTERNATIONAL CONSENSUS HAS BEEN REACHED TO HELP CUT CIGARETTE SMOKE.

Women's rights

Groups such as the League of Women Voters and the National Organization for Women pushed — unsuccessfully — for the passage of an Equal Rights Amendment to the Constitution during the 1970s and 1980s. They have remained very active in US politics, campaigning on such issues as equal pay and job opportunities for women. In addition, they have been involved in the debate over attempting to root out sexual harassment in the workplace, with some high-profile cases in the US military. This latter issue received much public debate in connection with President Clinton's relationships with women such as Paula Corbin Jones and Monica Lewinsky. Some criticised women's groups for not being more vocal in their condemnation of President Clinton's treatment of these women.

Women's groups have also been deeply involved in moves to try to increase the number of women being elected to Congress. The pressure group EMILY's List — an acronym for 'Early Money Is Like Yeast' — supports female candidates early in the election process so that they will be able to demonstrate their ability to raise money later on in the electoral cycle and win seats.

Abortion rights

Both the 'pro-choice' and 'pro-life' lobbies have been active in US politics during the past three to four decades. Since the 1973 *Roe v. Wade* decision by the Supreme Court, pro-choice pressure groups have fought to preserve the constitutional right of women to have an abortion, whereas pro-life groups have fought to have it both narrowed and overturned. Most recently, they have been involved in the debate over the practice of so-called 'partial birth abortions'. When Congress tried to ban such types of abortion, President Clinton vetoed the bills, once in 1996 and again in 1997. In 2000, the Supreme Court refused to allow states to ban this type of abortion. In pursuing their respective agendas, both sides in the debate have lobbied the Senate over presidential judicial appointments, most clearly seen in the fights over the nominations to the Supreme Court of Robert Bork in 1987 and Clarence Thomas in 1991.

Gun control

The National Rifle Association (NRA) is arguably one of the most powerful pressure groups in US politics, with a membership of some 3 million. It was formed in 1871 as a group dedicated to teaching Americans how to use guns. Since the 1960s, however, it has been influential in stopping what it sees as encroachment on citizens' rights to own and use legal firearms. It seeks to uphold the strictest interpretation of the 2nd Amendment

Roadside hoarding advertising the National Rifle Association

right to 'keep and bear arms'. It also works to oppose tougher gun control laws put forward at any level of government. The NRA opposed the Brady Bill and the assault weapons ban, as well as laws requiring background checks on those purchasing guns and the mandatory sale of trigger locks with handguns. It became involved in a national debate on the availability of guns following the 'Washington sniper' incident in October 2002.

Health

An area in which pressure groups played a decisive part during the 1990s was that of Bill Clinton's proposed healthcare reforms. The Health Insurance Association of America, representing the small and medium-sized health insurance companies, complained about the plan's complexity and the large role that would be played by the federal government. They aired an extremely effective series of television commercials in which a fictitious elderly couple — 'Harry' and 'Louise' — discussed the matter over breakfast or in their living room. Louise, for example, would be worriedly reading a copy of the Healthcare Bill when Harry arrived home. According to Elizabeth Drew (1994), they 'did more damage than any of the president's real-life opponents'.

Impact on Congress

Pressure groups seek to influence the way House and Senate members vote. They do this by a number of methods. First, they make direct contact with members of Congress as well as senior members of their staff. Second, they make contact with the relevant congressional committees — especially those who chair or are ranking minority members on those committees. Committee staff are another target of pressure group activity.

Third, pressure groups attempt to organise constituents to write to, telephone, fax, e-mail or visit their member of Congress to express either support for or opposition to a certain policy. This is most likely to occur just before a high-profile committee hearing, floor debate or final passage vote. Fourth, pressure groups publicise the voting records of House and Senate members, sometimes offering their own rankings. At election time, they endorse supportive and oppose non-supportive incumbents by fundraising and media advertising.

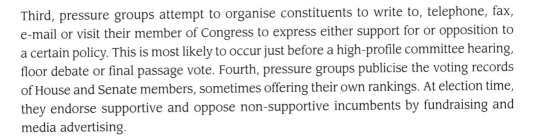 **Box 4.1 American Civil Liberties Union**

The following description appears on the website of the American Civil Liberties Union:

> The American Civil Liberties Union (ACLU) is our nation's guardian of liberty, working daily in the courts, legislatures and communities to defend and preserve the individual rights and liberties guaranteed to all in this country by the Constitution and laws of the United States.

> In 1920, when the ACLU was founded, civil liberties were in a sorry state. Activists were languishing in jail for distributing anti-war literature. Foreign-born people suspected of political radicalism were subject to summary deportation. Racial segregation was the law of the land and state-sanctioned violence against African-Americans was routine. Constitutional rights for lesbians and gay men, the poor and many other groups were virtually unthinkable. Moreover, the US Supreme Court had yet to uphold a single free speech claim under the First Amendment.

> Since our founding in 1920, the non-profit, non-partisan ACLU has grown from a roomful of civil liberties activists to an organisation of nearly 400,000 members and supporters, with offices in almost every state. The ACLU has also maintained, since its founding, the position that civil liberties must be respected, even in times of national emergency. In support of that position, the ACLU has appeared before the Supreme Court and other federal courts on numerous occasions, both as direct counsel and by filing *amicus* briefs.

> The ACLU's mission is to fight civil liberties violations wherever and whenever they occur. Most of our clients are ordinary people who have experienced an injustice and have decided to fight back. The ACLU is also active in our national and state capitals, fighting to ensure that the Bill of Rights will always be more than a 'parchment barrier' against government oppression and the tyranny of the majority.

> The ACLU is supported by annual dues and contributions from its members, plus grants from private foundations and individuals. We do not receive any government funding.

Source: **www.aclu.org**

Impact on the executive

Pressure groups seek to maintain strong ties with relevant executive departments, agencies and regulatory commissions. This is especially the case when it comes to the regulatory work of the federal government — regulations, for example, regarding health and safety at work, business, the transport and communications industries, and the environment.

Problems can emerge when regulatory bodies are thought to have too cosy a relationship with the particular group that they are meant to be regulating. Are they acting as 'watchdogs' or 'lapdogs'?

Box 4.2   The Sierra Club

The following passage is from the website of the Sierra Club:

Sierra Club members are 700,000 of your friends and neighbours. Inspired by nature, we work together to protect our communities and the planet. The Sierra Club is America's oldest, largest and most influential grassroots environmental organisation. Through grassroots activism, public education, lobbying and litigation, the Sierra Club works to protect the health of our environment and to preserve our remaining wild places. Here are just a few of the accomplishments that the Sierra Club has helped to bring about:

➤ establishment of Yosemite and Yellowstone national parks

➤ enactment of the Clean Water Act and the Endangered Species Act

➤ the Alaska National Interest Lands Conservation Act, designating more than 100 million acres of parks, wildlife refuges and wilderness areas

The mission statement of the Sierra Club is to explore, enjoy and protect the wild places of the earth; to practise and promote the responsible use of the earth's ecosystems and resources; to educate and enlist humanity to protect and restore the quality of the natural and human environment; and to use all lawful means to carry out these objectives.

The Sierra Club's first outing drew 96 people to Yosemite National Park in 1901. Today, our national outings programme offers more than 330 outings each year — from backpacking in the Sierra Nevada to whale watching in Hawaii. In addition, chapters and groups offer tens of thousands of outings every year led by Sierra Club volunteers — from hikes to bicycle rides to rafting trips. Most are free and have no membership requirement. Local outings are published in chapter and group newsletters and websites. In 50 US and Canadian cities, Sierra Club volunteers lead Inner City Outings, providing low-income, inner-city youth with trips to wilderness areas.

The Sierra Club's website has a 'take action' page where you can send faxes, e-mails and letters to public officials. Writing letters to the editor of your local newspaper can reach thousands of people in your community with the Sierra Club's message. The Sierra Club also works to build alliances with other groups like labour unions, religious groups, hunters and anglers, and poor and minority communities. For example, in the spring of 2003, the Sierra Club and the United Steelworkers began the first of 30 joint trainings focused on energy solutions that provide good jobs and curb global warming.

A great director can sometimes wring a good performance out of a bad actor. But it makes more sense to cast the right person in the role from the start. That's the reason behind the Sierra Club's political programme: invest in getting pro-environment champions elected to office and it's easier to get pro-environmental legislation passed. Nationwide, the Sierra Club endorses and works for thousands of candidates, from city council members to US Senators and presidential hopefuls. 'Receiving the Sierra Club endorsement was the turning point in my campaign,' acknowledged Minnesota Mayor R. T. Rybak, elected with Club support in 2002.

Source: **www.sierraclub.org**

Edward Ashbee and Nigel Ashford (1999) identify another close link, between 'producer groups' — such as companies, labour unions or small business federations — and relevant government departments and agencies seeking protection, funding, subsidies or price guarantee mechanisms.

Impact on the judiciary

Pressure groups can hope to influence the courts by offering *amicus curiae* briefings. Through these, pressure groups have an opportunity to present their views to the court in writing before oral arguments are heard. Pressure groups have used this method to great effect in recent decades, in such areas as the civil rights of racial minorities, abortion and 1st Amendment rights.

Impact on state government

Because of federalism, many important governmental and political decisions are taken not in Washington DC but in the capitals of the 50 states. Different states have a different manufacturing base to their economy: the high-tech industries of Silicon Valley in California; the tobacco industry of states such as Virginia and the Carolinas; sugar in Florida; oil in Alaska; coal in West Virginia; the logging industry in Oregon and Washington. Business, trade and labour groups therefore focus their lobbying in those states where their interests are most centred. They lobby state governors, state legislators and their staff, and state judges. States also vary as to how relatively weak or powerful the state governor is. Likewise the state legislature varies and in some states is in session for only a few weeks of each year.

Summary

The impact of pressure groups

➤ US pressure groups have had a significant impact in recent years on some key policy areas.

➤ They have had an impact on the three branches of the federal government.

Regulation of pressure groups

In a nation where 1st Amendment rights are the very breath of politics, it is difficult to regulate anything that fundamentally concerns freedom of speech and expression. The 1st Amendment states that: 'Congress shall make no law...abridging the freedom of speech, or of the press; or the right of the people to peaceably assemble, and to petition the government for a redress of grievances.' For over 100 years, pressure groups have sheltered under the protection of this amendment and have successfully pleaded its guarantees in court.

It was not until the passage of the Federal Regulation of Lobbying Act in 1946 that Congress started to regulate significantly the activities of pressure groups. This act required lobbyists to register with the clerk of the House of Representatives and the secretary of the Senate if they raised money 'to be used principally to aid the passage or defeat of any legislation by the Congress of the United States', but its provisions went largely ignored. Thirty years later the Lobby Disclosure Bill failed to make it onto the statute book — because of powerful lobbying from pressure groups.

It was largely as a consequence of the Watergate affair and the subsequent passage of campaign finance reform legislation that the regulation of pressure groups came about. The campaign finance reform of the 1970s gave rise to the huge growth of PACs. There was public disquiet over buying influence in Congress as a consequence of a congressional scandal known as 'Abscam' — the attempts of influential Arab interests to bribe leading members of Congress.

In the 1990s, Congress passed further regulatory legislation by expanding the definition of what qualified as a pressure group and thereby making more groups register. Congress also passed significant restrictions on lobbyists by banning gifts to members of Congress, including the 'wining and dining' of members and the paying of honoraria — writing or speaking fees paid by pressure groups to members of Congress.

All this legislation, which was not entirely effective anyway, was aimed at regulating only the activities of pressure groups in relation to Congress. Their lobbying of the executive branch went entirely unchecked.

Summary

Regulation of pressure groups

➤ Congress has made a number of attempts to regulate pressure groups but with varying degrees of success.

Arguments against pressure groups

Pressure groups can come in for something of a bad press. Do they enhance democracy? Are they a 'good thing' or merely a 'necessary evil'? Several arguments are made against the activities of pressure groups.

The revolving-door syndrome

Many pressure groups work through hired lobbyists employed by lobbying firms — many based in Washington DC — whose full-time job is to lobby government. There is nothing inherently wrong with that. A criticism that can be made, however, is that a high proportion of these professional lobbyists are former members of Congress or former congressional staff members. This is what is known as the revolving-door syndrome: people walk out of the political door, so to speak, perhaps having just been defeated in an election, but immediately re-enter the political world as a Washington lobbyist. Federal law forbids former public officials from taking up a job as a lobbyist within a year of leaving public office, but after that year has elapsed, the traffic through the revolving door from public official to professional lobbyist is quite heavy.

Critics argue that this constitutes an abuse of public service. People exploit their knowledge of and contacts within Congress or the executive branch of government in order to further the interests of their pressure group clients and in so doing make large sums of money for themselves. It is alleged that serving politicians may favour particular group interests because they are hoping for a job representing that interest, should they lose their public office.

A research article by Jill Abramson entitled 'The business of persuasion thrives in [the] nation's capital' (*New York Times*, 29 September 1998) identified 128 former members of Congress working as lobbyists in Washington DC. This number represented 12% of all members who had left Congress since 1970 and included former House members John Anderson and Ed Derwinski. Anderson represented an Illinois District in the House for 20 years before running unsuccessfully for the presidency in 1980 as a third-party candidate: he is now President of the World Federalist Association. Derwinski was a member of the House for 24 years, then became an under-secretary at the State Department before being appointed Secretary of Veterans' Affairs in 1989, a post he held for the next 3 years: he is now owner of the Washington lobbying firm Derwinski and Associates. Former Ohio Senator Howard Metzenbaum followed a career of 18 years in Congress by becoming chairman of the Consumer Federation of America.

The iron-triangle syndrome

The **iron triangle** is a term used to describe a strong relationship that many commentators of US politics see existing between pressure groups and the relevant congressional committees on the one hand and the relevant government department or agency on the other. This cosy relationship — the term 'cosy triangle' is sometimes used — guarantees policy outcomes to the benefit of all three parties involved. One example is what might be called the 'veterans' iron triangle'. On one side of the triangle would be veterans' groups such as the Vietnam Veterans of America, the Disabled American Veterans, the Veterans of Foreign Wars and the American Legion. On another side would be Veterans' Affairs committees of the House and the Senate. The Department of Veterans' Affairs would constitute the third side of this particular iron triangle. Such an iron triangle can become so powerful that it constitutes almost its own sub-government. This is particularly the case in such policy areas as agriculture and national defence.

Key term

> **Iron triangle.** A term used to describe a strong relationship between pressure groups, the relevant congressional committees and the relevant government department or agency in an attempt to guarantee the policy outcomes to the benefit of all three parties involved.

The iron triangle is linked with the revolving-door syndrome. A Pentagon general might, after the lawful waiting period, end up as a lobbyist for a missile manufacturer. Similarly, a former staff member from the Senate Armed Services Committee might get a job lobbying for a defence contractor.

The existence of these iron triangles raises the question of whether pressure group activities are compatible with a pluralist society. A pluralist society is one in which political resources such as money, expertise and access to both government and the mass media are spread widely and are in the hands of many diverse individuals and groups. Many see pressure groups as fostering an elitist view of society in which the aforementioned political resources are in the hands, not of the many, but of the few.

Inequality of groups

Defenders of pressure groups would have us believe that at the very least pressure groups operate within a series of 'competing elites'. They see US politics as a system in which pressure groups, along with political parties, bureaucrats, business people, trade unions, the media, educators, lawyers and so on, compete for influence over those who make policy. They would argue that, because each group represents the interests of its own clients, this is entirely compatible with a democratic society. Such an argument is associated with those on the right of the political spectrum.

Those on the left criticise pressure groups because they see this 'competition' as being one that is often unequal. As early as the 1950s, President Eisenhower warned against what he saw as the power of the 'military-industrial complex'. At around the same time, the noted American political philosopher C. Wright Mills continued this theme in his 1956 book *The Power Elite*.

There are a number of policy areas in which pressure groups representing the opposing sides of the argument are clearly unequal, for example the area of the environment. Many would argue that the resources of big business often outweigh the resources of the environmental protectionists. In the policy area of gun control, a battle between the National Rifle Association on the one hand and Handgun Control Inc. on the other is clearly unequal. In the debate over health issues and tobacco smoking, the resources of one side have traditionally outweighed the resources of the other. The tobacco industry spent $67.4 million on lobbying in 1998.

Special interests v. the public interest

A criticism levelled at pressure groups is that they tend to put the interests of a small group before the interests of society as a whole. The pressure groups that represent various ethnic groups within American society are a good example; the National Association for the Advancement of Colored People (NAACP), the American Jewish Congress, the Indian American Center for Public Awareness, the Organization of Chinese Americans and the National Association for Hispanic Health, to name but a few. Critics see this as pressure groups adding to a splintering, or 'atomisation', of US society.

Pressure groups tend to accentuate 'me' rather than 'we'. They spend too much time fighting for their special interest and little time working for the wider public interest. Provided their client group is satisfied, they rarely consider the implications for society as a whole. They can also lead to group stereotyping, by making it appear as if all blacks, or all Jews, or all Latinos — or women, or teachers, or airline pilots, or whoever — think the same way and want the same policy outcomes. Some would argue that part of the reason for the criticism heaped upon Supreme Court nominee Clarence Thomas in 1991 was that he was a *conservative* black who did not fit the group-think of liberal politics as espoused by the NAACP and most other black pressure groups.

Buying political influence

Senator Edward Kennedy once famously remarked that America has 'the finest Congress that money can buy'. You have to 'pay to play'. According to the Center for Responsive Politics, the year 1999 saw $1.45 billion spent on lobbying activities; and the lobbying business is growing at a staggering 7.3% a year. In the 2002 mid-term elections, PACs donated a total of just short of $215 million to House candidates and just over $60 million to Senate candidates. That is well over a quarter-of-a-billion dollars spent in just one mid-term election cycle.

What do lobbyists get for their money? The short answer for the critics of pressure groups is 'a disproportionate level of influence'. In her account of the 104th Congress, Elizabeth Drew (1997) claims that lobbyists acting on behalf of business corporations wrote legislation for members of Congress. She quotes a *Washington Post* story that a lobbyist for the energy and petrochemical industries wrote the first draft of a bill during that Congress and that lobbyists working for a group called Project Relief were given a Capitol Hill office to use as a 'war room' during an energy debate showdown. Meanwhile, the *New York Times* was reporting a story that a bill to weaken the Clean Water Act was written by a taskforce of lobbyists representing groups such as the Chemical Manufacturers Association and International Paper. House Speaker Newt Gingrich, asked about the role that pressure groups played in Congress, was quoted in the *Wall Street Journal* as saying: 'As long as it's out in the open, I have no problem.' Not everyone would agree.

Using 'direct action'

A final criticism levelled at pressure groups is their use of 'direct action' which is deemed by others to be inappropriate. This criticism is brought about whenever pressure groups use what most consider unacceptable levels of violence to pursue their political agenda. In recent years it has been associated with pro- and anti-abortion groups, environmentalists, anti-capitalist groups and groups of the extreme right

Anti-capitalists demonstrate in Seattle, 1999

pursuing their anti-government agenda. Violence — even shootings, bombings and murders — conducted around abortion clinics by 'pro-life' groups hit the headlines in the 1990s. Anti-capitalist demonstrations that disrupted a meeting of the World Trade Organization in Seattle, Washington, in 1999, followed by demonstrations outside the World Bank in Washington DC in 2000, brought similar condemnation, as did the bombing of the federal government building in Oklahoma City in 1995.

Summary

Arguments against pressure groups

➤ There are particular concerns about the revolving-door syndrome and iron triangles.
➤ In some policy areas, there is a clear inequality between pressure groups on opposite sides of the argument.
➤ Concerns exist that pressure groups promote 'special interests' over 'public interest'.
➤ The influence of money and the results of direct action raise further concerns.

Arguments for pressure groups

The arguments in favour of pressure groups tend to follow the functions they may usefully perform, as discussed on pp. 96–97. They provide legislators and bureaucrats with useful information and act as a sounding board for legislators at the policy formulation stage in the legislative process. They bring some kind of order to the policy debate, aggregating views and channelling the wishes of the clients and members whom they seek to represent, and they broaden the opportunities for participation in a democracy and make government more accountable.

The US political process is one that is conducive to pressure group activity. There are many 'access points' in the democratic process where pressure groups can have their say. This is especially the case in Congress, where the decentralisation of power, the autonomy of committees and the lack of strict party discipline when it comes to voting all make Congress an institution that is far more open to persuasion by pressure groups than most national legislatures. The number of 'access points' is merely increased by the federal division of powers, which allows many important decisions to be made in the host of state and local governments across the USA.

Summary

Arguments for pressure groups

➤ Pressure groups perform a number of useful functions.
➤ Pressure groups flourish in a political system that has many 'access points' and where party discipline is relatively weak.

Exercises

1 Describe the different types of pressure group found in the USA.
2 Explain the main functions performed by US pressure groups.
3 What methods do pressure groups use to further their aims?
4 Explain the terms: (a) political action committee; (b) the K Street corridor; (c) issue advertising.
5 Explain the impact that US pressure groups have had recently in any four policy areas.
6 Use the material on the American Civil Liberties Union (Box 4.1) and the Sierra Club (Box 4.2) to illustrate the different ways in which pressure groups work.
7 Explain the impact of US pressure groups on: (a) the three branches of the federal government; (b) state government.
8 Explain how pressure groups are regulated.
9 Explain the following terms: (a) revolving-door syndrome; (b) iron triangles; (c) pluralist; (d) competing elites; (e) atomisation; (f) direct action.

Exam focus

1 Examine the claim that pressure groups in US politics are undemocratic and work for narrow goals against the national good.
2 Are US pressure groups too powerful?
3 Analyse the factors that are likely to bring success to pressure groups in the USA.
4 Have pressure groups become more important than political parties in US politics?

References

Ashbee, E. and Ashford, N., *US Politics Today* (Manchester University Press, 1999).
Drew, E., *Showdown: The Struggle between the Gingrich Congress and the Clinton White House* (Simon and Schuster, 1994).

Further reading

Grant, A., 'Pressure groups and PACs in the USA', *Politics Review*, vol. 10, no. 3, February 2001.
Herrnson, P., *The Interest Group Connection: Electioneering, Lobbying and Policymaking in Washington* (Chatham House, 1998).
Peele, G., 'Pressure groups in the USA', *Politics Review*, vol. 12, no. 4, April 2003.

Chapter 5

Congress

The three branches of the US federal government are Congress, the presidency and the Supreme Court. Congress is the legislative branch of the federal government. Its home is in the building known as the Capitol, situated in the area of Washington known as Capitol Hill. The Capitol is a graceful domed building, the backdrop and the venue for many national occasions both joyful and sad. Presidential inaugurations occur on its west steps. The inside of the rotunda has witnessed the lying-in-state of many presidents, most notably that of President Kennedy following his assassination in November 1963.

Principally, Congress is the place where America's laws are made. It is where the 535 members of Congress work, 100 of them in the Senate, 435 of them in the House of Representatives. Their work is conducted both on the floor of the two great chambers and in the numerous committee rooms and offices that are to be found in the buildings adjacent to the Capitol.

The work of Congress can appear slow. Often it seems highly unproductive. Sometimes it is characterised by apparent gridlock. However, the Founding Fathers wanted a federal government characterised by 'limited government' and by 'checks and balances'. It was not meant to resemble the British Parliament, where a government pushes through its policy programme almost at will. The casual observer, therefore, must not be too quick to criticise Congress for what might appear to be inaction. Congress has a built-in negative bias — it was intended.

Questions to be answered in this chapter

➢ What is the structure of Congress?
➢ How are members elected?

> What is the make-up of Congress?
> What powers does it possess?
> How do the House of Representatives and the Senate compare in terms of power and prestige?
> What leadership exists in Congress?
> How important are congressional committees?
> How are laws made?
> What determines the way members of Congress vote?
> What reforms are suggested for Congress?

The structure of Congress

Congress is bicameral: it is made up of two houses — the House of Representatives and the Senate. This arrangement for the legislative branch of government was one of the compromises devised by the Founding Fathers at the Philadelphia Convention. Some delegates to the convention had wanted the states to be equally represented in the legislature, while others had wanted representation to be proportional to population. The compromise was to have a two-chamber structure. In the lower house (the House of Representatives) the states would be represented proportionally to their population, but in the upper house (the Senate) the states would be represented equally. This kept both the states with large populations and those with small populations content.

Another compromise was made. Some delegates wanted to see the legislature directly elected by the people, while others thought the legislators should be indirectly elected. The Founding Fathers decided that the House of Representatives would be directly elected but the Senate would be indirectly elected — appointed by the state legislatures. This arrangement for the Senate continued until 1914 when, as a result of the 17th Amendment, the first direct elections for the Senate were held.

Today, the House of Representatives is made up of 435 members. Each state has a certain number of members proportional to its population. The number of Representatives for each state is reapportioned after each 10-yearly census, which is held in the zero-numbered years (e.g. 1990, 2000, 2010). Some states gain House seats, while others lose them. For example, following the 2000 census, California's House delegation rose from 52 to 53, while New York's fell from 31 to 29. Except in states that have just one Representative, each member represents a sub-division of the state known as a congressional district.

The Capitol, east facade

With 50 states in the Union and each state having two Senators, there are today 100 members of the Senate.

Summary

Structure of Congress

➢ Congress is bicameral — made up of two houses.
➢ The House of Representatives benefits the large-population states.
➢ The Senate benefits the small-population states.
➢ This was one of the compromises worked out at the Philadelphia Convention.

Congressional elections

Congressional elections occur every 2 years. Members of the House of Representatives serve 2-year terms while Senators serve 6-year terms, but one-third of Senators are up for re-election every 2 years. Thus, in every cycle of congressional elections, the whole of the House of Representatives and one-third of the Senate are up for re-election. These elections, like those for the president, are held on the Tuesday after the first Monday in November. In years divisible by four (e.g. 2000, 2004), congressional elections coincide with the presidential election. Elections in the years between presidential elections (e.g. 2002, 2006) are therefore called **mid-term elections**, as they fall midway through the president's 4-year term of office.

The Constitution lays down certain requirements regarding age, citizenship and residency for those wishing to be elected to the House and the Senate. These are set out in Table 5.1. In terms of residency, many large states have passed a state law requiring Representatives to be resident in the **congressional district** that they represent. This is known as the **locality rule**.

Table 5.1 Constitutional requirements for Representatives and Senators

Category	Representative	Senator
Age	At least 25 years old	At least 30 years old
Citizenship	US citizen for at least 7 years	US citizen for at least 9 years
Residency	Resident of state they represent	Resident of state they represent

The first task for someone wishing to gain a seat in Congress is to secure the nomination of one of the two major parties. Third-party candidates very rarely win seats in Congress (see Chapter 3). Securing the nomination might mean running in a congressional primary. These differ from presidential primaries in that the winner of the congressional primary automatically becomes that party's candidate in the general election. Congressional primaries are held in the months prior to the November election, usually between May and September.

Sometimes even an incumbent Senator or Representative might be challenged for the nomination in the upcoming election and therefore will have to contest a primary. For incumbent Senators, defeat in a primary is highly unusual. In the elections between 1982 and 2002, only three incumbent Senators were defeated in primaries: one was a Senator who had been appointed to fill the vacancy of a retired Senator; Alan Dixon (D–Illinois) in 1992 and Bob Smith (R–New Hampshire) in 2002 were the only two elected incumbent Senators defeated in primaries.

Key terms

➢ **Mid-term elections.** The elections for the whole of the House of Representatives and one-third of the Senate that occur midway through the president's 4-year term of office.

➢ **Congressional district.** A geographic division of a state from which a member of the House of Representatives is elected. Congressional districts within a state are denoted by numbers; thus a House member represents, for example, the 32nd district of California or the 10th district of New York.

➢ **Locality rule.** A state law that requires members of the House of Representatives to be resident not just within the state but also within the congressional district they represent.

During the same 20-year period, 54 incumbent Representatives were defeated in primaries, including 19 in a single year — 1992, but considering that every 2 years around 400 Representatives seek re-election, an average of only five primary defeats for incumbents is not high. In the 2002 mid-term elections, only four incumbent Representatives were defeated by challengers in the primaries. (A further four were defeated by other incumbents in incumbent-versus-incumbent primaries caused by redistricting.) One of these four was Gary Condit (D–California), who had been questioned by police in connection with the murder of a female member of his congressional staff with whom Condit had belatedly admitted having an affair. Another was Cynthia McKinney (D–Georgia), who had drawn nationwide criticism for voicing a suggestion that President Bush might have known in advance about the attacks of 11 September 2001 on New York and Washington but had done nothing to stop them. It would appear that a Representative has to do something fairly unusual to merit losing a congressional primary.

Trends in Congressional elections

Because congressional elections coincide in every alternate cycle with the presidential election — people may be voting at the same time for president, Senator, Representative — it is difficult to separate voting intentions in these elections from the votes that people cast for the presidency. As a consequence, most analysis of congressional elections comes from the mid-term elections, in which voters are not casting a presidential ballot. Five trends are discernible when it comes to voting in congressional elections.

➢ It is sometimes possible to discern a **coat-tails effect,** which occurs when a strong candidate for a party at the top of the ticket — for president, or in mid-term elections for state governor — can help other party candidates get elected at the same time. The picture is of these other candidates riding into office clutching the coat-tails of the presidential or gubernatorial candidate. Few modern-day presidents have enjoyed much in the way of a coat-tails effect. The only clear example was Ronald Reagan for the Republican Party in 1980. In that November the Republicans gained 33 seats in the House and a staggering 12 seats in the Senate, when no fewer than nine incumbent Democrat Senators were defeated.

In some recent elections, there has been a reverse coat-tails effect. In 1992, for example, Democrat Bill Clinton won the presidency, but in the same election Democrats lost nine seats in the House and made no gains in the Senate.

A coat-tails effect can occur in mid-term elections, when a strong gubernatorial candidate can help others of the same party. This was the case for Texas Republicans in 1998 when Governor George W. Bush's popularity helped to sweep other Republicans into office across the state.

Key term

> **Coat-tails effect.** The effect of a strong candidate for a party at the top of the ticket helping other candidates of the same party to get elected at the same time.

> There is evidence of split-ticket voting, which occurs when someone votes for the candidates of different political parties for different offices at the same election. People might vote for a Republican president but a Democrat member of Congress. At the mid-term election, they might vote for a Democrat governor but a Republican member of Congress. Because elections in the United States are more candidate- and issue-orientated than simply party-orientated, ticket-splitting does not seem odd to American voters. There is some evidence that voters think in terms of divided government — a president of one party but Congress controlled by the other party. In 1996, the Republicans, having virtually admitted that their presidential candidate Bob Dole would lose, appealed to voters in the last days of the campaign to re-elect a Republican-controlled Congress. They did just that.

> There is evidence of losses by the president's party in mid-term elections. Since the Senate became directly elected, the president's party has lost an average of 31 House seats and four Senate seats in mid-term elections. As Table 5.2 shows, on only two occasions in this 90-year period — in 1934 and 2002 — has the president's party gained seats in both houses in the mid-term elections. The reasons are twofold. If a president has had a coat-tails effect in the presidential election 2 years before, it is likely that his party's House candidates, now devoid of his presence on the ticket, will do less well. The years 1966 and 1982 are examples of this phenomenon. Furthermore, voters often see the mid-term elections as a chance to express their disappointment or disapproval with the president's previous 2 years in office. In 1994, voters clearly

Table 5.2 Losses by president's party in mid-term congressional elections, 1914–2002

Year	Party holding presidency	Gains/losses for president's party in: House	Senate
1914	D	−59	+5
1918	D	−19	−6
1922	R	−75	−8
1926	R	−10	−6
1930	R	−49	−8
1934	D	+9	+10
1938	D	−71	−6
1942	D	−55	−9
1946	D	−45	−12
1950	D	−29	−6
1954	R	−18	−1
1958	R	−48	−13
1962	D	−4	+3
1966	D	−47	−4
1970	R	−12	+2
1974	R	−48	−5
1978	D	−15	−5
1982	R	−26	+1
1986	R	−5	−8
1990	R	−8	−1
1994	D	−52	−8
1998	D	+5	0
2002	R	+5	+2

expressed their disappointment with, among other things, President Clinton's failure to deliver his flagship policy of healthcare reform.

➤ There is evidence of strong support for incumbents, with high re-election rates during the past two decades, especially in the House. The early 1990s showed a temporary blip in this trend with the rise — but almost as quick fall — of the term limits movement and a 'throw the bums out' mentality among many voters. Even at this time, although Congress as an institution and members of Congress in general were held in low esteem, voters often thought that *their* Senator or Representative was doing a good job and deserved to be re-elected. It was as if the voters' slogan was: 'Throw the bums out — but *my* member of Congress isn't a bum!' In the House, re-election rates have exceeded 95% in 7 of the last 11 congressional elections, as shown in Table 5.3.

➤ There is debate over voting behaviour in congressional elections. The difficulty comes in differentiating voting behaviour in congressional elections that do coincide with

Table 5.3 House members: retired, defeated, re-elected, 1982–2002

Year	Retired	Sought re-election	Defeated in primary	Defeated in general election	Total re-elected	% re-elected who sought re-election
1982	40	393	10	29	354	90.1
1984	22	409	3	16	390	95.4
1986	38	393	2	6	385	98.0
1988	26	409	1	6	402	98.3
1990	27	407	1	15	391	96.1
1992	67	368	19	24	325	88.3
1994	48	387	4	34	349	90.2
1996	50	383	2	21	360	94.0
1998	33	401	1	6	394	98.3
2000	32	403	3	6	394	97.8
2002	38	397	8	8	381	96.0

Table 5.4 Senators: retired, defeated, re-elected, 1982–2002

Year	Retired	Sought re-election	Defeated in primary	Defeated in general election	Total re-elected	% re-elected who sought re-election
1982	3	30	0	2	28	93.3
1984	4	29	0	3	26	89.6
1986	6	28	0	7	21	75.0
1988	6	27	0	4	23	85.2
1990	3	32	0	1	31	96.9
1992	7	28	1	4	23	82.1
1994	9	26	0	2	24	92.3
1996	13	21	1	1	19	90.5
1998	5	29	0	3	26	89.6
2000	5	29	0	5	24	82.8
2002	5	28	1	3	24	85.7

presidential elections from voting behaviour in those that do not. Data on voting behaviour in presidential election years tend to focus on how voters cast their *presidential* ballot, not their congressional ones. When it comes to mid-term elections, there is evidence of voting being both 'national' and 'local'. In 1994 and 2002, the Republicans in particular attempted — with some success on both occasions — to 'nationalise' the mid-term elections. In 1994 they achieved this through their ten-point policy document called the Contract with America, a policy programme to which nearly all House Republican candidates signed up. It became the nationwide focus of the 1994 campaign.

In 2002, the Republicans sought to turn the mid-term elections into a referendum on President George W. Bush's first 2 years in power and specifically on the 'war on terrorism' and 'regime change' in Iraq. President Bush embarked on a 5-day, 16,000-kilometre, 15-state, 17-city campaign tour in the final days of the election. The tour included all the states with key Senate races. 'The blitz was a major, and perhaps determining, factor in several key elections,' commented *Congressional Quarterly*'s Bob Benenson. The Republican National Committee spent millions of dollars to identify likely Republican voters and then bombarded them with phone calls, mailshots and doorstep visits.

That having been said, however, voters in congressional elections tend to cast their ballots upon local issues and the record of the incumbent. Farm subsidies decide votes in Kansas and Iowa, but not in New Jersey. The regulation of the logging industry decides votes in Oregon and New Hampshire, but not in Texas. Policies to stop illegal cross-border immigration decide votes in Texas and New Mexico, but not in Kansas. Levels of money being committed to interdict coastal drug smuggling decide votes in Florida, but not in Colorado. Even in 2002, a piece in the *New York Times* showed that not everyone was focusing on possible war with Iraq (see Box 5.1).

Box 5.1 'Maine race is focused on region, not on Iraq', by Adam Clymer

Brewer, Maine, 28 September — For all the talk in Washington about war with Iraq, some congressional races out in the country are focused on local issues and the economy. One is here in Northern Maine's Second District, where it did not take the latest recession to put people out of work.

State Senator Michael H. Michaud, the Democratic candidate, boasted of his 28 years' membership in the paper workers' union in East Millinocket as he warmed up union workers who were about to go knocking on doors Saturday...

His Republican opponent Kevin L. Raye blamed high state taxes for the loss of jobs, and said that Mr Michaud, president of the State Senate, had always voted with labour and helped to create a bad business climate.

Source: **www.nytimes.com**, 5 October 2002.

Voters consider carefully the record of incumbent members of Congress — especially their attendance at roll-call votes in the House or Senate and how they cast those votes. The senior Senator from Kentucky, Republican Mitch McConnell, first won his seat back in 1984 by defeating two-term Democrat Walter Huddleston. McConnell, a 42-year-old county judge at the time, little known state-wide, defeated Senator Huddleston on the issue of his frequent absences from votes in the Senate and his failure to look after the state's interests. 'I can't think of a single thing that Huddleston has done for Kentucky, and no one else can either,' ran McConnell's slogan. He aired a series of state-wide television commercials which showed a pack of bloodhounds trying, in vain, to track down the Senator around Washington. 'Has anyone around here seen Senator Huddleston?' the commercials asked repeatedly. The Senator had missed almost a quarter of all the roll-call votes in the Senate that year. In 1992, Senator Alan Dixon (D–Illinois) was defeated mainly for just one vote he cast during 1991 — to confirm Clarence Thomas as an associate justice of the Supreme Court.

Summary

Congressional elections

➤ Congressional elections occur every 2 years.
➤ Some presidents help the congressional candidates of their party through what is known as the coat-tails effect.
➤ Split-ticket voting often results in divided government, in which the president and the majority of Congress are of different parties.
➤ The president's party usually loses seats in both houses of Congress in the mid-term elections.
➤ Congressional elections are characterised by high rates of re-election.
➤ Local rather than national issues tend to dominate, especially in mid-term elections.

Membership of Congress

The Constitution lays down certain qualifications to become a member of either the House or the Senate, but what does Congress look like in terms of gender, race, age, occupation and religion?

Women have been persistently under-represented in Congress. In 1992, the Democrats tried to focus on this issue and declared 1992 'the Year of the Woman'. The title might have struck some as contrived, but the effect was dramatic, virtually doubling the number of women in Congress in just one election. Gains in the last decade have been rather more modest, as Table 5.5 shows. The majority of the women in both houses are Democrats — the party that tends to attract the female vote. The 2002 mid-term elections were the first elections for over 20 years that resulted in no overall gains in the number of women in either house. Thus, women make up only 14% of each house, which, needless to say, is hardly representa-tive of American society as a whole. In this sense, Congress certainly does not 'look like America'.

Table 5.5 Women in the House and Senate, 1973–2003

Year	Women in House	Women in Senate
1973–74	14	1
1975–76	19	0
1977–78	18	0
1979–80	16	0
1981–82	19	1
1983–84	21	2
1985–86	22	2
1987–88	23	2
1989–90	25	2
1991–92	28	2
1993–94	47	7
1995–96	48	8
1997–98	51	9
1999–2000	56	9
2001–02	59	13
2003–04	59	14

Figure 5.1 North Carolina's 12th Congressional District (shaded area)

Representation by race is much better in the House of Representatives because the federal courts have allowed states to draw congressional district boundaries to create districts that are likely to return a Representative from an ethnic minority group. These so-called 'majority-minority districts' are often geographically distorted as they attempt to group together sometimes scattered pockets of minority voters. Figure 5.1 shows North Carolina's 12th Congressional District, which links small towns scattered for 100 miles along Interstate 85. The district is currently represented by African-American Democrat Melvin Watt. The redrawing of district boundaries following the 1990 census clearly boosted African-American representation in the House, as Table 5.6 shows. By 2003, all the 38 African-American Representatives were Democrats.

Table 5.7 indicates that much of Congress is middle-aged, highly educated and from a professional background. A typical Representative is a 54-year-old Protestant white male who has at least a master's degree and is from a professional background. A typical Senator is much the same, but 5 years older.

One final point, which is covered later in this chapter, is the number of former members of the other house in each chamber. In 2004 there were no former Senators in the House, but there were 49 ex-Representatives in the Senate. The 2002 mid-term elections saw House members Saxby Chambliss of Georgia and Jim Talent of Missouri elected to the Senate. The reasons why House members seek election to the Senate have a lot to do with the powers of the respective houses.

Table 5.6 African-Americans in the House and Senate, 1973–2003

Year	African-Americans in House	African-Americans in Senate
1973–74	15	1
1975–76	15	1
1977–78	16	1
1979–80	16	0
1981–82	17	0
1983–84	21	0
1985–86	20	0
1987–88	23	0
1989–90	24	0
1991–92	25	0
1993–94	38	1
1995–96	38	1
1997–98	38	1
1999–2000	35	0
2001–02	36	0
2003–04	38	0

Table 5.7 Age, educational, professional and religious background of House and Senate members

Characteristic	House of Representatives	Senate
Average age	54	59
Number under 40	26	2
Hold advanced degree	285	77
Been in the military	121	35
Lawyer	161	60
Academia	88	12
Roman Catholic	124	25
Jewish	26	11

Summary

Membership of Congress

➢ Women and African-Americans are under-represented in Congress despite some gains for both groups in recent decades.

➢ Congress remains a white, somewhat elderly, highly educated and professional body.

Powers of Congress

The powers of Congress are laid down in Article I Section 8 of the Constitution. Some of the powers are explicit: for example, Congress is given the power 'to coin money'. Other powers are vague: for example, Congress is given the power 'to provide for the common defence and general welfare of the United States.' Another way of categorising the powers of Congress is as exclusive and concurrent powers: some powers are exclusive to one house while other powers are concurrent to both houses (see Table 5.8).

Table 5.8 Powers of Congress

Nature of powers	House of Representatives	Senate
Exclusive powers	Initiate money bills Impeachment Elect president if Electoral College is deadlocked	Confirm appointments Ratify treaties Try cases of impeachment Elect vice-president if Electoral College is deadlocked
Concurrent powers	Pass legislation Override the president's veto Initiate constitutional amendments Declare war Confirm a newly appointed vice-president	

Exclusive powers of the House

The House of Representatives has three exclusive powers. First, it is given the power to initiate money bills. This is because at the beginning of the nation's history only the House was directly elected and the Founding Fathers believed that the people's directly elected representatives should have the first say in spending the people's money. Second, perhaps the House's most significant exclusive power is the power of impeachment. The House can impeach — that is, formally accuse — any member of the executive and judicial branches of the federal government. It has used this power 17 times since 1789. In the 1980s, the House impeached three federal judges. In 1998, the House impeached President Clinton. Third, if the Electoral College is deadlocked — if no candidate wins an absolute majority of Electoral College votes — then the House is charged with electing the president. The power has been used only twice — in 1800 and 1824.

Exclusive powers of the Senate

The Senate's exclusive powers are seen as more prestigious than those of the House. Two of them, in particular, give the Senate significantly more power than the House. First, the Senate alone has the power to confirm — by a simple majority — many appointments made by the president. These include all the president's appointments to the federal judiciary and a great many — though not all — of the appointments to the executive branch. As a result, whenever the president wishes to fill a vacancy in the trial, appeal or supreme courts of the federal government, the Senate must give its consent. Similarly, an incoming president must have many of his new appointments to the executive approved by the Senate, including all the heads of the executive departments who make up the president's cabinet. Whenever a vacancy occurs, the president must seek the Senate's approval for replacement appointments. In late 2002, when Treasury Secretary Paul O'Neill resigned, President Bush had to gain the approval of the Senate to appoint John Snow to replace him. An informal agreement called 'senatorial courtesy' allows a president to confer with any Senator of his party from a particular state before he makes a nomination to fill a vacancy for a federal office affecting that state. This is important when it comes to appointments that the president makes to the federal trial courts.

The second significant exclusive power of the Senate is its power to ratify — by a two-thirds majority — all treaties negotiated by the president. This means that the president needs to keep the Senate fully informed throughout treaty negotiations, to avoid concluding treaties that the Senate is unlikely to ratify.

Once the House has impeached someone, the Senate has the power to try that case of impeachment. This Senate trial is to determine whether the person is guilty of the offence of which they have been accused by the House. If they are found guilty by a two-thirds majority, the person is removed from office. All three federal judges impeached by the House in the 1980s were found guilty by the Senate, but President Clinton was acquitted by the Senate in 1999.

If the Electoral College is deadlocked, the Senate must elect the vice-president.

Concurrent powers of the House and Senate

Despite the significance of the Senate's exclusive powers, it is important to remember that in many ways the two houses of Congress are co-equal, for they have five concurrent powers. First, and most importantly, the two houses are co-equal in the passage of legislation. All bills must pass through all stages in both houses; neither house can override the wishes of the other. Both must agree the same version of the bill before that bill can be sent to the president for his signature. Second, both houses must vote — by two-thirds majorities — to override the president's veto of a bill. Third, the two houses are co-equal when it comes to initiating constitutional amendments. A constitutional amendment must be approved by a two-thirds majority in both houses before it can be sent to the states for their ratification. Fourth, both houses must concur in a declaration of war. This has occurred on only five occasions — the last one being 1941, when America declared war on Japan in the Second World War. Finally, the 25th Amendment (1967) gave to both houses the power to confirm a newly appointed vice-president. This has occurred twice — in 1973 (Gerald Ford) and 1974 (Nelson Rockefeller).

Summary

Powers of Congress

➢ Both houses of Congress have exclusive and concurrent powers.

The relative importance and prestige of the House and the Senate

It is often suggested that the Senate is more powerful and prestigious than the House. There are some significant reasons why this may be the case. While House members represent only a congressional district, Senators represent the entire state. For example, Representative David Dreier represents only the 26th Congressional District of California, but Senator Dianne Feinstein represents the entire state of California. She also enjoys a 6-year term in the Senate, whereas Mr Dreier has only a 2-year term in the House. Senator Feinstein is one of only 100 in the Senate whereas Congressman Dreier is one of 435 in the House. She is likely to get more of the action. Because of the smaller size of the Senate, a Senator is likely to gain a leadership position more quickly than a Representative in the House. In January 2003, Senator Bill Frist (R–Tennessee) became majority leader after only 8 years in the Senate. At the same time, Representative Nancy Pelosi (D–California) became House minority leader. But Ms Pelosi has been in the House since 1987. Senators are known statewide; House members are not. Senators may even be known nationwide. A typical American sitting in the public gallery in the Senate will probably have little difficulty in picking out such Senators as Edward Kennedy, Elizabeth Dole and John McCain. In the House, however, most people would be unlikely to recognise anyone but their own Representative.

Box 5.2 Is the Senate more prestigious than the House?

Yes, because:

> Senators represent the entire state

> Senators serve longer terms

> Senators are one of only 100

> Senators are more likely to chair a committee or sub-committee or hold some leadership position

> Senators enjoy greater name recognition state-wide and even nationwide

> the Senate is seen as a recruiting pool for presidential and vice-presidential candidates

> Senators enjoy significant exclusive powers

> House members frequently seek election to the Senate

No, because:

> both houses have equal power in the passage of legislation — Congress's key function

> both houses must approve the initiation of constitutional amendments

> members of both houses receive equal salaries

The Senate is seen as a launching pad for a presidential campaign. Presidents Harry Truman, John Kennedy, Lyndon Johnson and Richard Nixon were all former members of the Senate. Four Senators launched campaigns for the 2004 presidential race: John Kerry, John Edwards, Bob Graham and Joseph Lieberman. The Senate is seen as a recruitment pool for vice-presidential candidates too. Walter Mondale, Dan Quayle and Al Gore — three of the last five vice-presidents — were former members of the Senate. In 2000, Al Gore chose an incumbent Senator, Joseph Lieberman, as his running mate.

Senators enjoy significant exclusive powers — especially those concerned with the confirmation of appointments and the ratification of treaties. The simple evidence of career patterns shows that there are currently no ex-Senators in the House while there are 49 ex-House members in the Senate.

However, when it comes to the passage of legislation, Senators and Representatives enjoy equal powers. The same goes for those other concurrent powers. Finally, it is worth noting that members of both houses receive the same salary — in January 2003, $154,950.

Summary

The relative importance and prestige of the House and the Senate

➤ The Senate is regarded as more powerful and prestigious than the House of Representatives.

➤ Their concurrent powers, especially in the passage of legislation, make them more equal than at first appears.

Leadership in Congress

The main leadership posts in Congress are the Speaker of the House of Representatives, the majority and minority leaders and the standing committee chairs in both houses.

The House Speaker

The House Speaker is elected by the entire House membership at the start of each Congress: that is, every 2 years. With this method of election, it is likely that the person chosen will be the nominee of the majority party in the House at the time. The Constitution does not require the Speaker to be a serving member of the House, although all Speakers have been. Each of the last three Speakers has left office under unusual circumstances. Democrat Speaker Jim Wright was forced to resign in June 1989 after the House Ethics Committee announced it would charge him with 69 violations of the House's ethics rules. His successor was another Democrat, Tom Foley. In 1994, Foley became the first Speaker to be defeated in an election since 1862 when he lost his seat in that year's mid-term elections to a Republican with no previous experience of elective office. His successor was Newt Gingrich, who himself resigned in 1998 after his party's poor showing in that year's elections. His eventual successor was the current Speaker, Dennis Hastert. Wright and Gingrich were highly partisan figures — that was part of their problem. Hastert plays the Speaker's role in a much more low-key and behind-the-scenes fashion.

That said, the Speaker is a potentially powerful figure in the House. The Speaker has a number of specific powers:

➢ to act as the presiding officer of the House
➢ to interpret and enforce the rules of the House and decide on points of order
➢ to refer bills to standing committees
➢ to appoint select committee and conference committee chairs
➢ to appoint the majority party members of the House Rules Committee

According to the Constitution, the Speaker is next in line to the presidency after the vice-president. The passage of the 25th Amendment made this less significant, as it required the office of the vice-presidency to be filled if a vacancy should occur.

The Speaker has the power to exercise influence on the flow of legislation through the House, as well as to award committee assignments to majority party members and select House standing committee chairs. When the president and the majority of Congress are of different parties — which these days they often are — the Speaker may become a kind of 'leader of the opposition' figure, acting as spokesperson for the party not currently controlling the White House. This was the role that Republican Speaker Newt Gingrich played to Democrat President Clinton between 1995 and 1998.

Majority and minority leaders

In both the House and Senate, there is a majority and minority leader. Their respective party groups in each house elect them every 2 years, at the start of each Congress. In both houses, the majority and minority leaders:

➢ act as day-to-day 'directors of operations' on the floor of their respective houses
➢ hold press briefings to talk about their party's policy agenda
➢ act as liaison between the House/Senate and the White House

The Senate majority leader plays a key role in bringing bills for debate to the Senate floor. The House majority leader plays a 'number two' role to the Speaker. The importance of these posts can be gauged by the fact that they can be used as a launching pad for a presidential candidate. Democrat Lyndon Johnson (President: 1963–69) was Senate majority leader from 1955 to 1961. Republican Bob Dole was Senate majority leader when he launched his presidential bid in 1996. More recently, Democrat Dick Gephardt had served 8 years (1995–2003) as House minority leader before launching his unsuccessful bid for the 2004 presidential nomination.

The other significant leadership posts are connected with the work of the congressional committees.

Summary

Leadership in Congress

➤ Leadership in Congress is provided by the House Speaker, along with the majority and minority leaders in both chambers.

➤ Those who chair congressional committees, especially the standing committees, have leadership potential too.

Congressional committees

Writing in 1885, Woodrow Wilson — 28 years later to become president — said this about Congress:

> The House sits, not for serious discussion, but to sanction the conclusions of its committees as rapidly as possible. It legislates in its committee rooms; not by the determination of majorities, but by the specially-commissioned minorities [the committees]; so that it is not far from the truth to say that Congress in session is Congress on public exhibition, whilst Congress in its committee rooms is Congress at work.

In the 107th Congress (2001–02) there were 199 permanent committees and sub-committees (see Table 5.9). The most important types of congressional committee are: standing committees, the House Rules Committee, conference committees and select committees.

Box 5.3 Committee facts and figures

Number of permanent committees: 44
Number of permanent sub-committees: 155
Total number of permanent committees and sub-committees: 199
Largest committees: House Transportation & Infrastructure (75); House Financial Services (69)
Smallest committees: Senate Ethics (6); House Administration (9); House Rules (13)
Committees with most sub-committees: House Appropriations (13); Senate Appropriations (13)

Standing committees

Standing committees exist in both houses of Congress. They are permanent, policy-specialist committees (see Table 5.9). Most standing committees are divided into sub-committees, examples of which are shown in Table 5.10. A typical Senate standing committee comprises around 18 members, while a typical House standing committee is made up of around 40–50 members. The party balance in each standing committee is in the same proportion as that which exists within the chamber as a whole. At the beginning of the 108th Congress (January 2003), the Republicans had a small majority in both houses. Thus, each standing committee in each house had a small Republican majority.

Table 5.9 Congressional standing committees

Standing committee	Chair
Senate	
Agriculture, Nutrition and Forestry	Thad Cochran (Mississippi)
Appropriations	Ted Stevens (Alaska)
Armed Services	John Warner (Virginia)
Banking, Housing and Urban Affairs	Richard Shelby (Alabama)
Budget	Don Nickles (Oklahoma)
Commerce, Science and Transportation	John McCain (Arizona)
Energy and Natural Resources	Pete Domenici (New Mexico)
Environment and Public Works	James Inhofe (Oklahoma)
Finance	Charles Grassley (Iowa)
Foreign Relations	Richard Lugar (Indiana)
Governmental Affairs	Susan Collins (Maine)
Health, Education, Labor and Pensions	Judd Gregg (New Hampshire)
Judiciary	Orrin Hatch (Utah)
Rules and Administration	Trent Lott (Mississippi)
Small Business	Olympia Snowe (Maine)
Veterans' Affairs	Arlen Specter (Pennsylvania)
House of Representatives	
Agriculture	Bob Goodlatte (Virginia)
Appropriations	Bill Young (Florida)
Armed Services	Duncan Hunter (California)
Budget	Jim Nussle (Iowa)
Education and the Workforce	John Boehner (Ohio)
Energy and Commerce	Billy Tauzin (Louisiana)
Financial Services	Michael Oxley (Ohio)
Government Reform	Tom Davis (Virginia)
International Relations	Henry Hyde (Illinois)
Judiciary	James Sensenbrenner (Wisconsin)
Resources	Richard Pombo (California)
Rules	David Dreier (California)
Science	Sherwood Boehlert (New York)
Small Business	Donald Manzullo (Illinois)
Standards of Official Conduct	Joel Hefley (Colorado)
Transportation and Infrastructure	Don Young (Alaska)
Veterans' Affairs	Christopher Smith (New Jersey)
Ways and Means	Bill Thomas (California)

House and Senate members seek assignments on committees that are closest to the interests of their district or state. Re-elected members are routinely reappointed to their former committees unless they have asked for a new assignment. Some committees — for example, Judiciary, Armed Services and Appropriations — are more prestigious than others. New members might have to wait some years to get assigned to these more sought-after committees.

Table 5.10 Examples of congressional sub-committees

Committee	Sub-committees
House Science Committee	• Environment sub-committee • Research sub-committee • Energy sub-committee • Space sub-committee
House Transportation Committee	• Aviation sub-committee • Coast Guard and Maritime Transport sub-committee • Economic Development, Public Buildings and Emergency Management sub-committee • Highways and Transit sub-committee • Railroads sub-committee • Water Resources and Environment sub-committee

Standing committees have two functions in both the House and the Senate, and a third function in the Senate only. The first common function — and the most important one — is to conduct the committee stage of bills in the legislative process. This involves holding 'hearings' on the bill at which 'witnesses' appear. These witnesses might be:

➤ other members of Congress
➤ members from the relevant executive departments or agencies, or even from the White House
➤ representatives from interest groups or professional bodies likely to be affected
➤ ordinary members of the public

Witnesses make prepared statements in front of the committee and are then subjected to questioning from committee members. The length of such hearings is determined largely by the length of the bill itself and the level of controversy that it engenders. Short, non-controversial bills attract short hearings lasting no more than a few hours. But long, controversial bills are given hearings that might last — on and off — for weeks or even months. The committee hearings on President Clinton's Healthcare Reform Bill began in the summer of 1993 and were still unfinished a year later. At the conclusion of these hearings, a vote is taken by the committee on whether or not to pass the bill on to its second reading — the next stage in the legislative process.

The second common function of standing committees in both houses is to conduct investigations within the committee's policy area. Such investigations are often launched into perceived problems, as shown by examples given in Table 5.11. They attempt to answer such questions as 'Why did this happen?', 'Is current legislation proving effective?' and 'Is new legislation required?' Investigations might be held into crises or perceived policy failures. The format is much the same as for legislative hearings, with witnesses being summoned and questions asked.

Table 5.11 Examples of standing committee investigations during the 107th Congress

Committee	Investigation
House Financial Services Committee	Corporate accounting practices
House Agriculture Committee	Wild fires
Senate Banking Committee	How to encourage more Americans to open a bank account
Senate Foreign Relations Committee	The Peace Corps; Afghanistan; Cuba's pursuit of biological weapons
Senate Armed Services Committee	Iraq

In the Senate, standing committees have a third function: to begin the confirmation process of numerous presidential appointments. The two committees that are particularly busy in this regard are the Senate's Judiciary and Foreign Relations committees. The former must hold hearings on all the federal judicial appointments made by the president; the latter holds hearings on all ambassadorial appointments. Other Senate standing committees oversee appointments made within their particular policy areas. Hearings are held at which supporters, and possibly critics, of the nominee are heard from before a vote is taken. The vote is not decisive — only recommendatory — but it is a very important clue to the likely outcome of the nomination. Because these committees are regarded as the policy specialists in their particular areas, their recommendations are rarely overturned. An overwhelming — possibly unanimous — 'yes' vote by the committee indicates that the nominee will receive easy passage on the floor of the Senate, but a close vote will indicate problems ahead. Should the majority of a committee vote 'no', the nomination is certain to be defeated, if it even gets to the Senate floor (see Table 5.12).

Table 5.12 Senate standing committee and floor votes on various presidential nominees

Nominee	Post	President	Committee vote	Senate floor vote
Robert Bork	Supreme Court	Ronald Reagan	5–9	42–58
John Tower	Defense Secretary	George Bush	9–11	47–53
Clarence Thomas	Supreme Court	George Bush	7–7	52–48
Ruth Bader Ginsburg	Supreme Court	Bill Clinton	18–0	96–3
John Ashcroft	Attorney General	George W. Bush	10–8	58–42

Summary

Functions of standing committees

➤ To conduct the committee stage of the legislative process.
➤ To conduct investigations within the committee's policy area.
➤ In the Senate only, to begin the confirmation process of numerous presidential appointments.

The standing committees of Congress have considerable power to help the parent chambers to manage their huge workloads, but there are limits to their power. As congressional scholar Burdett A. Loomis (2000) points out:

> Committees are powerful but not all-powerful: they cannot legislate; they cannot require the executive to comply with their wishes; they cannot implement policies once they have been approved.

House Rules Committee

The House Rules Committee is one of the standing committees of the House of Representatives, but it performs a different function from the others. It is responsible for prioritising bills coming from the committee stage on to the House floor for their second reading. Because there is a huge queue of bills waiting for a second reading on the House floor, the Rules Committee has a vital legislative role to play. Its name comes from the 'rule' it gives to a bill, setting out the rules of debate by stating, for example, whether any amendments can be made to the bill at this stage. Most bills must go through the House Rules Committee if they are to reach final passage.

The Rules Committee is unusual in that its membership is much smaller and more skewed to the majority party than other standing committees. In 2004, the House Rules Committee had just 13 members — nine Republicans and only four Democrats — chaired by David Dreier. Chair of the House Rules Committee is considered one of the most influential posts in Congress.

Conference committees

Conference committees are required because of two important characteristics of the legislative process in Congress. First, both houses have equal power. Second, bills pass through both houses concurrently, rather than consecutively. As a consequence, there are two different versions of the same bill — a House version and a Senate version. By the time the bill has passed through each house, the two versions are likely to be different. If, after the third reading in each house, the two versions of the bill are different, and if these differences cannot be reconciled informally, then a conference committee is set up.

All conference committees are ad hoc — set up to consider only one particular bill. The members, known as 'conferees', are drawn from both houses. Their sole function is to reconcile the differences between the House and Senate versions of the same bill. Once a conference committee has come up with an agreed version of the bill, this version must be agreed to by a vote on the floor of each house. If agreement is not forthcoming, the same conference committee may be reconvened. Another compromise will be drawn up and sent to the floors of both houses. Should that be unacceptable to one or both chambers, the bill will be sent back to the *standing* committees that first considered it.

Conference committees are important because they are likely to draw up what will become the final version of the bill. Their power is checked, however, by the ability of the House and Senate to refuse to sign up to their compromise version.

Select committees

Select committees are sometimes known as 'special' or 'investigative' committees. Nearly all are ad hoc, set up to investigate a particular issue. But why are select committees needed when, as we have already seen, the standing committees have an investigative function? A select committee is set up when the investigation either: does not fall within the policy area of one standing committee; or is likely to be so time-consuming that a standing committee would become tied up with it, thus preventing the standing committee from fulfilling its other functions.

In recent decades, there have been a number of high-profile select committees, such as the Senate select committee on the Central Intelligence Agency (CIA); the House select committee on political assassinations; and joint select committees on both the Iran–Contra affair and the events of 11 September 2001.

Committee chairs

Those who chair standing committees are always drawn from the majority party in that house. Thus, in the 108th Congress, all the standing committees are chaired by Republicans. The **seniority rule** states that the chair of the standing committee will be the member of the majority party with the longest continuous service on that committee. The same applies for what are called the 'ranking minority members' of each committee. Referred to by its critics as the 'senility rule', it has been modified in recent years. From the 1970s, both parties gradually introduced secret ballots for committee chairs and ranking minority members. However, it is still usually the member with the longest continuous committee service who is elected.

Key term

> **Seniority rule.** A rule stating that the chair of a congressional standing committee will be the member of the majority party with the longest continuous service on that committee.

Further reforms came in the 1990s, when the Republicans placed a 6-year term limit on committee and sub-committee chairs. House Republicans started the term-limit clock in 1995; the Senate Republicans 2 years later. Hence, in January 2001, 14 of the 17 House standing committees had to select new chairs. These term limits were introduced partly as a concession to the early 1990s term limit movement and partly because Republicans had for many years been critical of Democrat committee chairs who had held their posts unchallenged, in some cases, for decades. Congressman Jamie Whitten (D–Mississippi) chaired the Appropriations sub-committee on Agriculture for 43 years. Critics of committee chair term limits say that the institutional memory of the committees is lost and that power is ceded to unelected committee staff upon whom new and inexperienced chairs have to rely more heavily.

Those who chair standing committees have a number of important powers. They:

➤ control the committee's agenda
➤ decide when the committee will meet
➤ control the committee's budget
➤ influence the membership, meetings and hearings of sub-committees
➤ supervise a sizeable committee staff
➤ serve as spokesperson on the committee's policy area within Congress, to the White House and in the media
➤ make requests to the House Rules Committee (in the House) and the party leadership (in the Senate) for scheduling of legislation on the House floor
➤ report legislation to the floor of their respective chamber on behalf of the full committee

Chairing a congressional committee brings power, perks and publicity. For many, this is the pinnacle of their congressional career.

Summary

Congressional committees

➤ Much of the work of Congress is done in committee.
➤ Standing committees perform important functions in both the legislative process and the investigation of the executive branch.
➤ In the Senate, standing committees begin the confirmation process of presidential appointments.
➤ The House Rules Committee plays an important role prioritising bills in the House.
➤ Conference committees play an important role towards the end of the legislative process.
➤ Select committees may play an important investigative role.
➤ Seniority is still important in selecting committee chairs, though not the all-important factor it once was.

The legislative process

The legislative process in Congress is best thought of in seven stages:

1 First reading
2 Committee stage
3 Timetabling
4 Second reading
5 Third reading
6 Conference committee (*optional*)
7 Presidential action

① with key positions

② cong commns most importantly

③ House senate overrides passed by house

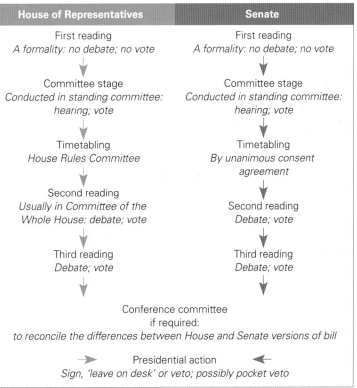

House of Representatives	Senate
First reading *A formality: no debate; no vote*	First reading *A formality: no debate; no vote*
Committee stage *Conducted in standing committee: hearing; vote*	Committee stage *Conducted in standing committee: hearing; vote*
Timetabling *House Rules Committee*	Timetabling *By unanimous consent agreement*
Second reading *Usually in Committee of the Whole House: debate; vote*	Second reading *Debate; vote*
Third reading *Debate; vote*	Third reading *Debate; vote*

Conference committee
if required:
to reconcile the differences between House and Senate versions of bill

Presidential action
Sign, 'leave on desk' or veto; possibly pocket veto

Figure 5.2 The legislative process in Congress

To be successful, all bills must pass through stages 1–5 and 7. Stage 6 — the conference committee — may be avoided if both houses pass the bill in the same form or if any differences can be resolved amicably. To be successful, a bill must pass through all these stages during a Congress — that is, 2 years. The 108th Congress ran from January 2003 until late 2004. Any bills not completed in one Congress must start the process again at the beginning of the next Congress.

First reading

The first reading — or introduction — is a pure formality. There is no debate and no vote. In the House, the first reading involves nothing more than placing a copy of the bill in a 'hopper' — a tray — on the clerk's desk. In the Senate, the first reading involves reading out the title of the bill on the Senate floor. Bills are then numbered, printed, circulated and sent on to the appropriate standing committee.

The most important fact to comprehend at this stage is the sheer volume of legislation that is introduced in Congress. As Table 5.13 shows, in a typical Congress, anything between 9,000 and almost 11,000 bills are introduced. Of these, only around 4–5% actually make it into law. The process explains largely why this percentage is so small.

Table 5.13 Number of bills introduced and laws enacted, 1997–2002

	105th Congress 1997–98	106th Congress 1999–2000	107th Congress 2001–02
Bills introduced	9,075	10,840	8,948
Laws enacted	394 (4%)	580 (5%)	377 (4%)

Source: *Congressional Quarterly*

Committee stage

This is the most important stage. Far more bills fail here than at any other stage. Hundreds of bills are referred to each of the standing committees in both chambers in each Congress. This is far more than they can handle. A significant number are pigeon-holed — put to one side, with no action taken on them at all, no hearings and no vote. It is those with a good deal of support — from members of Congress, the White House, the administration or interest groups, for example — that are given hearings. The hearings may be either in the full committee or in the relevant sub-committee.

There are other reasons why this stage is so important. The committee stage comes very early in the legislative process — *before* the second reading. The full House and Senate have not yet debated the bill. The standing committee members are regarded as the policy specialists in their policy area and they have the full power of amendment — anything can be added to and anything removed from the bill at this stage. Professor Vile (1999) stated that 'it is difficult to exaggerate the importance of these [standing] committees, for they are the sieve through which all legislation is poured, and what comes out, and how it comes out, is largely in their hands'.

Once the hearings have been completed, the committee holds a mark-up session — making the changes it wishes — before reporting out the bill, effectively sending it on to its next stage. The report written by the committee does four things: states the main aims of the bill; reviews the amendments made by the committee; estimates the cost of implementation; recommends future action to be taken by the full chamber.

Timetabling

By the time Congress has been in session for a few months, a huge number of bills will be waiting to come to the floor of both chambers for their second reading. While there are dozens of committee and sub-committee rooms, there is only one floor in each house. Something of a legislative traffic jam develops, with bills queuing for their turn on the House and Senate floors. Each house has its own procedure for dealing with this potential problem.

The Senate deals with it through what are called 'unanimous consent agreements'. These are, in effect, agreements between the Senate majority and minority leaders on the order in which bills will be debated on the Senate floor.

The House of Representatives deals with it through the House Rules Committee. The 'prioritising' role of the House Rules Committee makes it a kind of legislative 'gatekeeper' or 'traffic cop' — allowing some bills through but holding others back. If the Rules Committee fails to give a rule to a popular bill, House members may resort to the discharge process. A discharge petition must be signed by an absolute majority of House members — 218. Once that demanding requirement has been fulfilled, the bill is 'discharged' from the Rules Committee and comes automatically to the House floor for debate. This process was used successfully in 2001–02 on the Shays–Meehan Campaign Finance Reform Bill (see Bennett (2003), chapter 3).

Second reading

This is the first opportunity for the full chambers to debate the bill. In the House, most bills are debated at the second reading in the 'Committee of the Whole House', which permits rules of debate to be in force, allowing for as many members to take part as possible. In both houses, further amendments can usually be made. Votes are taken both on amendments and on the whole bill at the end of the debate. Simple majorities are required. Votes can be either by

The chamber of the House of Representatives

'voice vote' or by 'recorded vote'. In the former, members merely call out 'aye' or 'no': this is used mostly for non-controversial bills. In a recorded vote, a record of each member's vote is made. In the House this is done electronically; in the Senate by a roll-call vote with the clerk alphabetically calling the roll of the 100 Senators from Mr Akaka to Mr Wyden. Both procedures take 15 minutes.

In the Senate, there is the possibility of a **filibuster** taking place. Stamina is more important than relevance in conducting a filibuster. Senators have been known to read out extracts from the Constitution, the Declaration of Independence, the Bible and even the telephone directory. In 1957, Strom Thurmond conducted a filibuster against a Civil Rights Bill that lasted for over 24 hours. In 1992, Senator Alfonse D'Amato (R–New York) conducted a filibuster for more than 15 hours over the fact that a tax break for a New York typewriter manufacturer had been removed from a bill.

Key term

> **Filibuster.** A device by which an individual Senator, or group of Senators, can attempt to talk a bill to death by using delaying tactics. It derives from Senators' right of unlimited debate. A three-fifths vote (i.e. 60 votes) is required to end a filibuster.

A filibuster can be ended by a procedure known as 'closure' (or 'cloture'). To be successful, a closure petition must be signed by 16 Senators and then voted for by at least three fifths (60) of the entire Senate. In 1988, Senator Robert Byrd (D–West Virginia) brought a record eight closure votes to try to stop a Republican filibuster of a Campaign Finance Reform Bill. All eight failed.

Third reading

This is the final opportunity to debate the bill. If substantial amendments were made at the second reading and/or the final vote was close, then the third reading would be likely to occur some weeks or months later and require another substantial debate. If, however, few amendments were made at the second reading and/or the final vote showed a substantial majority in favour, then the third reading would follow on almost immediately after the second reading and be very brief. At the end of the third reading, a further vote is taken.

Conference committee

Conference committees can be avoided, either by the two houses passing identical bills, or by any differences being resolved amicably. Once a version of the bill has been agreed by both houses — with or without the offices of a conference committee — the bill is ready to be sent to the president.

Presidential action

The president always has three options as to what to do with a bill. At times, he has a fourth.

First, he may sign the bill into law. This he does with bills he fully supports and for which he wishes to claim some credit. An example of this would be the December 2002 signing by President Bush of the Homeland Security Bill. A bill-signing ceremony is arranged, usually at the White House, where a number of key House and Senate members who have supported the bill through its passage are present for a photo opportunity with the president. This is an opportunity for both credit claiming and political thank-yous. The president may also decide to sign bills out of political expediency. In this category would come the March 2002 signing by President Bush of the Campaign Finance Reform Bill.

Second, the president may decide to 'leave the bill on his desk'. He does this for bills upon which he takes no position at all, or which he would like to veto but knows his veto would be overridden. These bills will become law without his signature within 10 congressional working days.

Third, the president may **veto** the bill using a regular veto. He does this to bills that he strongly opposes. Presidents use the threat of a veto as a bargaining tool with Congress. The president hopes that the threat of the veto will cause Congress to make the changes in the bill the president has demanded. To veto the bill the president must act within 10 congressional working days of receiving it, sending it back to its house of origin with a message explaining his objections. He must veto the whole bill, not just parts of it.

Table 5.14 Regular vetoes and overrides, 1961–2003

President	Years in office	Regular vetoes used	Vetoes overridden
John Kennedy	1961–63	12	0
Lyndon Johnson	1963–69	16	0
Richard Nixon	1969–74	26	7
Gerald Ford	1974–77	48	12
Jimmy Carter	1977–81	13	2
Ronald Reagan	1981–89	39	9
George Bush	1989–93	29	1
Bill Clinton	1993–2001	36	2
George W. Bush	2001–	0*	0*

used

*To the end of 2003

Key term

➤ **Presidential veto.** A power vested in the president by Article II of the Constitution, by which he may return a bill to Congress unsigned, along with the reasons for his objection. Congress may override a presidential veto by a two-thirds vote in both houses.

Congress then has three options. It can put right the 'wrongs' identified by the president in his veto message and return the bill for his signature: this is unlikely, as they will have been well aware of his objections during the bill's passage. The second option is to attempt to override the veto. This requires a two-thirds majority in both houses — a demanding and difficult requirement that is rarely achieved. Third, they may realise that they do not have the votes to override the veto, do nothing and accept that the president has won. The last is by far the most likely option.

During his 8 years as president, Bill Clinton used the regular veto on 36 occasions. On 13 of those vetoes, Congress attempted to override the veto. It failed in 11 and succeeded in just 2. On the other 23 occasions when Clinton used the regular veto, neither house attempted to override the president's veto. Thus, President Clinton won on 34 out of 36 occasions when he vetoed legislation. The two bills that were passed over his veto were the Securities Bill (1995) and the Military Construction Appropriations

Table 5.15 Congressional overrides of President Clinton's vetoes

Bill	Final passage vote in:		Date of presidential veto	Veto override vote in:	
	House	Senate		House	Senate
Securities Bill	325–99	65–30	19/12/95	319–100	68–30
Military Construction Appropriations Bill	352–64	69–30	13/11/97	347–69	78–20

Bush hasn't used any

Bill (1998) (see Table 5.15). A president whose own party is not in control of Congress is more likely both to use the veto and to have a veto overridden. None of Democrat President Clinton's 36 vetoes was used during his first 2 years in office (1993–94) when the Democrats controlled both houses. Fellow Democrat Jimmy Carter used 13 vetoes against a Democrat-controlled Congress. Twice, they overrode his veto — the ultimate humiliation.

The president rarely loses on a veto for two reasons. First, the cards are stacked so much against Congress. The president needs only 34 supporters in the Senate to win. Second, the president will study the final passage votes of bills. If they have passed by huge majorities in both houses at the third reading or on the conference report, then he will rarely veto. If, however, the majorities have been small, he can veto with confidence, knowing that he will prevail.

The president may have a fourth option — to use a 'pocket veto'. If the bill is awaiting the president's action when the legislative session ends, the bill is lost: this is a pocket veto and cannot be overridden by Congress. A late rush of bills may arrive on the president's desk just as the legislative session ends, so this can be a significant power. President Clinton pocket-vetoed only one bill in his 8 years — the Consumer Bankruptcy Overhaul Bill in December 2000.

For a brief period during 1997 and 1998, President Clinton had the power of so-called 'line-item veto' until the Supreme Court declared it unconstitutional in 1998. This was the power to sign parts of a bill, but to veto sections or items within it.

An assessment of the legislative process

> The cards are stacked against action by Congress. As a result, those who seek action in Congress face a far more difficult task than those whose purpose is negative (Carr, 1974).

The beginning of this section on the legislative process showed that it is difficult to get bills passed through Congress successfully. It is possible to identify eight specific reasons for this.

➤ A vast number of bills are introduced. This immediately makes the process crowded.

➤ The process itself is complicated. Professor R. V. Denenberg (1976) describes Congress as a 'bastion of negation', the process of passing laws as a 'legislative labyrinth' and the legislative process as 'a built-in negative bias'.

➤ There is the need at some stages for super-majority votes: a three-fifths majority to stop a filibuster in the Senate; a two-thirds majority in both houses to override the president's veto.

➤ Power in Congress is decentralised. Much power resides with the standing committees and especially with those who chair them. Party leaders have limited powers — former Senate majority leader Bob Dole once described himself as the 'majority pleader'.

➤ The fact that both houses possess equal power makes the process more difficult. If, as in the UK Parliament, one house can virtually override the wishes of the other, legislation is generally more easily accomplished.

➤ These two equal houses may not be controlled by the same party. Between 1981 and 1987 and again from June 2001 to December 2002, the two houses were controlled by different parties. In the 1980s, the Republicans controlled the Senate, but the Democrats controlled the House. In the more recent example, it was the other way around.

➤ Even if the two houses of Congress are controlled by the same party, it may not be the president's party. He is therefore likely to find it difficult to pass the bills he wants.

➤ Even when party control of both the presidency and Congress does coincide, it may not count for much. Party discipline in Congress has tended to be weak. Members of Congress do not simply toe a party line.

Summary

The legislative process

➤ The legislative process in Congress is long and complicated, with many hurdles at which bills may 'fall'.

➤ At the start of the process, the standing committees hold significant power over bills, especially through pigeonholing and by having full power of amendment.

➤ Later, conference committees may play a significant role in drawing up what will probably be the final version of the bill.

➤ The president's power of veto is difficult for Congress to overcome and is therefore a formidable weapon.

➤ Only a very small proportion of bills introduced make it through the whole process and become law.

Voting in Congress

House and Senate members are called upon to cast a large number of votes each year (see Table 5.16). They might be voting on budgets, amendments to bills, second or third readings, bills from conference committees, constitutional amendments or — in the Senate — on treaties or appointments made by the president. They will probably be rushing to the floor to cast their vote, having just broken off a committee hearing or a meeting with constituents or staff.

Table 5.16 Number of recorded votes in the House and Senate, 1993–2003

	1993	1994	1995	1996	1997	1998	1999	2000	2001	2002	2003
House	615	507	885	455	640	547	611	603	512	483	675
Senate	395	329	613	306	298	314	374	298	380	253	459

Source: *Congressional Quarterly*

Recorded votes in the House of Representatives are nowadays taken 'by electronic device' in which members have 15 minutes to cast their votes. These were introduced to cut down the time it took to read out the names of the 435 members, which is how the recorded votes used to be carried out in the House. Entering the House chamber, each member places an electronic card into a small machine affixed to the back of the bench. As the member votes by pressing one of the buttons on the machine, a matching-coloured light appears next to the name on the roll of members displayed on the front wall of the chamber above the Speaker's chair. A 'score box' on the side of the press gallery shows the tally of votes and time remaining.

What factors make members of Congress vote as they do?

There are six factors to consider. The relative importance of each factor varies from one member of Congress to another and from one vote to another.

Political party

Political party is one of a number of determinants of voting in Congress. For some members, on some issues, it may be the most important determinant. 'Party votes' sometimes occur in Congress when the issue is a contentious, ideological matter, such as civil liberties, taxation, gun control, abortion or school prayers. Votes in the Senate to confirm the president's nominations can become partisan. Since the mid-1990s there has been a rise in partisanship in Congress. In 1995, the Republicans pushed their 'Contract with America' policy items, and Democrats voted to oppose them. In that year, the percentage of roll-call votes that were 'party votes' was 73% in the House and 69% in the Senate, the highest percentages in each chamber since 1910 and 1922 respectively. In the late 1990s, the impeachment and trial of President Clinton had an effect on each house.

The parties have few 'sticks' or 'carrots' to encourage party voting. 'Sticks' such as the threat of de-selection do not work in a system in which voters decide on candidates in primary elections. 'Carrots' such as executive branch posts do not work in a system of 'separated institutions', in which posts in the executive and legislature do not overlap.

A 'party vote' in Congress is simply a vote in which the majority of one party votes against the majority of the other party. Despite this very low threshold for qualifying as a 'party vote', in recent years only around 50% of votes in each chamber have been party votes, as Table 5.17 shows. Table 5.18 gives two examples of party votes — one in each chamber — on the passage of campaign finance reform in 2002. In both votes, the majority of Democrats voted 'yes', while the majority of Republicans voted 'no' — a 'party vote'.

Table 5.17 Party votes as a proportion of all recorded votes, 1993–2003 (%)

Year	House	Senate
1993	65	67
1994	62	52
1995	73	69
1996	56	62
1997	50	50
1998	56	56
1999	47	63
2000	43	49
2001	55	40
2002	43	45
2003	52	67

Table 5.18 Final passage votes on the Campaign Finance Reform Bill (2002)

	House of Representatives		Senate	
	Yes	No	Yes	No
Totals	240	189	60	40
Republicans	41	176	11	38
Democrats	198	12	48	2
Independents	1	1	1	0

Source: *Congressional Quarterly*

Constituents

House and Senate members place a high premium on representing the interests of their constituents — and with good reasons. First, the Constitution states that they must be residents of the state they represent, so this gives them a good understanding of what 'the folks back home' are saying. Second, a number of states go further by insisting — through the 'locality rule' — that House members reside in the congressional district that they represent. Third, typical House or Senate members do not just reside in the state or district; they will have been born, raised and educated and will have worked there. Fourth, House members are especially careful about constituents' views because they have to face the electors every 2 years.

There are various methods by which members of Congress can find out about their constituents' views. While they are in Washington DC they receive visits, phone calls, letters, faxes and e-mails from constituents. They keep in touch through phone and e-mail with their offices back in the state or district. They read the local newspapers published back home — usually on line.

They discover what their constituents want by making regular visits back home. The frequency depends on how far 'home' is from Washington DC. Congressman Doc Hastings (R–Washington), for example, represents a district nearly 3,125 miles (5,000 kilometres) from the nation's capital. A flight from Washington DC to Seattle — the nearest large airport — takes 6 to 7 hours, the equivalent of flying from London to Boston. Hastings therefore makes use of the longer recess periods — for example, around Christmas, Easter, Memorial Day (May) and Independence Day (July).

Back home, House and Senate members have a variety of engagements, including:

➤ holding party and 'town hall' meetings
➤ conducting 'surgeries' with individual constituents
➤ making visits around the state/district
➤ appearing on local radio phone-in programmes
➤ interviews with representatives of the local media
➤ addressing groups such as chambers of commerce, professional groups and Round Table lunches
➤ visiting local schools, hospitals and businesses

On most issues, constituents' views are likely to be divided, with some in favour and others against. Through town hall meetings and constituency mail, the views of the discontented are more likely to be heard than those of the content. One Democrat Congressman described his constituency mail as 'what folks don't like from the folks who don't like it'. It is usually not a representative cross-section of constituency opinion. Finally, members of Congress are meant to be more than just 'delegates' of their constituents and may need to balance other factors as well as the national good against what is perceived as being merely locally popular or electorally expedient.

The administration

The term 'the administration' refers to members of the executive branch, including the president. Much legislation voted on in Congress has been initiated by the administration. Cabinet members — the heads of the 15 executive departments — have a keen interest in the passage of legislation affecting their policy areas. So members of the administration — from the departments and agencies as well as the White House itself — keep in contact with members of Congress through phone calls as well as meetings in an attempt to persuade them to cast their votes in certain ways. They talk with members of the relevant committees as well as with staff on Capitol Hill. Often the White House gets involved through the Congressional Liaison Office as well as directly in the person of the president (see Chapter 6).

Any persuasion needs to be regular, reciprocal and bipartisan. It is important that members of Congress are approached not only just before an important vote comes up. It is important, too, that those from the departments and the White House are willing to do favours in return, offering a two-way street of mutual cooperation. All this needs to be done with members from both parties. For an administration to talk only with members of its own party is usually a recipe for disaster. Success tends to occur in Congress when there is a bipartisan coalition.

Pressure groups

Pressure groups use a number of different ways to try to influence how members of Congress vote (see Chapter 4). They make direct contact with members as well as with their staff. They attempt to generate public support favourable to their position. They make visits and phone calls, provide evidence to committees, organise rallies, demon-strations and petition drives, and engage in fundraising and campaigning. Money raised is used to fund politicians who support their cause and to seek to defeat those who do not. Certain policy areas have seen significant pressure group activity in recent years, including the environment, abortion, gun control, healthcare and welfare reform.

Colleagues and staff

Because of the huge numbers of votes that members of Congress have to cast, they cannot personally know the details of all of them. They therefore rely on others to help them make a decision on a vote.

Box 5.4 Voting in Congress: different members' views

'As a member of the Democratic Whip team, I try to persuade others to support the party position. We need to develop better tools of persuasion. By that I mean that if members don't support the party, then they should not be given the more prestigious committee and sub-committee assignments. We ought to demand a higher level of party discipline. We are too much of an assortment of free agents.'

A Democrat House member from Colorado

'I'm in the grocery store, the baker's shop, walking down the high street, at the ball game. If constituents get fractious, you have to consider whether they have anywhere else to go — would they actually vote against you in the primary or in the general election?'

A Republican House member from New Mexico

'There are a number of inputs: the views of my staff and mail from the district, for example. There is the material coming out of the House Republican Conference, which meets every 1–2 weeks. We usually check with neighbouring Republicans, especially with Porter Goss. He represents a very similar district to the south of ours and we are both conservative Republicans. I might be influenced by [Florida Congressman] Bill Young — what you might call the Dean of the Republican state delegation in the House. There will also be those votes where I have strong personal opinions.'

Former Congressman Dan Miller (R–Florida)

'In my opinion, too many House members see themselves as 'delegates', not 'representatives'. I believe in the Burkean view of representation and agree with the Founding Fathers that 'the passions of the day should be dampened'. That's why I need to exercise my own judgement. This sometimes gets me into trouble with some folks in my district. Indeed, after a recent town hall meeting, I received a letter from one irate constituent annoyed that I didn't seem to care what he thought.'

A Democrat House member from Colorado

'First, there is my own personal philosophy. I ask myself whether this bill offers a real solution to the problem. Secondly, there are the views of my district. Thirdly, there is the Democratic Party, and this particular factor has gradually diminished to the extent that party loyalty is of little or no use as a guiding principle. I'm not the most popular person with the party leadership. But the feeling is mutual.'

A Democrat House member from Ohio

Other colleagues can be helpful. A Congressman might turn to fellow members of the same chamber and of the same party who share the same philosophy and views. Some senior members act as 'mentors' to newer members, offering advice and suggestions on votes. In the House, one could look out fellow members of the state delegation, especially those from neighbouring districts. Members of the relevant committee can be a help — especially those who chair committees or who are the ranking minority members.

Senior staff members — the chief of staff or legislative director — at the weekly staff meeting in a Capitol Hill office of a Republican House member, might be heard telling their Congressman: 'You'll want to support this', or 'This plays well in the district'. One Republican House member talked thus of the importance of his senior staff:

> You can always tell those who don't know how things work here on Capitol Hill. When they leave my office after a meeting, they thank me and then hand me copies of all their papers so that I can follow up on whatever it was we were talking about. They don't know how things work. Those who *do* know how things work thank me and then give the papers to *my staff*. I remember getting an invitation from someone in the Clinton administration and the invitation stated: 'Members only. No staff.' Who do they think it is that I talk with just before I make a decision on how to vote?

Personal beliefs

On certain votes, House or Senate members may vote according to their own personal beliefs. Issues such as abortion, capital punishment, taxation (increases or cuts), federal subsidies and defence spending are likely to bring a member's own personal philosophy to the fore. There are, for example, members of Congress who will never vote for a federal subsidy to any industry or group, while others will never vote to deny life to a fellow human being, whether through capital punishment or war.

Summary

Voting in Congress

➤ Voting by members of Congress is affected by a number of important factors.

➤ The most important factors are likely to be party, constituents, the administration, pressure groups, colleagues and staff, and personal beliefs.

Reform of Congress

Congress is a very different institution from what it was 30 years ago. If Lyndon B. Johnson or Gerald R. Ford returned to the institution in which they spent a good deal of their political life, they would find much that they would not recognise.

What has changed and why has it changed?

Committee organisation

There are significant differences in the way the committees are organised and operate. The method of choosing committee chairs has been democratised by secret ballots. No one can chair more than one committee, and committees with more than 20 members must have at least four sub-committees. These sub-committees choose their own chairs, have their own budgets and hire their own staff. Committee hearings are held in public unless members vote for a 'closed' hearing. The Republicans have placed 6-year term limits on the holding of committee chairs in both houses.

Television

Television has arrived, not only in the chambers but also in the committee rooms. Cable television (C-SPAN) offers gavel-to-gavel coverage of both chambers and the most important committee hearings. This has had considerable implications for the 'folks back home', often thousands of miles from Washington DC, allowing them to see and hear their House and Senate members.

Levels of staffing and support

There has been a significant increase in congressional staffing and congressional agencies. In 1961, when Lyndon Johnson left the Senate to become vice-president, there were around 4,000 staff members working directly for House and Senate members. That figure has now almost tripled. During the same period, the Congressional Research Service has expanded significantly. The Congressional Budget Office was created in 1974.

Oversight of the executive branch

Congressional oversight of the executive branch has become more assertive. This can be seen in the passage of such presidency-curbing legislation as the Case Act (1972), the War Powers Act (1973) and the Budget and Impoundment Control Act (1974). Committees have stepped up the level of oversight too. This can be seen in the investigations of President Nixon over Watergate, President Reagan over the Iran–Contra affair, and the investigation — and eventual impeachment and trial — of President Clinton over the Monica Lewinsky scandal. Presidential nominees to both the executive and the judiciary have sometimes received a rough ride in the Senate confirmation process — Robert Bork (1987), John Tower (1989) and Clarence Thomas (1991) stand out in this regard.

Ethics rules tightened

There has been a tightening of the ethics rules of Congress. There is now an almost total ban on members of Congress receiving gifts, and 'honoraria' — fees for writing articles or making speeches — are banned. Two members of Congress have been expelled, and a House Speaker was forced to resign over infringement of ethics rules.

Why did these changes come about?

The debacles of Vietnam and Watergate were seen as congressional politics uncovering the failure of presidential politics. Having put the spotlight firmly on the executive branch, however, Congress had to admit that its house, too, needed putting in order. A new, younger, more independent breed of member began to arrive in Congress in the 1970s. They focused on changing Congress into a more open, modern, better-equipped, democratic and accountable institution.

What have been the consequences of these reforms?

Despite all the reforms, Congress has declined in public esteem. By 1992, a CBS/*New York Times* poll found that 71% of Americans disapproved of the way Congress was doing its job. Voters regard 'Washington politicians' with great scepticism. In six of the seven presidential elections from 1976 to 2000, the winner was a former state governor, not a Washington insider. In the minds of many, Congress is epitomised by gridlock and a 'do-nothing' mentality. Significant policy concerns such as gun control, social security and healthcare remain unresolved. Many Americans' view of Congress can be summed up in the bumper sticker that reads: 'What's the opposite of progress? **Congress!**'

Summary

Reform of Congress

➤ Significant changes have taken place in Congress in recent years.

➤ Many of these reforms were the result of political events such as Vietnam and Watergate.

Exercises

1 Explain how Congress came to be made up of two houses.

2 What are the constitutional requirements to be a member of Congress?

3 Explain the following terms: (a) locality rule; (b) coat-tails effect; (c) ticket splitting.

4 What usually happens to the president's party in mid-term congressional elections?

5 To what extent do national or local issues decide mid-term congressional elections?

6 How well are (a) women and (b) ethnic minorities represented in the make-up of Congress?

7 Outline the principal powers of Congress, indicating the difference between exclusive and concurrent powers.

8 Explain the roles of (a) the House Speaker; (b) majority and minority leaders.

9 Explain the role of congressional standing committees.

10 Why is the House Rules Committee so important?

11 What is the role of conference committees in Congress?

12 Explain what congressional select committees do.

13 Explain how people come to chair congressional committees.

14 Write a brief synopsis of the legislative process in Congress.

15 Explain what options the president has once bills are passed to him.

16 What factors affect voting by members of Congress?

17 How has Congress changed in recent decades?

Exam focus

1 Examine the way people vote in mid-term congressional elections.
2 Is Congress truly representative of America?
3 Why is the Senate regarded as more prestigious than the House of Representatives?
4 How important a role do political parties play in Congress?
5 Examine the claim that it is in the committee rooms that the real work of Congress is done.
6 Why is it so difficult to pass legislation in Congress?
7 How do members of Congress decide how to vote?

References

Bennett, A. J., *US Government & Politics 2003: Annual Survey* (Philip Allan Updates, 2003).

Carr, R. K., *Essentials of American Democracy* (Dryden Press, 1974).

Denenberg, R. V., *Understanding American Politics* (Fontana, 1976).

Loomis, B. A., *The Contemporary Congress* (Bedford-St Martin's, 2000).

Vile, M. J. C., *Politics in the USA* (Routledge, 1999).

Further reading

English, R., *The United States Congress* (Manchester University Press, 2003).

Smith, S. S., *The American Congress* (Houghton Mifflin, 1999).

Wadden, A., 'Congress and law-making in the US', *Politics Review*, vol. 11, no. 3, February 2002.

Chapter 6

The presidency

The office of the US president is often misunderstood by casual observers for two reasons. First, they tend to see the president as a one-man band when in fact he is part — though admittedly an important part — of an orchestra. Hence, this chapter is entitled 'The presidency' rather than 'The president', drawing to our attention the organisation rather than simply the person. Second, they tend to think of the president as 'the most powerful man in the world'. Maybe this mistake is even more common today, when the USA appears on the world stage as the only superpower — a kind of megapower. True, the president does have a considerable amount of power, more in foreign policy than in domestic policy. Whereas in foreign policy the president can use his formidable commander-in-chief powers, when it comes to domestic policy, he is far more limited — hedged around with numerous checks and balances, especially from Congress. President Johnson was once heard to remark: 'The only power I've got is nuclear, and I'm not allowed to use that.'

The US presidency is therefore something of a paradox: power and weakness. The president has to be both commander-in-chief and 'bargainer-in-chief'. He has considerable formal powers, but there are formidable limits on his use of those powers. To run the federal bureaucracy, mould public opinion and get on with Congress, the president needs to be an effective administrator, communicator, persuader and leader.

Questions to be answered in this chapter
  ➤ What kind of presidency did the Founding Fathers envisage?
  ➤ What are the formal powers of the president?
  ➤ How may the vice-president, the cabinet and the Executive Office of the President help, or hinder, the president in his job?
  ➤ How can the president get his way with Congress?
  ➤ What is 'presidential power' and what limits exist upon it?

The creation of the presidency

The Founding Fathers created a president who would be both head of state and head of the government. This is important to remember. The US president is not just another politician; he — and perhaps one day, she — is the personification of the nation. 'I am both king and prime minister,' remarked President Theodore Roosevelt. The arrival of the president at a formal, public function is greeted by a military band playing 'Hail to the Chief'. The White House may not have the grandeur of Buckingham Palace, but it is certainly a good deal more imposing than 10 Downing Street.

Second, the Founding Fathers created a singular executive. 'The executive power shall be vested in *a* president of the United States of America' are the opening words of Article II of the Constitution. It is important to remember this when considering the president's cabinet, for it is not — and cannot be — a decision-making body. President Truman had on his Oval Office desk a sign that read simply: 'The buck stops here.'

Third, they created an indirectly elected president. The president was to be chosen by the Electors — the great and the good — in an Electoral College. As Chapter 2 explains, this system has been adapted into a direct election, although the mechanism of the Electoral College still survives.

Finally, they created a limited — a checked — president. The Founding Fathers feared tyranny, and especially they feared tyranny by the executive branch. As a result, they hedged the president with a host of checks and balances (see Chapter 1). Thomas Cronin and Michael Genovese (1998) have written:

> The men who invented the presidency did not wish to create a ruler. Instead they hoped to create conditions where leadership might from time to time flourish. A ruler commands; a leader influences. A ruler wields power; a leader persuades.

Students of the US presidency need to understand that the office is often a limited and, for its main occupant, a frustrating one.

Table 6.1 American presidents since 1961

President	Party	Years in office
John Kennedy	Democrat	1961–63
Lyndon Johnson	Democrat	1963–69
Richard Nixon	Republican	1969–74
Gerald Ford	Republican	1974–77
Jimmy Carter	Democrat	1977–81
Ronald Reagan	Republican	1981–89
George Bush	Republican	1989–93
Bill Clinton	Democrat	1993–2001
George W. Bush	Republican	2001–

Summary

The creation of the presidency

➤ The intentions of the Founding Fathers regarding the presidency still affect the office today.

➤ This is especially the case in their creation of a 'limited' office, for which checks and balances are important.

The powers of the president

The powers of the president are his tasks, functions or duties. They are laid out in Article II of the Constitution. Essentially, they have been the same for every president — from George Washington to George W. Bush, and all the 41 presidents in between.

Propose legislation

Article II of the Constitution states: '[The president] shall from time to time give to the Congress information of the State of the Union, and recommend to their consideration such measures as he shall judge necessary and expedient.' This gives the president the power to propose legislation to Congress, which he may do through the annual State of the Union Address. This late-January event, which is carried live on television, is a chance for the president to address a joint session of Congress, setting out his legislative agenda for the coming year. The president can propose legislation at any time by, for example, calling a press conference or making an announcement at a public event. In the first 2 years of his presidency, George W. Bush proposed legislation to deliver education reform, tax cuts and anti-terrorist measures.

Vice-President Dick Cheney and House Speaker Dennis Hastert applaud as President George W. Bush delivers the State of the Union Address, 2002

Submit the annual budget

The budget is really just another piece of legislation, but it is potentially the most important. The Office of Management and Budget (OMB) draws up the annual federal budget for the president. The OMB is part of the president's own bureaucracy, which is known as the Executive Office of the President (EXOP). The president then submits the budget to Congress. This is followed by a lengthy bargaining process between the president and Congress — especially lengthy if the presidency and Congress are controlled by different political parties.

Sign legislation

Once bills have been passed through a lengthy and complicated legislative process in Congress (see Chapter 5), they land on the president's desk. He has a number of options, but the most likely is that of signing the bill into law. He will do this to bills for which he wishes to take some credit. Elaborate bill-signing ceremonies are often held, attended by House and Senate members who have been particularly supportive, relevant members of the administration, as well as interested parties who will be affected by the new legislation. At the bill-signing ceremony for the 2001 Education Reform Bill, Democrats Senator Edward Kennedy and Representative George Miller were both present, having been especially helpful to the President in getting the bill passed. Some Republican members of Congress as well as Education Secretary Rod Paige attended too.

Veto legislation

As well as signing bills into law, the president has the option of vetoing them. The regular veto is a much-used presidential weapon. Even the threat of it can be an important bargaining tool. Altogether, from George Washington to Bill Clinton, presidents have used over 2,500 regular vetoes. Congress may attempt to override the president's veto, but is rarely successful.

The president may have the power of pocket veto at his disposal, too, but this can be used only at the end of a congressional session. Pocket vetoes cannot be overridden by Congress. President Reagan (1981–89) used 39 pocket vetoes, President Bush (1989–93) 17, and President Clinton (1993–2001) just one.

Act as chief executive

The opening 15 words of Article II of the Constitution grant the president all executive power. Thus, the president is chief executive — in charge of running the executive branch of the federal government. This, as Chapter 7 explains, is a huge job and much of the day-to-day running is delegated to those who run the federal government's principal departments and agencies. Modern presidents have needed their own bureaucracy — EXOP — to help them to coordinate the work of the federal government.

Nominate executive branch officials

The president has the power to nominate hundreds of officials to the executive branch of government. A newly elected president — such as George W. Bush in 2001 — has a host of such posts to fill. The most important of these are the heads of the 15 executive departments such as the Treasury, State and Agriculture. In addition, there are lower-level officials in all these departments, as well as ambassadors, agency heads and members of regulatory commissions. The Senate must confirm all these appointments by a simple majority vote. Appointments continue to be made throughout the president's term of office.

Nominate all federal judges

Nomination of judges involves the president in making hundreds of appointments. He must fill vacancies not only on the federal Supreme Court, but also on the federal trial (district) and appeals (circuit) courts. All judicial appointments are for life and therefore assume a special importance. They must be confirmed by a simple majority vote in the Senate.

Act as commander-in-chief

This power was particularly important for presidents in office from the 1940s to the 1980s. Whether it was Franklin Roosevelt fighting the Second World War, Harry Truman in Berlin and Korea, Kennedy in Cuba, or Lyndon Johnson and Richard Nixon in Vietnam, presidents were seen as playing a highly significant role as commander-in-chief. Then came the demise of the Soviet Union and the break-up of the communist bloc in eastern Europe during the presidencies of Reagan and the first Bush. It was the same Bush who successfully fought the Persian Gulf War in 1991. The post-Cold War era saw a diminution of the president's commander-in-chief role. The decade from 1991 to 2001 brought no significant foreign policy engagement by a US president, nothing on the scale of Korea, Vietnam or the Gulf War. The events of 11 September 2001 changed all that, however. The second President Bush found himself thrust into the role of a wartime president.

In this area, Congress's checks are more questionable. The Constitution gives Congress the power to declare war, but that power has not been used since 1941. The president now asks Congress to 'authorise' his use of troops. Congress passed the Gulf of Tonkin Resolution in 1964, giving President Johnson the power 'to take all necessary measures' in Vietnam. Congress passed authorising resolutions in 1991 and 2002 before US troops were used in Kuwait and Iraq respectively. Congress also has the 'power of the purse' with which to check presidential war making, but this has not always proved effective.

Negotiate treaties

The president's seal of office (right) shows an eagle clutching a bundle of arrows in one claw, symbolising the commander-in-chief role, and an olive branch in the other to symbolise his peace-making role. Modern-day presidents have used this power to negotiate such treaties as the Panama Canal Treaty (Jimmy Carter), the Strategic Arms Reduction Treaty (Ronald Reagan) and the Chemical Weapons Ban (George Bush).

The president's power is checked by the Senate, which must ratify treaties by a two-thirds majority. Table 6.2 shows that during the twentieth century the Senate rejected seven treaties. The first and last were significant in that they were major treaties. In 1999, President Clinton failed even to gain a simple majority for the Comprehensive Test Ban Treaty, let alone the two-thirds majority required.

Table 6.2 Senate rejection of treaties during the twentieth century

Date	President	Treaty	Senate vote
19 March 1920	Woodrow Wilson (D)	Versailles	49–35
18 January 1927	Calvin Coolidge (R)	Commercial rights	50–34
14 March 1934	Franklin Roosevelt (D)	St Lawrence Seaway	46–42
29 January 1935	Franklin Roosevelt (D)	World Court	52–36
26 March 1960	Dwight Eisenhower (R)	Law of Sea Convention	49–30
8 March 1983	Ronald Reagan (R)	Montreal Protocol	50–42
13 October 1999	Bill Clinton (D)	Comprehensive Test Ban	48–51

Pardon

Presidents possess the power of pardon. Mostly used in uncontroversial cases, this power has occasionally been used in high-profile and controversial ones. In 1974, President Ford pardoned his predecessor, Richard Nixon, over all Watergate-related matters. President George Bush caused controversy with his 1992 pardon of former Defense Secretary Caspar Weinberger over his possible involvement in the Iran–Contra affair. President Clinton caused a storm on his final day in office in January 2001 when his pardon list included fugitive Mark Rich, whose former wife had made large monetary donations to Clinton's election campaigns and had given expensive personal gifts to the president and first lady.

Summary

The powers of the president

➤ The president possesses ten significant powers: to propose legislation, submit the annual budget, sign legislation, veto legislation, act as chief executive, nominate executive branch officials, nominate federal judges, act as commander-in-chief, negotiate treaties and grant pardons.

➤ These powers are subject to checks from Congress.

The vice-president

Selection, election and appointment

The selection of vice-presidential candidates is now made by the party's presidential candidate at, or usually just before, the National Party Convention. George W. Bush chose Dick Cheney in the summer of 2000. The presidential and vice-presidential candidates then run together, on what is called a 'joint ticket'.

When choosing the vice-presidential candidate, it is often said that a presidential candidate looks for a **balanced ticket**. 'Balance' might be looked for in terms of

Table 6.3 US vice-presidents since 1961

Vice-president	Party	Years in office
Lyndon Johnson	Democrat	1961–63
Hubert Humphrey	Democrat	1965–69
Spiro Agnew	Republican	1969–73
Gerald Ford*	Republican	1973–74
Nelson Rockefeller*	Republican	1974–77
Walter Mondale	Democrat	1977–81
George Bush	Republican	1981–89
Dan Quayle	Republican	1989–93
Al Gore	Democrat	1993–2001
Dick Cheney	Republican	2001–

*Appointed

geographic region, political experience, age and ideology, maybe even gender, race and religion. The best recent example of such a balanced ticket was the choice by Democrat Michael Dukakis of Lloyd Bentsen in 1988. Dukakis was a liberal governor from the northeastern state of Massachusetts. At 54 he had no experience of Washington politics. He was a Greek-American by birth and Greek Orthodox by religion. Bentsen, on the other hand, was a conservative senator from the South — Texas. He was 67 and had spent his entire political career in Washington. He was a 'WASP' — white, Anglo-Saxon, Protestant.

Key term

> **Balanced ticket.** A tactic used by a presidential candidate in selecting the vice-presidential candidate in an attempt to increase voter appeal for their 'ticket'.

On election day in 2000, people voted for the ticket of, for example, Bush–Cheney or Gore–Lieberman. In other words, the people elect the vice-president along with the president.

Since 1967 and the passage of the 25th Amendment, there are circumstances under which the vice-president may be appointed rather than elected. Should the vice-presidency become vacant, the president has the power to appoint a new vice-president who must be confirmed by a simple majority vote of both houses of Congress. This has occurred twice. In 1973, Vice-President Spiro Agnew resigned, having pleaded 'no contest' to a charge of income tax evasion. President Nixon then appointed Congressman Gerald Ford as vice-president. Ford was duly confirmed by votes of 92–3 and 387–55 by the Senate and House of Representatives respectively. Less than a year later, Nixon resigned from the presidency over the Watergate affair. Vice-President Ford therefore became president. He then appointed the former governor of New York, Nelson Rockefeller, as the new vice-president. Rockefeller was confirmed by congressional votes of 90–7 and 287–128.

Powers of the vice-president

The Constitution originally gave four powers to the vice-president.

- He is the presiding officer of the Senate, but this is a function that the vice-president rarely performs. The Senate deputes usually junior members of its chamber to chair debates.
- The vice-president is granted the power to break a tied vote in the Senate. Indeed, it is only to perform this function that a vice-president will usually attend the chamber. Dick Cheney cast a tie-breaking vote in April 2001 to protect President Bush's $1.6 trillion tax cut. More than 2 years passed before Cheney was called upon to vote again.
- The vice-president is given the task of counting and then announcing the result of the Electoral College votes. Thus in January 2001, outgoing Vice-President Gore had to announce his own defeat in the previous November's election.
- The first three powers are either of little importance or occur rarely — or both. It is the final power that gives the office of vice-president its potential importance. The vice-president becomes president upon the death, resignation or removal of the president from office. This has occurred on nine occasions: four times following the assassination of the president; four times following the natural death of the president; and once following the resignation of the president (President Nixon in August 1974). The insignificant powers of the office, coupled with this potential importance, led the first vice-president, John Adams, to remark of the post: 'In this I am nothing; but I may be everything.'
- More recently, the vice-president has acquired a fifth power: to become acting president if the president is declared, or declares himself, disabled. This is another provision of the 25th Amendment passed in 1967. The power has been used twice: first in July 1985 when President Reagan was hospitalised briefly; and again in June 2002 when President George W. Bush underwent sedation for some routine medical tests. On the latter occasion, Dick Cheney became acting president for all of 2 hours.

The increasing importance of the vice-presidency

The list of those who have held the office of vice-president falls into three distinct groups. Initially, the vice-president was seen as the 'president in waiting'. During much of the first two decades of the nation's history, the vice-president was the person who came second in the balloting of the Electoral College. Thus, the office was held by such prominent politicians as John Adams and Thomas Jefferson. The 12th Amendment (1804), however, changed all that. From then on, the vice-president was elected on a joint ticket with the presidential candidate. For the next century and a half, the vice-presidency was either filled mostly by people who were nonentities or was not filled at all. A list of vice-presidents between 1805 and the mid-twentieth century looks like an extract from 'who *wasn't* who'. Since then the vice-presidency has grown in importance for several reasons.

➤ As the role of the federal government and the president's responsibilities grew, presidents began to see the vice-presidency as a source of help in running the executive branch of government. Beginning with the Eisenhower–Nixon administration (1953–61), vice-presidents were given more high-profile tasks and became in some cases significant presidential advisers. Since Nixon's time as vice-president, all vice-presidents have been ex officio members of the cabinet. Walter Mondale (1977–81) was the first vice-president to be shown the presidential daily briefing (PDB) — the intelligence briefing given to the president at the start of each day. Mondale was also the first vice-president to be given an office in the West Wing — the building that houses the Oval Office. All his successors have seen the PDB and had the same office.

➤ This has had the effect of attracting more significant people to seek the office, which is now always occupied. Over the past 50 years, therefore, the list of vice-presidents has been a distinguished one, including such famous names as Lyndon Johnson, Hubert Humphrey and Al Gore. Of the ten vice-presidents who held office between 1953 and 2000, four went on to become president, while a further three were selected as their party's presidential candidate.

➤ Modern-day vice-presidents have taken on new roles. Many have played a key role in legislative liaison with Congress. This is a role that Dick Cheney — himself a former member of the House of Representatives — played for President Bush.

➤ The vice-president often becomes the party worker, electioneer and fund-raiser. Cheney played this role in the run-up to the 2002 mid-term elections, as Eric Schmitt commented in the *New York Times*:

> At event after event, Mr Cheney is drawing packed crowds and raking in millions of dollars for Republican candidates. Today, just a few days after lending a critical hand in shaping President Bush's speech on the Middle East, Mr Cheney slipped into his job as vice-fundraiser-in-chief, speaking to 300 Republican faithful at a $500-a-plate luncheon for [North Carolina Senate candidate] Elizabeth Dole. In this mid-term election year, Mr Cheney has become not only a marquee attraction but also a behind-the-scenes player in Republican electoral politics. He often squeezes in two or three events a week and has raised more than $11 million at some 30 events so far. Mr Bush usually pulls in more money per event. 'When people meet George W. Bush, they get giddy,' said Frank Luntz, a Republican pollster. 'When they meet Cheney, it's more reverence. It's the difference between meeting Britney Spears and meeting the Pope.'

➤ The vice-president may become a major spokesperson for the administration. This has certainly been the case with both Al Gore and Dick Cheney. Mr Gore became a regular face at the podium on environmental issues as well as over government efficiency drives. Mr Cheney has spoken out a good deal on foreign policy issues.

➤ Finally, in an era of Washington-outsider presidents — Governors Carter, Reagan, Clinton and George W. Bush — vice-presidents have often played the Washington-insider role, guiding the president around the potential pitfalls of Washington politics. These four presidents were ably served in this regard by their respective insider vice-presidents: Walter Mondale, George Bush, Al Gore and Dick Cheney.

Summary

The vice-president

➤ Vice-presidential candidates are nowadays usually chosen by the presidential candidates before the election and they run together on a 'joint ticket'.

➤ The 25th Amendment allows the president to appoint a new vice-president, should the office fall vacant.

➤ Vice-presidential powers are mostly administrative, except those relating to the vice-president becoming president or acting president.

➤ Recently, the office of the vice-presidency has grown significantly in importance and now attracts many politicians of considerable stature.

The cabinet

Historical background

The cabinet is an advice-giving group selected by the president, membership of which is determined by both tradition and presidential discretion. The traditional members are the heads of the executive departments. Originally there were just three — State, War and the Treasury. Now there are 15. The president has the discretion to award cabinet rank to other administration officials, too.

The cabinet is not mentioned in the Constitution. As we have already seen, the Founding Fathers created a *singular* executive — no councils or cabinets. However, the Constitution does state in Article II that the president 'may require the opinion in writing of the principal officer in each of the executive departments upon any subject relating to the duties of their respective offices'.

Four words or phrases in this brief extract indicate precisely what the president can require from the heads of the executive departments. First, the word 'may' is significant. This means that, whatever the Constitution prescribes in this section is voluntary, not obligatory. Constitutions are usually about 'shall', not 'may'. Second, the president may require 'opinions' — this is a very low-level word. These are not 'decisions' or even 'recommendations', merely 'opinions'. Third, he may require these opinions 'in writing'. No meeting is envisaged. Finally, there is the restriction as to what these 'opinions in writing' may be about: not 'upon any subject', but rather 'upon any subject *relating to the duties of their respective offices*'. In other words, the secretary of the treasury will offer opinions only on Treasury matters; the secretary of state only on State Department matters. This is certainly not the recipe for what students of UK politics understand by a 'cabinet meeting'.

Why, then, do presidents have a 'cabinet'? In 1789, President Washington thought it would be helpful to have a meeting with the secretaries of War, the Treasury and State, plus the attorney general. The press called them 'cabinet meetings'. Every president since then has had a cabinet and held cabinet meetings. According to presidential scholar Richard Fenno (1959), it is 'institutionalised by usage alone'. In other words, it's used because it's used.

It is important to differentiate between the cabinet as individuals and the cabinet as a group. Failure to see these two different uses of the term can lead to misunderstandings. The answer to the question 'Was President Clinton's cabinet important?' is impossible to answer until we have established in which sense the term is being used. As individuals, cabinet members were important: some, like Secretary of State Madeleine Albright and Treasury Secretary Robert Rubin, were very important. On the other hand, cabinet meetings were hardly ever held, so, as a group, the cabinet was unimportant.

Recruitment and membership

A new president needs to recruit a completely new cabinet. In a presidential system such as in the USA, there is no 'shadow cabinet' waiting to take office. Furthermore, in a 'separated' system, in which members of the legislature cannot at the same time serve in the executive, the president must cast his net more widely for potential cabinet members. There are four major pools of recruitment.

First, the president may try to recruit from Congress. Unfortunately, asking serving members of Congress to give up their seats to take up a cabinet post, where both prestige and job security are often in short supply, is rarely successful. The president is therefore more likely to have to invite former or retiring members of Congress. In January 2001, incoming President George W. Bush invited into his cabinet two former Republican senators who had just been defeated in the 2000 elections: John Ashcroft of Missouri to become Attorney General and Spencer Abraham of Michigan to become energy secretary. In the 40 years from John Kennedy to George W. Bush, however, fewer than one in five cabinet officers have had any experience at all in Congress.

Second, the president may recruit from among serving or former state governors. In 2001, Governor Tommy Thompson of Wisconsin was appointed as secretary of health and human services (HHS).

A third pool of recruitment is that of big city mayors. Bill Clinton appointed the former Mayor of Denver, Federico Peña, as secretary of transportation. Academia is a fourth possible source of recruitment. Rod Paige, appointed as secretary of education in 2001, was formerly a professor at the University of Cincinnati.

What the president is really looking for in cabinet officers is policy specialists. Bush's education secretary, Rod Paige, was not only a former professor; he had for 6 years been schools superintendent in Houston, Texas. His secretary of veterans' affairs, Anthony Principi, is himself a Vietnam veteran. His secretary of transportation, while serving in the House of Representatives, had chaired the House Transportation Committee.

Table 6.4 President George W. Bush's cabinet: year of appointment and Senate confirmation votes

Post	Cabinet officer	Appointed	Senate vote
Secretary of State	Colin Powell	2001	Voice vote
Secretary of Defense	Donald Rumsfeld	2001	Voice vote
Secretary of the Treasury	John Snow	2003	Voice vote
Secretary of Agriculture	Ann Veneman	2001	Voice vote
Secretary of the Interior	Gale Norton	2001	75–24
Attorney General	John Ashcroft	2001	58–42
Secretary of Commerce	Donald Evans	2001	Voice vote
Secretary of Labor	Elaine Chao	2001	Voice vote
Secretary of Health and Human Services	Tommy Thompson	2001	100–0
Secretary of Education	Rod Paige	2001	Voice vote
Secretary of Housing and Urban Development	Alphonso Jackson	2004	Voice vote
Secretary of Transportation	Norman Mineta	2001	100–0
Secretary of Energy	Spencer Abraham	2001	Voice vote
Secretary of Veterans' Affairs	Anthony Principi	2001	100–0
Secretary of Homeland Security	Tom Ridge	2003	94–0

A balanced cabinet

Presidents like to have a 'balanced' cabinet. President-elect Clinton in 1992 talked about having a cabinet that 'looked like America'. There are five principal factors that presidents usually consider to balance their cabinet.

➢ Presidents like to balance their cabinet in terms of region. In Bush's initial cabinet, there were representatives from all of the major regions within the United States: Gale Norton from Colorado (the Rockies); Rod Paige from Texas (the South); Tommy Thompson from Wisconsin (the upper Midwest); and Norman Mineta from California (the West Coast).

➢ Presidents look for balance by race. President Lyndon Johnson was the first president to appoint an African-American to his cabinet when Robert Weaver was appointed as Secretary of Housing and Urban Development (HUD) in 1966. Expectations had therefore been set, and incoming President Richard Nixon was criticised in 1969 when he appointed an all-white cabinet. Every president since Nixon has appointed an ethnically diverse cabinet. George W. Bush's 2001 cabinet was the most ethnically diverse cabinet ever appointed. It included Norman Mineta (a Japanese-American), Spencer Abraham (a Lebanese-American) and Elaine Chao (a Chinese-American), as well as Colin Powell and Rod Paige (both African-Americans).

➢ Gender is an important factor in appointing the cabinet. Once Gerald Ford had become the first modern-day president to appoint a woman to the cabinet, with his appointment of Carla Hills as HUD Secretary in 1975, successive presidents felt obliged to follow suit. When, in 1981, President Reagan appointed no women as heads of the executive departments, he faced considerable criticism. In 2001, Bush appointed three women as heads of department: Gale Norton (Interior), Elaine Chao (Labor) and Ann Veneman (Agriculture).

In terms of both race and gender, some would point out that female and ethnic minority nominations rarely head the so-called 'upper-tier' departments — State, Defense, the Treasury and Justice (see Table 6.5). President Clinton broke this trend by appointing Janet Reno at Justice in 1993 and Madeleine Albright at State in 1997. President George W. Bush did likewise by appointing Colin Powell secretary of state in 2001.

Table 6.5 Appointments of women and ethnic minority cabinet officers by department, 1961–2002

Department	Women	Ethnic minorities
'Upper-tier' departments		
State	1	1
Treasury	0	0
Defense	0	0
Justice	1	0
'Lower-tier' departments		
Agriculture	1	1
Interior	1	0
Commerce	2	1
Labor	5	1
Health and Human Services	3	2
Education	1	1
Housing and Urban Development	2	3
Transportation	1	2
Energy	1	1
Veterans' Affairs	0	2

➤ Age is yet another factor. As a rule of thumb, the average age of the cabinet usually reflects the age of the president. The youngest ever cabinet was that of President Kennedy — the youngest elected president. Their average age was just 47. However, that rule was broken when George W. Bush appointed the oldest cabinet in modern times — possibly the oldest ever. Its average age was 58. When they were sworn into office in January 2001, six of them (Rumsfeld, Paige, Powell, Mineta, O'Neill and Principi) were over 60, and a seventh (Thompson) was 10 months away from his sixtieth birthday. Only three — Norton (46), Chao (47) and Abraham (48) — were under 50.

➤ A fifth factor is political ideology. Whether it is a Democrat or a Republican cabinet, the president will want to have the different ideological wings of his party represented: liberal Democrats, conservative Democrats and New Democrats; conservative

Republicans and moderate Republicans. George W. Bush had campaigned in the 2000 election as a 'compassionate conservative'. His 2001 cabinet looked more 'compassionate' than 'conservative'. The obvious exception was Attorney General John Ashcroft, who had a solid conservative record during both his 8 years as Governor of Missouri and his 6 years in the Senate. Gale Norton at Interior probably fell into the conservative category too. But with the appointments of Colin Powell (State) and Tommy Thompson (HHS) — as well as Christine Todd Whitman, with cabinet rank, to head the Environmental Protection Agency — this certainly did not look like a conservative cabinet. It is not unusual for a president to pick someone from the other party. In his second term, Democrat President Clinton appointed former Republican Senator William Cohen as Secretary of Defense. In 2001, Republican George W. Bush kept former Democrat Congressman Norman Mineta from Clinton's cabinet, moving him from Commerce to Transportation.

Replacement appointments

Inevitably, presidents have to make replacement appointments to their cabinet. Members resign or sometimes get fired. Table 6.6 shows that over a full term of office, presidents tend to make around 8 cabinet replacement appointments — or about one every 6 months. Presidents Johnson and Ford, who inherited their predecessors' cabinet, had an understandably higher-than-average turnover. By the time Richard Nixon resigned after just over $5\frac{1}{2}$ years as president, not a single member of his original cabinet was still in office. In contrast, four members of Bill Clinton's cabinet served through all 8 years of his administration: Attorney General Janet Reno, Interior Secretary Bruce Babbit, HHS Secretary Donna Shalala and Education Secretary Richard Riley. Some departments seem more prone to turnover than others. Between 1961 and 2003, there were only 12 secretaries of agriculture but 17 secretaries of labor and 19 secretaries of commerce.

Table 6.6 Frequency of replacement cabinet appointments, 1961–2004

President	Months in office	Number of replacement cabinet appointments	Average months per replacement
John Kennedy	34	3	11.3
Lyndon Johnson	62	13	4.8
Richard Nixon	67	19	3.5
Gerald Ford	29	12	2.4
Jimmy Carter	48	8	6.0
Ronald Reagan	96	20	4.8
George Bush	48	8	6.0
Bill Clinton	96	16	6.0
George W. Bush*	36	2	18.0

*George W. Bush figures to January 2004.

Cabinet meetings

The frequency of cabinet meetings varies from one president to another. During his first year in office, Ronald Reagan held 36 cabinet meetings, while in his first year Bill Clinton held only 6. There is a trend to hold fewer cabinet meetings the longer the president remains in office. Reagan's 36 meetings in his first year became 21 in the second year and just 12 in each of the third and fourth years. The reasons for this decline seem to be threefold. First, some of the functions of the cabinet are no longer applicable. Second, presidents have increasing calls made upon their time, not least when they have to start running for re-election. Jimmy Carter, who had held 36 cabinet meetings in 1977, held just 6 in 1980. In 1980, however, he had to spend time fending off a challenge in the Democratic primaries from Senator Edward Kennedy as well as fight the general election campaign later that year. Third, presidents tend to become disillusioned with their cabinet officers, often believing them to have become disloyal: Presidents Richard Nixon and Jimmy Carter are prime examples. President George W. Bush holds cabinet meetings about every 6–8 weeks.

Who attends cabinet meetings and what does the scene look like? All the heads of the executive departments, the vice-president and all other administration officials granted cabinet rank are expected to attend. The cabinet room contains a huge mahogany table which tapers to both ends, allowing the president — seated in the middle of one side — to see all the participants. All regular attendees are assigned places around the table according to seniority. Opposite the president sits the vice-president. To the president's right and left are, respectively, the secretary of state and secretary of defense. To the vice-president's right and left are, respectively, the

| Box 6.1 | **Comments from cabinet officers regarding cabinet meetings** |

'The president listened to the group with thinly disguised impatience.'

J. Edward Day, postmaster general in Kennedy's cabinet

'I always went to cabinet meetings thinking "I wonder how soon I can get away from this so I can get on with all the work I've got to do." And I think most of my colleagues had the same idea.'

A cabinet officer to President Johnson

'Nothing of substance was discussed. There was no disagreement because there was nothing to disagree about. Things over which one might have disagreed were not discussed.'

Elliot Richardson, attorney general in Nixon's cabinet

'Carter cabinet meetings were almost useless. The discussions were desultory. There was no coherent theme to them, and after a while they were held less and less frequently.'

Zbigniew Brzezinski, national security advisor in Carter's cabinet

'Very often they were a waste of time. You could get very bored.'

A cabinet officer to President George Bush

secretary of the treasury and the attorney general. Other attendees — mostly senior members of the White House staff — sit around the room, looking in towards the cabinet table.

Meetings of the president with the full cabinet tend to get a bad press. Many describe them as 'boring' and 'a waste of time' (see Box 6.1). Part of the trouble is that so many of the people sitting round the table are policy specialists. They have little or nothing to contribute to discussions in other policy areas. As Reagan's labor secretary, Bill Brock, put it:

> The problem with the cabinet is that it has become too large. We keep adding new departments, so there are too many issues that come up where people have neither jurisdiction nor competence.

Since Brock sat in the cabinet, two more departments have been created — Veterans' Affairs (1989) and Homeland Security (2002).

However, formal meetings held in most organisations are probably described by at least some of the participants in deprecating terms. It does not necessarily mean that such meetings should not be held or that they perform no useful functions. The same is true of the president's cabinet, for the cabinet meeting performs many useful functions, both from the president's perspective and from that of the cabinet officers.

The functions of cabinet meetings for the president

Cabinet meetings can potentially perform several functions from the president's perspective.

➤ They can engender team spirit. This is especially important at the beginning of an administration. Presidents do not have a 'shadow cabinet' waiting to come into office. Many of the president's cabinet officers will be complete strangers to him. Cabinet meetings can help to weld them into *his* team to move forward *his* agenda. Once this has been achieved — probably within the first year — this function ceases. This may partly explain why cabinet meetings decline in number from that point in most administrations.

➤ It is important for presidents to appear collegial and consultative. This is particularly important for presidents post-Nixon. The Nixon administration was notorious for its lack of openness. A political novel written of the era was famously titled *Washington: Behind Closed Doors*. Cartoonists drew Nixon's Oval Office with guards outside dressed in Prussian-style military uniforms holding 'no entry' signs. Cabinet meetings with a media photo opportunity either before or after the meeting are a good way for the president to send reassuring signals that he is running an open administration. To this extent, cabinet meetings can be a public relations exercise and an opportunity for the president to make some comments that will receive coverage in the media.

➤ Cabinet meetings provide opportunities for both information giving and information gathering. The president can make statements at a cabinet meeting knowing that every member has heard them and he can go round the table asking cabinet officers what is going on in their departments. President Carter's cabinet meetings usually took the form of the president going clockwise — the next time, anticlockwise — round the cabinet table, asking each member to give a brief report on current departmental issues and activity. Cabinet meetings can be an efficient method by which the president keeps in touch with what is going on in the vast federal bureaucracy.

➤ Some presidents have liked to use cabinet meetings as a forum in which to debate policy. Reagan's defense secretary, Frank Carlucci, remembered that 'cabinet meetings were often vigorous, such as the one on the pros and cons of building the Russian oil pipeline — it was quite a shouting match'. Michael Jackson, a senior member of President George Bush's Office of Cabinet Affairs who attended meetings as an observer, stated:

> At the meeting prior to the Malta summit [with Soviet president Gorbachev in December 1989], the president engaged the cabinet in a very significant discussion of foreign policy. It allowed the president to broaden his consultations.

➤ At cabinet meetings the president can present so-called 'big picture items' that affect all cabinet officers: the budget; up-coming elections; a major legislative initiative or foreign trip. For example, President George W. Bush called a cabinet meeting on 26 February 2001, the day before his first address to a joint session of Congress. He held another on 9 April 2001, the day he submitted his first budget to Congress. Yet another was called on 3 August 2001 to review the accomplishments of the administration's first 6 months.

➤ Some presidents have used cabinet meetings to check up on legislation going through Congress in which they have a particular interest. Willard Wirtz, labor secretary to President Johnson, stated:

> If the Congress was in session, and you knew there was a cabinet meeting coming up in a day or two, you tried to make sure that there was some progress to report to the president. He knew the system so well. He could often embarrass you. Johnson would often pressurise you into making sure things moved quicker.

President George W. Bush used his 24 September 2002 cabinet meeting to push for congressional action on three key issues: authorisation for military action against Iraq; the passage of the Homeland Security Bill; and the budget.

➤ Finally, cabinet meetings provide an opportunity for the president to see cabinet members whom he would not otherwise be likely to see. Whereas the 'first-tier' cabinet officers — such as the secretary of state and the secretary of defense — are likely to have fairly frequent meetings with the president, this will not be the case for such 'second-tier' cabinet officers as the secretary of veterans' affairs and the secretary of agriculture. Again, whereas the Treasury Department is only half a block from the White House, other departments are situated in far-flung parts of downtown Washington. There is no obvious reason for the president to see many cabinet officers except at a cabinet meeting. The president might even forget who is in the cabinet. HUD Secretary Sam Pierce never lived down the story of when President Reagan spotted him one day at a White House reception for visiting city mayors and mistook Pierce for a visitor: 'How are you, Mr Mayor?' asked the president of his housing secretary. 'How are things in your city?'

The functions of cabinet meetings for cabinet officers

There are good reasons for cabinet officers, too, to see cabinet meetings as potentially useful occasions, despite their frequent critiques of them.

> They provide initial get-to-know-you opportunities. Not only will the president not know many of them; they will often not know each other.

> Cabinet meetings can be used to resolve interdepartmental disputes. Ford's secretary to the cabinet, James Connor, remembers a cabinet meeting in which a dispute about affirmative action for African-Americans was aired. 'It was one hell of a show,' stated Connor.

> Meetings in many organisations are often as useful for what goes on before and after them as what occurs during them. The same can be true for the president's cabinet meetings. They can prove a useful opportunity to speak with other cabinet officers, and as there are precious few other opportunities to run into one's cabinet colleagues — unlike in a parliamentary system — these can be valuable occasions.

> It may even be possible to catch the president after the meeting, should he linger in the cabinet room. However, such situations can present danger for a president who agrees too readily to what may appear to be an innocent, off-the-cuff request from a cabinet officer. George W. Bush's secretary to the cabinet explained how he would be 'hovering [around the president] at the end of a meeting, not exactly eavesdropping, but at a respectful distance' to ensure that no cabinet officer took advantage of the president in such an unscheduled moment.

> Finally, attendance at cabinet meetings gives cabinet officers increased standing back at their departments. They have just heard the president. They know what he wants, today, as opposed to what others might *think* he wanted, yesterday. President George Bush's agriculture secretary, Clayton Yeutter, summed up a number of these functions this way:

> [Cabinet meetings] were useful for being informative. You got an insight on the top stories. It was for some just the thrill to have a meeting with the president. The 'second tier' cabinet officers don't get to see him that often. They would go back to their departments and be able to say: 'I just came from a cabinet meeting.' They would then hold their own staff meetings and the stories would be passed out to sub-cabinet people and so to the rest of the department. They were evangelistic.

Cabinet councils

There is a problem with using full cabinet meetings for policy discussion, because most cabinet members are policy specialists. To overcome this problem, some presidents developed a series of policy-specific cabinet councils. These existed during the presidencies of Ronald Reagan, George Bush and George W. Bush. In the administration of George W. Bush there were three: the Economic Policy Council; the Domestic Policy Council; and the National Security Council. As a result, full cabinet meetings were held less frequently and used for 'big picture' items. Commenting on this arrangement, Secretary to the Cabinet Albert Hawkins stated:

> The president is using a series of three cabinet councils which will mean that full cabinet meetings will not get bogged down on the minutiae of policy. Each cabinet council has designated membership but others will be invited to attend as required. The president will attend as necessary.

Mr Hawkins, however, also remarked that George W. Bush's cabinet included four former state governors, 'who, as experienced chief executives, are used to looking at policy issues much more broadly'.

An assessment of the president's cabinet

How important, then, is the president's cabinet? Individually, its members are very important — they all run large departments and spend large budgets. Some, however, are more important than others. Collectively, there are five structural reasons why the president's cabinet can never be of prime importance.

First, the Constitution grants 'all executive power' to the president. Cabinet officers have no executive power vested in them directly. Second, there is no doctrine of collective responsibility. The president is not 'first among equals'. He is simply 'first'. As Professor Anthony King put it: 'He doesn't sum up at the end of the meeting; he *is* the meeting.' Third, cabinet officers are not the president's political rivals. The cabinet is not seen as a stepping stone to the presidency. This is not to say that some former cabinet officers have not harboured presidential ambitions. Lamar Alexander and Jack Kemp, both of whom served in the cabinet of President George Bush in the early 1990s, made unsuccessful bids for the presidency. The last person to step from the cabinet directly to the presidency was Herbert Hoover in 1929. Hoover had served as commerce secretary to Presidents Warren Harding and Calvin Coolidge. Fourth, the members of the president's cabinet have loyalties other than to the president. Charles Dawes (Vice-President 1925–29) once remarked that members of the cabinet are 'a president's natural enemies'! They also do not work in the White House. Some of them may see the president rarely.

One more significant limit to the cabinet's importance is the existence, since 1939, of the Executive Office of the President (EXOP). In the EXOP, the cabinet has something of a rival, and a rival with a number of key advantages.

Summary

The cabinet

➢ There is no mention of the president's cabinet in the Constitution.

➢ The president has a wide pool of recruitment for cabinet officers.

➢ Presidents may try to appoint a 'balanced' cabinet.

➢ Cabinet officers are mostly policy specialists.

➢ Cabinet meetings, although often given a bad press, may fulfil some important functions both for the president and for cabinet members.

➢ There are some significant reasons why the cabinet cannot become all that important.

The Executive Office of the President (EXOP)

EXOP is an umbrella term for an organisation that consists of the top presidential staff agencies that provide help, advice, coordination and administrative support for the president.

In 1939, the Brownlow Committee reported to President Franklin Roosevelt (FDR) that 'the president needs help'. Why did presidents from the mid-twentieth century 'need help' in running the federal government? First, there had been a huge increase in the size and scale of the federal government, caused mainly by the westward expansion and industrialisation of the nineteenth century. In 1789, there were just three executive departments of the federal government — State, War and the Treasury. By 1939, a further five had been added: Interior (1849), Justice (1870), Agriculture (1889), Commerce and Labor (both 1903).

President George W. Bush meets in the Oval Office with three senior White House advisers

Second, when the great depression hit the USA in the late 1920s, the states looked to the federal government for help. FDR responded to this with his 'New Deal' programme — a whole raft of federal government schemes to promote employment, agriculture, industrial expansion and a huge building programme of schools, roads, hydroelectric schemes and the like.

Third, the USA was about to become a major player on the stage of world politics. This added considerably to the president's role as commander-in-chief. The presidents of the second half of the twentieth century had to spend much of their time dealing with the consequences of the Cold War — in southeast Asia, eastern Europe and Central America.

As a result, presidents found more demands made on them. Overload became a real danger. So EXOP was established to help the president cope with these increased demands. Through the second half of the twentieth century, EXOP grew to include around a dozen offices, the most important being the White House Staff, the National Security Council and the Office of Management and Budget. Altogether, EXOP came to number some 1,500 staff. The most important EXOP personnel, including the key presidential advisers, work in the West Wing of the White House, which is where the Oval Office is located.

The White House Staff

The White House Staff includes the president's most trusted and closest aides and advisers. (In 2004, these included Karl Rove (senior policy advisor) and Scott McClellan (press secretary). In charge of running the White House Staff was the White House chief of staff, Andrew Card.) Their principal function is to provide advice and administrative support for the president on a daily basis. Whether in the White House, travelling within the United States or out of the country, these people are never far from the president. When the second plane hit the World Trade Center in New York on 11 September 2001, it was Chief of Staff Andrew Card who was pictured whispering the awful news into the president's ear as he sat in front of a class of schoolchildren in Sarasota, Florida, that morning.

Specifically, the White House Staff are responsible for a host of duties. They act as liaison between the White House and the vast federal bureaucracy. George W. Bush's cabinet secretary — himself a White House Staff member — explained that if a cabinet officer wanted to talk one-to-one with the president, then that cabinet officer would first talk either with himself or with Chief of Staff Andrew Card. They act as liaison between the White House and Congress, too. The Congressional Liaison Staff is a branch of the White House Staff with that sole responsibility. The staff member designated as head of congressional liaison is the person who arranges for members of Congress to meet with the president. Anyone whose job description includes deciding on who has a meeting in the Oval Office with the president of the United States is a potentially important person.

Even telephone calls to the president are screened by the White House Staff to decide who should and who should not be put through to the president. The same goes for paperwork. President Eisenhower was known to read only those documents that included the letters 'OK. SA' on them — indicating that his chief of staff, Sherman Adams, had 'okayed' them. The White House Staff are responsible for drawing up the president's daily schedule, for the day-to-day running of the White House and for personnel management. They ensure that decisions are arrived at in an orderly fashion — that all relevant options, pros and cons have been presented to the president for him to make his decision. They deal with crisis management and act as 'lightning conductors' — taking the blame when things go wrong. As White House chief of staff to President Ford, Dick Cheney, remarked: 'He takes the credit; I take the blame.'

In order to fulfil these important functions, members of the White House Staff are meant to act as 'honest brokers', not as policy-makers. They are meant not to be always in the media spotlight, but to have something of what the Brownlow Report called 'a passion for anonymity'. If senior members of the White House Staff are thought to be pursuing their own rather than the president's agenda, this can lead to trouble. In President George Bush's administration, Chief of Staff John Sununu was thought by many to be pursuing his own conservative policy agenda rather than what the president wanted. Sununu's access to the president put him at a significant advantage over other policy players, who came to resent Sununu's role. Bush had to fire him eventually.

The role of the White House chief of staff is the most crucial job of all within the White House Staff. Some, like Don Regan (Reagan: 1985–87) and John Sununu (Bush: 1989–92), became too obtrusive — almost a kind of 'deputy president'. Others, such as Thomas 'Mack' McClarty (Clinton: 1993–94), were overwhelmed by the job because of their lack of Washington experience. The best model is that of someone who always seeks the president's best interests rather than his or her own, and who protects the president from political harm. Jack Watson, who served as chief of staff to President Carter, described his job as being like that of a 'javelin catcher' — protecting the president from incoming missiles that could hurt him. Watson continued:

> The chief of staff's role is to see that all the relevant people have a full and fair opportunity to present their views to the president. To act as an honest broker means that I view my role as a fulcrum rather than being a weight on one end. I must ensure that the president hears conflicting views, and not seek to make the judgement for him.

In a May 1993 *Washington Post* article on the role of the White House chief of staff, Lloyd Grove stated:

> It is the hottest seat in town and its occupant is the orchestrator of presidential paper flow, the 'honest broker' of ideas and opinions, the fearsome disciplinarian of wayward staffers, the president's trusted adviser and sounding board, the White House's apologist and occasionally, when necessary, the president's fall guy.

Nixon's chief of staff, Bob Haldeman, once famously said: 'Every president needs a son-of-a-bitch, and I'm Nixon's!' Those who have received high marks for their chief-of-staff role include Dick Cheney (Ford: 1975–77), James Baker (Reagan: 1981–85), Leon Panetta (Clinton: 1994–97) and Andrew Card (George W. Bush: 2001–). Ultimately, though, it is the president who largely decides how he wants the White House organised and run. Staff are there essentially to carry out presidential instructions.

There are fundamentally two different ways of organising the White House, or any organisation, come to that. The first is described as the 'spokes of the wheel' system. In this organisational structure, the president is at the centre — the hub — of the White House with many different advisers — spokes — having direct access to the Oval Office. This system was popularised by President Kennedy and adopted by such presidents as Jimmy Carter and Bill Clinton. The advantage is that the president is accessible. The potential hazard is that he is too accessible and that some advisers take advantage of their access to the president.

The second method of organising the White House is described as the 'pyramid' system. In this structure, the president sits at the apex of the pyramid. Only a few key advisers — possibly only one or two — have direct access to the president. The others have to pass their views up through the different layers of the pyramid. The advantage is that it leads to a highly disciplined White House. The potential hazard is that the president becomes isolated and hears only what he wants to hear, not what he needs to hear. This system was adopted most notably by President Nixon. His three senior advisers — Henry Kissinger, Bob Haldeman and John Ehrlichman — were collectively nicknamed 'the Berlin Wall'. Ronald Reagan and George Bush used the same basic White House structure.

The National Security Council

The National Security Council (NSC) was established in 1947 to help the president coordinate foreign, security and defence policy. Headed by the national security advisor (NSA), the NSC began life as an in-house think-tank for the president. The NSC would coordinate information coming to the White House from the State Department, the Defense Department, the Central Intelligence Agency (CIA), the Joint Chiefs of Staff and American ambassadors around the world. It would liaise with the relevant congressional committees, too. Like the White House Staff, the NSC was designed to operate as an 'honest broker', a 'facilitator', presenting carefully argued options for presidential decision making.

President Nixon changed the way the NSC worked. Distrustful of the State Department, which he saw as too liberal and establishment-orientated, Nixon decided to run foreign policy from the White House. He appointed Henry Kissinger as his NSA to act as a roving foreign policy-maker, largely cutting out the State Department's traditional role. But this enhanced and politicised role for the NSC caused grave problems for subsequent presidents.

President Carter's NSA, Zbigniew Brzezinski, feuded with Secretary of State Cyrus Vance over a rescue mission to free 52 American hostages held in Iran. The mission — backed by Brzezinski but opposed by Vance — was an utter disaster. Vance resigned in protest at the way Carter had allowed Brzezinski to influence the policy-making process. Then, in the Reagan administration, NSA John Poindexter was discovered to be running a secret — and illegal — foreign policy in the so-called Iran–Contra affair. Poindexter was forced to resign.

Subsequently, Presidents George Bush, Bill Clinton and George W. Bush have returned the NSC to its 'honest broker' role. In the 1991 Persian Gulf War, George Bush was skilfully served by NSA Brent Scowcroft. He acted as a behind-the-scenes coordinator of policy advice arriving from Secretary of State James Baker, Defense Secretary Dick Cheney and Chairman of the Joint Chiefs of Staff Colin Powell. For Bill Clinton, Samuel 'Sandy' Berger played a similar role. Writing in *The New Republic* in April 1998, Jacob Heilbrunn described Berger as 'the chief coordinator and adviser to the President; the glue that holds the foreign policy team together'. For George W. Bush, NSA Condoleezza Rice plays a similarly important but facilitating role. Bob Woodward (2003) said of Rice:

> She saw her job as twofold: first to coordinate what Defense, State, the CIA and other departments and agencies were doing by making sure the President's orders were carried out; and second, to act as counsellor — to give her private assessment to the President, certainly when he asked, perhaps if he didn't. In other words she was the President's trouble-shooter.

Condoleezza Rice, George W. Bush's National Security Advisor

The Office of Management and Budget

President Nixon created the Office of Management and Budget (OMB) in 1970 when he revamped what was previously called the Bureau of the Budget. The OMB has two principal functions: first, to advise the president on the allocation of federal funds in the annual budget; second, to oversee the spending of all federal departments and agencies.

It is headed by the OMB director — just about the only EXOP post that requires Senate confirmation. The job of the OMB director is both to run the Office and to give advice to and speak on behalf of the president on budgetary matters. Some have performed the job with distinction and thereby the president has received the credit. Others have been less competent and have thereby caused problems and embarrassments. Notable in the first category was Bill Clinton's first OMB director, Leon Panetta. Panetta had served in Congress, rising to become the chair of the House Budget Committee. He was widely credited with getting President Clinton's first budget through Congress — by the narrowest of margins. 'Clinton could not have had a better salesman,' one media commentator said in praise of Panetta. On the other hand, it was OMB director Richard

Darman who persuaded Republican President George Bush to break his 'no new taxes' pledge. Bush had made the pledge during the 1988 election campaign, turning it into a famous catchphrase: 'Read my lips: no new taxes.' Yet 2 years later, Darman persuaded Bush to break the pledge in order to get his 1990 budget through a Democrat-controlled Congress. It was akin to political suicide and cost the president dearly in his re-election campaign in 1992.

Summary

The Executive Office of the President

➢ The EXOP is a crucial source of help for modern-day presidents.
➢ It contains the president's key aides and advisers.
➢ The White House chief of staff plays a decisive role in running the administration efficiently.

EXOP–cabinet rivalries

Presidents must guard against the development of unhealthy rivalries and distrust between those who work in the EXOP, on the one hand, and the heads of the executive departments — the cabinet — on the other. Such rivalries and distrust can inflict serious wounds on a presidency, as Presidents Richard Nixon and Jimmy Carter discovered.

There is a danger that those who work in the White House might come to regard cabinet officers as distant and disloyal. Similarly, cabinet officers might come to regard those who work in the White House as too close and too loyal to the president. Some of these feelings are born of natural circumstances. Cabinet officers are, physically, distant from the White House. The office of the secretary of state, for example, is on the seventh floor of the State Department building in Foggy Bottom — an area of Washington about seven blocks west of the White House, making it a good 10 minutes away from the Oval Office. The secretary of defense is even further away. The Pentagon — the department's headquarters — is over the other side of the Potomac River, 15–20 minutes away. In comparison, the national security advisor's office is a 30-second walk from the Oval Office. It is hardly surprising that the secretaries of state and defense seem — and feel — a bit distant. Those who work in the EXOP have the key advantage of proximity. Daniel Patrick Moynihan, who served in the White House under President Nixon, commented: 'Never underestimate the power of proximity.'

It is understandable to some extent that cabinet officers sometimes appear disloyal. Although they are appointed by the president and serve only at his pleasure, they have other loyalties. They have a loyalty to Congress, whose votes decide their departmental budgets and whose committees can call them to account in person. They have a loyalty to their own departmental bureaucracy to interest groups with which their department has close links. This, often cosy, relationship between the executive departments, congressional committees and interest groups is referred to as 'the iron triangle'. They often work together on policy making to the mutual benefit of all three groups, but their interests might not always coincide with the president's interests. In the words of Nixon White House aide John Ehrlichman, the trouble with the cabinet is that they go off and 'marry the natives'. On the other hand, those who work in the EXOP have only one loyalty — to the president. They are *All the President's Men* — the title of a 1970s book (and a film starring Robert Redford and Dustin Hoffman) about the Nixon White House and the Watergate affair.

Friction between the cabinet and the White House was clearly identifiable in the Nixon administration. Even the nicknames used by each group to refer to the other were revealing. The cabinet referred to senior White House aides as 'the Berlin Wall' and 'the palace guard'. The White House Staff showed contempt for cabinet members when referring, for example, to Postmaster General William Blount as 'the postman' and to Transportation Secretary John Volpe as 'the bus driver'.

When President Carter was trying to sort out the sheep from the goats in his cabinet in mid-1979, the two tests of 'breeding' were, first, 'loyalty to the president' and, second, 'ability to work with the White House Staff'. He called all the cabinet to the presidential retreat of Camp David. In a rambling statement, the president — his eyes scanning those who were seated at the table — observed: 'There are times when you do not support the White House policy. I need your absolute loyalty.' For their part, the cabinet bitterly resented the powerful White House Staff members who had the proximity and access to the president that they clearly did not. Landon Butler, a senior aide in the Carter White House, pointed out that there is a danger of the White House coming to see cabinet officers as mere dogsbodies and that this poses serious difficulties. Interviewed in 1980, Butler stated:

> I think every [White House] staff can succumb to the temptation to treat cabinet officers as simply a group of people who we trot out to make speeches when we want them to make speeches, to say what we want them to say and then go quietly back to their offices. Whenever this happens, it always results in political disaster. It is the cabinet officer's role to provide leadership on the major issues. It is the staff's job to carry out decisions.

How can these problems be guarded against? First, it is critically important that the president clearly explains to each group what are, and what are not, its functions. Professor Richard Neustadt (2000) stated:

> The president must prepare the cabinet members against the shocking discovery that most of them are not the principal advisers to the president, are not going to be, and never will be.

Similarly, staff must be staff. Helmut Sonnenfeldt, an aide to Henry Kissinger in the Nixon and Ford administrations, identified the problem and the solution thus:

The staff capability, in order to be credible and accepted by the cabinet, has to be a neutral capability. The cabinet officer has to be certain that the paper he sends to the president gets to the president as he wrote it. If it's doctored, if it's changed, because you have strong policy advocacy in the White House staff, the credibility gets lost and you have chaos.

Second, it is important that the cabinet officers really do think about what the president wants and do not become ensnared by the iron triangle. One-time Transportation Secretary William Coleman put it this way:

Too many cabinet officers go away and become advocates of their departmental views and wishes. It's very easy to do that. But a cabinet officer should look only at the issues as *the president* sees them. It is the president who appointed him. Of all the other people President Ford could have had as transportation secretary, he chose me. So I saw it as my first job to do what the president wanted.

Third, it is helpful if the two sides meet regularly and are made to work together. This is why the use of cabinet councils by Reagan and Bush — both George and George W. — can be helpful. Cabinet councils are made up of both cabinet officers and those from EXOP. The Economic Policy cabinet council had 271 meetings during Reagan's first term — that's almost 70 meetings a year. This can help with the loyalty factor. Martin Anderson, a White House aide to President George Bush, stated:

Just the act of having to leave their fiefdoms, get into a car, and be driven to the White House, was a powerful reminder to every member of the cabinet that it was the president's business they were about, not theirs or their department's constituents.

Summary

EXOP–cabinet rivalries

➤ Because of their advantages of loyalty and proximity to the president, those who work in EXOP have distinct advantages over cabinet officers.
➤ This often leads to friction, distrust and harm to the president.
➤ The president needs to take steps to keep EXOP–cabinet rivalry to a minimum.

The president's relations with Congress

Almost every power that the president possesses is checked by Congress. The president, therefore, needs Congress's agreement. However, in a system of 'separated institutions sharing powers' this is by no means easy. Party links may not help much. The president and the majority of Congress may well be of different parties, as shown in Table 6.7. Even when the two branches are controlled by the same party, there is no guarantee of success

Table 6.7 Party control of Congress and the presidency, 1969–2004

Years	Party: President	House	Senate
1969–70	R: Nixon	D: 243–192	D: 57–43
1971–72	R: Nixon	D: 255–180	D: 55–45
1973–74	R: Nixon/Ford	D: 244–191	D: 57–43
1975–76	R: Ford	D: 291–144	D: 62–38
1977–78	**D: Carter**	**D: 291–143**	**D: 62–38**
1979–80	**D: Carter**	**D: 276–159**	**D: 59–41**
1981–82	R: Reagan	D: 243–192	R: 53–47
1983–84	R: Reagan	D: 269–166	R: 54–46
1985–86	R: Reagan	D: 253–182	R: 53–47
1987–88	R: Reagan	D: 258–177	D: 55–45
1989–90	R: Bush	D: 260–175	D: 55–45
1991–92	R: Bush	D: 267–167	D: 56–44
1993–94	**D: Clinton**	**D: 258–176**	**D: 58–42**
1995–96	D: Clinton	R: 230–204	R: 54–46
1997–98	D: Clinton	R: 227–207	R: 55–45
1999–2000	D: Clinton	R: 223–211	R: 55–45
January–May 2001	**R: George W. Bush**	**R: 221–212**	**R: 50–50**
June 2001–2002	R: George W. Bush	R: 221–212	D: 50–49
2003–2004	**R: George W. Bush**	**R:229–205**	**R: 51–48**

Note: **Bold** type indicates years during which House and Senate were controlled by the same party as the president

— witness the difficulties experienced by Bill Clinton in his failed attempt to pass health-care reforms in 1993–94. As Richard Neustadt (1960) stated: 'What the Constitution separates, the political parties do not combine.'

As Table 6.8 shows, the president can do very little without the agreement of Congress. There is an intricate system of checks and balances devised by the Founding Fathers, who wanted it to be difficult for the president to get his way in Congress. As Nelson Polsby (1976) put it: 'Conflict and cooperation between Congress and the president are not merely the result of whim or wilfulness at one end or the other of Pennsylvania Avenue.' Professor S. E. Finer (1970) has likened the president and Congress to 'two halves of a bank note, each useless without the other'. However, the Founding Fathers' desire for cooperation and compromise between these two branches of government — 'ambition must counteract ambition', as James Madison put it — often leads to inaction and gridlock.

There is a famous story of President Truman sitting at his Oval Office desk in December 1952, contemplating what it would be like for his successor coming into office in just a few weeks' time. His successor was to be Dwight Eisenhower — a former army

Table 6.8 Powers of the president and checks by Congress

Powers of the president	Checks by Congress
Propose legislation	Amend/block legislation
Submit the annual budget	Amend budget
Veto legislation	Override veto
Act as chief executive	Investigation/impeachment/removal
Nominate executive officials	Confirmation (Senate)
Nominate federal judges	Confirmation (Senate)
Negotiate treaties	Ratification (Senate)
Commander-in-chief of the armed forces	Declare war/power of the purse

general, affectionately known as 'Ike'. Truman was contemplating how strange it would be for the general-turned-president.

> He'll sit here and he'll say, 'Do this! Do that!' And nothing will happen. Poor Ike, it won't be a bit like the army. He'll find it very frustrating.

It would be 'not a bit like the army' because in the army Eisenhower could get what he wanted by issuing commands. As president, Eisenhower would learn that little happens as a result of command; most happens as a result of persuasion. Truman knew that. Earlier in his presidency he had remarked:

> I sit here all day trying to persuade people to do the things they ought to have the sense to do without my persuading them. That's all the powers of the president amount to.

As Richard Neustadt (1960) so succinctly put it: 'Presidential power is the power to persuade.' So how does the president persuade? There are essentially two methods: he can use other people; or he can get involved himself.

Persuasion through other people

The president, if he is to be a successful persuader, must work through a number of other people. He cannot — nor should he — try to do it all himself. There are four groups of people he can use. First, he can use the vice-president. All of the last five vice-presidents — covering a period of more than 25 years — have been former members of Congress. Bush's vice-president, Dick Cheney, spent 10 years as a member of the House of Representatives, rising to be minority whip — the second most senior House Republican. He was widely liked and respected on both sides of the aisle. Congressman Jerry Lewis (R–California), who was elected to Congress in 1978 with Cheney, put it like this:

> He's a great asset for the administration, especially in dealing with the House. He's always been a really great person to deal with legislators. He knows them well and has their confidence.

As President of the Senate, the vice-president has a foothold in Congress too. He has an office there, where he can meet with members of both houses.

Second, the president uses his own Congressional Liaison Staff. They are members of the White House Staff who work as full-time lobbyists for the president on Capitol Hill. They meet with members of Congress as well as with senior members of their staff. The Congressional Liaison Staff are usually organised in such a way that some work on the House side and others on the Senate side, hoping to build up good relationships with people whom they will get to know well.

Third, the cabinet officers can be deployed by the White House to talk with members of Congress in their own policy areas. George W. Bush used Education Secretary Rod Paige to sell his education reform package to Congress in 2001. The following year, Secretary of State Colin Powell was dispatched to Congress to help persuade members to support the authorisation of use of US troops against Iraq.

Finally, the president can work through the party leadership in Congress: the House Speaker; the majority and minority leaders of both houses; the party whips; the committee chairs and ranking minority members. The importance that the White House places on these people could be seen when, in December 2002, President George W. Bush quickly withdrew his support from the Republican leader in the Senate, Trent Lott, in December 2002 after Lott had made some unfortunate remarks about racial policy in America. Bush did not want to reduce the chances of his policy agenda being passed through the Senate by having Lott as the spokesman for it. The White House was clearly behind the plot to force Lott to resign and have him replaced by Senator Bill Frist, a close friend and political ally of the president.

Presidential persuasion

Any of these people, however, may report back to the president that, in order to secure the vote of a particular member of Congress, the president himself needs to get involved. As David Mervin (1993) stated:

> The president must bargain, he must make deals, he must negotiate with those with whom he shares power. Bargaining skill is therefore indispensable in a president.

The president may, for example, make a personal phone call to certain members of Congress. In an important budget vote in the House in August 1993, President Clinton phoned Democrat House member Marjorie Margolies-Mezvinsky in a hallway just off the chamber of the House of Representatives. She cast the crucial 218th vote to ensure passage of his budget by 218 votes to 216.

The president might offer help with legislation that benefits that member's state or district. He might offer to look more favourably on a judicial or executive branch appointment of interest to the member. The president might invite members of Congress for an Oval Office meeting — either individually or in a small group. He might even go to Capitol Hill to meet with a selected group of members of Congress there. If a member whose support is sought is of the president's party, the president might offer to campaign for them in the next congressional elections. A popular president can use this perk to great effect. If all else fails, the president might go on national television to appeal over the heads of Congress directly to the people. This is what President Johnson called 'putting Congress's feet to the fire'.

However, persuasion needs to be a two-way street. If members of Congress get the idea that the only time they hear from the president — either directly or indirectly — is when he wants them to cast a difficult vote for him, cooperation will soon dry up. Small courtesies from the White House can pay off. An invitation to a bill-signing ceremony, dinner with the president at the White House, a trip on Air Force One — all these small perks can help to make the wheels of cooperation turn more smoothly.

The results of presidential persuasion

David Mervin (1993) described the US president as 'bargainer-in-chief'. Presidents bargain for a purpose: that their legislation is passed, their appointments are confirmed, their budgets are agreed to, their vetoes are sustained and their treaties are ratified. As Mark Peterson (2000) stated: 'Leaders are those who make things happen that otherwise would not come about.' The president's success rate is measured each year in what is called the presidential support score. This annual statistic measures how often the president won in recorded votes in the House and Senate on which he took a clear position, expressed as a percentage of the whole.

Table 6.9, which shows the presidential support score since it was first published in 1953, reveals some interesting information. Presidential support tends to decline during a presidential term. Having one's party control both houses of Congress usually results in a high support score. Loss of control of Congress means a dip in the president's support score: witness Reagan in 1987 and Clinton in 1995. The score is a useful guide to presidential success, but it does have certain limitations.

First, the score does not measure the importance of votes. The president might win trivial votes while losing important ones or vice versa. Second, presidents can avoid low scores by simply not taking positions on votes they expect to lose. There has been a significant decline in recent years in the number of votes on which presidents have declared a position. In 1978, President Carter announced a position on 306 votes; in 1998, President Clinton announced a position on just 154; and in 2002, President George W. Bush announced a position on a mere 98 votes. Third, the score does not count bills that fail to come to a vote on the floor in either house. President Clinton's high score in 1994 took no account of the failure of his Healthcare Reform Bill even to reach the floor of either house, yet this was his flagship policy.

It is worth keeping in mind that changes in Congress — and more widely in the US political system — make the president's job of trying to build support for his legislation more difficult than was the case in the 1950s or 1960s. There are five possible reasons to consider.

Table 6.9 Presidential support score, 1953–2003

Year	President	Support score (%)	Year	President	Support score (%)
1953	Eisenhower	89.0	1978	Carter	78.3
1954	Eisenhower	82.8	1979	Carter	76.8
1955	Eisenhower	75.0	1980	Carter	75.1
1956	Eisenhower	70.0	1981	Reagan	82.4
1957	Eisenhower	68.0	1982	Reagan	72.4
1958	Eisenhower	76.0	1983	Reagan	67.1
1959	Eisenhower	52.0	1984	Reagan	65.8
1960	Eisenhower	65.0	1985	Reagan	59.9
1961	Kennedy	81.0	1986	Reagan	56.1
1962	Kennedy	85.4	1987	Reagan	43.5
1963	Kennedy	87.1	1988	Reagan	47.4
1964	Johnson	88.0	1989	Bush	62.6
1965	Johnson	93.0	1990	Bush	46.8
1966	Johnson	79.0	1991	Bush	54.2
1967	Johnson	79.0	1992	Bush	43.0
1968	Johnson	75.0	1993	Clinton	86.4
1969	Nixon	74.0	1994	Clinton	86.4
1970	Nixon	77.0	1995	Clinton	36.2
1971	Nixon	75.0	1996	Clinton	55.2
1972	Nixon	66.0	1997	Clinton	53.6
1973	Nixon	50.6	1998	Clinton	50.6
1974	Nixon	59.6	1999	Clinton	37.8
1974	Ford	58.2	2000	Clinton	55.0
1975	Ford	61.0	2001	George W. Bush	87.0
1976	Ford	53.8	2002	George W. Bush	87.8
1977	Carter	75.4	2003	George W. Bush	78.7

Source: *Congressional Quarterly*

First, recent decades witnessed declining levels of party discipline in Congress, although the mid-1990s did see a return to higher levels of partisanship in Congress. Second, it is less likely these days that the president and a majority of both houses of Congress will be of the same party. Third, members of Congress are now more aware of constituents' wishes — through the effects of such factors as C-SPAN and e-mail — and therefore are perhaps less willing merely to go along with what the president wants. Fourth, changes in the methods of selecting presidential candidates have resulted in

Washington outsiders becoming president — Governors Carter, Reagan, Clinton and George W. Bush. They know less about the workings of Congress than did presidents who had worked in Congress — Truman, Kennedy, Johnson, Nixon and Ford — and do not have the personal ties to members of Congress that presidents such as Truman and Johnson enjoyed. Finally, there has been a significant fragmentation of power within Congress. The power of the leadership has been eroded as Congress has become more democratic and power more diffused.

All this can make life frustrating for presidents. From Congress's perspective, former House Speaker Tom Foley looked back to the system of the 1950s:

> It isn't possible any more for the Speaker of the House — then Sam Rayburn — to call up the majority leader in the Senate — then Lyndon Johnson — and say, 'Lyndon, come on over.' And Lyndon would come over to the Speaker's office and they would agree on the legislative programme for the rest of the year. Then they would go down and visit President Eisenhower and tell him which bills would be passed and which would not. And the President would negotiate a bit with them, and they'd make some agreement and go back and it was done. Now, you have to negotiate with literally hundreds of members and this is an infuriating thing for the president to try and deal with.

The situation doesn't look any better from the White House perspective. Former Nixon White House aide John Ehrlichman saw similar frustrations:

> Every time President Nixon turned round there were new restraints on what he could do as president — in the conduct of the war in Vietnam, in dealing with domestic violence, in trying to balance the budget and things of that kind. So he was continually building coalitions in the Congress: on every issue that came up a new coalition — a few southerners, some Republicans, some interested Democrats who needed a judge approved in their District, or a bridge built, or a canal dug, or something of this kind — laborious step by step work, like putting together tiles in a great mosaic.

Summary

The president's relations with Congress

➤ The president faces significant checks from Congress and therefore needs to persuade members to support him.

➤ This is especially true during periods of 'divided government' when Congress is controlled by a different party from the president's.

➤ The president can use a number of persuasive methods.

➤ Presidential success in Congress has varied significantly both between and during different administrations.

Theories of presidential power

How powerful an office is the US presidency, if its limits, weaknesses and frustrations are taken into account?

The presidency has evolved significantly since the time of George Washington. Presidential scholars have used various terms to signal this evolution. The 'modern presidency' and the 'institutionalised presidency' both had their birth in the administration of Franklin Roosevelt (FDR). It was during FDR's presidency that the role of the federal government expanded significantly, EXOP was established and the USA took on its full-time world leadership role. The pendulum swung in the direction of presidential power and away from congressional authority. Congress seemed to become more subservient to the president. This trend continued with FDR's Democratic successors — Truman, Kennedy and Johnson — as well as with Republican Richard Nixon, who succeeded them.

The imperial presidency

Critics of this presidential assertiveness soon materialised. The one whose criticism received the widest recognition was Pulitzer prize-winning author and professor, Arthur Schlesinger. In 1973 he published *The Imperial Presidency* and the term became a catch-phrase for critics of the growth of presidential power. According to Schlesinger's thesis, 'the **imperial presidency** was essentially the creation of foreign policy'. He traces its origins to the Japanese attack on Pearl Harbor in December 1941 — a crisis that allowed FDR to break free from Congress's conventional ties on the executive.

Key term

> **Imperial presidency.** A term, popularised by the book of that title written in 1973 by Arthur Schlesinger, used to refer to a presidency characterised by the misuse and abuse of the powers of the presidency. In particular, it referred to excessive secrecy — especially in foreign policy — and high-handedness in dealing with Congress. The term was most widely used in reference to the presidencies of Lyndon Johnson (1963–69) and Richard Nixon (1969–74).

To see how quickly presidential power had increased, there is no need to look further back than 1950. When North Korea invaded South Korea that year, President Truman immediately sent US troops to South Korea without any congressional authorisation, and Congress raised barely a murmur. In 1958, President Eisenhower sent 14,000 US troops to Lebanon. Again, there was no congressional authorisation. In 1961, President Kennedy launched the disastrous attack on the Bay of Pigs in Cuba without congressional authorisation. Congress played no role at all in the Cuban missile crisis the following year. In 1964, Congress signed a virtual blank cheque — the Tonkin Gulf Resolution — to allow President Johnson to take 'all necessary measures' to sort out the problems in Vietnam. In 1970, President Nixon bombed Cambodia without even the knowledge, let alone the authorisation, of Congress.

The imperial presidency might have been the creation of foreign policy, but it soon spread to the conduct of domestic policy. President Nixon's policies to clamp down on the anti-Vietnam War protests smacked to some of excessive use of power. Even the way he organised and conducted business in the White House looked to some more like an emperor's court than a presidential office. The Watergate affair, which broke in 1972 and forced Nixon to resign in August 1974, added fuel to the fire. Watergate was about illegal bugging and break-ins, the payment of hush money, secrecy, impoundment of congressional funds and obstruction of justice — all at the very highest levels of the Nixon administration.

Was the 'imperial presidency' a reality or merely something conjured up by Nixon's critics? David Mervin (1990), one of a number of presidential scholars who are sceptical of the Schlesinger thesis, wrote:

> In the wake of Watergate and other scandals, the pejorative connotations of the imperial presidency gained added weight, but the concept was always something of a cliché. The word 'imperial' summons up images of the president as an emperor, a supreme sovereign authority, a master of all he surveys. Roosevelt, at the beginning of the 1930s and at the height of World War II, may have briefly approached such a position of pre-eminence, but none of his successors has come even close to such a situation.

Indeed, one could argue that Nixon's forced resignation was proof that the imperial presidency did *not* exist. In his resignation statement, Nixon said he was resigning because 'I no longer have a strong enough political base in the Congress.' Nixon resigned, forced out by Congress. In his own memoirs, Nixon (1978) stated that he believed that:

> The 'imperial presidency' was a straw man created by defensive congressmen and disillusioned liberals who in the days of FDR and John Kennedy had idolised the ideal of a strong presidency. Now that they had a strong president who was a Republican — and Richard Nixon at that — they were having second thoughts.

In 1986, even Schlesinger recanted his thesis to some extent.

Congress's reaction to the 'imperial presidency' was re-assertiveness. They passed a number of pieces of presidency-curbing legislation, especially in the field of foreign policy. The Case Act (1972) forced presidents to inform Congress of all executive agreements made with foreign states. The War Powers Act (1973) attempted to limit presidents' use of troops unless Congress declared war or gave 'specific statutory authorisation'. Thus, Presidents Ford and Carter — the immediate post-Watergate presidents — found their hands much more tied. In 1975, President Ford found he was impotent when the North Vietnamese communists finally overran the South Vietnamese capital, Saigon, including the US embassy compound in the city. Ford complained of congressional meddling in presidential powers. During his campaign for re-election in 1976, Ford protested: 'Our forefathers knew you could not have 535 commanders-in-chief and secretaries of state, it just would not work.' In an article for *Time* magazine 4 years later, Ford wrote:

> Some people used to complain about what they called an 'imperial presidency'. But now the pendulum has swung too far in the opposite direction. We have not an imperial presidency but an imperilled presidency. Under today's rules, which include some misguided 'reforms', the presidency does not operate effectively. That is a very serious development, and it is harmful to our overall national interests.

Ironically, Ford's article was published in the edition of *Time* magazine (10 November 1980) which announced the defeat of President Carter by Governor Ronald Reagan in the previous week's election.

The post-imperial presidency

Reagan's 8 years in the White House meant that the 'imperilled presidency' thesis had to be rewritten. In contrast to the 'failed', one-term presidents Ford and Carter, Reagan launched an ambitious legislative programme at home, restored America's damaged self-confidence abroad and was re-elected by a landslide in 1984. He even managed to pass on the mantle to his vice-president, George Bush, in the 1988 election.

At home the economy boomed — though so did the federal budget deficit. It was 'morning again in America', according to Reagan's 1984 television commercials. Abroad, Reagan called the Soviet Union 'the evil empire'. In 1987, Reagan even went to Berlin's Brandenburg Gate and declared: 'Mr Gorbachev, open this gate! Mr Gorbachev, tear down this wall!' His call did not have instant effect, but the Berlin Wall eventually fell. The Soviet Union collapsed. The USA was the world's only superpower. Presidential power was back.

George Bush's presidency, successful in foreign policy, fell on the economic recession at home in the early 1990s and Americans' growing concerns about the ballooning federal budget deficit. Enter Bill Clinton, under whose stewardship the economy boomed. Clinton's contribution to the presidency, however, was to repeat Nixon's sin and besmirch its aura and compromise its integrity. Monica Lewinsky was not Watergate. Clinton survived his impeachment trial in the Senate and became the first Democrat president to serve two terms since FDR. But the tawdry affair, the lying, the attempts at concealment, the hair-splitting legalisms all served to diminish the office of the presidency. Political commentator Elizabeth Drew (1999) wrote:

> The presidency must have a certain aura of majesty and mystique. Clinton's lack of dignity, not to mention his sexual recklessness, was an assault on the office itself.

It also harmed his ability to work effectively.

The events of 11 September 2001 may well have implications for the office of the presidency. In a crisis, Americans traditionally look to the president, rather than Congress, for both action and reassurance. But the history of presidential power over the last 50 or so years tells us that power is a variable, and that presidential power is cyclical. It varies according to the personality of the president as well as the 'state of the Union'.

What we can say is that presidential power is limited — the Founding Fathers intended it to be so. All this makes being a successful and effective president exceedingly difficult.

Box 6.2 Quotations on presidential power

'Weakness is still what I see; weakness in the sense of a great gap between what is expected of a man (or, some day, a woman) and assured capacity to carry through.'

Richard Neustadt (2000)

'The presidency is not a powerful office... . Presidents cannot command obedience to their wishes but must persuade.'

James Pfiffner (2000)

'Leadership is difficult precisely because the framers of the Constitution wanted it to be so. ...Opportunities to check power abound; opportunities to exercise power are limited.'

Thomas Cronin and Michael Genovese (1998)

'Novelist Somerset Maugham once said, "There are three rules for writing a good novel. Unfortunately, no one knows what they are." We are tempted to conclude that there are three rules to being an effective president, yet no one knows exactly what they are.'

Thomas Cronin and Michael Genovese (1998)

Summary

Theories of presidential power
- ➤ The theory of the 'imperial presidency' was popular in the 1960s and 1970s.
- ➤ Later, commentators worried about what they called the 'imperilled presidency'.
- ➤ Presidential power is limited; it is also a variable that inevitably goes through discernible cycles.

Limits on presidential power

There are limits on the president's powers, which fall into seven broad areas.

Congress
The checks and balances that Congress has on the president are highly significant, even to the ultimate check of removal from office.

The Supreme Court
The Supreme Court (see Chapters 8 and 9) can declare the actions of any member of the executive branch, including the president, to be unconstitutional. Nixon felt this in *United States v. Richard M. Nixon* (1974), the court judgment that led within days to his

resignation. Clinton felt it in *William Jefferson Clinton v. Paula Corbin Jones* (1997), the judgment that resulted in President Clinton having to answer questions from Ms Jones's lawyers. They asked about a certain Monica Lewinsky, and the rest, as they say, is history.

These two branches provide the constitutional limits on presidential power, but there are extra-constitutional limitations too.

Public opinion

Public opinion is a limitation. President Clinton discovered how important public approval was to his continuing in the White House. He survived his many scandals mainly because his public opinion ratings remained high. President Nixon saw the other side of the coin. President George W. Bush's approval rating rose from 51% in the first week of September 2001 to 86% in the second week. When the 2002 mid-term elections came round, he enjoyed the highest public opinion rating of any president at that point in his term of office since polling began and saw gains for his party in both houses of Congress in those elections.

Pressure groups

Pressure groups can mobilise public opinion either for or against the president himself or his policies (see Chapter 4).

The media

The media have a role to play here too. Presidents today live in an era of the 24-hour news cycle. As a result, what the media report and say can profoundly limit what presidents can do: examples are Johnson in Vietnam, Carter in Iran and Clinton in the area of healthcare reform.

The federal bureaucracy

The federal bureaucracy limits the president's powers. The president is only one person in an executive branch made up of 15 executive departments and around 60 other federal government agencies, boards and commissions employing some 3 million civil servants. Getting the federal bureaucracy to *do* something can be a challenge to any president. Moreover, it is not just the federal government that limits the president. Many federal government programmes are implemented — or not — by state and local governments across the USA. Some southern state governors were able to frustrate Presidents Eisenhower, Kennedy and Johnson over civil rights reforms.

Other factors

As if these were not enough, there are other potential limitations on the president's power. One is his own professional reputation — what members of Congress, state governors and city mayors think of him. The quality of the staff he chooses for the executive branch — especially in the White House — is vital. President Clinton got himself into all kinds of political problems in the first year of his presidency because he had appointed some people to top White House jobs who were ill-qualified to do them. 'This White

House is arrogant, lying, incompetent and stupid. Not the president, I mean those jerks he has around him,' one disgruntled political observer commented in 1993.

The level of unity displayed by the president's party is important too. President Clinton would have got his healthcare reforms through Congress, had his party been united behind them. Equally, he would not have survived impeachment had the Democrats deserted him.

Crises can limit what a president can do. What might President Carter have achieved, had not the last 14 months of his presidency been given over to trying to solve the Iranian hostage crisis? Even luck can take a hand. It was surely bad lack that American hostages were taken prisoner by the Iranians on 4 November 1979. It just so happened that 4 November 1980 — the day marking the hostages' full year in captivity — was election day. It is not hard to guess what the media spent their time talking about, just as people were going to the polls.

The test for any president is both to work within these limitations and to ensure that they do not shackle him. He needs to persuade Congress, to woo public opinion, to use the media to his advantage, to control the federal bureaucracy and to unite his party even as he works to divide the opposition. The electorate does not want to hear that the president could not deliver his promises because of the limits upon his office. As David Mervin (1993) stated: 'Given the plethora of potential obstacles that stand in their way, it sometimes seems almost miraculous that presidents accomplish anything at all.'

Summary

Limits on presidential power
➢ Presidents face significant limits on their power from a variety of sources.
➢ Some are more within the president's control than others.
➢ The test of presidential success is to be able to achieve stated goals despite limitations.

Exercises

1 What kind of presidency did the Founding Fathers create?
2 Outline the principal powers of the president.
3 How do vice-presidents come to office?
4 What are the vice-president's powers?
5 Explain why modern vice-presidents have become more important.
6 Explain how the president's cabinet came into existence.
7 What are the major pools of recruitment for the president's cabinet?
8 Explain in what ways a president might seek to appoint a 'balanced' cabinet.
9 How often are cabinet meetings held? Who attends them?

10 Explain the functions that cabinet meetings can fulfil — both for the president and for cabinet officers themselves.

11 Explain how cabinet councils work.

12 What are the main reasons why the president's cabinet can never be especially important?

13 Explain how and why the Executive Office of the President (EXOP) came into existence.

14 What are the functions of: (a) the White House Staff; (b) the National Security Council; (c) the Office of Management and Budget?

15 Explain why there are often rivalries and difficulties between the EXOP and the cabinet.

16 Who might the president use in trying to persuade members of Congress to support his proposals?

17 What methods of persuasion might the president use on members of Congress?

18 Explain what the 'presidential support score' is.

19 What are the main changes that have occurred in Congress which make it more difficult these days for the president to get his way in Congress?

20 What was meant by 'the imperial presidency'?

21 How did Congress react to the so-called 'imperial presidency'?

22 Briefly assess the success or failure of the presidents who held office between 1974 and 2000: Ford, Carter, Reagan, Bush and Clinton.

23 What are the main limits on presidential power?

Exam focus

1 Does the president's cabinet fulfil any useful functions?

2 Examine the importance of the Executive Office of the President.

3 How can a president successfully coordinate the work of his administration?

4 Assess the difficulties that presidents face in their dealings with Congress.

5 How accurate is it to describe the president as 'bargainer-in-chief'?

6 Examine the claim that 'the president's power is the power to persuade'.

7 Assess the accuracy of Pfiffner's claim that 'the presidency is not a powerful office'.

References

Cronin, T. E. and Genovese, M. A., *The Paradoxes of the American Presidency* (Oxford University Press, 1998).

Drew, E., *The Corruption of American Politics* (Birch Lane Press, 1999).

Fenno, R. F., *The President's Cabinet* (Harvard University Press, 1959).

Finer, S. E., *Comparative Government* (Penguin, 1970).

Mervin, D., *Ronald Reagan and the American Presidency* (Longman, 1990).

Mervin, D., *The President of the United States* (Harvester-Wheatsheaf, 1993).

Neustadt, R. E., in Felzenberg, A. S. (ed.) *The Keys to a Successful Presidency* (The Heritage Foundation, 2000).

Nixon, R. M., *RN: The Memoirs of Richard Nixon* (Sidgwick and Jackson, 1978).

Peterson, M. A., 'Presidential power and the potential for leadership', in Shapiro, R. Y. et al. (eds), *Presidential Power: Forging the Presidency for the 21st Century* (Columbia University Press, 2000).

Pfiffner, J., *The Modern Presidency* (Bedford-St Martin's, 2000).

Polsby, N. W., *Congress and the Presidency* (Prentice-Hall, 1976).

Schlesinger, A. M., *The Cycles of American History* (Houghton Mifflin, 1986).

Woodward, B., *Bush At War* (Simon and Schuster, 2003).

Further reading

Bennett, A. J., 'A heartbeat away from the presidency', *Politics Review*, vol. 11, no. 2, November 2001.

Bennett, A. J., 'What makes a good president?', *Politics Review*, vol. 13, no. 1, September 2003.

Busby, R., 'The American presidency: imperial or imperilled?', *Politics Review*, vol. 12, no. 2, November 2002.

Gould, L. L., *The Modern American Presidency* (Kansas University Press, 2003).

Peele, G., 'The Clinton legacy and the US presidency', *Politics Review*, vol. 10, no. 2, November 2000.

Pfiffner, J., *Understanding the Presidency* (Addison Wesley Longman, 2000).

Chapter 7

The federal bureaucracy

At the beginning of Chapter 6, we observed that the president is not a one-man band. Indeed, it would be quite impossible for the president to try to run the executive branch of government single-handedly. We have already seen in the previous chapter all that exists within the White House — the president, the vice-president, the cabinet, cabinet councils and the Executive Office of the President. But the executive branch of government is more than just the White House. There is a vast federal bureaucracy, which those who work in the White House are trying to coordinate. Some of that federal bureaucracy is based in downtown Washington, but there are significant parts spread throughout all 50 states.

The federal bureaucracy grew significantly during the twentieth century as the size and scope of the federal government itself expanded. This expansion was brought about by a number of important developments in US society, such as industrialisation, immigration, westward expansion, the New Deal and the development of modern means of communication such as road, rail and air, as well as the telephone, radio and the new electronic media. Furthermore, the USA's development into a world power from the 1950s — and into the world's sole superpower by the end of the century — added to the responsibilities laid at the door of the federal government. Such a rapid and significant expansion brought problems to presidents from Franklin Roosevelt onwards which would have been almost — if not entirely — unknown to their predecessors. Even in the last two decades, two new executive departments have been created, reflecting the growing importance of the policy areas for which they have oversight — Veterans' Affairs and Homeland Security. The federal bureaucracy has now grown to a size quite unimaginable at the beginning of the twentieth century.

Questions to be answered in this chapter

➤ What is the structure of the federal bureaucracy?

➤ Why has the size of the federal bureaucracy grown?

➤ What are its principal functions?

➤ How are the personnel recruited and organised?

➤ What problems are associated with the federal bureaucracy?

➤ How is the power of the federal bureaucracy checked?

The structure of the federal bureaucracy

The federal bureaucracy can be defined as the administrative system of the national government that carries out policy. The term is synonymous with 'the executive branch of government' or 'the administration'. To some, 'bureaucracy' is also synonymous with excessive red tape, delay, over-manning, inefficiency and waste, as well as an over-commitment to routine, hierarchy and 'process', and a resistance to change.

By 2001, the federal bureaucracy had 2,697,602 civilian employees and an annual payroll of $11,369,841,107. Needless to say, these nearly 3 million civil servants are not all based in Washington DC. The city isn't big enough — only 11% of federal civil servants work in the Washington area. The federal bureaucracy is spread throughout the length and breadth of the United States. This was most dramatically brought home to ordinary people when the *federal* government building in Oklahoma City was blown up in 1995. Almost every respectable-sized city in America contains such a building. These facts of size and geographic dispersal throughout America bring significant managerial problems.

The federal bureaucracy can be divided into four broad categories.

Executive departments

The executive departments might be thought of as the 'giants' of the federal bureaucracy. Initially, there were only three — State, War and the Treasury. Today there are 15 (see Table 7.1), with a great range in size, both of personnel and budget. The heads of these executive departments are designated as the 'secretary' — secretary of state, secretary of defense and so on — with the exception of the head of the Justice Department, who has the title of attorney general. These 15 heads of the executive departments are ex officio members of the president's cabinet (see Chapter 6).

Within these executive departments, there are two 'tiers' — the first tier made up of State, Treasury, Defense and Justice; the second tier comprising all the rest. The first-tier departments are regarded as the most prestigious and important parts of the federal bureaucracy.

The State Department conducts foreign policy, represents the United States abroad and conducts treaty negotiations on the president's behalf. The influence of the State Department varies considerably, depending upon the importance given to foreign policy in any administration, the degree to which the president himself wishes to be involved in the development and conduct of foreign policy, and the forcefulness of its secretary. Some secretaries of state have been significant persons who have played an important role in shaping and conducting foreign policy, notably George Marshall (1947–49), John Foster Dulles (1953–59), Dean Rusk (1961–69), George Shultz (1982–89) and Colin Powell (2001–). Others have had a lower profile, notably William Rogers (1969–73) and Warren Christopher (1993–97).

The Treasury Department deals with tax policy and collection, public debt management, and coin and currency manufacture. Nearly three-quarters of its employees work for the Internal Revenue Service (IRS). However, it does not have the oversight of either budgetary or monetary policy: the former is the territory of the Office of Management and Budget within the White House, while the latter is overseen by the Federal Reserve Board. Some secretaries of the treasury have played pivotal roles in recent administrations, such as Lloyd Bentsen and Robert Rubin during the Clinton administration.

Table 7.1 Creation of executive departments

Department	Created
State	1789
Treasury	1789
Defense[a]	1949
Interior	1849
Justice	1870
Agriculture	1889
Commerce[b]	1903
Labor[c]	1903
Health and Human Services[d]	1953
Housing and Urban Development	1965
Transportation	1966
Energy	1977
Education[e]	1979
Veterans Affairs	1989
Homeland Security	2002

[a] Formerly War Department (created 1789); amalgamated with Navy (1798) and Air Force (1947). [b] Commerce and Labor created as a joint department (1903); separated in 1913. [c] Commerce and Labor created as a joint department (1903); separated in 1913. [d] Formerly Health, Education and Welfare; Education separated in 1979. [e] Formerly part of Health, Education and Welfare (created 1953); separated in 1979.

The Defense Department is often referred to by the name of the building that houses it — the Pentagon. Its importance has waxed and waned as the defence policy of various administrations has changed. Under interventionist Republican administrations — such as those of Nixon, Reagan and Bush — the Defense Department has swallowed a large segment of the federal budget and played a significant part in the USA's 'world policeman' role. The names of secretaries of defense such as Caspar Weinberger (1981–87), Dick Cheney (1989–93) and Donald Rumsfeld (2001–) are synonymous with increased defence spending and the use of the US military abroad. During the Carter and Clinton administrations, Harold Brown, Les Aspin, William Perry and William Cohen played a more restrained role.

The Justice Department offers legal advice to the president and represents the executive branch of the federal government in court. It investigates federal crimes, enforces federal law and operates federal prisons. In recent decades it has had to deal with a number of hot political issues, such as abortion, gun control, immigration, discrimination and topics concerning civil rights and liberties. Through the 1960s, 1970s and 1980s, the post of attorney general — the head of the Justice Department — became synonymous with 'cronyism', appointing friends to political office. John Kennedy even went as far as appointing his brother Robert to the post. Nixon appointed long-time friend John Mitchell. Carter followed suit with Griffin Bell; Reagan with William French Smith. This pattern was broken by Clinton's appointment of Janet Reno — the first woman to head the department. Under George W. Bush, the role of Attorney General John Ashcroft was much enhanced by the events of 11 September 2001.

Executive agencies

The executive agencies are almost indistinguishable from the executive departments, except that their heads — known usually as 'directors' — are not ex officio members of the cabinet. Like the heads of the executive departments, they are appointed by the president with the advice and consent of the Senate. A number of executive agencies — such as housing and veterans' affairs — have, over the years, been upgraded into executive departments.

The Environmental Protection Agency (EPA) was created by President Nixon in 1970. It regulates air and water pollution controls, deals with the clean-up and disposal of hazardous wastes and toxic substances, and regulates drinking water, noise and radiation. The EPA has become something of a 'Cinderella agency' — incoming presidents have promised much but have often produced little in the way of effective environmental policy. Both Carol Browner under Bill Clinton and Christine Todd Whitman under George W. Bush were appointed amid a blaze of publicity but quickly faded into obscurity. The agency has frequently been mentioned for full department status, but as long as Republicans remain in control of Congress this seems unlikely.

The Federal Reserve Board — known colloquially as 'the Fed' — conducts the monetary policy of the federal government, oversees the supervision of banks and enforces the laws to protect consumers in financial dealings. The Fed has of late become closely associated with the name of its chairman Alan Greenspan, appointed in 1987 by President Reagan and reappointed by Presidents Clinton and George W. Bush.

The National Aeronautics and Space Administration (NASA) conducts space exploration and aeronautic research. After the heady days of the moon programme in the 1960s and 1970s it was seen during the 1980s and 1990s as something of a falling star. The loss of the Challenger (1986) and Columbia (2003) missions led to further questioning of its efficiency and viability. The space station project is now struggling to obtain adequate funds from Congress.

Independent regulatory commissions

The independent regulatory commissions (IRCs) occupy a special status in the federal bureaucracy, for they are administratively independent of all three branches of the federal government. They operate behind barriers created by Congress to shield them from direct presidential control. In practice, however, they are subject to pressures not only from the White House, but also from Congress and the industries and groups they are meant to regulate. An IRC might regulate railways, airlines, radio and television, banks, Wall Street, labour unions, business corporations or federal elections.

The first IRCs were created towards the end of the nineteenth century, after the Sherman Act (1890) ushered in the era of 'trust busting' — legal action taken to break up monopolies or trusts which under law were determined to be illegally restraining competition. It was the coming of the New Deal in the 1930s that really pushed the federal government into the regulation business.

The Consumer Product Safety Commission (CPSC), created in 1972, sets safety standards for products and has the ability to ban the sale of those products that do not satisfy them. Toy safety and bicycle helmets have been two high-profile issues.

The Federal Election Commission (FEC), created in 1975, was one of the chief products of the post-Watergate reforms. The FEC enforces federal election laws and administers the distribution of 'matching funds' to presidential candidates as well as overseeing the financial disclosures of fundraising and spending by candidates and their campaign committees.

The Federal Trade Commission (FTC) is a product of an earlier era, established in 1914. It deals with consumer protection and anti-trust law enforcement. It is backed by a federal law that states simply: 'Unfair competition in commerce is hereby declared illegal.' It investigates allegations of price fixing, deceptive advertising, mislabelling and false packaging.

Government corporations

Beginning in the 1930s, the federal government established various corporations, some quite high profile, to perform principally commercial functions that might otherwise have been carried out by the private sector. The United States Postal Service was created in 1970 out of the former Post Office Department. The Federal Deposit Insurance Corporation (FDIC) insures savings deposits in commercial banks; outside every bank in the USA is a sign that reads simply: 'Member FDIC.' If you take a passenger train from, say, Washington DC to New York or Boston, your journey will be on AMTRAK, the corporation that runs the nationwide passenger train system.

Summary

Structure of the federal bureaucracy

➢ The federal bureaucracy is organised into four different categories: executive departments, agencies, independent regulatory commissions and government corporations.

➢ The executive departments are the 'giants' of the federal bureaucracy, employing millions of people and spending huge budgets.

Growth of the federal bureaucracy

This subject was touched on in two previous chapters — when looking at the changing relationship between the federal and state governments in Chapter 1, and, briefly, in accounting for the need of the president to expand his in-house support in the White House in Chapter 6.

From Table 7.1 above, it can be seen that the number and range of the federal government's executive departments expanded significantly during the last decade of the twentieth century. At the birth of the nation, three executive departments — State, War and the Treasury — were sufficient to look after the scope of the federal government. In other words, in the late eighteenth century, the federal government handled principally three things: diplomacy, war and money. Everything else, such as it was, was the job of the state governments. There were a significant number of policy areas that concern the federal government today but which did not then concern any level of government — federal, state or local.

The first factor that caused the growth of the federal government was the nation's growth. As the nation spread westwards in the nineteenth century, land, law and order, and agriculture became issues for the federal government. This brought about the birth of three new departments: Interior, Justice and Agriculture. Because of industrialisation in the first decade of the twentieth century, the departments of Commerce and Labor were created — initially as one department, then separated 10 years later.

It was not until the second half of the twentieth century that the effects of Roosevelt's New Deal and America's position as a world power were truly felt in the organisation of the federal bureaucracy. By this time, the federal government was taking over responsibility for the running of such policy areas as health, education, housing, cities, transport and energy. These policy areas generated five new executive departments in just over 25 years. Meanwhile, America's world power status and emergence as a superpower brought about the reorganisation of the departments of the Army, Navy and Air Force into the huge Department of Defense (1949), together with the two most recently created executive departments — one to oversee provision for the USA's war veterans, another to coordinate domestic security. While all this was going on at the very top of the federal bureaucracy, lower down there were equally dramatic changes in the creation of dozens of new federal agencies, regulatory commissions and government corporations.

Summary

Growth of the federal bureaucracy

➤ The growth of the federal bureaucracy reflects the significant changes that have taken place in US history over the past two centuries.

➤ Most significant are those changes that have occurred in the last 50 years associated with Roosevelt's 'New Deal' and the USA's emergence as a superpower.

Functions of the federal bureaucracy

The federal bureaucracy has three principal functions: executing laws, creating rules and adjudication.

Executing laws

The Constitution states in Article II, Section 2 that the president shall 'take care that the laws be faithfully executed'. This is the main reason why the president needs the federal bureaucracy. It is also one of the reasons why, as Congress has legislated in more and more policy areas over the decades, the federal bureaucracy has of necessity become larger. Congress passes bills; the president signs them into law. The federal bureaucracy must then see that they are carried out: that mail is delivered

The Pentagon — headquarters of the US Department of Defense

(the United States Postal Service); taxes are collected (the IRS); planes are inspected (the Federal Aviation Administration); the country protected (the Pentagon); and the national parks preserved (the Department of the Interior). This is the principal function of the executive departments — carrying out the laws within their own policy areas.

Creating rules

Legislators usually establish only the broad principles of policy. It is the bureaucrats who are required to write the specific rules that decide how the laws will be executed. The more complex society has become, the greater the need for specialist bureaucrats to create specific rules. It is in this function that the regulatory commissions of the federal government play a significant role.

Adjudication

In executing laws and creating rules, disputes inevitably arise. One party will consider that a law is not being applied rigorously, while another will consider that its application has been partial or unfair. It is a function of the federal bureaucracy to adjudicate in such disputes.

Summary

Functions of the federal bureaucracy

➤ The federal bureaucracy has three principal functions: executing laws; creating rules; and adjudication.

Personnel of the federal bureaucracy

It is a widely accepted belief that recruitment to and promotion within the federal bureaucracy should be on the basis of merit, not political favouritism. Thus, the Civil Service Reform Act (1978) established the Office of Personnel Management (OPM) to manage those who work within the federal bureaucracy. The OPM develops the rules, regulations and policies for federal personnel management. It oversees recruitment, evaluation, investigation, training and retirement programmes. It also supervises affirmative action programmes and the requirements of the Ethics in Government Act (1978) as it pertains to federal employees.

However, federal civil service recruitment is more decentralised and politicised than these basic rules of thumb seem to imply. First, in recent years, the OPM has offloaded many of its recruitment responsibilities to individual agency heads. Second, recruitment to upper- and middle-level jobs is more political than appears at first glance.

At the upper level, some posts — comprising some 3% of the federal bureaucracy — are appointed on grounds of politics rather than purely on merit. First and foremost are those appointments, authorised by the Constitution and by law, that the president can make of cabinet and sub-cabinet officials, judges, attorneys, ambassadors and various members of boards and commissions. These appointments are subject to confirmation by the Senate. In addition, 'Schedule C' appointments to jobs in the departments and agencies, described as being of a 'confidential or policy-determining character', are available to an incoming president to fill with so-called political appointees. In 1961, President Kennedy had 451 such posts to fill. President Clinton in 1993 had well over 2,000.

Even in the middle-level appointments, there is a certain degree of political appointment in what is known as the 'buddy system'. This is based on what is called the 'name-request job'. This process is similar to one used by most private businesses or organisations. A person learns of a job from someone who already has one, or the head of an agency decides in advance whom they wish to recruit to a certain post. The agency must still send a form describing the job to the OPM, but it also names the person whom it wishes to appoint.

The overwhelming majority of people who work in the federal bureaucracy are career civil servants recruited on the basis of competitive examinations and for the particular skills that they possess, be they economists, nuclear physicists, statisticians or computer programmers. This has been the case ever since the old 'spoils system' was replaced by a merit system in the Civil Service Reform Act of 1883, known as the Pendleton Act. The act was a direct result of the assassination of President James Garfield in 1881 by someone who would forever be described in history books as 'a disappointed office seeker'.

President-elect Bill Clinton claimed in 1992 that he wanted a cabinet that 'looked like America'. Few thought that his initial cabinet looked much 'like America', but what about the federal bureaucracy? By the time Clinton entered the White House, the federal civil service certainly looked much more like America than it had done when President Kennedy arrived in the Oval Office 32 years earlier. In 1961, only 25% of the civil service was female. By 1993, that figure had risen to 43%. In 1961, it would have been hard to find any ethnic minorities in the federal civil service. Kennedy even commented, apparently disapprovingly, on their absence from his inaugural parade. By 1993, ethnic minorities made up 28% of the federal civil service. However, a civil servant from an ethnic minority is more likely to be a lower- than a higher-grade worker. Recent figures show that, whereas in the lower grades (GS 1–4) 31% of civil servants are black and 8% Hispanic, in the higher grades (GS 13–15) only 8% are black and just 3.5% Hispanic. The Department of Veterans' Affairs appoints significantly from among war veterans, with disabled veterans being given some preference.

Summary

Personnel of the federal bureaucracy

➤ While most posts in the federal bureaucracy are filled on merit, a number of upper-level posts are political appointments.

➤ Recruitment to the federal bureaucracy has recently been decentralised.

➤ But the overwhelming number of federal civil servants are careerists who remain in place under administrations of both parties.

➤ Appointment of women, racial minorities and disabled persons is an issue in the federal bureaucracy.

Problems of the federal bureaucracy

Robert Singh (2002) described six main problems commonly identified with the federal bureaucracy. To these, it is possible to add a further two.

Clientelism

Agencies tend to serve the interests of those whom they are supposed to be overseeing. This is seen as a particular problem with the regulatory commissions, as these watchdog agencies often turn out to be lapdogs. Special interests are protected at the expense of the public interest.

Imperialism

Agencies invariably seek to expand their powers and responsibilities at the expense of other agencies. Political interests become paramount, sometimes regardless of the public interest. Imperialism sometimes manifests itself in 'turf battles' between agencies over who has jurisdiction over which policy area. This was seen in the battles that ensued at the time of the creation of the new Department of Homeland Security in the second year of the George W. Bush administration.

Parochialism

Agencies tend to focus narrowly on their own goals rather than on the 'big picture' of the administration as a whole, and departmental interest often triumphs at the expense of national interest.

Incrementalism

Most agencies are known for acting slowly and cautiously, with a tendency to resist change. This can make life frustrating for an incoming president who wants to see radical policy changes being made. Agencies are seen as overly conservative, too resistant to change.

Arbitrariness

In applying rules and regulations, agencies often ignore the particular concerns or specific merits of those who will be affected by the rules. Bureaucracy is seen as inhuman and over-committed to form and process.

Waste

Because of their size and dedication to routine, agencies tend to use resources less efficiently than private sector organisations. This is sometimes linked to a perceived lack of accountability.

Iron triangles

The term **iron triangle** is used to describe a strong, resilient relationship between three distinct political bodies: special interests (often represented by interest groups); congressional committees; and the related agency. This relationship results in policies being made and executed to the mutual benefit of the three parties involved. Such iron triangles are generally considered to have a negative impact on the policy-making and policy-execution processes. An example is the relationship between defence contractors, the House and Senate Armed Services Committees and the Defense Department, which results in a large national defence budget.

Key term

> **Iron triangle.** A strong relationship between pressure groups, congressional committees and federal agencies in a given policy area for the mutual benefit of these three parties.

'Going native'

There is always a fear in the White House of the political appointees in the federal bureaucracy '**going native**'. This means that, rather than imposing the president's wishes on the bureaucracy, they become advocates of the bureaucracy's wishes to the president and start to resist his policy preferences. The term derives from a comment made by John Ehrlichman, a senior aide in the Nixon administration, who complained that members of Nixon's cabinet had gone off and 'married the natives'. The picture here is perhaps that of Christian missionaries going to foreign countries to 'convert the natives'. Under this scenario, rather than converting them to their beliefs, they marry them and adopt the native customs and ways of looking at the world.

Key term
> **'Going native'.** A term used to refer to the situation in which political appointees cease to be advocates for the politician who appointed them — in this case, the president — and instead become advocates for the bureaucracies and special interests associated with their policy area.

Richard Fenno likewise noted that the president's influence over the bureaucracy 'becomes splintered and eroded as [members of the bureaucracy] respond to political forces not presidential in origin and direction'. One way round this problem is to appoint close and trusted friends to key posts in the federal bureaucracy. Both Presidents Bush have adopted this strategy with some success.

Summary

Problems of the federal bureaucracy
> There are a number of significant problems identified with the federal bureaucracy.
> As well as those problems associated with bureaucracies in most political systems, two give further cause for concern: iron triangles and 'going native'.

Checking the power of the federal bureaucracy

The power of the federal bureaucracy is checked in the main by Congress. It is Congress that has the legislative power to establish, merge or abolish departments and agencies. Congress has reorganised the federal bureaucracy on a number of occasions, as shown in Table 7.1. There was a substantial reorganisation in 2002 when Congress extracted 170,000 current federal government employees from 22 different agencies — including the departments of Justice, Treasury, Agriculture, Transportation, Health, Energy, Defense and Commerce — and merged them to form the new Department of Homeland Security. A number of big-name agencies were drawn into the new department, including the Federal Emergency Management Agency (FEMA), the US Customs Service, the US Coast Guard, the Immigration and Naturalisation Service (INS) and the Secret Service.

Congress can use its appropriations power — the 'power of the purse' — to finance the various departments and agencies within the federal bureaucracy. During the Reagan–Bush era (1981–93), for example, the budget of the Consumer Product Safety Commission was cut from $42 million to just over $30 million. A staff of 812 in 1981 was down to 519 by 1989.

Congress can use its power of oversight to investigate federal departments and agencies. Such oversight is conducted largely in the policy specialist standing committees of both houses of Congress (see Chapter 5). Here, members build up policy expertise over many years. Given the high rates of incumbency — especially in the House of Representatives — bureaucrats have every reason to fear the spotlight of key members of the relevant congressional committees, who are likely to remain in office long after a president and his entourage have vacated the White House.

In contrast, most modern-day presidents have gone on record as saying that they found it well nigh impossible to control the federal bureaucracy. Harry Truman (1945–53) once commented: 'I thought I was the president, but when it comes to these bureaucracies, I can't make them do a damn thing.' Lyndon Johnson (1963–69) made this remark about members of his cabinet:

> When I looked at the heads of my departments, I realised that while all of them had been appointed by me, not a single one was really mine. Here I was working night and day to build the Great Society...and I couldn't even count on my own administrative family for complete support.

Jimmy Carter (1977–81) found that the situation had changed little by the time he arrived in the Oval Office — he was driven to commenting: 'Before I became president, I was warned that dealing with the federal bureaucracy would be one of the worst problems I would have to face. It has been even worse than I had anticipated.'

Following Jimmy Carter into the White House, Ronald Reagan was determined to try to check the power of the federal bureaucracy through a more controlled appointment process. First, he tried to ensure that his cabinet members were ideologically attuned to his own policy goals. Then, instead of leaving cabinet officers to appoint their own sub-cabinet officials, the Reagan White House insisted on making those appointments too. He then used the powers given to him by the newly passed Civil Service Reform Act (1978) to reassign senior bureaucrats whom he deemed insufficiently supportive of his administration's policy objectives. It was widely reported that when President Reagan was wheeled into the operating theatre at the George Washington Hospital in Washington DC, following the assassination attempt on him in March 1981, the president jokingly asked the surgeons: 'I hope all you guys are good Republicans?' Reagan might have posed the same question, but in a more serious fashion, to the senior echelons of the federal bureaucracy.

Reagan arrived in Washington determined to cut the size of the federal bureaucracy, too. During his election campaign, Reagan had often asked his audience which were the most frightening words in the English language. The answer was: 'I'm from the federal government, and

Ronald Reagan tried to limit the power of the federal bureaucracy

I'm here to help!' In his inaugural address, Reagan claimed: 'Government isn't the solution: government is the problem.'

Despite all these strategies and slogans, Reagan achieved nowhere near as much as he would have wished in limiting the power of the federal bureaucracy. Although he made political appointments further down the bureaucratic structure than any of his predecessors had ever done, he found himself having to appoint some, who, lacking the organisational skills and inside knowledge of Washington politics, had to rely on career civil servants.

President Clinton set about trying to reorganise the federal government and make it more efficient with his 'Reinventing Government' initiative, of which Vice-President Gore was put in charge. Although Gore undertook the task with his usual thoroughness, the Clinton administration found it no easier than its predecessors to make significant reforms of such a large organisation as the federal bureaucracy.

This might not be good news for governmental efficiency, but it might be good news for democracy. A president who really did have total control over the federal bureaucracy might be in a terrifyingly powerful position. After all, President Nixon did try to use the IRS, the FBI and the CIA in his attempts to destroy those who featured on his 'enemies list' as well as to effect the cover-up of the Watergate scandal. Fortunately, he failed. The problems of control of the federal bureaucracy are therefore matters not only of efficiency, but also of the checks necessary for democratic government.

Summary

Checking the power of the federal bureaucracy

➤ Congress can check the power of the federal bureaucracy by legislation and appropriations, and by its power of oversight and investigation.

➤ Presidents have found it more difficult than they expected to control the federal bureaucracy.

Exercises

1 How large and geographically dispersed is the federal bureaucracy?
2 How many executive departments are there? List those created since 1950.
3 Describe the responsibilities of four of the executive departments.
4 Describe the role of the executive agencies.
5 Explain what is the main function of the independent regulatory commissions.
6 Give three examples of government corporations.
7 What are the main reasons for the growth of the federal bureaucracy?
8 What are the three main functions of the federal bureaucracy?
9 Explain how federal civil servants are recruited.
10 What are the main problems associated with the federal bureaucracy?
11 What checks exist on the federal bureaucracy?

Exam focus

1 How accurate would it be to describe the US federal government as 'an over-large and out-of-control bureaucracy'?
2 How effectively does the US federal government recruit and organise its civil service?
3 Analyse the claim that, far from serving the president, the federal bureaucracy is decentralised, fragmented and out of control.
4 How successful have recent presidents been at directing and controlling their administrations?

References

Singh, R., *American Politics and Society Today* (Blackwell, 2002).

Further reading

Pfiffner, J. P., *The Modern Presidency* (Bedford-St Martin's, 2000).
Pfiffner, J. P., *Understanding the Presidency* (Addison Wesley Longman, 2000).

Chapter 8

The Supreme Court

On the northwest corner of Capitol Hill in Washington DC stands the ornate building which for the past 70 years has been the home of the United States Supreme Court. While the Capitol — which stands just across the road — houses the 535 members of Congress, the Supreme Court is home to only nine people, the total membership of the USA's highest court. The building is imposing and does justice to the importance of the decisions handed down by the members of the Supreme Court, which plays an extremely important political role in the life of the USA. Many of the Court's decisions in recent decades have affected US society profoundly.

This chapter looks at the institution itself, while Chapter 9 deals with the Court's important role as defender of the laws, the Constitution and the very rights and liberties of US citizens.

Questions to be answered in this chapter
➢ What is the structure of the federal courts in the USA?
➢ What is the membership of the Supreme Court?
➢ How does the appointment process work?
➢ What is the power of judicial review?
➢ What checks exist on the Court's power?

The structure of the federal courts

The United States Supreme Court sits at the top of the federal judiciary. According to the original Constitution, the Supreme Court was to be the only federal court. Article III, Section 1, begins:

The judicial power of the United States shall be vested in one supreme Court and in such inferior Courts as the Congress may from time to time ordain and establish.

By passing the Judiciary Act of 1789, Congress immediately set up a system of lower federal courts. Below the Supreme Court are 13 Courts of Appeals, known as Circuit Courts, and below those are the 94 trial courts known as District Courts (see Figure 8.1). The vast majority of federal cases begin in the District Courts. Once the case has been

The west front of the Supreme Court

decided there, it may be appealed to one of the Circuit Courts and from there to the United States Supreme Court. Cases may also arrive at the United States Supreme Court from the state Supreme Courts, if questions involving the federal government are raised. The United States Supreme Court hears only those cases that it wishes to hear. There is no automatic right to have one's case heard before the United States Supreme Court. The Court rejects over 96% of cases that seek to be heard there. It hears only those cases that it believes are of major constitutional significance.

United States Supreme Court
1 court with 9 justices

⬆

United States Courts of Appeals
1 in each of 11 'circuits' (regions)
plus 1 in Washington DC
plus 1 federal Circuit Court

⬆

United States District Courts
1 in each of 94 districts

Figure 8.1 The structure of the federal courts

Summary

The structure of the federal courts

➤ The federal court is a three-tier structure of trial courts at the bottom, appeal courts in the middle and the United States Supreme Court at the top.

Membership of the Supreme Court

Today there are nine members of the Supreme Court — one chief justice and eight associate justices. The number is fixed by Congress and has remained unchanged since 1869. They are appointed by the president and must be confirmed by a simple majority vote in the Senate. Once appointed and confirmed, they hold office for life — 'during good behaviour', as Article III, Section 1 of the Constitution puts it. This means that members of the Court can be removed only through the impeachment process. The House must impeach a justice by a simple majority and the Senate must then try that justice. If found guilty by the Senate by a two-thirds majority, the justice is

Members of the Supreme Court, 2003

removed from office. However, no Supreme Court justice has ever been impeached, although Associate Justice Abe Fortas resigned from the Supreme Court in 1968 rather than face impeachment. Thus, barring impeachment, justices leave the Court only as a consequence of voluntary retirement or death.

When the Supreme Court is sitting, the justices sit along a bench in high-back chairs with a backdrop of a plush red curtain. Sitting in the middle of the nine justices is the chief justice. Although his powers are in most respects the same as those of his colleagues, the chief justice has the opportunity to set the tone of the Court. The current chief justice, William Rehnquist, is only the fifteenth person to hold the office in over 210 years. His predecessors include a number of illustrious names, such as John Marshall (1801–35), Roger Taney (1836–64), William Howard Taft (1921–30) and Charles Evans Hughes (1930–41), but students need to be familiar only with Chief Justice Rehnquist and his two immediate predecessors — Earl Warren (1953–69) and Warren Earl Burger (1969–86). Commentators often use the name of the chief justice to denote an era in the Court's history. Thus, we talk of the 'Warren Court', the 'Burger Court' and the 'Rehnquist Court'. The membership of the Supreme Court in 2003 is set out in Table 8.1.

Table 8.1 Supreme Court membership, 2003

Justice	Date appointed	President appointing
Chief Justice		
William Rehnquist	Associate Justice 1971	Nixon (R)
	Chief Justice 1986	Reagan (R)
Associate Justices		
John Paul Stevens	1975	Ford (R)
Sandra Day O'Connor	1981	Reagan (R)
Antonin Scalia	1986	Reagan (R)
Anthony Kennedy	1987	Reagan (R)
David Souter	1990	Bush (R)
Clarence Thomas	1991	Bush (R)
Ruth Bader Ginsburg	1993	Clinton (D)
Stephen Breyer	1994	Clinton (D)

Summary

Membership of the Supreme Court

➤ The Supreme Court is made up of one chief justice and eight associate justices.

➤ They are appointed by the president.

➤ They are confirmed by a simple majority vote of the Senate.

➤ They have life-term appointments, 'during good behaviour'.

The appointment process

The vacancy

First, the president must wait for a vacancy to occur. There have been 118 vacancies to fill on the Supreme Court since 1789 — which is around one every 2 years. Thus, a president might expect to make two such appointments in a 4-year term, and three or four appointments in two terms. Reagan made three Supreme Court appointments in his 8 years in office and George Bush made two appointments in his 4 years (1989–93). However, some presidents are not so fortunate. Clinton was able to make only two appointments during his 8 years and Carter made none at all in his 4 years. No vacancies occurred on the Court for almost 10 years between the summer of 1994 and spring 2004 — the longest period since the Court remained unchanged for 12 years between 1812 and 1824.

Box 8.1 The appointment process of Supreme Court justices

1 A vacancy occurs through voluntary retirement, death or impeachment.

2 The president instigates a search for possible nominees and interviews short-listed candidates.

3 The president announces his nominee.

4 The Senate confirmation process begins in the Senate Judiciary Committee and ends on the floor of the Senate.

Second, because of the life tenure that the justices enjoy and the great importance of the Supreme Court, presidents regard Supreme Court appointments as the most important of their entire presidency. Most other appointments that presidents make last only for as long as the president remains in office. Cabinet officers, for example, are lucky to serve more than 2 or 3 years, and all of them will almost certainly leave office the moment the president departs. The same goes for most other appointees — ambassadors, agency heads and Executive Office personnel. But Supreme Court justices will, politically speaking, almost certainly outlive the president. Indeed, they may even outlive him physically. President Eisenhower left office in 1961 and died in 1969. Justice William J. Brennan, whom Eisenhower appointed to the Supreme Court in 1956, retired only in 1990. President Nixon left office in 1974 and died in 1994, but Justice William Rehnquist, whom Nixon appointed to the Supreme Court in 1971, was still serving in April 2004. In this sense, the Supreme Court can often appear to be something of an 'echo chamber', through which the voices and views of earlier decades can still be heard to speak.

Table 8.2 Supreme Court appointments, 1961–2001

President	Years in office	Number of Supreme Court appointments
John Kennedy (D)	2½	2
Lyndon Johnson (D)	5½	2
Richard Nixon (R)	5½	4
Gerald Ford (R)	2½	1
Jimmy Carter (D)	4	0
Ronald Reagan (R)	8	3
George Bush (R)	4	2
Bill Clinton (D)	8	2

The search and pools of recruitment

Once a vacancy has occurred, the president commissions a search for suitable candidates. Of course, if a vacancy has been anticipated, this search might have been going on surreptitiously for some time. The president seeks advice from different sources. First, he asks his political advisers — senior White House aides and top officials in the Justice Department — for possible nominees. In addition, he might hear some names being mentioned by key members of Congress of his own party — possibly from members of the influential Senate Judiciary Committee, who have a more formal role to play later in the process. Second, the president — especially Democrats — might seek advice from professional groups such as the American Bar Association (ABA). Third, the president might turn to personal friends and confidants.

US Courts of Appeals

The vast majority of Supreme Court justices are recruited from the federal Courts of Appeals — the courts one tier below the Supreme Court and the courts that will usually have heard cases before they arrive at the Supreme Court. Of the current Court membership, seven of the nine justices were recruited from the federal Courts of Appeals, including both the Clinton appointees.

State courts

Alternatively, the president might look to the state courts. When President Reagan had his first opportunity to fill a vacancy on the Supreme Court back in 1981, he nominated Sandra Day O'Connor, who was then a judge on the Arizona state Court of Appeals. David Souter, nominated by President Bush in 1990, had been on a federal Court of Appeals for only 3 months. Before that he was a member of the New Hampshire state Supreme Court.

Executive branch

Another possible pool of recruitment is the Justice Department. In 1971, President Nixon nominated William Rehnquist to the Supreme Court. Rehnquist was then serving as the number two at the Justice Department.

Congress

Presidents might consider members of Congress — former Senate majority leader George Mitchell was often mentioned as a possible nominee during the Clinton administration.

Academia

A president might turn to academia — a law professor from a distinguished university. In 1987, President Reagan nominated Harvard law professor Douglas Ginsburg to the Supreme Court, although the nominee later withdrew.

The announcement

Once a shortlist has been drawn up, FBI background checks are conducted on all the possible nominees and the president personally interviews two or three finalists. Having decided on the nominee, the president makes the formal announcement (before the identity of the nominee is leaked to the press). The public announcement is a major political event attended by the nominee, members of his or her family, key members of Congress and the executive branch, as well as members of the press.

There then follows a part of the appointment process that is entirely unofficial but has become accepted by tradition: this is the rating by the ABA. Nominees are given one of three ratings: 'well qualified'; 'qualified'; 'not qualified'. As this is a nomination to the USA's highest court, a 'well qualified' rating would be expected. Not to gain that rating would be a significant problem. The only recent Supreme Court nominee to be given a rating other than 'well qualified' was Clarence Thomas, who, when nominated by George Bush in 1991, was awarded a rating of 'qualified' by the ABA.

The confirmation process

The focus moves to Capitol Hill for the confirmation process. The nominee first has to appear before the Senate Judiciary Committee. Hearings are held at which the witnesses include not only the nominee but also supporters, and maybe critics, of the nominee. Witnesses might be individuals with close knowledge of the nominee or representatives of interest groups who support or oppose the nomination. In the hearings conducted on Clarence Thomas's nomination in 1991, the appearance of Professor Anita Hill, a long-time work associate of Judge Thomas, proved explosive because she accused Thomas of sexual harassment. Thomas, a conservative African-American, thought he detected some ulterior motives in his critics' actions.

If the process goes badly for the nominee, he or she might be tempted to withdraw. Alternatively, the president might be tempted to call a halt to the nomination to save further embarrassment and a possible defeat on the Senate floor. This is what happened in 1987 over the nomination of Professor Douglas Ginsburg — no relation to Justice Ruth Bader Ginsburg, who joined the Court in 1993. Just 9 days after being nominated by President Reagan, Ginsburg withdrew following revelations before the Senate Judiciary Committee that he had smoked marijuana.

Once the hearings have concluded, the committee votes on whether or not to recommend further action. This is therefore only a recommendatory, not a decisive, vote. However, the committee vote is a clear pointer to the likely outcome when the full Senate makes the final decision. If the Senate Judiciary Committee votes unanimously or overwhelmingly in favour of a nominee, the nomination is near certain to be confirmed. If, however, the committee vote is close or is lost, defeat on the floor is a near certainty. The 1987 defeat of the nomination of Robert Bork in the Judiciary Committee was a prelude to his defeat on the Senate floor (see Table 8.3). When the committee voted 7–7 on the nomination of Clarence Thomas, it was clear that he was in for a fight on the Senate floor. The Senate did eventually confirm Thomas, but only by a margin of 4 votes. However, Ruth Bader Ginsburg (1993) followed her unanimous approval by the committee with a 96–3 vote on the Senate floor. A simple majority is required for confirmation.

Table 8.3 ABA ratings and Senate votes on selected Supreme Court nominees

Nominee	Year	ABA rating	Senate Judiciary Committee vote	Senate vote
Robert Bork	1987	Well qualified	5–9	42–58
David Souter	1990	Well qualified	13–1	90–9
Clarence Thomas	1991	Qualified	7–7	52–48
Ruth Bader Ginsburg	1993	Well qualified	18–0	96–3

The Senate has rejected 29 nominations since 1789, but only three in the last 65 years. The most recent example was the rejection in 1987 of Reagan nominee Robert Bork by 42 votes to 58. Bork's critics regarded him as being both too conservative and too closely associated with former president Richard Nixon. Bork had played a role in the Watergate affair when, at the orders of President Nixon, he had fired the independent prosecutor, Archibald Cox, who was investigating the Watergate cover-up.

The two other modern-day examples of rejections were both nominees of President Nixon: Clement Haynesworth (1969) by 45 votes to 55 and Harrold Carswell (1970) by 45

Robert Bork's links to the Watergate affair contributed to his rejection

votes to 51. Both Haynesworth and Carswell were regarded by a Democrat-controlled Senate as too conservative. It is no coincidence that all three rejections occurred when the president faced a Senate controlled by the opposing party.

Table 8.4 Senate action on recent Supreme Court nominees

Nominee	President	Date	Result	Vote
Thurgood Marshall	Johnson (D)	1967	Confirmed	69–11
Abe Fortas	Johnson (D)	1968	Withdrawn	–
Warren Burger	Nixon (R)	1969	Confirmed	74–3
Clement Haynesworth	Nixon (R)	1969	Rejected	45–55
Harrold Carswell	Nixon (R)	1970	Rejected	45–51
Harry Blackmun	Nixon (R)	1970	Confirmed	94–0
Lewis Powell	Nixon (R)	1971	Confirmed	89–1
William Rehnquist	Nixon (R)	1971	Confirmed	68–26
John Paul Stevens	Ford (R)	1975	Confirmed	98–0
Sandra Day O'Connor	Reagan (R)	1981	Confirmed	98–0
William Rehnquist*	Reagan (R)	1986	Confirmed	65–33
Antonin Scalia	Reagan (R)	1986	Confirmed	98–0
Robert Bork	Reagan (R)	1987	Rejected	42–58
Douglas Ginsburg	Reagan (R)	1987	Withdrawn	–
Anthony Kennedy	Reagan (R)	1987	Confirmed	97–0
David Souter	Bush (R)	1990	Confirmed	90–9
Clarence Thomas	Bush (R)	1991	Confirmed	52–48
Ruth Bader Ginsburg	Clinton (D)	1993	Confirmed	96–3
Stephen Breyer	Clinton (D)	1994	Confirmed	87–9

* As Chief Justice

Philosophy of justices

It is often suggested that presidents wish to appoint justices who share their judicial philosophy. From a philosophical perspective, justices can be classified as 'conservatives' or 'liberals'. Another classification used is that of **strict constructionists** and **loose constructionists**.

Key terms

> **Strict constructionist.** A justice of the Supreme Court who interprets the Constitution in a strict, literal or conservative fashion, and who tends to stress the retention of as much power as possible by the governments of the individual states.
> **Loose constructionist.** A justice of the Supreme Court who interprets the Constitution in a loose or liberal fashion, and who tends to stress the broad grants of power to the federal government.

Strict constructionist judges are usually conservative in outlook. In their decisions they tend to interpret the Constitution in a strict or literal fashion. They often favour states' rights over the power of the federal government, and they tend to be appointed by Republican presidents. Chief Justice Rehnquist and Associate Justices Scalia, Thomas and Kennedy fall into this category. Strict constructionist judges focus on the text of the Constitution. For them, the language is supreme and the Court's job is to derive and apply rules from the words chosen by those who framed the Constitution. For them, constitutional principles are fixed, not evolving. Justice Scalia declared:

> The Constitution that I interpret and apply is not living but dead. Our first responsibility is not to make sense of the law — our first responsibility is to follow the text of the law.

Loose constructionist judges, on the other hand, are usually liberal in outlook. Their decisions tend to interpret the Constitution in a loose fashion — reading elements into the document that they think the framers of the Constitution would approve. They tend to favour the power of the federal government over states' rights, and they are usually appointed by Democratic presidents. Currently, Associate Justices Ginsburg and Breyer fall into this category, as do Justices Stevens and Souter, although they were both appointed by Republican presidents.

In contrast with Justice Scalia, a loose constructionist such as Justice Breyer would say that he looks at 'context'. The language of the text is only the starting point of an inquiry in which a law's purpose and a decision's likely consequence are the more important elements. He sees Scalia's approach as 'too legalistic' and one that 'places too much weight upon language, history, tradition and precedent alone'.

This leaves Associate Justice Sandra Day O'Connor as what is called the 'swing' justice. In recent years, when the Court has decided cases by 5–4, the decision of Justice O'Connor has been the deciding factor. In the Court's 2002–03 session, of the 71 cases, 14 were decided by a 5–4 majority. Justice O'Connor was in the majority in 12 of those 14 cases. She was in the majority in most decisions in the six consecutive sessions from 1996–97 to 2002–03 and on 63 of the Court's 71 decisions in 2002–03.

Assessment

Most modern-day criticism of the appointment process centres on accusations of politicisation — by the president, by the Senate and by the media that cover the process. Although presidents always deny any political consideration in the appointment process, it seems nonetheless to underlie the choosing of Supreme Court justices. Presidents are tempted to choose a justice whose political and judicial philosophy reflect their own. Republican presidents want to pick a justice who is conservative and takes a strict and literal view of the Constitution. Democrat presidents, on the other hand, want to choose a justice who is liberal and takes a looser, adaptive view of the Constitution. There is always the danger that presidents use a 'litmus test' on Court nominees, often scrutinising their previous judgments on controversial cases, such as those regarding affirmative action, capital punishment or abortion.

When President Bush announced his nomination of David Souter to the Supreme Court in 1990, the first question he was asked by the press after he had delivered his introductory statement was: 'Did you ask Judge Souter his views on abortion?' Bush said that he had not, stating: 'It would have been inappropriate to ask him his views on specific issues.' Then, for good measure, the president added:

> What I am certain of is that he will interpret the Constitution and not legislate from the federal bench.... You might think the whole nomination had to do with abortion.... I have too much respect for the Supreme Court than to look at one specific issue.

On this occasion, however, the president might indeed have been right to deny any political considerations in his choice. Justice Souter has, in more than a decade on the Supreme Court, made decisions which would find little favour with President Bush in particular or conservative Republicans in general. He has proved to be one of the most consistently *liberal* members of the Court.

Most presidents pick politically, and it is no coincidence that the two Clinton appointees on the Court deliver opinions that are consistently of a liberal position. It is no coincidence that the most conservative members of the Court are appointees of Richard Nixon and Ronald Reagan. Given the opportunity to choose a member of the nation's highest court and thereby have the chance to shape the Court's thinking for the next 15–20 years or more, most presidents understandably take it.

The Senate, too, has been accused of politicising the confirmation process. The defeat of Robert Bork, one of the most outstanding jurists and scholars of his generation, is a case in point. Democrat opponents on the Senate Judiciary Committee mobilised an array of liberal interest groups against Bork's nomination. The National Abortion Rights Action League and the National Organization for Women, to name but two, weighed in against Bork. Even a television advertising campaign was mounted against his nomination, costing a sum in the region of $15 million. Conservative groups mounted a counterattack, but to little avail.

A similar situation arose when President Bush nominated another conservative, Clarence Thomas, in 1991. In this case, the Senate could justifiably have questioned Thomas's nomination on his lacklustre qualifications. It chose instead to concentrate on his conservative philosophy and the allegations of sexual harassment brought against him by a black female work colleague. Thomas was unimpressed by the confirmation process, issuing a forthright denunciation of the Senate's work:

> This is a circus. It's a national disgrace. From my standpoint as a black American, it is a high-tech lynching for uppity blacks who in any way think for themselves.... No job is worth what I've been through — no job. No horror in my life has been so debilitating. Confirm me if you want. Don't confirm me if you have been so led. But let this process end. Let me and my family regain our lives.

When the process ended and the Senate finally voted on Thomas's nomination, the vote was almost entirely along party lines. Only 11 Democrats — mostly southern conservatives — voted in favour, and only two Republicans voted against. This does little to rebut the allegation that Thomas's nomination was considered in a partisan fashion by both sides.

The media came out of the Thomas hearings with little credit. Their 'feeding frenzy' on the allegations made against Thomas was liberally interspersed with sexual details that bordered on the prurient. Rather than have an informed debate about judicial philosophy and qualification, much of the media chose to compete over who could come up with the most lurid allegations and the most tasteless details. Thomas's use of the word 'lynching' was intended to have racist overtones.

With the Court so finely balanced between conservatives and liberals — witness the large number of 5–4 decisions in recent years — it is unlikely that either the president or the Senate of either party is going to give up on trying to get its way. Vacancies on the Court are bound to arise in the near future — including that of the chief justiceship — so Court watchers could be in for an interesting time.

Summary

The appointment process

- ➢ A new appointment to the Supreme Court occurs, on average, every 2 years.
- ➢ The main pool of recruitment for Supreme Court justices is the federal Appeal Courts.
- ➢ The Senate has rejected a significant number of Supreme Court nominees.
- ➢ Justices can be classified as 'strict constructionists' or 'loose constructionists'.
- ➢ Accusations have been made that the appointment and confirmation processes have been politicised.

The power of judicial review

Judicial review is the power of the Supreme Court to declare acts of Congress, or actions of the executive — or acts or actions of state governments — unconstitutional, and thereby null and void. The power is not mentioned in the Constitution; it might be said that the Supreme Court 'found' the power for itself in the 1803 case of *Marbury v. Madison*. This was the first time that the Supreme Court declared an act of Congress unconstitutional.

Key term

- ➢ **Judicial review.** The power of the Supreme Court to declare acts of Congress, or actions of the executive — or acts or actions of state governments — unconstitutional, and thereby null and void.

Since then, the Supreme Court has used this power on numerous occasions — against both federal and state laws. The Court has gone through periods of both judicial activism and judicial restraint. During the 1980s, for example, the Court declared 16 federal and 161 state laws unconstitutional. On the other hand, during the 1940s the Supreme Court declared only two federal laws and 58 state laws unconstitutional.

By using its power of judicial review the Court can, in effect, update the meaning of the words of the Constitution, most of which were written over two centuries ago. Hence, the Court decides what the phrase in the 8th Amendment (written in 1791) forbidding 'cruel and unusual punishments' means today. Likewise, it decides whether the 1st Amendment right of 'freedom of speech' applies to the internet, for example. As former Chief Justice Charles Evans Hughes once remarked: 'We are under a Constitution, but the Constitution is what the judges say it is.'

Using its power of judicial review, the Supreme Court has involved itself in a host of political issues. It is this that helps give the Court its political importance, because many of the issues dealt with by the Court are the key political issues of the day — matters over which political parties disagree and elections are fought. For example, political commentator Mark Shields has been quoted as saying that America's two major parties are 'separated [only] by the issue of abortion'. Which branch of government decides women's rights concerning abortion? As Chapter 9 shows in detail, the answer is the Supreme Court. In addition, the Supreme Court has handed down landmark decisions in recent years on such politically contentious issues as the rights of racial minorities, capital punishment, gun control and freedom of speech.

The political importance of the Court is demonstrated in the case of *George W. Bush v. Albert Gore Jr* (2000). Five weeks after the presidential election, on 11 December 2000, the Supreme Court ruled that the manual recount scheme devised by the Florida state Supreme Court was unconstitutional because it violated the 'equal protection' clause of the Constitution's 14th Amendment. In the same decision, the Court also ruled that because of the time constraints, 'it is evident that any recount seeking to meet the December 12 [deadline] will be unconstitutional'. The Court was seen by some to be handing the election to George W. Bush.

The power of judicial review not only gives the Court political importance, but is also said to turn it into a quasi-legislative body. This is because the decisions that the Court hands down have almost the effect of a law having been passed by Congress. So, for example, when in its 1973 decision in *Roe v. Wade* the Court stated that women have a constitutional right to choose an abortion, the effect was comparable to an abortion rights law having been passed by Congress. In this sense, the Court has been described as 'a third house of the legislature'.

Summary

The power of judicial review

➤ The power of judicial review significantly increases the importance of the Supreme Court.

Checks on the Supreme Court

Just as the legislature (Congress) and the executive (the president) are subject to the system of checks and balances that pervades the US system of government, so is the judiciary.

Checks by Congress

The Supreme Court is subject to four checks by Congress.

➤ The Senate has the power to confirm or reject appointments to the Court. In having a hand in who does and who does not sit on the Court, Congress therefore acts as a check. This is clearly seen when the Senate rejects nominations as, for example, it did over the nomination of Robert Bork in 1987.

➤ Linked with this is Congress's power to decide how many justices sit on the Court. Congress could, for example, decide to increase the number of justices, thereby obliging the president to make new appointments and potentially altering the philosophical make-up of the Court. Congress refused President Franklin D. Roosevelt's plan to increase the number of Supreme Court judges from 9 to 15 for just this reason — that by agreeing to such a plan, the nature of the Court would be altered.

➤ Congress has the power of impeachment. Even the threat of its use can be effective. In 1968 Associate Justice Abe Fortas resigned rather than face almost certain impeachment.

➤ Congress can initiate constitutional amendments that can have the effect of negating a decision by the Court. The clearest example of this was in the Court's 1895 decision of *Pollock v. Farmers' Loan and Trust Company*, when it declared federal income tax to be unconstitutional. Congress then initiated — and the states ratified — the 16th Amendment (1913), which stated: 'The Congress shall have the power to lay and collect taxes on incomes.' However, recent attempts by Congress to initiate constitutional amendments to overturn the Court's decisions on such matters as flag desecration, school prayers, abortion rights and congressional term limits have all failed.

Checks by the president

The president has two important checks on the Court.

➤ The president has the power to nominate justices. By choosing justices of a certain political and judicial philosophy, the president may seek to change the nature of the Court. The outlook of the Court has changed since the 1960s from one appointed mostly by Democratic presidents — Roosevelt, Truman, Kennedy and Johnson — to one appointed mostly by Republican presidents — Nixon, Reagan and George Bush.

➤ The president can decide either to throw his political weight behind a decision of the Court or to criticise it openly. President Eisenhower gave his political support to the Court's 1954 decision in *Brown v. Board of Education of Topeka*. In this decision, the

Court had declared that segregated schools were unconstitutional. In 1957, Eisenhower used his power as commander-in-chief to send federal troops to Arkansas to enforce the desegregation of the Little Rock Central High School. Contrast that with President George Bush's response to the Court's 1989 decision in *Texas v. Johnson*. In this decision, the Court declared a Texas state law forbidding the burning of the US flag to be unconstitutional. An irate President Bush publicly described the Court's decision as 'wrong, dead wrong'.

Other checks

- The Supreme Court has no power of initiation. It must wait for cases to come before it. Many presidents, politicians and commentators have been of the view that the War Powers Act (1973) may be unconstitutional. However, the Court has been unable to rule on the matter because no case regarding this act has appeared before it.
- The Court does not possess any enforcement powers. The Court is reliant upon either enforcement by other branches of government or majority acceptance by law-abiding Americans. When in 1954 the Court announced in *Brown v. Board of Education of Topeka* that states should desegregate their schools 'with all deliberate speed', there was little the Court could do in practical terms to ensure that this occurred. Some years later the Court complained that desegregation was subject to 'too much deliberation and not enough speed'.
- This links with a further potential check on the Court — public opinion. While a judicial body should be thought immune to public opinion, the Court often seems to be mindful that, were the public to view its decisions as lacking credibility, the Court's legitimacy could be at risk. The Court's attitude towards public opinion seems to vary, however. In some instances, the Court seems to want to mould and lead public opinion: this is what it seemingly wanted to do in its 1954 decision on school deseg-regation. In other instances, it apparently ignores public opinion altogether, as in the 1989 flag desecration decision. In yet other instances, the Court seems to be careful to try to mirror public opinion, as in its 1992 abortion decision — *Planned Parenthood of Southeastern Pennsylvania v. Casey*. In this case, the Court decided neither that women had no constitutional right to choose an abortion nor that such a right was unlimited. Its decision, probably in line with the less vocal majority of public opinion, was that a woman's right to choose an abortion did exist in the Constitution but could be subjected to reasonable limitations by state legislatures.
- The Court is also checked by itself, for Court decisions can amend — even overturn — decisions of earlier Courts. For example, the 1954 *Brown v. Board of Education of Topeka* decision stated that 'separate educational facilities are inherently unequal'. However, the Court's decision in the 1896 *Plessy v. Ferguson* case laid down what became known as the 'separate but equal' doctrine, which was then accepted as law for almost 60 years.

➤ Finally, the Constitution is a check on the Supreme Court. Although certain parts of the Constitution are open to interpretation by the Court — such as the 1st Amendment — other parts of the document are unambiguous, allowing little, if any, room for modern-day interpretation by the Court.

Summary

Checks on the Supreme Court

➤ Just like the other two branches of the federal government, the Supreme Court is subject to significant checks and balances.

Exercises

1 Explain the structure of the federal courts.
2 Describe the membership of the Supreme Court.
3 Explain how appointments are made to the Supreme Court.
4 Explain the Senate's role in confirming Supreme Court appointments.
5 Explain the terms: (a) strict constructionist; (b) loose constructionist.
6 Briefly explain the power of judicial review.
7 What checks exist on the Supreme Court?

Exam focus

1 Examine the claim that the most important appointments a president makes are to the Supreme Court.
2 Is the process for appointing Supreme Court justices in need of reform?
3 To what extent can a president hope to mould and influence the Supreme Court?
4 Does the Supreme Court have too much unchecked power?

Further reading

Pacelle, R. L., *The Role of the Supreme Court in American Politics* (Westview, 2002).

Peele, G., 'The US Supreme Court: politicians in disguise?', *Politics Review*, vol. 11, no. 4, April 2002.

Chapter 9

Civil rights and liberties

The United States is a nation of great ethnic diversity. There are the American Indians (Native Americans) — nowadays making up a tiny proportion of the US population; the WASPS — white, Anglo-Saxon Protestants — who arrived in the New World from the Old from the seventeenth century onwards; the African-Americans, whose initial life of slavery became one of increasing freedom from the 1860s; followed by the great wave of nineteenth- and twentieth-century immigration — initially from Europe, but then increasingly from Central and South America, Asia and Africa. The USA is therefore seen as a 'melting pot' of races, culture, languages and religions.

Many who fled to America over the centuries did so seeking refuge from intolerance and persecution at home: English Puritans, French Huguenots, Jewish exiles from Hitler's Germany, or political exiles from Castro's Cuba. The Declaration of Independence in 1776 was an attempt by suppressed colonists to throw off what they saw as the tyrannical rule of Great Britain. The new nation was not going to exchange one tyranny for another. The Founding Fathers who wrote the Constitution and the Bill of Rights that it eventually contained wanted above everything to devise a system in which government would be limited and citizens' rights — as far as they were understood in the late eighteenth century — would be protected.

Civil rights are positive acts of government designed to protect people against discriminatory treatment, either by the government or by other individuals or groups within society. Civil liberties are those liberties that guarantee the protection of persons and property from the arbitrary interference of government officials. Restraints on civil liberties are permissible in a free society only in so far as they are imposed to prevent the abuse of such liberties by groups or individuals and to protect public welfare.

This chapter looks at how US government has adapted to the changes that have taken place in US society, and the institutions of government to which Americans can look to safeguard their rights and liberties. It also considers how effective these institutions have been in protecting Americans' rights and liberties.

Questions to be answered in this chapter
➤ How ethnically diverse is the USA?
➤ How are minorities represented?
➤ How effectively are rights and liberties protected by the three branches of the federal government?

Ethnic diversity and minority representation

In the beginning, the USA was a creation of white European Protestants. Black people were, in most cases, slaves; American Indians were not regarded as citizens either. The story of westward expansion — as depicted in Hollywood 'westerns' — was the story of the white 'Cowboys' depriving the 'Indians' of their land, livelihood and women. Catholics and Jews were initially a tiny minority and were often persecuted.

However, the nineteenth and twentieth centuries changed all that. The end of the Civil War (1861–65) brought emancipation for the slaves and a slow march towards equality in politics, at home, at school and in the workplace. Immigration brought a flood of new settlers — including Irish Catholics fleeing from the potato famines of the mid-nineteenth century, and European Jews fleeing from religious persecution in the mid-twentieth century. Then came the political and economic Hispanic migrants from Mexico and other Central American countries, and refugees from Africa, the Middle East and Asia. Not all were legal, and certainly not all were white Protestants. Buddhists and Muslims arrived along with people of many other faiths and cultures.

During the 1990s, the combined population of African-Americans, Native Americans, Asians, Pacific Islanders and Hispanics/Latinos grew at 13 times the rate of the non-Hispanic white population. The 2000 census was the first to show Hispanics as a larger proportion of the US population than blacks (see Table 9.1). It was also the first to allow Americans to indicate their belonging to more than one ethnic group — what Tiger Woods calls 'Cablinasian'. It was after Woods' 1997 Golf Masters win that he first used the term in public to denote his white, black, Thai, Chinese and American Indian heritage. As Figure 9.1 shows, population estimates suggest that by 2025 the Hispanic and Asian communities will constitute more than one-quarter of the entire US population.

Table 9.1 US population by ethnic groups, 1980–2000 (%)

Ethnic group	1980	1990	2000
White	79.6	75.7	69.1
Black	11.5	11.8	12.2
Hispanic	6.4	9.0	12.6
Asian	1.5	2.8	3.8
Indian	0.6	0.7	0.7

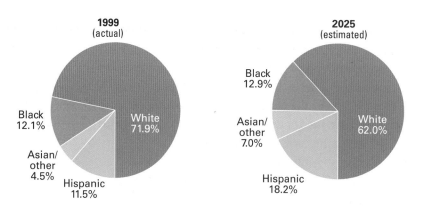

Figure 9.1 Racial and ethnic composition of the USA, 1999 and 2025 (estimated)

Ethnic diversity itself is a challenge to any society. Diversity needs both protection and adequate representation; so do minorities. How to move US society from one that was 'half slave and half free' to one in which the interests of minorities are both protected and represented has raised many problems. As this chapter explains, there has been a role for all three branches of the federal government in this. Over the past half-century, many different policies and approaches have been adopted. Some have been more successful than others. Some have stirred up controversy among both minority and majority groups. Some have been favoured by the right; others by the left.

Developments in minority representation

➤ The nineteenth century had seen attempts to use the Constitution to guarantee rights and representation for racial minorities. The 13th, 14th and 15th Amendments, passed immediately after the Civil War, were meant to put right the wrongs of slavery. For almost a century, however, little changed in practice. Segregation remained rife, especially in the Deep South. The twentieth century brought another type of segregation — what might be called 'residential segregation'. With the onset of the Great Depression in the 1930s, blacks moved increasingly to the big cities — and especially those of the northeast — to seek work. Cities such as Chicago, Philadelphia and Washington DC saw the arrival of large numbers of ethnic minorities, which tended to congregate in inner-city regions, leaving the suburbs still largely — if not exclusively — white. The result was to create two Americas — metropolitan America, which is multi-racial, and suburban and rural America, which is largely white or, in the case of the southeast, biracial.

➤ The twentieth century brought two further developments regarding minority rights and representation. From the 1950s, the Supreme Court saw itself as having a major role to play in this area. From the 1960s, Congress too plunged into the area of civil rights. For the Supreme Court, the watershed came in 1954 with its landmark decision in *Brown v. Board of Education of Topeka*. For Congress, it came with the passage of the major civil rights legislation from 1964.

➤ The twentieth century also saw an on-going argument between what has been called 'equality of opportunity' on the one hand and 'equality of results' on the other. From the middle of the century, many civil rights advocates — whether in the areas of ethnicity or gender — came to believe that minority rights and representation could not be guaranteed solely by 'giving' rights to people — 'equality of opportunity'. This would merely give the *theory* of rights and equality. If people wanted to see the *practice* of rights and equality, they had to work towards 'equality of results'. The only way to overcome racial *disadvantage* was by introducing racial *advantage* through such policies as **busing**, **quotas**, **affirmative action** and majority-minority districts for elections to the US House of Representatives.

Key terms

➤ **Busing.** The mandated movement of schoolchildren between racially homogeneous neighbourhoods — white suburbs and black inner cities — to create racially mixed schools in all neighbourhoods.

➤ **Quotas.** A set-aside programme to benefit previously disadvantaged minorities in such areas as higher education and employment. A certain percentage — quota — of places is reserved for people of the previously disadvantaged group. The Supreme Court found quotas unconstitutional in a number of decisions during the 1980s and 1990s.

➤ **Affirmative action.** A programme that entails giving those members of a previously disadvantaged minority group a headstart in such areas as higher education and employment. The term is often regarded as being synonymous with 'positive discrimination'. Affirmative action is now required by law for all federal government agencies and for those organisations in receipt of federal funds.

➤ A late-twentieth-century innovation was the devising by state governments of congressional districts — electoral districts in which members of the House of Representatives are elected — in which a majority of residents are from a specific racial minority group. These are the so-called 'majority-minority districts'. The adoption in the early 1990s of such strategies for the drawing of electoral boundaries resulted in a significant increase in House members from minority groups in the 1992 congressional elections — the first to be fought under the new boundaries (see Chapter 5).

Summary

Ethnic diversity and minority representation

➤ There have been significant changes in the ethnic make-up of the US population in recent decades.

➤ America has attempted various means to improve minority representation.

The protection of rights and liberties by the Supreme Court

To which institutions of government might Americans look for the protection of their rights and liberties? The simple answer is that all three branches of the federal government — as well as state governments — have a role to play. However, in a nation with a written Constitution, which itself includes a Bill of Rights, it is the courts — and in the end the Supreme Court — that is likely to play the most significant role in the protection of rights and liberties.

Most of the Constitution dates from the eighteenth and nineteenth centuries and was written at a time when the understanding and public expectations of civil rights and liberties were very different from what they are today. It is the role of the Supreme Court, using its power of judicial review, to interpret the meaning of that document in today's society. The Supreme Court pronounces on what those fundamental rights and liberties enshrined in the Bill of Rights in 1791 mean in practice today — freedoms regarding speech, religion and the press, as well as freedoms from arbitrary arrest and cruel punishment.

The history of the Supreme Court contains numerous landmark decisions that have had the effect of deciding the extent to which these rights and liberties are — or are not — protected (see Table 9.2).

The rights of racial minorities

Since the 1950s, the Supreme Court has been at the centre of attempts to protect the rights of racial minorities. The early cases centred upon the rights of black Americans, but as US society has become more diverse, cases relating to other racial minorities have been heard too.

In 1954, the Supreme Court handed down one of the most important decisions of the twentieth century. In the case of *Brown v. Board of Education of Topeka*, the Court ruled that a law of the state of Kansas was unconstitutional because it transgressed the 'equal protection' clause of the 14th Amendment. In so doing, the Court ruled that schools — and, by implication, other public facilities such as railway carriages, parks and restaurants — could not be segregated by race. The case overturned the Court's 1896 decision, which had set in place what became known as the 'separate but equal' doctrine. For the previous 60 years, many facilities — including schools — had been designated as being only for whites. The potential implications of the 1954 decision were huge. The case was sponsored by the National Association for the Advancement of Colored People (NAACP), which believed that poor schooling opportunities for blacks lay at the root of black poverty and disadvantage.

This case dealt with *de jure* segregation — segregation that resulted from laws passed usually by state legislatures in the South — but it did nothing about *de facto* segregation — segregation that resulted from neighbourhood schooling, mainly in the cities of the northeast. In cities such as Boston, New York, Newark, Philadelphia and Washington DC, there were schools that were attended exclusively or mostly by pupils of only one race.

Table 9.2 Landmark decisions on civil rights by the Supreme Court

Civil rights area	Supreme Court decisions
Rights of racial minorities	*Brown v. Board of Education of Topeka* (1954) *Swann v. Charlotte-Mecklenburg Board of Education* (1971) *Adarand Constructors v. Peña* (1995) *Gratz v. Bollinger* (2003)
Rights of arrested persons	*Gideon v. Wainwright* (1963) *Miranda v. Arizona* (1966) *Atkins v. Virginia* (2002)
Capital punishment	*Furman v. Georgia* (1972) *Ring v. Arizona* (2002)
Abortion	*Roe v. Wade* (1973) *Webster v. Reproductive Health Services* (1989) *Planned Parenthood of Southeast Pennsylvania v. Casey* (1992)
Freedom of religion	*Engel v. Vitale* (1962) *School District of Abington Township v. Schempp* (1963) *Lynch v. Donnelly* (1984) *Wallace v. Jaffree* (1985) *Allegheny County v. American Civil Liberties Union* (1989) *Lee v. Weisman* (1992) *Zelman v. Simmons-Harris* (2002)
Freedom of speech and expression	*Buckley v. Valeo* (1976) *Rankin v. McPherson* (1987) *Texas v. Johnson* (1989) *United States v. Eichman* (1990) *Reno v. American Civil Liberties Union* (1997) *Ashcroft v. Free Speech Coalition* (2002) *Watchtower Bible and Tract Society of New York Inc. v. Village of Stratton, Ohio* (2002)
Freedom of the press	*New York Times v. United States* (1971)
Freedom to bear arms	*United States v. Lopez* (1995)
Freedom from unreasonable searches	*United States v. Drayton* (2002) *Board of Education v. Earls* (2002)

In predominantly black inner-city neighbourhoods, schools were mainly black. The opposite was true in white suburban neighbourhoods. In the 1971 case of *Swann v. Charlotte-Mecklenburg Board of Education*, the Court decided that *de facto* segregation was unconstitutional too. This led to the introduction of school busing programmes to provide racially mixed schools in all areas.

In *Adarand Constructors v. Peña* (1995), the Court struck down a federal government affirmative action programme on the employment of minority workers. The federal Department of Transportation had a policy that gave road-building contractors a bonus if they hired subcontractors which employed minority workers. In Colorado, a firm employing white workers put in a bid to erect road safety barriers. However, despite putting in the lower bid, they lost out to a firm employing minority workers. In its decision, the Supreme Court refused to say whether such an affirmative action programme was constitutional. Associate Justice O'Connor, writing for the 5–4 majority, stated that in order to survive a court challenge, such affirmative action programmes must be 'narrowly tailored measures that further compelling governmental interests'. The use of the words 'narrowly' and 'compelling' were meant as signals that the Court would not sanction affirmative action programmes *per se*. The case was much debated during the 1996 presidential election, with President Clinton stating in his re-election campaign that it was his opinion that affirmative action programmes should be 'mended, not ended'.

At the heart of the *Adarand* decision were three fundamental questions about civil rights. First, should racial advancement be on the basis of merit alone? Second, how can the conflict between 'individual rights' on the one hand and 'group rights' on the other be reconciled? And third, is there a moral difference between 'advantageous discrimination', such as affirmative action programmes, and 'invidious discrimination', such as the old segregation laws? Put another way, is affirmative action just a form of 'racial paternalism'? The latter question was debated in this judgment by the conservative Justice Thomas on the one hand and the liberal Justice Stevens on the other. Writing for the majority, Justice Thomas stated:

> I believe that there is a moral and constitutional equivalence between laws designed to subjugate a race and those that distribute benefits on the basis of race in order to foster some current notion of equality. Government cannot make us equal. It can only recognise, respect and protect us as equal before the law. That these [affirmative action] programmes may have been motivated, in part, by good intentions cannot provide refuge from the principle that under our Constitution, the Government may not make distinctions on the basis of race. As far as the Constitution is concerned, it is irrelevant whether a government's racial classifications are drawn by those who wish to oppress a race or by those who have a sincere desire to help those thought to be disadvantaged. There can be no doubt that the paternalism that appears to lie at the heart of this programme is at war with the principle of inherent equality that underlies and infuses our Constitution.

For Justice Thomas, the Constitution is 'colour-blind'. Writing for the dissenting minority though, Justice Stevens argues quite the opposite:

> The consistency that the Court espouses would disregard the difference between a 'No Trespassing' sign and a welcome mat. It would equate a law that made black

citizens ineligible for military service with a programme aimed at recruiting black soldiers... . It is one thing to question the wisdom of affirmative action programmes; there are many responsible arguments against them. It is another thing altogether to equate the many well-meaning and intelligent lawmakers and their constituents, whether members of majority or minority races, who have supported affirmative action over many years, with segregationists and bigots.

In *Gratz v. Bollinger* (2003) the Court ruled (6–3) that the University of Michigan's affirmative action-based admissions programme for its undergraduate students was unconstitutional because it was too 'mechanistic'. All black, Hispanic, and American-Indian applicants were automatically awarded 20 of the 150 points required for admission. But in *Grutter v. Bollinger* (2003), the Court ruled (5–4) that the University Law School's admissions programme was constitutional because it used a more 'individualised' approach in considering the racial profile of its applicants.

The net effect of these two rulings will be to permit universities to continue to use race as a 'plus factor' in evaluating applicants, provided they take sufficient care to evaluate each applicant's ability individually. A majority of the Court also signed up to the idea that affirmative action programmes should not be seen as a permanent fixture of US society, urging universities to prepare for the time when it should no longer be necessary. The Court suggested that this might occur within the next 25 years. It was 25 years ago in *Regents of the University of California v. Bakke* (1978) that the Supreme Court ruled out racial quotas in university admissions programmes but left the door open to race being considered in admissions procedures.

At the centre of the debate in these cases was swing justice Sandra Day O'Connor. It was O'Connor who announced the majority opinion in the Law School case, describing for a hushed audience the grounds of the majority opinion thus:

> Effective participation by members of all racial and ethnic groups in the civic life of our nation is essential if the dream of one nation, indivisible, is to be realised. Moreover, universities, and in particular law schools, represent the training ground for a large number of our nation's leaders. In order to cultivate a set of leaders with legitimacy in the eyes of the citizenry, it is necessary that the path to leadership be visibly open to talented and qualified individuals of every race and ethnicity.

In his dissenting opinion, Chief Justice Rehnquist, joined by Justices Scalia, Thomas and Kennedy, denounced the law school admissions plan as a 'sham' and a 'naked effort to achieve racial balancing', seeing it as 'a carefully managed programme designed to ensure proportionate representation of applicants from selected minority groups'. Justice Clarence Thomas, the only black member of the Court, reverted to his typically colourful language in denouncing racial diversity programmes as 'the faddish slogan of the cognoscenti' that do 'nothing for those too poor or uneducated to participate in elite higher education'.

Many commentators remarked on how closely these judgements on affirmative action reflected the majority opinion of ordinary Americans. A recent poll by the Pew Research Centre, for example, found that — by a margin of two to one — Americans approve of 'programmes designed to increase the number of black and minority students' in universities. But the same people disapproved — by a three to one margin — of 'giving minorities preferential treatment'. As David Von Drehle pointed out in his *Washington Post* article (24 June 2003), it isn't often that the Supreme Court in its imposing black robes and marbled halls can be said to 'look like America', but on this occasion it did just that. The Court's double judgement mirrored Americans' approval and wariness of affirmative action.

In his summing up of these two seemingly contradictory decisions, Justice Antonin Scalia used the metaphor of the way US newspapers often lay out their front pages, calling the Court's judgements 'a split double-header'.

The rights of arrested persons

In two landmark decisions in the 1960s, the Supreme Court attempted to protect the rights of arrested persons. In *Gideon v. Wainwright* (1963) the Court interpreted the 14th Amendment as guaranteeing the right of arrested persons to legal representation. In *Miranda v. Arizona* (1966) the Court interpreted the 5th Amendment right to remain silent as extending to the right to be reminded of that right when arrested. What have become known as 'Miranda rights' have been read to people arrested by state police across America ever since that judgment.

Capital punishment

Linked to these rights are those guaranteed by the 8th Amendment against 'cruel and unusual punishments'. In the case of *Furman v. Georgia* (1972), the Court decided that the death penalty, as it was then imposed, was a 'cruel and unusual punishment' and thereby violated the 8th Amendment. The Court made its decision based on the methods used for executing convicted criminals and the arbitrary and unfair way in which, the Court believed, the punishment was handed down. The consequences of this case included the more widespread use of lethal injection and of the two-stage trial. The latter was meant to try to reverse the trend by which the death penalty was more likely to be given to poor members of racial minorities than to more wealthy whites. During a second stage of the trial, mitigating circumstances are considered before the sentence is decided.

In *Ring v. Arizona* (2002) the Court declared that death sentences imposed by judges, rather than by juries, were unconstitutional because they infringed the 6th Amendment right to trial by jury. In *Atkins v. Virginia* (2002) the court decided that the execution of mentally retarded criminals infringed the 8th Amendment ban on 'cruel and unusual punishments'. Of the 38 states permitting capital punishment in 2002, 20 of them — including Virginia — still allowed the execution of the mentally retarded. Daryl Atkins had been on the state's death row for 4 years for the murder of a US airman. Atkins was reported to have an IQ of just 59. His sentence was altered to life imprisonment.

Abortion rights

Supreme Court decisions concerning a woman's right to choose an abortion have dominated the argument about rights and liberties in America for over 30 years. In 1973 the Court announced in *Roe v. Wade* that the 14th Amendment right of 'liberty' included 'freedom of personal choice in matters of marriage and family life' and that this right 'necessarily includes the right of a woman to decide whether or not to terminate her pregnancy'. The case centred upon Norma McCorvey — identified in the case only by the alias of 'Jane Roe' — who had been denied an abortion by the state law of Texas. (Henry Wade was a Dallas County district attorney.) The *Roe v. Wade* decision was one of the most politically important decisions of the twentieth century. It came at a time when the issue of women's rights was gaining importance and support in the USA. It took on political significance as the 'pro-choice' lobby (those who supported the decision) became closely associated with the Democratic Party, while the 'pro-life' lobby (those who opposed the decision) became closely associated with the Republicans.

The issue of abortion did not stand still over the next 30 years. In *Webster v. Reproductive Health Services* (1989) the Court upheld a Missouri state law forbidding the involvement of any 'public employee' or 'public facility' in the performance of an abortion 'not necessary to save the life of the mother'. Pro-choice supporters regarded this as the Court nibbling away at *Roe v. Wade*.

In 1992, in *Planned Parenthood of Southeastern Pennsylvania v. Casey*, the Court upheld a Pennsylvania state law that required a married woman seeking an abortion to notify her husband beforehand, receive counselling on the risks and alternatives, and wait 24 hours after receiving that counselling. Women under 18 also had to have parental consent for an abortion. This again was opposed by the pro-choice lobby. Thus, it is clear that the Supreme Court has been at the forefront of the debate over abortion rights.

Freedom of religion

The 1st Amendment begins with this statement: 'Congress shall make no law respecting an establishment of religion, or prohibiting the free exercise thereof.' It is a right that is grounded in the wish of the eighteenth-century framers of the Constitution to preserve a level of religious freedom within the United States which had been noticeably lacking in those countries from which many of their forebears had come. However, these opening 16 words of the 1st Amendment contain something of a conundrum: how to ensure that there is no established religion while preserving citizens' rights to practise their religion freely. It has posed a seemingly insuperable problem for the Court in its attempts to protect religious freedoms. Critics of the Court — these days mainly evangelical Christians — believe that the Court has been too attentive to the first half of this opening phrase while ignoring the second half.

For a long time, the Supreme Court declined to enter this particular area of civil liberties. But in 1962, in *Engel v. Vitale*, the Court declared a New York state law to be unconstitutional because it provided for a prayer written by the New York Board of Regents to be used in the state's public (i.e. state-run) schools. In the Court's view, this violated the 1st Amendment clause against 'an establishment of religion'. Reasoning that they could not write special prayers, states resorted to the use of the Lord's Prayer or the recitation of passages from the Bible, yet these too were declared unconstitutional in *School District of Abington Township v. Schempp* (1963). In this case, the Court argued that the study of religion could be part of a school curriculum, but that public schools could not be used for praying, which the Court argued was essentially a religious act. The Court ruled that the fact that students could excuse themselves from the time when prayers were being recited was irrelevant — it was the act of praying that constituted 'an establishment of religion', not who or how many actually decided to participate.

The next strategy adopted by schools in certain states, especially in the South, was to set aside a short period of the school day for 'silent reflection' by students. But in *Wallace v. Jaffree* (1985), the Court declared unconstitutional an Alabama state law which provided for such a period. Then, in 1992, in *Lee v. Weisman*, the Court declared prayers recited at public school graduation ceremonies to be unconstitutional, even if these prayers were chosen and recited by students.

In 1989, in *Allegheny County v. American Civil Liberties Union*, the Court declared Allegheny (Pennsylvania) County's Christmas display unconstitutional because its inclusion of religious figures infringed the 1st Amendment. This contrasted with the Court's earlier decision in *Lynch v. Donnelly* (1984) that the City of Pawtucket's (Rhode Island) Christmas display, containing Santa Claus and a Christmas tree, was constitutionally acceptable.

Most of these decisions constitute attempts by the Supreme Court to strike some kind of balance between upholding the rights of those who wish to 'exercise' their religious beliefs and maintaining 'the wall of separation' between Church and state. The issue at stake in these decisions is the use of taxpayers' money. Private schools could have whatever religious observance they wished. If students at public schools wished to attend a church service *before* coming to their graduation ceremony, that would be fine. If, at Christmas, *privately owned* shops or shopping malls wanted to display nativity scenes featuring the holy family, the Court would have no problem with that. However, in the Court's view, US citizens have a right not to see public money used for the promotion of religious observance.

In what some saw as a change of emphasis, in *Zelman v. Simmons-Harris* (2002), the Court upheld a programme in Ohio giving financial aid to parents to allow them to send their children to religious or private schools. In a 5–4 decision, the Court upheld the so-called 'school voucher' programme being run in the state of Ohio, and so appeared to breach the wall of separation between Church and state. In this case, the four liberal members of the Court — Justices Stevens, Souter, Ginsburg and Breyer — all dissented. The programme was supported by the Bush administration, the Republican Party and ideological conservatives. They saw the voucher programme as the best way to help poor people whose children would otherwise have to attend failing inner-city schools. The opponents were the Democratic Party, the teachers' unions and ideological liberals. They saw the programme as a threat to the state-run school system.

The case was of particular interest because it involved not only issues of religious freedom but also issues of race, as most of the children involved in the voucher programme were African-Americans. Under the programme in Cleveland, Ohio, the parents of some 3,700 children had been given vouchers worth up to $2,250 to send them to private schools rather than the free, state-run, local school. Of these 3,700, around 96% had opted to send their children to religious schools.

In December 2000, the Federal Court of Appeals had declared that the programme had the 'impermissible effect of promoting sectarian schools' and thereby violated the 1st Amendment's prohibition against 'the establishment of religion'. The majority of the Supreme Court disagreed. The majority opinion authored by Justice Thomas was most striking. Justice Thomas is the Court's only African-American and he often credits his own rise from poverty to the rigorous education that he received in a Roman Catholic school in Savannah, Georgia. He wrote:

> The promise of public school [i.e. state-run] education has failed poor inner-city blacks.
> If society cannot end racial discrimination, at least it can arm minorities with the education to defend themselves from some of discrimination's effects.

Chief Justice Rehnquist wrote in this case for the majority, too, stating that the key issue was not that almost all of the students who used vouchers went to religious schools, but rather that the vouchers were just one part of an array of alternatives to the state-run schools. Rehnquist concluded:

> The question is whether Ohio is coercing parents into sending their children to religious schools, and that question must be answered evaluating all options Ohio provides Cleveland school children, only one of which is to obtain a [voucher] and then choose a religious school.

In other words, it didn't matter that 96% of these children with vouchers happened to enrol in religious schools. That was a choice made by their parents, not the government.

The dissenting minority were unimpressed by this logic. Justice Souter called the Court's decision a 'potentially tragic' mistake that could 'force citizens to subsidise faiths they do not share even as it corrupts religion by making it dependent on government'. Justice Breyer said that the Court 'risks creating a form of religious conflict potentially harmful to the nation's social fabric'. Justice Stevens claimed that the Court had 'removed a brick from the wall that was once designed to separate religion from government, increasing the risk of religious strife and weakening the foundation of democracy'.

Freedom of speech, freedom of expression and freedom of the press

The 1st Amendment talks about more than just freedom of religion. It goes on to state: 'Congress shall make no law...abridging the freedom of speech, or of the press.' Here again, the Supreme Court has played an important role in protecting these fundamental rights. In *Buckley v. Valeo* (1976) the Court declared unconstitutional part of the Federal Election Campaign Act (1974) that limited expenditure by presidential candidates. The Court claimed that such limits infringed the 'freedom of speech' provision of the 1st Amendment.

When a lone gunman tried to assassinate President Ronald Reagan in Washington DC in March 1981, a 19-year-old clerk, Ardith McPherson, was fired from his place of work after being overheard to say: 'If they go for him again, I hope they get him.' In *Rankin v. McPherson* (1987), the Court stated that McPherson's 1st Amendment rights had been infringed by his being sacked.

In the 2002 case of *Watchtower Bible and Tract Society of New York Inc. v. Village of Stratton, Ohio*, the Supreme Court sought to protect the rights of people to go from door to door, whether as hawkers, politicians or representatives of religious groups, without having to get a permit beforehand. The case involved the small town on Stratton, Ohio, which had passed a local law requiring permits, under the guise of protecting its elderly citizens from doorstep harassment and potential crime. The law was challenged by the Jehovah's Witnesses, whose members are renowned for their door-to-door visits. Writing for the majority, Justice Stevens proclaimed:

> It is offensive, not only to the values of the 1st Amendment but to the very notion of a free society, that in the context of everyday public discourse a citizen must first inform the government of [his or] her desire to speak to [his or] her neighbours and then obtain a permit to do so.

The case was heard against the background of media reports of a couple in New Hampshire, allegedly murdered by two teenagers who had called at their home claiming to be conducting a door-to-door survey on the environment.

The Court has extended the 1st Amendment right of freedom of speech to freedom of expression — none more controversial than the 'expression' made by protesters of burning an American flag. In 1984, Gregory Lee Johnson was arrested outside the Republican National Convention in Dallas, Texas, for burning an American flag. Texas, along with 47 other states, had a state law forbidding the desecration of the US flag. In *Texas v. Johnson* (1989), the Supreme Court said that such laws were unconstitutional, as they infringed the 1st Amendment rights regarding freedom of expression. When the United States Congress reacted to the Court's decision by passing a federal law banning flag desecration, the Court promptly declared it unconstitutional in the 1990 case of *United States v. Eichman*.

In 1997, the Supreme Court had to decide how the freedom of speech rights guaranteed in the 1st Amendment applied to the world of the internet. In *Reno v. American Civil Liberties Union*, the Court struck down as unconstitutional the Communications Decency Act (1996). The act had made it a crime to make 'indecent' or 'patently offensive' material available to minors on the internet. In the view of the Court, this infringed the 1st Amendment. In particular, the Court objected to the imprecision of 'indecent' and 'patently offensive', calling them 'vague contours'. The Court claimed that, in attempting to protect minors, the Act had infringed the constitutional rights of adults. Writing for the 7–2 majority in this case, Justice Stevens stated:

> The Communications Decency Act (CDA) lacks the precision that the 1st Amendment requires when a statute regulates the content of speech. In order to deny minors access to potentially harmful speech, the CDA effectively suppresses a large amount of speech that adults have a constitutional right to receive and to address to one another.

Civil rights groups, such as the American Civil Liberties Union that had brought the case, hailed the decision as 'the Bill of Rights for the 21st century'. The *Washington Post* headlined the decision: 'The 1st Amendment Goes Digital'.

It is clear to see the difficulty that the Court faced in balancing competing rights. Senator Patrick Leahy (D–Vermont), aware of the interpretations that could be put on the Court's ruling, commented: 'I hope that nobody thinks this is a victory for child pornographers.' Senator Dan Coats (R–Indiana) did not like the judgment at all, saying that it showed the Court as 'out of touch with the American people'.

In *Ashcroft v. Free Speech Coalition* (2002), the Court decided that the Child Pornography Protection Act (1996) was unconstitutional. The act banned 'virtual' child pornography and provided for prison sentences for those who sold, distributed or possessed images that 'appear to be' or 'convey the impression of' children engaged in sexually explicit conduct. Again, the Court ruled that the law had been too widely drawn. Writing for the majority, Justice Kennedy stated:

> Few legitimate movie producers or book publishers, or few other speakers in any capacity, would risk distributing images in or near the uncertain reach of this law. The Constitution gives significant protection from over-broad laws that chill speech within the 1st Amendment's vast and privileged sphere.

Justice Kennedy went on to give examples of such contemporary films as *Traffic* and *American Beauty*, which present sexual scenes involving minors. He even wondered how Shakespeare's *Romeo and Juliet* would fare under this law.

In these 'freedom of speech' and 'freedom of expression' cases, the Court can be seen trying to balance competing rights and freedoms. The Court in essence is saying: we cannot protect the rights of one group in society by limiting the rights of another group. The rights of gun owners must be set against the public safety of school students. The rights of children to be protected from pornography on the internet must be set against the rights of those adults who wish to view pornography. The rights of people wishing to visit door-to-door must be set against the rights of people to be safe in their homes.

The Supreme Court has dealt with cases involving the freedom of the press, too. In *New York Times v. United States* (1971), the Court upheld the right of the *New York Times* to publish the so-called 'Pentagon Papers' — secret Defense Department documents concerning the Vietnam War.

Freedom to 'bear arms' (gun control)

The 2nd Amendment guarantees American citizens' right to 'bear arms'. The Constitution reads: 'A well regulated Militia, being necessary to the security of a free State, the right of the people to keep and bear Arms, shall not be infringed.' Thus, the Constitution implies the right of revolution. The Founding Fathers believed that the ultimate check against tyranny was an armed citizenry. However, the assassination of presidents and leading political figures — President Kennedy (1963), Senator Robert Kennedy (1968) and Martin Luther King (1968), to name but three — not to mention an alarming rise in gun-related crime, aroused nationwide concern over the ease with which Americans can buy guns. On the other side, the National Rifle Association, gun clubs, and other citizens concerned to be able to defend themselves in their own homes, have argued against stricter gun control.

In the 1995 case of *United States v. Lopez*, the Supreme Court declared the 1990 Gun-Free School Zones Act to be unconstitutional. This widely popular law had made it an offence 'for any individual knowingly to possess a firearm at a place that the individual knows, or has reasonable cause to believe, is a school zone'. This was Congress's response to the increase in shootings at and in the vicinity of schools in which the lives of pupils had been endangered. In 1992, an 18-year-old Texas high school student had been caught carrying a handgun to school: the Court declared that, by passing the act, Congress had exceeded its power under Article I, Section 8 of the Constitution.

Freedom from unreasonable searches

The 4th Amendment states: 'The right of the people to be secure in their persons, houses, papers and effects, against unreasonable searches and seizures shall not be violated.' In *United States v. Drayton* (2002), the Supreme Court ruled in a case regarding 'unreasonable searches'. The case arose from an incident in 1999 when police officers questioned and searched two passengers on a Greyhound bus in Tallahassee, Florida. Both men were found to be carrying packets of cocaine and were later convicted and sentenced on drug charges. However, they claimed that their 4th Amendment rights had been violated.

Writing for the 6–3 majority, Justice Kennedy said the passengers did not have to be told that they weren't obliged to cooperate. 'It is beyond question that had this encounter occurred on the street it would be constitutional,' he wrote. 'The fact that an encounter takes place on a bus does not on its own transform standard police questioning of citizens into an illegal seizure.' In his dissent, Justice Souter likened the situation to one in an alley 'with civilians in close quarters unable to move effectively, being told their cooperation is expected'. The case took on added importance after 11 September 2001, as police attempted to prevent the hijacking of public transport by road, rail or air.

In *Board of Education v. Earls* (2002), the Supreme Court upheld a programme in Oklahoma that required students wishing to participate in after-school activities to submit to random drug tests. The tests required no suspicion of any drug use and applied to students in Grades 7–12: that is, those aged between 13 and 18. The Court had already ruled in 1995 on the constitutionality of drug testing for school athletes. This case, however, involved a programme of testing students who had signed up to such activities as cheerleading, singing in a choir, playing in a band or joining the Future Farmers of America Club. The drug-testing programme was challenged by Lindsay Earls, a student at Tecumseh High School, Oklahoma.

In a 5–4 decision, the Court found the drug testing constitutional because, in the words of Justice Thomas, 'this policy reasonably serves the school district's important interest in detecting and preventing drug use in its students'. According to dissenting Justice Ginsburg, the programme was 'unreasonable, capricious and even perverse' because it targeted for testing a student population unlikely to be at risk from illicit drugs — that is, students who volunteer for after-school activities.

Summary

The protection of rights and liberties by the Supreme Court

➤ The Supreme Court's power of judicial review allows it to play a significant role in the protection of rights and liberties.

➤ It has been particularly active in the last 50 years in such areas as the rights of racial minorities and women, as well as such 1st Amendment rights as freedom of speech, expression and religion.

The protection of rights and liberties by Congress

Although the Supreme Court has often taken the lead in the protection of civil rights and liberties, Congress has frequently been involved as well. This was especially true during the 40-year period between 1955 and 1994, when the Democratic Party controlled the House of Representatives and, with the exception of 6 years (1981–86), the Senate as well. Since the formation of the so-called 'New Deal Coalition' in the 1930s, the Democrats have been the party committed to passing laws to protect the rights of minorities.

The rights of racial minorities

It was the Supreme Court in its 1954 *Brown v. Board of Education of Topeka* decision which gave momentum to black civil rights in the twentieth century. Congress was not far behind, passing a raft of civil rights laws during the next four decades.

Martin Luther King Jnr (1929–68), American black civil rights campaigner

In 1957, Congress passed a law creating the Civil Rights Commission and making it a federal crime to try to prevent a person from voting in a federal election. The really significant civil rights legislation was passed in 1964 and 1965, following a number of important political developments. First of these were the civil rights demonstrations, initially in the South, but then spreading to other parts of the United States. A year-long bus boycott by blacks in Montgomery, Alabama, started in December 1955 to protest against segregation laws on certain buses. The protest began when a black woman, Rosa Parks, was arrested for failing to give up her seat on a bus to a white man. These early demonstrations were based on the philosophy of non-violent civil disobedience advocated by Martin Luther King, who emerged as the leader of black Americans.

In May 1961, so-called 'freedom rides' began across the South, in which blacks deliberately travelled in the 'whites only' sections of buses; and in September 1962, James Meredith — a black student — attempted to gain admission to the all-white University of Mississippi. Once the civil rights movement gained its momentum, it was difficult to keep it under control and violence erupted. There was violence as law officials attempted to stop both the 'freedom rides' and Meredith's admission to the University of Mississippi. Similarly ugly scenes were repeated in Birmingham, Alabama, in April 1963 as police used force to end a black demonstration in the city. It was here that the police chief, Eugene 'Bull' Connor, ordered his officers to attack protesters, using attack dogs and high-pressure fire hoses to disperse what were essentially peaceful demonstrations.

Second, significant political developments took place in Washington DC. The assassination of President Kennedy in 1963 had brought Lyndon Johnson to the White House. Johnson was elected in 1964 by an overwhelming majority and was determined to use this mandate to pass a series of civil rights laws through a Democrat-controlled Congress. There was, however, a political mismatch within the Democratic Party itself. Although both Presidents Kennedy and Johnson wanted to enact civil rights legislation, many of the powerful Democrats in Congress were conservatives from the South. For example, both the Senate Judiciary Committee and the House Rules Committee — two committees crucial to the passage of such legislation — were hostile, dominated as they were by conservative Democrats and Republicans.

A police dog attacks a black protestor in Birmingham, Alabama, in April 1963

The passage of the 1964 Civil Rights Act was Congress's most far-reaching attempt to improve the civil rights of African-Americans. It dealt with five areas of disadvantage and discrimination: voting, public accommodations, schools, employment and the allocation of federal funds. In voting, it made it more difficult for states to use such ploys as literacy tests and the payment of a poll tax to bar African-Americans from voting. It barred discrimination in public accommodations, whether rooms in hotels or tables in restaurants. It authorised the federal government to take legal action against school districts that failed to desegregate their schools. It established the right to equality of opportunity in employment, for any race or colour. It provided for the withholding of federal government funds to programmes that were administered by state or local governments in a discriminatory fashion. The Senate took 83 days to debate the bill — the longest time in congressional history. The year 1964 also saw the ratification of the 24th Amendment (see Box 9.1).

Box 9.1 The 24th Amendment

Section 1. The right of citizens of the United States to vote in any primary or other election for President or Vice President, for electors for President or Vice President, or for Senator or Representative in Congress, shall not be denied or abridged by the United States or any State by reason of failure to pay any poll tax or other tax.

Section 2. The Congress shall have the power to enforce this article by appropriate legislation.

The following year, Congress passed another major piece of civil rights legislation — the Voting Rights Act (1965). This act ended the use of literacy and other tests to debar African-American voters and introduced federal officials to register voters. The act had a profound effect on national elections, as well as elections held in the South, and led not only to thousands of minority voters being added to the electoral registers, but also to the election of an increasing number of office-holders from minority groups.

A third major piece of legislation was the Civil Rights Act of 1968, which dealt principally with discrimination in housing. It banned discrimination, based on race, religion or national origin, in the advertising of, financing of, sale or rental of houses. It was extended to discrimination on the basis of gender in 1974 and physical handicap in 1988.

The rights of women
The movement to deliver fundamental rights and freedoms to racial minorities was followed swiftly by a similar movement aimed at doing the same for women. Congress responded to the feminist movement by passing laws requiring equal pay for equal work, and prohibiting discrimination on the basis of gender in employment as well as student admissions to schools and universities that received federal funding.

In March 1972, Congress initiated the Equal Rights Amendment (ERA) to the Constitution, which would have debarred discrimination on the basis of gender (see Box 9.2). When the 7-year limit for ratification by the states expired in 1979, Congress, in an unprecedented move, extended the deadline for a further 3 years. However, by March 1982, only 35 states had voted to ratify this proposed amendment — three short of the three-quarters of all the states required by the amendment procedure. The ERA movement was angered when incoming President Reagan failed to support the proposed amendment, thus almost guaranteeing its failure.

Box 9.2 The proposed Equal Rights Amendment

Equality of rights under the law shall not be denied or abridged by the United States or any state on account of sex.

The 1970s saw Congress pass some significant legislation to advance the rights of women. The Education Amendments Act (1972) prohibited discrimination on the grounds of gender in schools or universities receiving federal funding. The Equal Credit Opportunity Act (1974) gave women the same workplace rights as men. The Pregnancy Discrimination Act (1978) forbade discrimination against women employees on the grounds of pregnancy-related absence from work. Such legislation had some significant effects on educational and workplace opportunities for women during the succeeding decade, as shown in Table 9.3.

Table 9.3 Women in selected occupations: 1982 and 1992 compared

Occupation	Percentage women 1982	Percentage women 1992
Financial managers	38.6	46.3
Personnel managers	43.9	58.9
Pharmacists	26.7	37.8
Accountants	38.7	51.2
Lawyers	15.3	21.4

More recently, Congress has enacted laws against sexual harassment. The issue came to the fore in Washington politics during the 1990s. In 1991, Clarence Thomas faced allegations of sexual harassment during the Senate confirmation hearings for his appointment to the Supreme Court. This was followed later in the decade by allegations of sexual harassment against President Clinton by Paula Corbin Jones.

The rights of disabled persons

In 1990, Congress passed and President Bush signed into law the Americans with Disabilities Act (ADA). This may well be regarded as the first President Bush's most significant legislative achievement. Under this law, a disabled person is defined as anyone having a physical or mental impairment 'that substantially limits one or more major activities of life'. It requires 'reasonable accommodations' to be made for disabled persons, whether in the workplace or in public facilities such as pavements and train stations and on public transport. It is in the latter area that the effects of the act have been seen most profoundly: wheelchair access is now commonplace on buses, trains and subway systems in the USA. Offices, hotels, restaurants, churches, universities, libraries and the like have been adapted to allow easy access for physically disabled persons, and telephone companies offer special facilities for people with speech and hearing disabilities.

The ADA has proved to be a significant step forward in efforts by the federal government to bring disabled people into the mainstream of US life and society. The act has become the major source of grievance claims filed against employers with the Equal Employment Opportunity Commission.

Summary

The protection of rights and liberties by Congress

➢ Congress has played a significant role in the protection of rights and liberties over the past 40 years, especially regarding racial minorities, women and disabled persons.

The protection of rights and liberties by the president

Presidents can play an important role in the protection of rights and liberties in a number of ways. First, through their role as commander-in-chief, they can use troops to enforce legislation as well as judgments of the Supreme Court. President Eisenhower sent federal troops to Little Rock, Arkansas, in 1957 to give weight to the Supreme Court's order to desegregate schools.

Second, presidents can use the office as what Theodore Roosevelt called a 'bully pulpit' — to converse with the American people about important issues such as the rights and freedoms of Americans. Both Kennedy and Johnson used the presidential office to try to lead the country in the direction of civil rights reform during the 1960s. President Clinton conducted a public debate about the role of affirmative action programmes in the USA in the mid-1990s. Presidents can lend their clear and unequivocal support to civil rights legislation being debated in Congress. This was seen most remarkably during 1964 and 1965 with President Johnson's wholehearted support for the civil rights acts of those years. The support of President George Bush was crucial to the enactment of the Americans with Disabilities Act in 1990. In 2003, President George W. Bush publicly praised the Supreme Court for its decision in *Gratz v. Bollinger*, describing it as 'a careful balance between the goal of campus diversity and the fundamental principle of equal treatment under the law'.

Equally, presidents can use their political clout against developments in rights and freedoms to which they are opposed. President Nixon came out clearly in opposition to the 'busing' decision by the Supreme Court in *Swann v. Charlotte-Mecklenburg Board of Education*. President Ronald Reagan opposed the ratification of the Equal Rights

Amendment. President George Bush criticised the Supreme Court's decision to permit the burning of the American flag in *Texas v. Johnson*. Presidents can also oppose civil rights legislation passing through Congress. President George Bush vetoed the so-called Brady Gun Control Bill.

A number of presidents have used executive orders to further the cause of civil rights and liberties. President Truman integrated the United States armed forces by executive order. President Kennedy instituted an affirmative action programme in federal employment by executive order. In 1993, President Clinton used an executive order to return abortion counselling to federally funded clinics. (In 2001 President George W. Bush issued another executive order to reverse it.)

Presidents can affect federal government policies on civil rights through the appointments that they make to such groups as the Civil Rights Commission and the Equal Employment Opportunity Commission. In 1983, President Reagan sought to replace members of the Civil Rights Commission who had been openly critical of his administration's civil rights policies. Appointments that the president makes to all federal courts — and especially the United States Supreme Court — affect the way in which civil rights and liberties may, or may not, be protected. The extent to which a president appoints people from a diversity of backgrounds sends clear signals too. President Nixon's cabinet was described as '12 grey-haired guys named George'. President Clinton, on the other hand, said he wanted a cabinet that 'looked like America' and, during his 8 years in office, he appointed both the first female attorney general — Janet Reno in 1993 — and the first female secretary of state — Madeleine Albright in 1997.

Summary

The protection of rights and liberties by the president

➤ Presidents may play a significant role in the protection of rights and liberties through the use of troops, lending political support, using executive orders and making key appointments.

Exercises

1 Explain the terms: (a) civil rights; (b) civil liberties.
2 What significant developments have occurred in the USA since the Civil War that have affected the representation of ethnic minorities?
3 Explain the terms: (a) busing; (b) quotas; (c) affirmative action.
4 Describe (with examples) how the Supreme Court has attempted to safeguard the rights of racial minorities.
5 What significant rulings has the Supreme Court made concerning capital punishment?
6 Explain the Supreme Court's role in the issue of abortion.

7 Explain the difficulties facing the Supreme Court in cases concerning freedom of religion.
8 Explain how the Supreme Court has sought to defend freedom of speech, of expression and of the press.
9 What rulings has the Supreme Court made on the issue of gun control?
10 What has the Supreme Court said on 4th Amendment rights?
11 How important a role has Congress played in the protection of civil rights and liberties?
12 Explain the role of recent presidents in attempting to protect civil rights and liberties.

Exam focus

1 Assess the impact that the three branches of the federal government have each had on the protection of the rights of ethnic minorities.
2 Examine the claim that the Supreme Court's power of judicial review makes it essentially unnecessary to amend formally the US Constitution.
3 To what extent can the Rehnquist Court be described as 'conservative'?
4 'A judicial body whose decisions are of major political importance.' Assess this comment on the US Supreme Court.
5 How effectively have the civil rights and liberties of US citizens been protected?
6 How effective is the Bill of Rights in securing liberty for individual Americans?
7 Examine the claim that the Supreme Court has a greater impact on US society than the reforms of either the president or Congress.

Further reading

Gillman, H., *The Supreme Court in American Politics* (Kansas University Press, 1999).
Pacelle, R. L., *The Role of the Supreme Court in American Politics* (Westview, 2002).

US/UK Comparative Government & Politics

Chapter 10

Constitutions, judiciaries, rights and liberties

Just off Pennsylvania Avenue in Washington DC — midway between the White House and the Capitol — is an imposing building with a cupola. Even in the hottest and most humid days of a Washington summer, you will see an orderly, and surprisingly hushed, line of American tourists waiting to enter. As they do so, shirts are put on and baseball caps are removed. Not much in America causes such reverential behaviour. What is this building? Does it have some sacred significance? No. It's much more important than that. It is the National Archives — the building that houses the Constitution of the United States of America. Americans are not known for queuing, and they are certainly not known for quietness, but the Constitution demands both. The Vietnam Memorial is perhaps the only other 'monument' in Washington that elicits the same response.

The Magna Carta might create a similar queue in Great Britain, but it is unlikely to be on many tourists' priority list. In the UK, the Constitution is rather like God — invisible and not highly regarded by most, though probably more important than people think.

If you walk up Pennsylvania Avenue from the National Archives, within a few blocks you are on Capitol Hill. Sitting just across the road from the Capitol is the building that for the past seven decades has housed the United States Supreme Court. It is imposing, with its Greco-Roman architecture adorned with marble and a multitude of statues both inside and out. It is not really possible to come up with a parallel in Britain. There is no Supreme Court in the British system yet. The Law Lords are accommodated within the Palace of Westminster. A similar arrangement used to be in place in Washington, where until the 1930s the Supreme Court was housed in the basement of the Capitol. Today, the third branch of government has its own separate and splendid quarters. It is perhaps symbolic of the UK's fused system of government that, when it comes to the head of the judiciary, even the buildings are fused.

The United States Supreme Court and the Law Lords in the UK pass what is usually the final judgment on the most important court cases involving fundamental rights and liberties. In both systems, however, the other two branches of government have a role to play.

A Constitutions

Questions to be answered in this section

➤ What is a constitution?
➤ How do constitutions originate?
➤ What are the differences between codified and uncodified constitutions?
➤ How important are the concepts of democracy and sovereignty in the US and UK constitutions?
➤ What are the differences between presidential and parliamentary systems of government?
➤ What are the differences between federal and unitary systems of government?
➤ What issues of constitutional reform are debated in the USA and the UK?

Terminology

A constitution is a framework within which a country's system of government is conducted — the rules that govern the relationship between the government and the governed. Constitutions establish the duties, powers and functions of the various institutions of government. They define the relationship between the state and the individual. Constitutions can be either codified, as in the USA, or uncodified, as in the UK.

Origins

Constitutions tend to be the product of either revolution or evolution. The US and UK constitutions are respectively examples of each. The US Constitution is largely the product of the late-eighteenth-century War of Independence. This one cataclysmic event produced a break with the colonial past and an entirely new system of government. The US Constitution was written to mark that break by people who were to become known as the Founding Fathers — the founders of the new nation.

As Malcolm Walles (1988) has put it, 'whereas the US Constitution appeared out of the smoke of gunpowder, the UK constitution appeared out of the mists of time'.

The kind of national and political upheaval seen in the USA in the late eighteenth century has not been seen in the UK since the eleventh century and the Norman Conquest. The English Civil War of the seventeenth century failed to have similarly long-lasting effects. The monarchy was quickly restored and the evolutionary pattern of development continued. Even the so-called Glorious Revolution of the 1680s, accompanied as it was by the drawing up of a Bill of Rights, failed to give birth to any new formal statement of governmental relationships. The UK constitution was left to evolve, piecemeal.

Codified and uncodified constitutions

The vast majority of democracies have codified constitutions: that is, they have a document in which most of the rules concerning the government of the nation are drawn together. The USA is therefore in line with other democracies. The UK is unusual in having an uncodified constitution.

Table 10.1 Features of the US and UK constitutions

Features of the US constitution	Features of the UK constitution
Codified	Uncodified
Federal	Unitary
Presidential	Parliamentary
Separation of powers	Fusion of powers
Popular sovereignty	Parliamentary sovereignty
High levels of democratic participation	Low levels of democratic participation

The USA has a single document, running to no more than 7,000 words — under 20 printed pages — which contains most of the country's constitutional arrangements. However, even a codified constitution often contains parts that are uncodified. For example, in the US Constitution, there is no mention of such important matters as political parties, primary elections or congressional committees. It is possible to regard certain fundamental Acts of Congress — for example, the War Powers Act (1973) — as being part of the Constitution. Nations with codified constitutions can even develop entirely unwritten conventions. When President George Washington declined to seek a third term of office in 1796, he put in place the unwritten convention of the

The Articles of the US Constitution

two-term presidency. It was only after Franklin Roosevelt broke that convention in 1940 — and again in 1944 — that the convention was formalised as part of the written document, in this case as the 22nd Amendment.

Similarly, although the UK is said to have an uncodified constitution, it is certainly not entirely unwritten. Indeed, much of the UK constitution is written down — in Acts of Parliament and in common law. It is simply that it is not collected together into a document called 'a constitution'. Thus, every constitution is in the end a blend of the written and the unwritten. It is the balance between the two that varies.

The advantages of codified constitutions

Codified constitutions are said to have certain advantages.

➤ The provisions within them are entrenched — hedged about with a deliberately difficult and demanding amendment process. To delay the general election due in 1940 during the Second World War, all the UK government had to do was pass an Act of Parliament. As a result, no general elections were held in the UK between 1935 and 1945. In the USA, the presidential and congressional elections both went ahead as usual in November 1944. Only the passage of a constitutional amendment could have stopped them. Likewise, the granting of votes to women and to 18 to 21-year-olds required only Acts of Parliament in the UK, but constitutional amendments in the USA.

➤ Codified constitutions are said to provide for more significant and effective checks and balances between the various branches of government. In the USA, the president finds himself subject to all kinds of checks — mainly by the legislature, but also by the judiciary — that are unknown to the UK prime minister.

➤ Codified constitutions are said to enhance both the awareness and the protection of civil rights and liberties. Prime Minister Margaret Thatcher deprived workers at the government's communications headquarters (GCHQ) of trade union membership rights in the 1980s on the grounds of national security. In the USA, 1st Amendment rights would have made such a move more difficult.

➤ Codified constitutions can be made surprisingly flexible by vague wording and judicial interpretation. The US Constitution's granting of power to Congress to 'provide for the common defence and general welfare of the United States' is an example of the former, and the Supreme Court's rulings on abortion rights an example of the latter.

The disadvantages of codified constitutions

Codified constitutions are said to have drawbacks too.

➤ They tend to elevate the importance of unelected judges over the elected legislature. In the USA this could be seen in the Supreme Court's power to declare Acts of Congress to be unconstitutional. Imagine the courts in the UK deciding the result of a general election, as occurred in the USA in December 2000.

➤ Codified constitutions can be inflexible and so fail to change along with society. Some would see the difficulties in the USA concerning the 2nd Amendment — the right to keep and bear arms — as an example of the Constitution being stuck in the eighteenth century to the disadvantage of those living in the twenty-first.

➤ The enumeration of rights does not necessarily safeguard those rights. The passage of the 15th Amendment in 1870 regarding the rights of African-Americans in the United States did little for many blacks for almost a century.

Summary

Codified and uncodified constitutions

➤ Most democracies have codified, rather than uncodified, constitutions.

➤ There are both advantages and disadvantages to codified constitutions.

➤ The US and UK constitutions have many significant differences.

Democracy and sovereignty

Here again, the US and UK constitutions differ significantly. Although both constitutions can nowadays be said to be based on the principle of democracy, the two constitutions have evolved at different speeds to different conclusions. In the USA, the concepts of direct democracy and popular sovereignty are — and have always been — more in evidence.

Americans play a greater role in the electoral processes of their nation than do people in the UK. Between the 1780s and the 1880s, the US House of Representatives was elected on a wider franchise than the UK House of Commons. Admittedly, slavery was permitted in the Constitution until the Civil War, but the Founding Fathers envisaged the House as being elected every 2 years by all free men over the age of 21. The Senate has been directly elected since 1914. The election of the president has evolved from an indirect to a virtually direct election. The significant growth of the direct primary through the twentieth century allowed ordinary voters to participate in candidate selection for elections at all levels of government. Moreover, in the states, the initiative, referendum and recall procedures allow a level of direct participation unheard of in the UK.

In the UK, the emphasis is on representative democracy and parliamentary sovereignty. British citizens — although, strictly speaking, they are merely 'subjects of the Crown' — have fewer opportunities for democratic participation than their US counterparts. While the Founding Fathers in Philadelphia were establishing a House of Representatives, elected every 2 years by most men over the age of 21, the UK had a House of Commons elected every 7 years — 5-yearly elections were introduced only after the 1911 Parliament Act — by an electorate that had to satisfy property-owning qualifications. It took the UK until the third Parliamentary Reform Act (1884) to reach anything like the levels of participation that had been practised in the USA by then for nearly 100 years. In the UK, only party members can participate in the selection of candidates for the lower chamber, the second chamber remains unelected, the prime minister is indirectly elected, there is a hereditary monarch and Parliament remains sovereign, not the people.

Summary

Democracy and sovereignty

> The US and UK constitutions differ considerably in terms of democracy and sovereignty. The US Constitution allows for higher levels of democratic participation than does the UK constitution. In the USA the people are sovereign; in the UK Parliament is sovereign.

Presidential and parliamentary systems

One of the most important differences between the US and UK constitutions is between the US presidential system and the UK parliamentary system. A presidential system is one in which there is a strict separation of personnel between the executive and the legislature. A parliamentary system is one in which the executive is derived from and can be removed by the legislature.

Table 10.2 Features of the presidential and parliamentary systems

Features of presidential systems	Features of parliamentary systems
Executive barred from the legislature	Executive derived from the legislature
Separation of powers	Fusion of powers
Co-equal branches	Parliamentary sovereignty

The US Constitution is characterised by what Neustadt called the doctrine of 'separate institutions, sharing powers', which is popularly known as the separation of powers. The UK constitution is characterised by a fusion of powers, under which government ministers who head up executive branch departments sit as members of the legislature at the same time. Until June 2003, when new institutions were announced, the Lord Chancellor sat in all three branches of government — the Law Lords (i.e. the judiciary), the House of Lords (i.e. the legislature) and the cabinet (i.e. the executive). However, given the 'sharing' of powers in the US system, the differences between the two systems are perhaps not as great as textbooks have traditionally stated. The US president *needs* Congress no less than the UK prime minister *needs* Parliament.

The US Constitution is based on the principle of co-equality between the three branches of government. This is at the heart of the checks and balances principle, which James Madison called 'ambition counteracting ambition'. The UK constitution is based on the principle that the legislature is supreme or 'sovereign'. It is Parliament to which government ministers — both collectively and individually — are accountable through the twin doctrines of collective and individual ministerial responsibility. Parliament is 'supreme' in the sense that no court can declare an Act of Parliament to be unconstitutional. As Malcolm Shaw (1968) concluded:

> The end result of executive–legislative–judicial relations in Britain is a concentration of authority facilitating party government and majority rule. The end result in America is a diffusion of authority obstructing party government and enhancing minority rights.

Summary

Presidential and parliamentary systems
> ➤ The US and UK constitutions differ significantly in that the former is based on a presidential system while the latter is based on a parliamentary system.

Federal and unitary systems

If the UK is out of synch with most modern democracies in terms of its uncodified constitution, it is very much in synch with most modern democracies in having a unitary form of government. A unitary system of government is one in which all political power is vested in a single national institution. All local or devolved governmental power exists only at the pleasure of the national government.

By contrast, the USA has a federal system of government in which political power is divided between a national government and state governments, each having its own area of substantive jurisdiction. Americans think of themselves very much as Floridians, Virginians, New Yorkers or whatever, in a way in which those in the UK do not regard themselves as much other than British, except to be English, Welsh, Scots or Northern Irish. Federalism is appropriate to a country as large and diversified — in race, culture, language, economy and climate — as the USA. 'Federalism' in UK politics is used only in reference to the politics of the EU.

The advantages of federalism

Federalism is said to have certain advantages.

- ➤ It safeguards against an over-strong central government and creates an additional set of checks of balances — those between the federal and state governments.
- ➤ It mitigates remoteness in geographically large countries, and it allows a greater measure of regional diversity.
- ➤ It helps maintain national unity in countries that might otherwise fracture into different nation states.
- ➤ The states can become policy incubators as well as training grounds for national politicians.

The disadvantages of federalism

There are disadvantages, however.

- The over-fragmentation of government can result in gridlock and frustration. Consider, for example, the way the southern states were able to frustrate civil rights reform in the 1950s and 1960s.
- Federalism does not necessarily overcome centralising tendencies. Consider the way the power of the federal government increased in the USA during the first two thirds of the twentieth century at the expense of the state governments.
- Federalism can also breed national divisions and encourage moves towards independence — witness the southern states in the 1860s, or the relationship between Canada and Quebec today.

The last 30 years of the twentieth century in the USA saw significant moves towards decentralisation, be it with Nixon's 'new federalism' or Clinton's declaration that 'the era of big government is over'. In the UK, modifications of the unitary form of government came with the devolution of power to the Scottish Parliament and the assemblies in Wales and Northern Ireland. The Blair government in 2003 was considering regional assemblies in England.

Centralisation or decentralisation

The 'centralisation versus decentralisation' debate is common in today's political science. On the one hand, centralisation is said to have four specific advantages. First, it promotes national unity to the benefit of the entire community. Second, it promotes uniformity because laws, levels of taxation, education and other social benefits are uniform across the entire nation state. Third, it promotes equality. It is easier, for example, to promote economic redistribution between rich and poor areas within a nation-state. Finally, a single currency and central control of taxation and the national infrastructure all tend to promote national prosperity.

On the other hand, decentralisation has its merits. First, it provides enhanced opportunities for democratic participation. Second, it promotes a higher degree of responsiveness, with governmental institutions being 'closer to the people'. Accountability is thereby enhanced. Third, by cutting down the physical distances between the government and the citizenry, legitimacy is enhanced. Finally, decentralisation guards against central government tyranny and provides a useful set of checks and balances.

Summary

Federal and unitary systems

- The US system of government is federal while the UK system is essentially unitary.
- There are both merits and demerits to federal systems of government.
- There are advantages and disadvantages to centralisation and decentralisation in governmental systems.

Constitutional reform

The debate concerning constitutional reform is alive and well in both the USA and the UK. However, the debate is often in different areas.

In the USA, constitutional reform usually comes in the shape of calls for further amendments to the Constitution. In recent years, there have been calls for constitutional amendments to pursue a number of clear policy — rather than specifically constitutional — objectives. These have included the proposal of constitutional amendments to balance the federal budget, ban flag desecration, permit prayers in state-run schools and preserve the traditional concept of marriage.

Most calls for specifically constitutional reform have recently centred on electoral practices and the relationship between the legislature and the executive. In the first category, there have been unsuccessful attempts to limit the number of terms that members of Congress may serve; however, the 'term limits' movement seemed to be a passing fad of the 1990s. Following the 2000 election débâcle, there were calls — again largely unheeded — to amend, or abolish, the Electoral College as the means of electing the president.

In the second category is the constitutional debate during the 1990s about whether the president should be granted the power of 'line-item veto'. A congressional attempt to grant the president something like this power merely by the passage of an Act of Congress was declared unconstitutional by the Supreme Court in 1998. Following talk of the 'imperilled presidency' in the 1970s, specifically after the so-called 'failed' presidencies of Nixon (1969–74), Ford (1974–77) and Carter (1977–81), there was some debate about wholesale constitutional reform of executive–legislative relations. Some scholars and commentators called for such reforms as: a one-term 6-year presidency; bringing together the elections for the president and both houses of Congress; and drawing the cabinet from Congress. There was some debate, too, about possible reform of both the budget process and the war-making powers, which would affect the balance of power between president and Congress. The stand-off between President George W. Bush and the Senate on judicial nominees brought calls for changes to the nomination and confirmation process. The events of 11 September 2001 brought calls for a constitutional amendment to allow Congress to cope better with an attack that might wipe out a significant number of House and Senate members.

This is all quite different from debate in the UK on constitutional issues. It is almost tempting to suggest that the UK is indulging in constitutional debates that the USA had decades — even centuries — ago. No wonder Americans find it difficult to understand the debate going on in the UK on the further reform of the House of Lords as well as debate about the future of the monarchy. Debate about electoral systems has been on the constitutional reform agenda in the UK for decades. Not since before the Second World War has there been any serious debate in the USA about abandoning or modifying the first-past-the-post electoral system. That members of Congress are elected in a first-past-the-post election is not, and never has been, a matter of debate within the USA. The lack of a national third party to push for a change that might be to its advantage is clearly a factor. The Republicans and Democrats — much like the Labour and Conservative parties in the UK — are satisfied with an electoral system that allows them to control the levers of power alternately. The Republicans' 40-year period of minority status in the House of Representatives between 1955 and 1995 brought many Republicans to support congressional term limits, but any enthusiasm for this soon waned once they had enjoyed majority status for a few years.

One area of constitutional reform common to both countries is that of decentralisation in the USA and devolution in the UK. There might be a parallel between moves towards decentralisation in the USA from the 1970s and those towards devolution in the UK during the same period. The debate in the USA, however, is strictly within the limits of a federal system, whereas not many British politicians are prepared to talk about the 'f-word'. In addition, moves towards devolution within the UK are no more than that. Devolution within a unitary system of government is not the same as decentralisation within a federal system of government. Devolution is simply the transfer of power from central government to *subordinate* regional governments. Sovereignty remains with the central government. To 'devolve' is to 'pass powers *down*', from a higher authority to a lower authority.

Finally, it is important to note that, while constitutional reform was a central plank of the two Blair governments (1997 and 2001), no modern US administration was elected on a platform that included constitutional reform and is unlikely to be. Despite the flurry of votes on constitutional amendments immediately after the Republican victories in the 1994 mid-term elections — 17 votes in 5 years — none resulted in Congress passing an amendment. (Even then, there would still remain ratification by three-quarters of the state legislatures.) Americans' reverence for the Constitution and their great reluctance to tinker with it contrasts significantly with the situation in the UK, where many see constitutional arrangements as being in drastic need of reform and where governments appear too timid to address the issues. Only another cataclysmic event on a par with the War of American Independence or the Civil War would trigger moves for significant constitutional reform in the USA. Not even events as significant as the disputed 2000 election or the attacks of 11 September 2001 were of sufficient magnitude to bring about reform of the US Constitution. Americans seem to have adopted the view of constitutional reform put forward in 1770 by Horace Walpole: 'Everybody talks of the Constitution, but all sides forget that the Constitution is extremely well, and would do very well, if they would but leave it alone.'

Meanwhile, in the UK, with its evolutionary tradition, constitutional reform will continue, whether it be wholesale, with a codified constitution, or piecemeal, with further reform of the electoral system, regional government, the second chamber and the monarchy.

Summary

Constitutional reform

➤ Constitutional reform tends to be less of an issue in the USA than in the UK.

➤ In the USA, the Constitution is regarded with some reverence.

➤ The UK constitution is seen by many as out-dated.

B Judiciaries

Questions to be answered in this section

➤ What is the judiciary and what are its functions?

➤ How are judges selected?

➤ Are the courts politicised?

➤ What checks are there on the judiciaries?

➤ Has 'judicial activism' increased in recent decades?

Definition and functions

The judiciary is the branch of government empowered to decide legal disputes. Once the legislature has 'made' the law, and the executive has 'carried out' the law, the judiciary both 'enforces' and 'interprets' the law. In nations that have a codified constitution, the judiciary finds itself interpreting 'the supreme law' too — that is, the constitution itself. It is this important function that distinguishes the judiciary in the USA from its UK counterpart. As a corollary to this, the US courts can declare Acts of Congress to be unconstitutional. The UK courts have no power to declare Acts of Parliament to be unconstitutional. To do so would infringe the doctrine of parliamentary supremacy.

Judiciaries therefore resolve disputes between individuals and between individuals and the state. In addition, they interpret the law, determining what it now means and how it should be applied. Judges act as guardians of the law, applying its rules fairly and impartially — giving 'equal justice under law', as the motto on the front of the US Supreme Court building has it. Judiciaries play an important role in safeguarding the rights and liberties of citizens, too — an area that is developed in greater detail later in this chapter.

Appointment of judges

In the USA, judges are appointed by the president for life and must be confirmed by a simple majority vote of the Senate. In the UK, senior judges are appointed by the prime minister on the advice of the Lord Chancellor. There is no formal check on such appointments. All federal judges in the USA and all judges in the UK are therefore appointed to office. The same is true in most of the states of the USA where the state governor has the power of appointment. In about a third of states, state judges are elected.

Both systems have potential problems. Appointment can lead to accusations of cronyism, nepotism and politicisation. Presidents and prime ministers can attempt to appoint judges whose judicial philosophy seems to match their own. This is more important in the USA, where judges quite simply have greater opportunity to exercise a political role by virtue of their power of judicial review. Presidents' attempts at such political manipulation do not always work out in practice, however. The Senate may reject their choices on these grounds — witness the Senate's rejection of Robert Bork in 1987 — or, more likely, the judges prove to be unpredictable in their judgments — witness the appointment by Presidents Gerald Ford and George Bush of what turned out to be liberal Supreme Court justices Stevens and Souter: both presidents thought they were appointing conservative justices. Some think that appointed judges are unrepresentative, too likely to be drawn from the wealthier and better-educated members of society. Appointed judges are often accused of being out-of-date, out-of-touch and overly conservative, more interested in protecting property rights than personal rights and unsympathetic to those who disturb the public order or challenge the status quo. Of course, these are generalisations, but there is evidence to substantiate the arguments.

However, election, while perhaps going some way towards making the courts representative, is no guarantee of judicial competence. Elected judges might be more tempted than their appointed counterparts to follow the latest popular whim.

Summary

Selection of judges

➤ All federal court judges in the USA and all judges in the UK are appointed to office.
➤ There are more stringent checks on these appointments in the USA than in the UK.

Politicisation

In democratic states where politicians appoint judges, there is a concern that judges may become politicised. The appointment process can clearly lead to politicisation. When, as in the USA, judges are appointed by a politician — the president — and confirmed by a vote of politicians — the Senate — politics is bound to get mixed up in the process. As a candidate in the presidential election in 2000, George W. Bush made clear the *kind* of judges he would appoint to the courts if elected.

The appointment process in the UK is undoubtedly less politicised than in the USA. It avoids the open partisanship of appointment that is so evident in both the appointed and elected judges in the USA. However, there is still potential for politicisation. Appointment to the bench is by the Lord Chancellor, who is appointed by the prime minister and is a member of the government, although the Blair government wishes to change this.

Courts with the power to declare acts passed by the legislature to be unconstitutional have inevitably brought the courts into the political arena. The US Supreme Court makes decisions on a host of issues that are the subject of political debate — issues that divide the major political parties. In 2000, it effectively had to decide the result of a presidential election. Interestingly, on both sides of the Atlantic during the second half of the twentieth century, judges seemed more willing to grasp political nettles, to enter the political arena more readily. This raises serious questions of representation and accountability.

Representation and accountability

Judges and their courts can claim to be politically independent if they are not subject to pressure from politicians in the decisions they reach. In the former Soviet Union or in Robert Mugabe's Zimbabwe, for example, the courts were — or are — not politically independent. The US Supreme Court has not been noted for being kind to presidents.

The judiciary can claim to be politically independent if the judges refrain entirely from involving themselves in party politics and electioneering. Here again, both the US and UK systems hold up pretty well. In this respect, the sight of the members of the Supreme Court sitting in the front row of the 'audience' at the president's State of the Union Address to Congress might be considered a little out of place. Political independence of judges is enhanced by their life tenure, which puts them above political pressure.

It is, nonetheless, probably true that Americans think of their courts — and especially the US Supreme Court — as part of the political apparatus of the federal government. When the Court makes decisions about abortion, crime and punishment, the content of the internet or even who becomes their president, it is hardly surprising that this institution is thought to be political. In the UK, most citizens probably do not see the courts as part of the political system, yet there are doubtless some who would urge the UK courts be more political as well as others who think they are at times already too political. There are certainly some who fear that, were the UK to adopt a written constitution or a modern bill of rights, its courts would follow the path of greater politicisation seen in the USA. Others, however, point out that such fears ignore the different political environments of the two countries. The concentration of power in the UK compared to the diffusion of power in the USA probably makes it more desirable to have some statement of citizens' rights and equally of constraints on government.

Summary

Politicisation

➤ Allegations of politicisation of the courts occur in both the USA and the UK.
➤ The federal courts in the USA have a much more significant political role to play than do their UK counterparts.
➤ Political independence of judges is safeguarded in both systems.

Checks on the judiciary

Like the other branches of government, the judiciary is subject to a number of checks. It is checked by the legislature, which may alter the laws and thereby alter the judgments that the courts may make. In the USA, the legislature may initiate constitutional amendments, thereby further limiting the ability of the judiciary to decide that something is unconstitutional. Furthermore, the legislature may be able to play a role not only in the appointment but also in the removal of judges. This is the case in the USA, where the Senate must agree by a simple majority vote to the appointment of all federal judges. The House may vote to impeach a judge and, should the Senate then find the judge guilty by a two-thirds majority, he or she is removed from office. Legislatures may be able to influence the number of judges that are appointed to any court, as is the case in the US federal courts.

The executive branch may be able to check the judiciary too. Chief executives usually have a role in the appointment process — possibly significantly, as for the president of the USA. The chief executive may seek to check the judiciary by deciding whether to throw his political weight behind a particular judgment of the courts.

Judiciaries must often rely upon the other two branches of government to give practical support to their decisions, otherwise they will remain judgments merely in theory rather than in practice. The extent to which the other two branches lend their practical support to the decisions made by judiciaries may well be decided by public opinion. Thus, public opinion can form an important check on the judiciary. Although judges are not meant to act as elected representatives of the people, they have to keep in mind that, if their decisions are to be regarded by the majority of citizens as both legitimate and worthy of obedience, they cannot afford to stray too far from what is acceptable in the mainstream of public opinion.

In countries with a codified constitution, the document itself can be a check on the judiciary. It may contain specific grants of power or may grant specific rights and liberties that a judiciary cannot reinterpret. Constitutions may be amended to curtail the power of the judiciary.

Summary

Checks on the judiciary

➤ Judiciaries are checked by the other branches of government and public opinion.

Judicial activism

Some would argue that both the USA and the UK have seen a growth in judicial activism in recent decades. In the USA, this would be dated from the Warren Court (1953–69), continuing with decisions such as *Roe v. Wade* (1973) and *Bush v. Gore* (2000).

In the UK, there has been a trend since the 1980s for the courts to be more willing to issue judgments that are critical of the actions of government ministers. The number of applications for 'judicial review' in the UK has increased sharply during the past 20 years and judges have become more willing to enter the political debate by declaring policy invalid or actions illegal. Although UK courts do not have the 'judicial review' power of their US counterparts to declare legislation unconstitutional, they do have a power of judicial review to declare actions of members of the executive branch *ultra vires* — beyond the powers vested in them. The UK courts have become increasingly willing to issue such decisions, mainly concerning areas of human rights and liberties. While home secretary in Margaret Thatcher's government, Kenneth Baker fell foul of the courts on anything from retrospective rises in television licences to the deportation of immigrants. His successor in the John Major government, Michael Howard, had an equally torrid time from the courts, being defeated by them on ten occasions, often over sentencing policy.

Michael Howard, when home secretary, was overruled on policy on a number of occasions by the courts

Summary

Judicial activism

➤ Both the USA and the UK have seen an increase in judicial activism in recent decades.

C Rights and liberties

Questions to be answered in this section
➤ What are rights and liberties?
➤ How can they be classified?
➤ Who protects rights and liberties?

Definition and types of rights

A right is something to which a person is entitled. A 'human right' is a right to which all human beings are entitled; a 'civil right' is a right to which all within a particular nation state are entitled. Hence, rights are often described as being 'fundamental' or 'inalienable' — that is, undeniable. John Locke (1632–1704) defined these fundamental rights as 'life, liberty and property'. For Thomas Jefferson (1743–1826) they were 'life, liberty and the pursuit of happiness'.

Rights can be classified into two distinct types: positive rights and negative rights. Positive rights are rights 'to' something. They include the right to life, liberty, security, a fair trial, assembly, religion, expression, thought and conscience as well as respect for private and family life. Negative rights are rights to be free 'from' something. They include the right to freedom from torture, inhuman or degrading treatment, imprisonment without trial, slavery and enforced labour as well as from various forms of discrimination based on such matters as race, colour, gender or religious belief and practice.

However, safeguarding and delivering rights is a different matter from simply announcing or listing them. Despite a constitutional guarantee of rights, a number of significant groups have been subject to discrimination. In the USA the treatment of Native Americans and blacks, as well as that of Japanese-Americans during the Second World War, comes to mind. In the UK, government attempts to tamper with trade union membership rights, the right to silence and the right to trial by jury have all led to lively political debate.

Summary

Definition and types of rights

➢ A right is something to which one is entitled.

➢ Rights can be classified as either 'positive' or 'negative'.

➢ Defining rights in a constitution is one thing; safeguarding them in practice is another.

Protecting rights and liberties

The protection of rights and liberties is a role played, potentially, by all three branches of government as well as by other parts of the political system, such as political parties, pressure groups and the media.

It is probably the judiciaries that play the most significant role in the protection of rights and liberties. This has certainly been the case in the USA, where the rights of such groups as women, racial minorities and arrested people have been the subject of important Supreme Court decisions. The Court has been to the fore in decisions about freedom of speech, religion and expression — so-called 1st Amendment rights. Whether the Court has always been effective in protecting these rights and liberties is a debatable point. Certainly, African-Americans got fairly short shrift from the Court until 1954. Some women might consider that some of the decisions by the Court on abortion rights have whittled away their 'right to choose', while pro-lifers might criticise the Court for its failure to protect the rights of unborn children. A similar debate could be had on the issue of school prayers — protecting the separation of church and state while at the same time protecting Americans' right to the 'free exercise' of their religion.

In the UK, similar points could be made to debate whether the courts have effectively protected the rights of women, trade unionists and racial minorities. In addition, several eminent UK judges argued publicly for the incorporation of the European Convention on Human Rights into British law — a goal that was achieved by the passage of the Human Rights Act (1998) by the first Blair government.

Legislatures have a significant role to play in the protection of rights and liberties. In the USA, Congress has passed civil rights legislation to promote the rights of minorities in such areas as education, housing and work, as well as voting rights. In the UK, Parliament has passed laws in such areas as abortion rights for women as well as equal opportunity rights for racial minorities. Equally, legislatures sometimes stand accused of infringing rights and liberties: the US Congress in its anti-terrorism legislation after 11 September 2001 and the UK Parliament in its attempts to limit trial by jury. In both countries, the balance between civil liberties on the one hand and domestic security on the other has been difficult to maintain, as the cartoon below depicts with 'Uncle Sam'.

Executives have a leadership role to play — what Americans call the 'bully pulpit'. Presidents and prime ministers can, by the use of their formal and informal powers, bring political weight to bear in the protection of rights and liberties. Consider, for example, President Lyndon Johnson's leadership in the promotion of black civil rights, Bill Clinton's support for affirmative action and Tony Blair's support of equal opportunity legislation. Equally, they can by their opposition be seen in the eyes of their critics to frustrate the promotion of certain rights and liberties. In this regard, consider President Richard Nixon's views on 'busing', the first President Bush's views on flag burning and Tony Blair's views on the right to silence. Both sides in the heated debate in British politics about hunting with dogs view the issue as one about rights.

Political parties may seek through their policy agendas to promote the safeguard of civil rights and liberties. Such agendas are most clearly associated with parties of the centre left — the American Democrats and the Liberal Democrats and the Labour Party in the UK — which have played a significant role in advancing the protection of rights in a number of the areas already mentioned.

Pressure groups have a significant role to play in that they seek to protect the rights and liberties of their own client group — be they minorities, motorists or medical staff, to give but three examples. Pressure groups lobby all three branches of government to see rights enacted, protected and enforced.

Finally, the media, through drawing attention to the failure of governments to safeguard certain rights and liberties, seek to bring pressure upon political leaders to strengthen the legal framework to support groups which they see as disadvantaged. For example, the media in both countries have from time to time highlighted what they perceive as racial prejudice within the police force, exhibiting itself either through violence (the Rodney King case in the USA) or through lack of interest (the Stephen Lawrence case in the UK).

Summary

Protecting rights and liberties

➢ All three branches of government have a potential role to play in protecting rights and liberties.

➢ Judiciaries tend to play the most significant role, especially in the USA.

➢ Parties, pressure groups and the media may play a role too.

Exercises

Constitutions

1 What is a constitution?

2 How do the constitutions of the USA and the UK differ in terms of their origins?

3 Explain the merits and demerits of a codified constitution.

4 Explain how the USA and the UK differ in their concepts of (a) democracy and (b) sovereignty.

5 Explain the essential differences between presidential and parliamentary systems of government.

6 Explain the essential differences between federal and unitary systems of government.

7 What are the merits and demerits of a federal system of government?

8 What are the arguments for (a) centralised government and (b) decentralised government?

9 Explain the differences in the debates on constitutional reform in the USA and the UK.

Judiciaries

10 (a) What is the judiciary? (b) What are its functions?

11 Explain the differences that exist in the selection of judges in the USA and the UK.

12 (a) What reasons could be put forward for suggesting that the judiciaries of the USA and the UK are politicised? (b) What are the counter-arguments?

13 Describe the checks that exist on judiciaries.

14 What evidence is there of increased judicial activism in the USA and the UK in recent decades?

Rights and liberties

15 Define the terms: (a) a right; (b) a human right; (c) a civil right.

16 Explain the terms (a) positive rights and (b) negative rights.

17 Explain how each of the following institutions may attempt to protect rights and liberties in the USA and the UK: (a) judiciaries; (b) legislatures; (c) executives; (d) political parties, pressure groups and the media.

Exam focus

1 Examine the arguments for and against codified constitutions.

2 'The main difference between the constitutions of the USA and the UK is that one is flexible and the other is not.' Discuss.

3 Discuss the merits and demerits of centralised and decentralised forms of government.

4 Assess the extent to which the judiciaries of the USA and the UK are politically independent.

5 What are the arguments for and against having judges appointed rather than elected?

6 Are the US and UK courts subject to effective checks?

7 Examine the means by which rights and liberties are safeguarded in both the USA and the UK.

References

Shaw, M., *Anglo-American Democracy* (Routledge and Kegan Paul, 1968).

Walles, M., *British and American Systems of Government* (Philip Allan/Barnes and Noble, 1988).

Further reading

Bennett, A. J., 'The British and American constitutions compared', *Politics Review*, vol. 11, no. 1, September 2001.

Chapter 11

Elections

In comparing nationwide elections in the USA and the UK, we come up against some significant difficulties. First and foremost, most of our study of elections in US politics has been of presidential elections. However, there is no comparable election in the UK. Whereas in US presidential elections voters are asked to choose the president and vice-president — the individuals who head the executive branch of government — in UK general elections voters are asked specifically to vote for a Member of Parliament to represent their constituency. That, of course, is comparable to the US *congressional* election. Thus, in comparing nationwide elections in the two countries, we must keep in mind these important differences.

Questions to be answered in this chapter
> What are the functions of elections?
> What electoral systems are used in the USA and the UK?
> How are candidates selected?
> How is the frequency and timing of elections decided?
> How are campaigns conducted?
> What factors affect voting behaviour?
> Why has voter turnout fallen in recent elections?

Functions of elections

Elections are said to have five principal functions. First, elections are the principal source of political recruitment, especially for legislatures. All legislators in the USA and all those in the House of Commons and regional assemblies in the UK are recruited through elections.

Second, elections are used in some nation-states to directly elect the government and the chief executive. This function occurs in the USA, as it does in France, but not in the UK.

Third, elections are used to facilitate representation. The concept of representation has a number of distinct meanings which are discussed in Chapter 13. Suffice it to say here that, while members of Congress tend to follow the trustee model of representation, the mandate model of representation fits better the role of the UK. There is also the so-called resemblance model of representation, which suggests that a legislative chamber should be as near as possible to a cross-section of the nation as a whole. This concept of representation would call for a legislative chamber to look like the society as a whole, in terms of gender, race, age and perhaps social class.

Elections have two further functions: influencing policy and educating voters. They tend to deter governments and legislatures from pursuing deeply unpopular policies or actions lest they fall foul of the voters at the next election — witness the treatment by US voters of the Democrats in the 1994 mid-term elections or the treatment by UK voters of the Conservatives in the 1997 general election. Elections also provide voters with a wealth of information about politics, policies, personalities and parties.

Summary

Functions of elections

➤ Elections perform five functions: political recruitment, election of the government, representation, policy influence and education of the electorate.

Electoral systems

There is a good deal of common ground between US and UK politics in the use of the first-past-the-post (FPTP), winner-takes-all electoral system. It is this system that decides how 48 of the 50 states cast their Electoral College votes for the presidency and how all 535 seats in Congress are filled. It is this system, too, that decides the results of the 659 seats in the UK House of Commons. There are a few variations. Maine and Nebraska award their Electoral College votes on a congressional district-based version of FPTP. Louisiana has a combined primary and general election in which the winner must gain more than 50% of the popular vote or face a run-off against their nearest opponent in a second ballot.

In the UK, elections for regional assemblies in Scotland and Wales use the additional member system. In Northern Ireland, all elections — Westminster parliamentary, regional assembly, local and European parliamentary — use the single transferable vote system. Elections to the European Parliament within Great Britain use the party list system.

The merits of the FPTP system

The FPTP system is said to have five advantages. First, it tends to lead to stable, single-party governments. This is especially important in parliamentary systems, such as the UK's, where electoral terms are not fixed. Governments elected with small majorities or elected as, or which become, minority governments often last for only short periods; the result is overly frequent elections. This occurred in the UK in 1974 with two elections that year — one in February and another in October. In the February 1974 election, the Labour Party won only 301 of the 635 seats in the House of Commons, which meant that it took office as a minority government. However, in 12 of the 16 UK general elections held between 1945 and 2001 — that is, 75% — the newly elected government was a single-party government with a sufficiently large parliamentary majority to allow it to run for at least 4 years.

Second, the FPTP system encourages the formation of broad-based, middle-ground political parties and discourages narrow, ideological, extremist parties. Parties that appear to have become too ideological tend to be seen as unelectable. This might be said to have been the case with the UK Labour Party in 1983 and 1987 and with the Conservatives in 2001. In the USA, the Republicans suffered a similar fate in 1964 and the Democrats in 1972.

Third, because the major parties are themselves coalitions, the need for coalitions to be formed after the election is lessened. Therefore the coalition — that is, the major party — puts its programme before the electorate. Under proportional systems, in which coalitions often have to be formed *between* parties *after* the election, party leaders decide the programme behind closed doors. As a former UK Labour cabinet minister once put it, under proportional systems 'the people vote first and then the politicians huddle together afterwards to decide what policies they are going to introduce in Parliament.'

Fourth, under the FPTP system, there is a close link between the elected members of the legislature and their constituents. This is seen in both the UK House of Commons and the US Congress. MPs and members of Congress represent geographically cohesive areas. In the USA, some 'constituencies' are geographically vast compared with their UK counterparts. Take, for example, the members of the House of Representatives who have to represent the entire state of Wyoming or Alaska, or the two Senators who must represent all of California.

Fifth, the FPTP system has the merit of simplicity. Essentially, it involves voters making a simple choice and marking that choice with a cross on a ballot paper or a fingered touch on a computer screen. Admittedly, in the USA there are other, more complicated varieties, including the machinations of the Electoral College and all-party primaries. These are nothing, however, compared with the complications of party lists, droop quotas or non-transferable votes.

The demerits of the FPTP system

On the other hand, the FPTP system has some demerits. First, it is possible to win constituencies with well below 50% of the popular vote. This can be seen in UK parliamentary constituencies as well as in elections to both houses of Congress and in presidential elections. In 1992, the Liberal Democrats won the constituency of Inverness with just 26% of the vote in a four-horse race with Labour, SNP and Conservative candidates, all of whom got more than 22% of the vote. In the US presidential election the same year, Bill Clinton won the state of Maine with just 39% of the vote, while his opponent, George Bush, won Kansas with the same percentage of the vote.

Second, the relationship between votes won and seats gained in the legislature is often poor. In the 1997 UK general election, the Labour and Conservative parties gained respectively 43% and 31% of the popular vote, but they gained respectively 64% and 25% of the seats. In the UK the outcome has sometimes been that the party that won the most votes in the election did not win the election in terms of seats in Parliament. This occurred in both 1951 and February 1974. The same phenomenon caused the oddity of the 2000 American presidential election, in which Al Gore polled more votes than George W. Bush but lost the election in the Electoral College.

Third, a significant number of votes are wasted. These could be votes cast for losing candidates or excess votes cast for candidates who win by huge majorities. Third parties often regard their votes as 'wasted' in FPTP elections. Indeed, the major parties use this by telling the electorate not to 'waste their vote' by voting for a third-party candidate.

Fourth, FPTP systems tend to produce legislatures that are unrepresentative in terms of women and ethnic minorities. This can be seen in the UK House of Commons and in both houses of Congress in the USA.

Reform of the electoral system has been a significant topic of debate in UK politics for the past 30 years, pushed mainly — though not exclusively — by the Liberals, now the Liberal Democrats. The Blair government introduced different electoral systems for some regional and local elections. In the USA, though, 'electoral reform', in the sense in which that term is used in Britain, is almost unknown. In the USA, reform of the electoral system means reform of the Electoral College, reform of voting procedures — touch-screen technology rather than voting machines — or campaign finance reform. It does not mean adopting alternative, and certainly not proportional, electoral systems for either the federal or state legislatures.

Summary

Electoral systems

➤ Both the UK and the USA essentially use the FPTP electoral system for national elections.

➤ In the UK, there have been recent moves towards more proportional systems in European, regional and some local elections.

➤ The FPTP system has both merits and demerits.

➤ Reform of the electoral system is a significant issue in UK politics, but not in the USA, at least not with reference to electoral systems.

Candidate selection

There is a simple rule of thumb in comparing US and UK candidate selection. In the UK, candidates are chosen by the parties. In the USA, candidates are chosen by ordinary voters in direct primaries.

Who has the power of selection?

There are essentially four potential groups which may have the power within a democracy to select candidates for election: the national party organisation; the local party organisation; individual party members; and ordinary voters. If the system is dominated by the party organisations — either national or local — we might regard candidate selection as being elitist and undemocratic. If, on the other hand, the system is dominated by party members or ordinary voters, then we might regard candidate selection as being pluralist, participatory and democratic.

In the UK, candidate selection procedures for parliamentary candidates have, during the past three decades, moved from elitist systems to more pluralist and participatory systems involving party members. This has been the case in the USA, too, in the selection of presidential candidates, with a significant increase in the involvement of ordinary voters in primary elections. However, primaries have a longer history in congressional races, having been widely used in most states from the beginning of the twentieth century.

The most significant changes in candidate selection have taken place in presidential candidate selection in the USA. The reforms that came out of the McGovern–Fraser Commission in the early 1970s significantly reduced the power of the national party organisation in presidential candidate selection. The power of the 'party bosses' in 'smoke-filled rooms' at the National Party Conventions was removed. Convention delegates would henceforth be chosen mostly as a result of a series of state-by-state presidential primaries in which any registered voter could take part. This significant change resulted in the likes of Jimmy Carter (1976) and Bill Clinton (1992) being chosen as presidential candidates, who would both have been unthinkable under the old 'party boss' system. The power of the national party still to promote its preferred candidate should not be underestimated, however: it was seen in the Republicans' selection of Governor George W. Bush, rather than Senator John McCain, in 2000, and in the Democrats' selection of Senator John Kerry rather than Governor Howard Dean in 2004.

In UK parliamentary elections, there have been some moves towards democratisation by the major parties in the selection of their candidates. In the Conservative Party, however, the selection of parliamentary candidates is still very much in the hands of the local party organisation, in the shape of the constituency Executive Council, the main decision-making body of the local Conservative Association. Would-be candidates must place their names on the party's candidates list, maintained by the national party headquarters. The Labour Party has undergone considerable democratisation in the selection of parliamentary candidates, although the short-list is still under the control of the Executive Committee of the local Constituency Labour Party. Whereas in the Conservative Party only committee members are allowed a vote on the choice of candidate, in the Labour Party all party members within the constituency get a vote in a one member, one vote system introduced in 1993. However, the locally selected candidate must still receive the endorsement of the party's National Executive Committee.

These procedures are not comparable to the direct primaries used in the USA for candidate selection in congressional elections. Whenever a House or Senate member faces the electorate, anyone may challenge them in a party primary. In the 20 years from 1982 to 2002, 54 House members and two Senators have been defeated in the primaries. Indeed, this can be a way for the supporters of a party to be rid of an unpopular incumbent but maintain control of the seat, as in the 2002 Senate race in New Hampshire.

Summary

Candidate selection

➢ Candidate selection is far more open and democratic in the USA than in the UK.
➢ However, both major parties in the UK have recently moved towards a greater degree of democratic participation in the selection of candidates.

Frequency and timing of elections

The USA has fixed-term elections: 2 years for the House of Representatives, 6 years for the Senate (with one third re-elected every 2 years) and 4 years for the presidency. In the UK, the only stipulation is the maximum lifetime of a parliament — 5 years, although

European Parliament, regional and local elections are fixed-term elections. The year 1992 saw general elections in both countries. Since then, the House of Representatives has been re-elected six times — in 1994, 1996, 1998, 2000, 2002 and 2004. The House of Commons has been re-elected only twice — in 1997 and 2002. General elections in the UK and presidential elections in the USA occur roughly in equal number. Between 1920 and 2004, there will have been 22 of each.

In the USA, not only is the number of years between each election fixed by the Constitution, but the date of each election is fixed by federal law as the Tuesday after the first Monday in November — in other words, some time between 2 and 8 November. Thus, US presidents have no flexibility in the calling of elections in which they will be a candidate. UK prime ministers, in contrast, do have flexibility, up to the 5-year maximum. As a result, US presidents cannot manipulate election dates to suit favourable political or economic factors. For example, in 1980 President Carter had to go to the polls on 4 November despite it being the precise anniversary of the still unresolved Iranian hostage crisis. In 1992 President George Bush had to go to the polls in November despite the fact that in a couple more months more favourable economic indicators would have been noticed by the electorate. Both Carter and Bush lost.

In the UK, prime ministers can use their discretion in the timing of the election. Some, like Margaret Thatcher in 1983 and John Major in 1992, seem to get it right. Others, like Harold Wilson in 1970 and Jim Callaghan in 1979, seem to get it badly wrong.

In both countries there are various arrangements for filling up vacancies in the legislature as they occur. In the UK House of Commons, this is done through by-elections. In the USA, vacancies in the House of Representatives are filled by special elections, similar to the British by-elections. In the Senate, the filling of vacancies varies according to state law. In most states, the state governor appoints a replacement until the next set of congressional elections. In others, such as Texas, a special election is held. Thus, when Rhode Island Senator John Chafee died in 1999, the state governor appointed the late Senator's son, Lincoln Chafee, to serve out the remainder of his father's term. However, when the Texas Democrat Senator Lloyd Bentsen resigned in January 1993, having been appointed to President Clinton's cabinet, a special election was held in June 1993 that was won by Republican Kay Bailey Hutchison.

Summary

Frequency and timing of elections
➤ The USA has fixed-term elections.
➤ In the UK, the timing of elections for the House of Commons is to some extent at the discretion of the prime minister, although European, regional and local elections are fixed-term elections.
➤ Both countries have arrangements for filling vacancies in their legislature.

Conduct of election campaigns

There are a number of significant differences between elections in the UK and the USA. The first noticeable difference between UK and US election campaigns is the difference in their length. In 1992, Prime Minister John Major announced the calling of the election on 11 March. Parliament was dissolved on 16 March. The election was held on 9 April. Thus, the entire election campaign lasted a mere 30 days, for the first 5 days of which Parliament was still in session.

Table 11.1 Features of US and UK elections

US elections have the following features	UK elections have the following features
Fixed terms (2, 4 or 6 years)	No fixed terms
Long campaign period	Short campaign period
Candidates travel huge distances	Candidates travel shorter distances
No automatic voter registration	Automatic voter registration
Huge amounts of money raised and spent	Smaller amounts of money raised and spent
Parties/candidates buy time on television	Buying of television time outlawed
Televised debates between major party presidential candidates	No televised debates between party leaders
Newspapers mostly local, city-based	Newspapers mostly national, London-based
Candidate-based elections	Party-based elections

In the USA, congressional races typically have a formal campaign lasting at least 9 weeks — from Labor Day at the beginning of September to polling day at the beginning of November. If a primary is held, the intra-party campaign begins a good deal earlier, with some congressional primaries being held as early as March.

When it comes to US presidential elections, campaigning — especially for the challenging party (the Democrats in 2004) — begins 18 months to 2 years before polling day. The first caucuses and primaries start in January of the election year — still a good 9 months or more before the general election.

The conduct of campaigns in each country is affected by the distance to be travelled by the candidates. Although a number of urban and suburban US congressional districts are similar in geographic size to many UK parliamentary constituencies, those in more rural states bear little comparison. The state of Wyoming — in geographic size about equal to the UK — has only one member of the House of Representatives and is therefore in itself one congressional district. All Senators, of course, represent their entire state, many of which are considerably bigger than the whole of the UK, let alone a parliamentary constituency. For the presidential election, candidates must travel the length and breadth of the country. In just the last 4 days of his 1996 presidential campaign, Bob Dole travelled 10,534 miles, visiting 20 different states in what he called his '96 Hours to Victory Tour' — and what *Time* magazine called a 'meandering political death march, a strange odyssey across a sleeping land that seemed, at times, to have forgotten that Dole was even out there'. Any criss-crossing of the UK, whether by train, plane or 'battle bus', could in no way compare with such distances.

The processes of voter registration in the UK and USA differ. In the UK, the government takes the initiative in trying to ensure that everyone eligible to vote is regis-tered to vote by sending a voter registration form to every household each year. A pre-paid envelope is even enclosed for its return once completed. In the USA, individual citizens must usually take the initiative to ensure that they are registered to vote, although this has been made easier with the passage of the Motor-Voter law. Low voter turnout in the UK is about registered voters not voting rather than, as is often the case in the USA, eligible voters not being registered.

Bob Dole: Republican presidential candidate, 1996

The difference in voter registration shows up a wider difference between the two countries in the conduct of their elections. There is more central government involve-ment in UK elections than in US elections — not surprisingly, as one is a unitary and one a federal system. Central government in the UK involves itself not only with voter registration but also with rules regarding the conduct of individual campaigns. This leads to greater uniformity in UK elections than in US elections.

In the UK, the government passed legislation to provide for the free delivery of one communication — called the 'election address' — from each candidate to each relevant voter. Each candidate is required by law to appoint an election agent — what in the USA would be called a campaign manager. The agent must authorise and account for all campaign expenses. Candidate expenditure is strictly limited by law. The limit varies according to the geographic size and type of constituency, but it is usually less than £7,000. Candidates for House or Senate seats in the USA would not only be staggered at the small sum, but would probably be dumbfounded to discover that most candidates spend only around three-quarters of the permitted amount. This compares with the often five-, six- or seven-figure sums that might be spent in House or Senate races and the hundreds of millions of dollars required for a successful presidential race.

In terms of the media coverage of election campaigns, elections in both countries have become increasingly 'made for television' affairs. Just as the 1960 presidential election marked a watershed in television's importance in the USA, so the elections of 1964 and 1966 marked a similar watershed in the UK. However, there are subtle differences. In the UK, neither candidates nor parties are allowed to buy time on any television channel, so there is no direct UK equivalent of the US 30-second campaign commercial. The parties are, however, allowed free time to put out party election broadcasts, and these are carried on both BBC and ITV. The parties' only expense comes in the production of the broadcast.

Parties are allotted time on the basis of the number of candidates fielded at the election. This usually means equal time for the major parties and less time for any minor parties that field at least 50 candidates.

The rise of the televised debate in the US presidential election — especially since 1976 — has had no parallel in UK general elections. Sitting prime ministers have always rejected any suggestion of a televised debate with the leader of the opposition.

A significant difference in media coverage of the two countries' elections is the UK national newspapers, which usually endorse a particular party during the election campaign. Although papers such as the *Washington Post* and *New York Times* have a national reputation, they do not enjoy the national readership of, say, *The Times* or *Daily Mirror* in the UK. Newspaper readership in both countries has declined in recent years.

UK general election campaigns have traditionally centred on the competition between political parties, but have come to resemble increasingly US presidential election campaigns by virtue of becoming more candidate-centred events. This may be a significant effect of television, which concentrates more easily on the candidate than on a party: a Labour Party election broadcast in 1992 concluded with the Americanised caption: 'Vote Kinnock'. UK general election campaigns are seen to some extent as elections about potential prime ministers.

Summary

Conduct of election campaigns

➤ There are significant differences between the conduct of election campaigns in the USA and the UK.

➤ These concern frequency, length of time, voter registration and expense, as well as the role of party, money and the media.

➤ Campaigns in the USA tend to be more candidate-based, whereas in the UK they are more party-based.

Voting behaviour

Comparisons of voting behaviour in UK and US elections are difficult, because like is not being compared with like. In the UK, a general election is a nationwide election to fill 659 seats in the lower house of the national legislature. In the USA, a nationwide election for seats in the House of Representatives and the Senate coincides on alternate occasions with the election of the president and vice-president. The mid-term elections, on the other hand, often attract such low levels of participation that a comparison with a UK general election is equally difficult.

It is worth keeping in mind, too, that a voter in the UK generally makes only one decision in the voting booth: for the Member of Parliament for their constituency. If, as occasionally happens, the general election coincides with other local or European

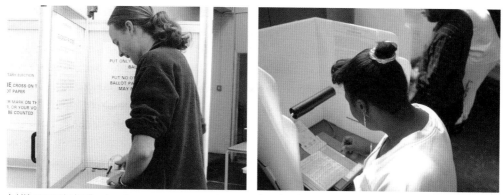

A UK general election booth   A voting booth in Berkeley, California, USA

elections, voters may be asked to make up to half-a-dozen choices at the same time; but this is nothing compared with the number of choices being made in one visit to the polling booth by voters in the USA. In a presidential election year, most voters are asked to choose a president, a member of the House of Representatives, possibly a US Senator, maybe the state governor and lieutenant governor, members of both houses of the state legislature, maybe state judges and the city mayor, all the way down to members of the local board of education and the ubiquitous mosquito control officer. There may, in addition, be a number of initiatives or propositions on the state ballot, such as proposed amendments to the state constitution, handgun control issues or tax proposals. Voters may well be confronted with 40 or 50 decisions in just one visit to the polling station. This may affect voting behaviour, especially if the technology allows people to vote what is called a 'straight ticket' — in other words, for the candidates of one particular party for every office on the ballot.

Four models of voting behaviour

Psephologists have come up with four major models of voting behaviour: the party identi-fication model; the sociological model; the rational choice model; and the dominant ideology model. They suggest that voting behaviour is influenced by both short- and long-term factors. Among short-terms factors are: the economy; the personality and public standing of the 'party leaders'; the record of the previous administration; and the effectiveness of the election campaign. Long-term factors include: social class; party identification; gender; race; and religion. Voting can also be considered in terms of negative voting, tactical voting and split-ticket voting.

The party identification model stresses the voter with a long-term attachment to a particular political party — one that is often handed down within the family. This creates stability and continuity in elections because these party attachments rarely change. However, this model might have been better suited to the more stable and less mobile society of the first half of the twentieth century — both in the USA and in the UK — than to the geographically and socially mobile societies of the modern-day USA and UK. Decline in party identification has led to the rise of third-party and independent candidate support in both countries as well as to 'independent' voters in the USA and 'floating' voters in the UK.

The sociological model stresses the link between the voter and membership of certain groups defined by class, gender, race, region or religion. This model might be considered past its sell-by date, given the significant breakdown in distinct boundaries between, for example, social class groups in the UK and racial and regional groups in the USA.

The rational choice model sees a voter acting in a rational way based on self-interest rather than habit. Models differ. Key (1996), for example, stresses what he calls 'retrospective voting', while others, such as Himmelveit (1985), see voters as 'consumers', shopping around for the best policies for them — so-called 'issue voting'.

The dominant ideology model stresses the importance of the media as a significant determinant of the political agenda. In this model, voters are significantly influenced by the policy areas that the media declare are the most important — healthcare, education or minority rights, for example.

Short-term issues in voting behaviour
The economy

Voters in both the USA and the UK can be said to be influenced by short-term factors. Uppermost seems to be the economy. This can be seen in terms of the *national* economy — interest rates, unemployment, and inflation — what Jimmy Carter in 1976 called 'the misery index' — or in terms of the *personal* economy — as Ronald Reagan asked of voters in 1980: 'Are *you* better off than you were 4 years ago?' Incumbent parties tend to lose elections at times of perceived economic hardship — Labour in 1979 in the UK; Carter (1980) and Bush (1992) in the USA. This is not an unbroken rule, however: witness the Conservatives' landslide victory in 1983 with 3 million unemployed and high inflation. Equally, incumbent parties tend to be rewarded with re-election at times of perceived economic prosperity: Clinton (1996) in the USA; Labour (2001) in the UK. There are exceptions: the Democrats lost the 2000 presidential and congressional elections in the USA even though the Clinton–Gore administration had presided over 8 years of almost unparalleled economic prosperity. Economic competence was viewed as important in recent UK general elections. In 1992, the Conservatives had a 21-point lead over Labour in answer to the question: 'Who can handle the economy best?' By 1997, that had become a 14-point lead for Labour and by 2001 a 22-point lead for Labour.

Personalities

One of the most interesting long-term factors by which to compare the USA and the UK is the role played by the 'party leaders'. The general rule of thumb suggests that this factor is more important in presidential (US) than in parliamentary (UK) systems. The truth, though, is perhaps more subtle. The role of the presidential candidates in US presidential elections varies, depending on what are the prevailing issues. In 1996, Republican Bob Dole tried to make the character of President Bill Clinton the salient issue, but he failed — and lost the election. In 2000, however, George W. Bush succeeded in making 'character' the issue with Gore and, to some extent, linking Gore with President Clinton's character flaws. In the UK, the picture is even more difficult to decipher. The experience of the Conservatives with Winston Churchill (1945) and Labour with Jim Callaghan (1979) shows that popular leaders cannot compensate for unpopular parties. On the other hand, the parties in the UK have come to believe that unpopular leaders can lose them elections. The Conservatives' ousting of Prime Minister Margaret Thatcher in November 1990 was clearly inspired by a belief that she had become an electoral liability. Some commentators are unconvinced, however. Anthony King (1992) writes: 'Like prospective diners in a restaurant, voters are more interested in the food, the décor and the standards of hygiene, not just in who happens to be the head waiter.'

Retrospective voting

The record of the previous administration — retrospective voting — is an important issue in both US and UK elections. In the USA, for example, Carter's defeat in 1980 and the Democrats' débâcle in the 1994 mid-term elections were votes of no confidence in what had occurred in the years immediately before the election. The 1997 rout of the Conservatives seemed to be the voters' judgment on 'Black Wednesday' and the 'sleaze' that had marred the Major (1992–97) administration. Equally, voters can react positively to what they see as a good administration record: for example, Reagan's landslide re-election in 1984, the Republicans' successes in the 2002 mid-term elections and Labour's re-election in 2001.

The campaign

The effectiveness of the campaign is a short-term issue that may affect voting behaviour. Campaigns need to be 'effective' in perhaps three different ways. First, a campaign must be competent and well run. The contrast between a competent Clinton campaign in 1996 and a far less well-run Dole campaign the same year comes to mind. A similar contrast was apparent in 1992 between a competent Conservative campaign and an over-confident but lacklustre Labour campaign that culminated in a somewhat optimistic 'victory' rally in Sheffield a few days before the election was held. Second, a campaign needs to excite and activate the voters. There is little point in voters agreeing with the party's position if they do not come out and vote on the day. Third, elections need to be effective at 'conversion' — persuading voters who began the campaign as supporters of one party to then support the opposing party. Campaigns that are plagued by poor organisation, lack of focus, disunity and ineffective, poorly thought-out or irrelevant policies usually go down to defeat — witness the UK Conservatives in 2001 and the American Democrats in 2002.

The role of the media in the campaign can be important in the extent to which they assist 'conversion' or merely facilitate 'activation'. The day after the Conservatives' surprise victory in 1992 the headline of the *Sun* claimed: 'It's the *Sun* wot won it!' This is clearly open to debate. The message that the media convey must have some agreement with voters' view of reality. Reagan's highly successful *It's Morning Again in America* campaign in 1984 was successful not because of the media, but because it tallied with most Americans' view of a buoyant economy.

Long-term issues in voting behaviour

Social class

There are five long-term factors in voting behaviour to be considered. First, the factor of social class in explaining voting behaviour was especially popular in voting studies of UK elections until the 1970s. In recent decades, however, many psephologists believe that class dealignment has made this factor less potent. By 2001, only 41% of the professional and managerial class were voting Conservative. David Sanders (1998) writes: 'The pattern of voting [in recent UK elections has] put paid to any lingering doubts that class-based voting plays anything like the role [now] that it did in previous decades.' In the USA, social class has never been regarded as an important factor, mainly because of the lack of class consciousness. There is some correlation of Democrat voting among blue-collar, unionised workers and of Republican voting among white-collar, non-unionised workers, but Democrat candidates are often reluctant to strike a 'haves versus have-nots' tone, lest all those potential Democrat voters who regard themselves as 'middle class' are put off.

Party identification

Party identification has been steadily declining in both countries over the past three or four decades. In the UK in the 1964 election, 81% of voters identified with one of the two major parties. By the 1997 election, this figure was down to just 39%. In the USA during the same period, the respective figures fell from 76% to 60%. Although party identification does not appear to have declined in the USA to the extent that it has in the UK, US elections in recent decades have been characterised by high levels of split-ticket voting and have often resulted in divided party control of government. In 2000, Democrat Congressman Charles Stenholm was re-elected to the House of Representatives. In the same election, his district voted 72–28 in favour of George W. Bush over Al Gore. Similarly, Republican Bill Janklow won his House race in South Dakota on the same day that 60% of voters in his district voted for Al Gore. That is both impossible and inconceivable in a UK general election.

Gender

There is no evidence of a so-called 'gender gap' in British politics. In 2001, men divided 49–27% in favour of Labour while women divided 46–29% in favour of Labour. Thus, Labour had a 22 and 17 percentage point lead among men and women respectively. In 2000, men divided 53–42% in favour of Bush while women divided 54–43% in favour of Gore. Thus, the Republicans had an 11% advantage among men but an 11% disadvantage among women. This gender gap in the USA is often explained in terms of the major parties' policies of particular interest to women. In the 1990s, Clinton's Democrats were said to be trying to appeal to 'soccer moms' on such family issues as crime, gun control, education and controls on scenes of violence and sex in the media.

Race

Racial minorities tend to support centre-left parties: Labour in the UK; the Democrats in the USA. This is linked to the centre left's support for civil rights issues, which are of particular interest to racial minorities.

Religion

Finally, as with gender, religion is far more important in the USA than in the UK. With the growing secularisation of western European countries, including the UK, levels of religious belief and of church attendance have fallen noticeably over the past five decades. Gone are the days when the Church of England could be called 'the Conservative Party at prayer'. In 2001, Anglicans — whatever and whoever that means these days — divided 41–39% in favour of Labour. But Labour held an even bigger lead among those who claimed no religious affiliation at all: 48–21%, with 23% voting Liberal Democrat.

In the USA, however, where 42% say they attend religious services weekly or more often, religion is a more important factor. Among that 42% of voters, Bush in 2000 won 60% of the vote, while of the 14% who said they never attended religious services, Gore won 60% of the vote.

Summary

Voting behaviour

➤ There are different models of voting behaviour.

➤ Factors affecting voting can be classified as either short-term or long-term issues.

➤ Short-term issues include such factors as the economy, party leaders, the record of the previous administration and the effectiveness of the campaign.

➤ Long-term issues include such factors as social class, party, gender, race and religion.

Voter turnout

Turnout in US and UK elections has declined significantly over the past four decades. In the 1964 US presidential election, the turnout was 69%. By 2000 it was 51%. As recently as the 1992 general election in the UK, the turnout was 77%. By 2001 it was down to just 59%. In one constituency — Liverpool Riverside — turnout was just 34%. Malcolm Walles (1988) has noted that: 'education is the single most significant factor in determining whether or not a person will vote: the higher the level of education, the more likely the citizen is to go to the polls.' Turnout tends to increase in both countries with age. It also increases with affluence: the rich vote more than the poor. The economically and socially secure vote in a higher proportion than those who are economically and socially threatened. It tends to be higher in competitive seats than safe seats, too. That said, in 2000 the closest presidential election in decades attracted only just over half of the registered voters.

Table 11.2 Reasons for voter turnout decline: USA and UK compared

Reasons for voter turnout decline in the USA	Reasons for voter turnout decline in the UK
Perception of there being little difference between the major parties	Perception of major parties having moved to the middle ground
Complicated registration process	Party decline
Party decline	Predictable elections
Fewer competitive races	Voter fatigue
Increased levels of distrust of politicians	Increased levels of distrust of politicians

What have been the principal reasons for the decline in voter turnout on both sides of the Atlantic? Five main reasons are suggested for decline in voter turnout in the USA. First, increased numbers of voters see little difference between the presidential candidates of the two major parties. Second, the registration process is complicated. Third, some see decline in turnout as linked to party decline — where party membership and identification has declined, voters feel less compelled to vote for *their* party's candidates, or for those of any other party. Fourth, few House races are now competitive. In 2002, in only 40 out of the 435 districts did the winner gain less than 55% of the vote. Finally, some analysts point to the increased levels of distrust of politicians, especially in the 'anti-Washington', 'kick the bums out', pro-term limits era of the 1990s. Voters, it is argued, have been turned off politics by any number of things: Vietnam, Watergate, Iran–Contra or the Clinton scandals.

In the UK, similar and different factors are put forward. First, many UK voters see the two main parties as having moved to the middle ground. There was consequently less of a choice in 1997 between Blair and Major than there was in, say, 1983 between Foot and Thatcher. UK politics has suffered from a decline in party membership and identification, and this is seen as a factor explaining the decline in turnout in the UK too. A third reason is the predictability of the outcome in four of the past five elections — 1983, 1987, 1997 and 2001. The electoral system, furthermore, creates a huge number of safe seats, resulting in large numbers of wasted votes. Fourth, voter fatigue may be taking its toll now that voters are asked to vote not only in parliamentary and local elections, but also in elections for the European Parliament and, in many parts of the UK, for regional assemblies and directly elected city mayors. UK politics, too, has had its share of distrust of politicians brought about by a range of factors, such as the Winter of Discontent, the poll tax, the débâcle of the exchange rate mechanism, 'sleaze' and 'spin'.

Some commentators see a low turnout as the politics of contentment: people don't vote because they are quite content with their life. Evidence suggests that it is a disaffected and disengaged underclass which does not vote, feeling that politics is remote, incomprehensible and irrelevant, that results in low turnout.

Politicians have devised various ideas for increasing voter turnout. The use of electronic voting is being tested in both the USA and the UK. Postal voting, too, is being encouraged on both sides of the Atlantic, as is setting up voting booths in more voter-friendly places, such as shopping malls and supermarkets. Some point to the need to improve the political education of the young, while, in the USA, some point to a continuing need to simplify registration practices. Others suggest more radical constitutional reform to try to make government and politics appear more relevant, coherent and up to date. Some are even advocating Australian-style compulsory voting laws.

Summary

Voter turnout

➤ Voter turnout has declined in both the USA and the UK.

➤ A range of possible factors might account for the decline, many of which are common to both countries, such as there being fewer competitive races and increased levels of distrust of politicians.

Exercises

1. Explain the functions of elections.
2. Explain the resemblance model of representation.
3. Which electoral systems are used in (a) the USA and (b) the UK?
4. Outline the merits and demerits of the first-past-the-post electoral system.
5. Which four groups may have power in a democracy to select candidates for election?
6. Explain how the process for selecting candidates for election has been democratised in both the USA and the UK in recent decades.
7. How do the frequency and timing of elections differ between the USA and the UK?
8. What are the main differences in the conduct of election campaigns in the USA and the UK?
9. Explain the four different models of voting behaviour and how each might apply in the USA and the UK.
10. Explain how voting behaviour in both the USA and the UK is influenced by (a) short-term and (b) long-term factors.
11. What are the main reasons for the decline in voter turnout in (a) the USA and (b) the UK?

Exam focus

1. Discuss the merits and demerits of the first-past-the-post electoral system.
2. Analyse the different methods used by political parties in the USA and the UK to select candidates for election.

3 Examine the most important factors that may determine the way people vote in US and UK general elections.

4 Discuss the extent, causes and possible solutions of low levels of voter turnout in the USA and the UK.

References

Himmelveit, H. T. et al., *How Voters Decide* (Open University Press, 1985).

Key, V. O., *The Responsible Electorate* (Vintage, 1996).

King, A. (ed.), *Britain at the Polls 1992* (Chatham House, 1992).

Sanders, D., in King, A. (ed.), *New Labour Triumphs: Britain at the Polls* (Chatham House, 1998).

Walles, M., *British and American Systems of Government* (Philip Allan/Barnes and Noble, 1988).

Further reading

Batchelor, A., 'UK and US electoral issues', *Politics Review*, vol. 12, no. 3, February 2003.

Farrell, D. M., *Electoral Systems: A Comparative Introduction* (Palgrave, 2001).

Jones, B., 'Apathy: why don't people vote?', *Politics Review*, vol. 12, no. 4, April 2003.

McNaughton, N., 'Evaluating electoral systems', *Politics Review*, vol. 10, no. 1, September 2000.

Chapter 12

Political parties
and pressure groups

Elections are the means whereby power is peacefully transferred within a nation-state. Political parties are the agencies that give some coherence to this process. Political parties seek to gain political power. There are, however, other political groups within democracies that seek not to gain political power, but to influence those who have it. In many ways, pressure groups fill the gaps left by political parties. They offer more opportunities for democratic participation, especially between elections.

Both political parties and pressure groups have come to exist in the USA and the UK. However, the paths they have trodden to be where and what they are today have been quite different in the two countries. Their relative importance within their own political system is different too. The UK has what can essentially be called party government. The USA does not. Both nations are said to have, or at least to have had, a two-party system, but, if that is so, they are very different two-party systems. Party ideology is different; so is party organisation. Political parties in the USA must operate within a federal system of government, while those in the UK operate within a unitary system with some recently devolved responsibilities.

Pressure groups in the UK enjoy fewer access points into the political system than do their US counterparts, neither do they enjoy the influence that big money and big membership bring to many US pressure groups. As in so many other aspects of government and politics, when the USA and the UK are compared, there are both similarities and differences.

A Political parties

Questions to be answered in this section

> What are political parties?
> How can political parties be classified?
> What are the major functions of political parties?
> How are parties organised in the USA and the UK?
> What differences are there between party leaders in the USA and the UK?
> How important is ideology in US and UK political parties?
> Do both the USA and the UK have a two-party system?
> What role is played by third parties in the USA and the UK?
> Do both the USA and the UK have 'party government'?
> How do the theories of party decline and renewal apply in US and UK politics?

Definitions and classifications

A political party is a group of people that is organised for the purpose of winning governmental power by electoral means.

Political scientists have four different ways of classifying political parties. First, they are either cadre parties or mass parties. Cadre parties are made up of and dominated by an elite. They see little purpose in extending the party into a mass membership, nationwide organisation. They are hierarchical, 'top-down' parties. They often exist in nation-states alongside a limited franchise. The UK Conservative Party of the nineteenth century could be described as a cadre party. Mass parties are the opposite. They are broad, nationwide, democratic, 'bottom-up' parties. The UK Labour Party has always been a mass party.

Second, parties can be classified as either representative or integrative parties. Representative parties see their main function as winning votes in elections and thereby gaining governmental power. They tend to reflect, rather than attempt to shape, public opinion and tend to believe in 'consensus' politics. They fit with Joseph Schumpeter's and Anthony Downs' rational choice model of political behaviour. 'New Labour' could be described as a representative party. Integrative parties, on the other hand, see their main functions as being to educate, inspire and mobilise the electorate rather than just respond to their wishes and concerns. They tend to want to change conventional wisdom and to believe in 'conviction' politics. It could be suggested that the UK Conservative Party under Margaret Thatcher's leadership took on this model in the 1980s.

Third, political parties can be either constitutional or revolutionary parties. Constitutional parties recognise the rights of other political parties to exist freely and are prepared to operate within a framework of constitutional and political rules and constraints. They recognise that there is an essential difference between 'the party' and 'the state' as well as between 'the party in power' and state institutions, such as the bureaucracy, the police, the judiciary and the media. This definition of constitutional parties explains why there is always concern when so-called constitutional parties appear not to adhere strictly to these criteria. Revolutionary parties, on the other hand, are anti-constitutional and either seek to gain power by seizing it rather than winning it, or having gained power legitimately, seek to remain in power by unconstitutional means. They often seek to develop a one-party state.

Finally, parties can be classified as either left wing or right wing. Left-wing parties include those of a progressive, socialist or communist ideology. They seek change and tend to be supported by the disadvantaged sections of society. Right-wing parties include those of a conservative, nationalist or fascist ideology. They seek to maintain the status quo and tend to be supported by business and middle-class interests. The terms 'left' and 'right' are drawn from the seating arrangements in most European legislatures — though not in the Westminster Parliament — of socialist parties sitting on the presiding officer's left, and nationalist and conservative parties sitting on the presiding officer's right.

Functions of political parties

Political parties have five principal functions. First, they fulfil the function of representation. This is usually seen as their principal function. They respond to and articulate the views of their members as well as those who vote for their candidates. Parties act as a link between the government and the governed. This links with the rational choice model of voting behaviour. Anthony Downs sees politicians as political entrepreneurs seeking votes, with the parties acting like economic businesses. Parties can also fulfil a representative function in terms of the resemblance model of representation (see Chapter 11). Hence, parties may seek to select candidates who resemble, in terms of gender, race, age and social background, those who vote for them.

Second, parties are said to have a function of providing leadership. Political parties are therefore seen as training grounds for national leaders. Would-be leaders join political parties so that they can learn and display the necessary skills of leadership. This is more the case in parliamentary than in presidential systems. In parliamentary systems, the route to leadership is often through the party. Jim Callaghan, for example, had been a Labour MP for 31 years before becoming UK prime minister. In contrast, Dwight Eisenhower had no party political links before becoming US president.

Third, parties are said to have the function of interest articulation and aggregation. They are seen as vehicles through which different groups seek both to advance and to defend their interests. By so doing, they bring some order and prioritisation to political choices at elections.

Fourth, parties have a mobilising function through a number of different methods, depending upon the type of party. Cadre and integrative parties seek to mobilise through rigid promotion of party dogma and through propaganda. Mass and constitutional parties seek to educate and persuade, but must often fight against high levels of cynicism and apathy among the electorate.

Finally, parties organise government. Indeed, in parliamentary systems, it is a 'party government'. Parties are thereby said to offer political stability. They also forge links between the executive and legislative branches, but in different ways in the parliamentary and presidential systems. Richard Neustadt, commenting on the US political system, said that 'what the Constitution separates [i.e. the three branches of government], the political parties do *not* combine.' Parties also provide opposition to governments and thereby hope to provide a government in waiting.

Party organisation

Power within parties

In considering party organisation, parties can be divided into two groups — those in which the power lies at the centre and those in which the power lies at the grassroots. Some parties entrench the dominance of leaders and elites, and limit the power of ordinary members. Some parties are closed and hierarchical. Others are open, democratic and participatory. Political philosopher Robert Michels (1911) famously stated that: 'he who says organisation says oligarchy.' Michels used his 'iron law of oligarchy' to explain what he saw as the inevitable failure of parties in a democracy to be themselves democratic. In his famous book *British Political Parties*, Robert McKenzie (1964) claimed similarly that the UK Conservative Party was elitist and leader dominated while the Labour Party was characterised by high levels of internal party democracy. Some might question the accuracy of this statement as a picture of 'New Labour' under Tony Blair's leadership. In the USA, the Democratic Party has often been regarded as more internally democratic than the Republican Party.

The two most important comparisons that can be made about US and UK political parties are that US political parties tend to be undisciplined and decentralised whereas those in the UK tend to be disciplined and centralised. There are reasons for these important differences. At first, political parties in England meant parliamentary parties. Only after the extension of the franchise in the nineteenth and early twentieth centuries did party organisation move outside parliament. The Labour Party was the first major party to begin as an extra-parliamentary party. In the USA, the beginnings of legislative party organisation were followed almost immediately by party organisation in the country. Moves towards universal adult suffrage also came earlier in the USA than in the UK.

The other significant contributory factor to differences in party organisation between the two countries was that US political parties existed within a federal state whereas British political parties existed within a unitary state. This important institutional difference had its effect on the development of party organisation in both countries. The federal system of the USA gave rise to a decentralised, state-based party system.

The unitary system in the UK gave rise to a centralised, Westminster-based party system. Constitutional changes in the UK involving both the European Union and devolution have led to changes within the UK party organisations, effectively making them rather less centralised.

The extent of central control in party organisations inevitably has an effect upon levels of party discipline. The more centralised the party, the more highly disciplined its politicians are likely to be. Hence, we have usually seen more highly disciplined parties in London than in Washington. A number of party procedures illustrate the centralisation of British parties and the decentralisation of US ones.

Table 12.1 Differences between US and UK parties

Parties in the US have:	Parties in the UK have:
decentralised power	centralised power
no centralised control of candidate selection	some centralised control of candidate selection
4-yearly National Party Conventions	annual party conferences
small national organisations	large national organisation
party 'platforms' (not seen as a list of specific commitments)	party 'manifestos' (seen as a list of specific promises)

Candidate selection

Methods of selecting candidates provide a second basis for comparing degrees of centralisation. Candidate selection is dealt with fully in Chapter 11. Suffice it to say here that decisions about party candidates in the USA are made locally. There are no 'approved lists' or possible vetoes from national party headquarters in Washington DC. In the UK, although candidate selection has become subject to increased local control in recent decades, national parties still have significant power and influence.

National gatherings

In the UK, parties hold annual party conferences. Although these gatherings may have become more about style and less about substance in recent years, the level of national party control over these events is almost legendary, and increasingly so in the Labour Party. In the USA, the parties hold National Conventions only once every 4 years. These are really no more than the coming together of *state* parties and are designed simply to 'rally the troops' ahead of the imminent presidential campaign.

Headquarters

All three major national parties in the UK have significant, permanent and professional organisations in London. 'Smith Square' and 'Millbank' — respectively the London locations of the Conservative and Labour Party headquarters — are synonymous with party control. In Washington DC, the premises housing the Democratic and Republican National Committees are both modest and almost anonymous in comparison with their London counterparts.

Platforms and manifestos

British parties put out important policy documents — the party manifestos — ahead of the general election. A 'manifesto promise' is regarded as a specific commitment to the voters, which will be implemented by any winning party. The US party 'platforms' are both more bland and more easily forgettable than their UK counterparts.

Summary

Party organisation

➤ The organisation of US and UK political parties is very different.

➤ This principally reflects the difference between federal and unitary states.

Party leaders

Here is another significant difference between political parties in the USA and those in the UK. To see this, we have only to ask the question: 'Who are currently the leaders of the Republican and Democratic parties?' We could suggest that President George W. Bush is leader of the Republican Party, but, even if he is, it is only because he is the president of the USA. Who then is leader of the Democratic Party: Bill Clinton? John Kerry? In the UK, the situation is quite the reverse. Tony Blair is prime minister only because he happens to be leader of the Labour Party and that party happens to be the largest single party in the House of Commons. Bush was elected president; Blair was elected party leader.

The choosing of 'party leaders' is more democratic and participatory in the USA than in the UK. In the United States, ordinary voters choose 'party leaders'. Anyone may put themselves forward for nomination. In 2004, General Wesley Clark sought the presidential nomination of the Democratic Party despite not being an elective office holder. In the UK, in contrast, only party members choose the party leaders, and that is a recent innovation in the Labour and Conservative parties. In both parties, candidates are nominated only by and from Members of Parliament. As was witnessed in the Conservative Party 'election' of Michael Howard as leader in November 2003, this system can be significantly controlled by the party's MPs.

US presidents have less control over their parties than UK party leaders have over theirs. Presidents have much less in the way of both sticks and carrots than UK party leaders. For the president, offers of cabinet jobs will not bring party compliance. Threats of legislative dissolution cannot be used at all. Indeed, the president has to face the electorate before many of his own party in the Senate. The president has no control over nominations for members of Congress, so threats of 'de-selection' are invalid. Members of Congress from the president's party may be able to ride above any unpopularity that comes the president's way. Pleasing 'the folks back home' may be more important to a member of Congress than pleasing the president. The electorate has real sanctions: it can deny a member either nomination or election.

In a candidate-centred election, US 'party leaders' are held more personally responsible for electoral defeat than are UK party leaders. Only Richard Nixon in modern times has been given a second chance after losing a presidential election, and he had to wait 8 years for that second chance. For most — Walter Mondale (1984), Michael Dukakis (1988), Bob Dole (1996) and Al Gore (2000) — one defeat is all that is allowed. There are no second chances, much, perhaps, to Al Gore's disappointment.

Summary

Party leaders

> US political parties do not have 'party leaders' in the same sense as party leaders exist in UK politics.
> The US president or, during election year, the presidential candidate(s) might be thought of as the 'party leader'.
> In UK politics, party leaders are nominated only from and by the party's elected officials in the legislature; in US politics, 'self-nomination' exists.

Party ideology

When it comes to ideology, the conventional wisdom is that parties in the USA are less ideological than their UK counterparts. Even the names suggest as much. The US parties took names of ideologies that are not mutually exclusive — democracy and republicanism. Parties in the UK have traditionally been associated with exclusive ideologies — conservatism, socialism, liberalism.

The fact that US parties have tended to be regarded as non-ideological while UK parties have tended to be regarded as ideological is often linked with the point already made about US parties being decentralised and UK parties being centralised. One factor that binds together UK politicians of the same party is their common ideology. That, so it is argued, is why they so often vote together in divisions in Parliament. This conventional wisdom, however, is open to question.

First, British parties are not ideological monoliths. For most of the time they pride themselves on being 'broad churches', not upturned ice-cream cones. Second, the divergent views that sometimes separate the two parties tend to involve more than ideology. Parties in both countries agree on as much as — if not more than — they disagree about. It was Churchill who remarked that 'four fifths of the two major British parties agree about four fifths of the things that need to be done'. Disagreements are often about degree, method and timing, but are masked in the over-inflated political rhetoric all too common in the politics of both nations.

Third, political parties are more like trees — changing to match the passing seasons — than mountain ranges. All parties face challenges as society changes. If the party fails to change, the party either declines or disappears altogether. In the USA both parties have undergone significant ideological change. The Democratic Party was reshaped by the depression, Vietnam, black civil rights, the decline of the 'solid South', and Clinton's 'New Democrat' and 'third way' ideology. The Republican Party was reshaped by Nixon's 'new federalism' and 'southern strategy' as well as by Reagan's conservatism. In the UK, the Conservative Party has gone from 'one nation' Toryism to Thatcherism and is currently looking for a new ideological angle. Labour has gone from the welfare state, nationalisation and unilateral nuclear disarmament to 'New Labour'. Having been trounced by the Conservatives in the 1983 and 1987 elections, many in the Labour Party realised that a party whose ideology was stuck in the UK of the 1940s and 1950s was unlikely to be a party that could still win elections.

Another piece of conventional wisdom that needs to be challenged is that the major parties — especially those in the USA — are now almost indistinguishable from one another in terms of ideology. True, differences may not be as marked as they were in the 1980s with Thatcher facing Foot and Reagan facing Mondale. It might be argued that such wide differences are the exception, not the rule. But in 2000 there were significant differences between Bush and Gore, and in 2001 there were equally significant differences between Blair and Hague. To be sure, the major parties in both countries want to appeal to the middle ground. That is why they are major parties in a first-past-the-post system and why the Green Party in both countries is a minor party. When the major parties forsake the middle ground, they cede victory to their principal rivals. Barry Goldwater's demand for 'a choice, not an echo' in the 1964 presidential election was laudable, but no one needs reminding that Goldwater did not make it to the White House — neither did fellow ideologue George McGovern. Michael Foot never made it to Number 10. Canny politicians may prefer to throw some ideological red meat to the party activists while governing as a centrist. That was partly the secret of Ronald Reagan's success.

How can we compare the four major parties: Conservative, Labour, Republican, Democratic? A Democrat member of the House of Representatives once gave this answer: 'Oh, that's easy. We in America have the Republican Party, which is like your Conservative Party, and then we have the Democratic Party, which is like your Conservative Party!' More seriously, if the four parties were graded from right to left in ideological terms, the list would probably read: Republicans, Conservatives, Democrats, Labour. In other words, the US Republicans tend to be to the right of the UK Conservatives and likewise the US Democrats tend to be to the right of the UK Labour Party. Ideological positions on political issues as varied as the war in Iraq (2003), tax cuts and capital punishment might show the accuracy of such an ideological spectrum.

A further difference between the major political parties in the USA and the UK may be that, whereas there is evidence that the Republicans and Democrats are becoming more ideologically cohesive, the Conservative and Labour parties are becoming less so.

The fact that the Democrats have all but lost their southern, conservative wing to the Republicans has contributed much to this greater ideological cohesion in the two major parties in the USA. It leaves the Democrats more clearly left of centre and strengthens the conservative strand of the Republican Party. Meanwhile, in the UK, both major parties appear less ideologically cohesive than they did 20 years ago — before the fall of Margaret Thatcher and the rise of 'New Labour'. On the other hand, recent US presidential elections have seen the Democrats move to the centre with Bill Clinton's 'New Democrat' credentials, and the Republicans try to do likewise with George W. Bush's 'compassionate conservatism'. Ideological signals are rather mixed.

Summary

Party ideology

➤ Conventional wisdom suggests that party ideology is weaker in the USA than in the UK.
➤ This conventional wisdom can be challenged, regarding both the non-ideological nature of US parties and the strength of ideology in UK parties.

Party systems

Political scientists generally admit to the existence of four different types of party system: one-party systems; two-party systems; dominant-party systems; and multiparty systems. Under normal circumstances, both the USA and the UK can best be described as two-party systems, though with subtle differences.

A two-party system is dominated by two 'major' parties that, over a period of time, have a roughly equal prospect of winning governmental power. Other, minor, parties exist but with no realistic chance of winning power. It might be possible to argue that the USA and the UK have not always fitted this definition. The Democratic Party's victory in five successive presidential elections between 1932 and 1952, followed by its control of the House of Representatives for 40 years (1954–94), does not fit easily with a definition including the phrase 'roughly equal prospect of winning power'. Likewise, the Conservatives' hold on power from 1979 to 1997 led some to think that the UK two-party system was not looking healthy or that the UK had a dominant-party system.

In a dominant-party system a number of political parties compete for power, but a single major party dominates, enjoying prolonged periods in power. Japan, with the Liberal Democrats in power from 1955 to 1993, is a case in point.

The demise of the two-party system on both sides of the Atlantic has often been predicted, but has never materialised. A book about Jim Callaghan, published in Britain in the early 1990s, was mischievously titled *Labour's Last Prime Minister*. An illustrious group of political scientists published a scholarly tome, following Labour's fourth successive election defeat in 1992, under the title of *1992: Labour's Last Chance?* Five years later, they were doubtless glad that they had included the question mark in the title.

Two-party systems are often linked to first-past-the-post electoral systems. They are praised for providing stable, responsible governments and for offering the voters clear choices at each election. They are criticised for causing complacency and moderation on the one hand, and polarisation and adversarial politics on the other.

Even if it is agreed that both countries normally have a two-party system, there are subtle differences.

First, there is greater representation of third parties in the UK Parliament than in the US Congress. This is largely to do with the regional parties dividing over nationalism in Scotland, Wales and Northern Ireland.

Second, whereas the two major parties in the USA can largely trace back their origins to the beginning of the republic, in the UK the Labour Party has come from being a third party to a major party and the Liberals (nowadays the Liberal Democrats) have moved from major to minor party status.

Third, there is much greater regional diversity among the major parties in the USA than in the UK.

Fourth, adversarial politics has been a more prominent feature of UK than US politics. There have been exceptions, such as the impeachment and trial of President Clinton, but US parties are — and need to be — more cooperative with their major rivals than their UK counterparts are with theirs. Even the seating arrangements in Parliament and Congress show this. In the House of Commons, members from opposing parties are seated opposite each other, a sword's length apart. In both chambers of the US Congress, only a gangway divides Democrats from Republicans (see picture on p. 139). There is considerable cooperation 'across the aisle'.

Summary

Party systems

➤ There are four different types of party system: one-party; two-party; dominant-party; and multiparty.

➤ Both the USA and the UK are said to have a two-party system, although there are subtle differences between them.

Third parties

While voters in both the USA and the UK have a number of third-party and independent candidates to turn to, only UK voters have any realistic chance that their third-party candidate will win a seat in the legislature.

Third parties in the UK

Both countries have a history of third-party and independent candidates. During the twentieth century in the UK these have included the Liberals, the SDP — eventually combining to form the Liberal Democrats — nationalist parties, unionist parties in Northern Ireland, Greens, socialists and communists, as well as single-issue candidates. Following the 2001 general election, candidates of nine third or independent parties won seats in the House of Commons, including 53 Liberal Democrats. There were 80 MPs who did not take either the Labour or Conservative Party whip.

This marks a significant change from the position just four decades ago. Until the 1960s, third-party representation in the UK House of Commons was minimal. So what changed? The electoral system — one that famously favours a rigid two-party system — still survives, at least for elections to the House of Commons. What has changed is the 'cleavage factor', which is said to be an important determinant of a country's party system. If a society has significant cleavages — usually to do with religion or nationalism — the party system is likely to reflect these cleavages. Of the UK population of some 60 million people, fewer than 1 million a week attended a church in 2003, so religion is unlikely to be thought of as an important cleavage in society.

However, two changes took place in the UK from the 1970s. First, nationalism grew in both Scotland and Wales, encouraged by the devolution referendums. This breathed life into the Scottish National Party and Plaid Cymru (the Welsh nationalists), giving the geographically concentrated support that can pay impressive dividends even under the first-past-the-post system. The second event was the splintering of Ulster unionism following the imposition of direct rule from Westminster in 1972 after the onset of 'the Troubles'. Up to that point, the Unionist Party had been united and an integral part of the Conservative Party. 'The Troubles' led to increased levels of support for nationalist parties in Northern Ireland, be they of the moderate type (SDLP) or the more radical type (Sinn Fein).

Third parties in the Westminster Parliament can encourage themselves with the hope that, whereas they may never *form* the government, as they will never be the largest single party, circumstances might allow them to *enter* or *influence* government in a hung parliament. The so-called 'Lib–Lab pact' between Jim Callaghan's Labour government and the handful of Liberal MPs in the late 1970s was such a case. This was not a full coalition government, because no Liberal MPs were included in the Callaghan cabinet. It seems unlikely that any third party would be willing ever again to give away so much for so little in return. Charles Kennedy's Liberal Democrats could, with 50+ MPs after a future election, realistically hope to form a left-of-centre coalition government with Labour.

Charles Kennedy, the Liberal Democrat Party leader, might hope to effect a coalition with Labour in the future

Third parties in the USA

Third and independent parties in the USA face significant problems: for a party to be taken seriously in a presidential system, it has to be able to mount a serious challenge in the race for the presidency. This occurred on only four occasions during the twentieth century — 1912, 1948, 1968 and 1992. However, after each of these third-party challenges, one or both of the major parties so realigned itself as to absorb most of those voters who had defected to the third party 4 years earlier. The demise of Perot and the Reform Party in 1996 and 2000 is an example of this, as is the Republicans' 'southern strategy' in 1972 following George Wallace's total of 46 Electoral College votes 4 years earlier.

Ross Perot — third-party US presidential candidate, 1992 and 1996

Major parties in the USA are more flexible and responsive than their UK counterparts. Their all-embracing nature in terms of ideology leaves little room for anything other than the more extreme — or regional — of third parties. Of equal importance is the use of the direct primary in US politics. Primaries make the parties more responsive to ordinary voters, who therefore have less reason to seek out third parties for a protest vote in the general election.

Politics in the USA is a more expensive arena to compete in than it is in the UK. Distances are greater. Organisational requirements are therefore far more demanding. US parties do not have the advantage of party election broadcasts on radio and television which their UK counterparts enjoy. As a result, third-party representation in both Congress and state government is minimal. In 2004, only two members of Congress — out of 535 — were not Democrats or Republicans.

Summary

Third parties

➤ Third parties in the UK stand a realistic chance of winning representation at constituency level in elections at European, national, regional and local levels.

➤ Third parties in the USA stand little chance of winning representation in any election.

➤ Third parties in the UK Parliament could be included in a coalition government; in the USA, there is no such thing as a 'coalition government'.

➤ Third parties in the USA face some formidable obstacles largely unknown to their UK counterparts.

Party government

In a UK general election, the major political parties seek a mandate to govern. To obtain this mandate, the parties go to the electorate with their manifesto — a detailed and specific list of what the party will do during the next 4–5 years if elected to government. To form a government, a party needs a 'working majority' in the House of Commons. Most recent UK elections have delivered such a majority to one of the major parties, often comfortably. The winning party then controls both the legislative and executive branches of government for a period of up to 5 years.

Implementation of the government's policies is carried out through strict party discipline in the House of Commons and the convention that the House of Lords will not ultimately thwart the government on a manifesto policy. The second largest party after the election becomes the official opposition and — along with other opposition parties — seeks to amend or defeat government proposals, but the government in almost all cases get its way. Of course, this is a shortened and over-simplified digest of UK government, but, be that as it may, the UK constitution can be said to encourage party government.

The USA Constitution cannot be said in any way to encourage party government. It does quite the opposite — it makes any kind of party government well nigh impossible. As Malcolm Shaw (1968) commented: 'Party government is precisely what the Constitution is designed, among other things, to prevent, and thus far it has succeeded.' The US Constitution seeks not to *merge* power into the hands of a responsible party government, but to *disperse* power and create separate branches of government competing for authority — what Edward Corwin once called 'an invitation to struggle'. Such an arrangement is incompatible with the party government associated with a parliamentary system. What is more, any efforts by the separate branches of government to cooperate are often frustrated, not facilitated, by the political parties. Federalism adds a further layer of frustration.

At a UK general election the entire House of Commons, prime minister, cabinet and government can be evicted in one clean sweep, at least in theory. No such occasion exists in US politics. Even in presidential election years, two-thirds of the Senate are not up for re-election and nor are most state governors, most of whose terms expire in the mid-term elections.

Parties in the USA are undisciplined. Even if a president enjoys a majority of his own party in both houses of Congress, there is no guarantee of it being what in the UK House of Commons would be called a 'working majority', as Jimmy Carter, Bill Clinton or George W. Bush would testify. Government in the USA is a government of individuals, not of party. The Congress is made up of 535 individuals. The president's cabinet is made up of 20 or more individuals, the majority of whom have no *party* political background at all.

What does all this mean for 'responsible' government? Some would argue that party government goes hand in hand with responsible government, while government by individuals leads to a lack of responsibility in government. To some extent this may be true. When governments in the UK return to the voters in a general election, it is clear to voters who has been responsible for the running of the government over the previous 4 or 5 years. Thus, there is a direct line of responsibility between the party of government on the one hand and the electorate on the other. The defeat of the Conservative government in 1997 is a clear example of responsible government in action.

In the USA, however, responsibility is usually much less clear. Because of staggered elections and the possibility of divided control both between the executive and the legislature and between the two co-equal houses of the legislature, US voters find it more difficult to know who has been responsible for success or failure during the previous 2–4 years. Yet it would be misleading to think there is no responsibility in US government. When one party does control both the presidency and both houses of Congress, responsibility can be more clearly attributed to that party. This goes some way to explain the loss by the Democrats of 52 House seats in the 1994 mid-term elections despite the fact that the voters could not be rid of President Clinton at that time. In addition, it could be argued that with congressional elections occurring every 2 years — rather than every 4–5 years for the UK House of Commons — there is more accountability in the USA than in the UK. Furthermore, where is the accountability of the members of the House of Lords, be they hereditary or appointed?

Summary

Party government

➤ In UK general elections, political parties seek a mandate to govern.
➤ In the USA, the Constitution actively makes 'party government' difficult or impossible.
➤ In the UK, voters can evict the entire government — legislature and executive — at one go.
➤ In the USA, the president and the two houses of Congress are elected for different lengths of time.
➤ 'Responsible government' is a feature of UK politics but rarely of US politics.

Theories of party decline and renewal

In both countries, the last few decades have seen a debate centred on theories of party decline and renewal. In both countries, the debate may have become polarised into an 'either–or' argument rather than a 'this-and-that' debate. Arguments on both sides have been too easily exaggerated.

It cannot be denied that party membership has declined in both countries over the past three decades. In the UK, party membership of over 9 million in the 1960s had fallen to under 2 million by the end of the 1990s. The same was true in most other European countries. Any revival in party membership numbers for a particular party — for example, for Labour in the mid-1990s — was short-lived. In addition, parties seemed to lose out in both countries to other vehicles of political expression and communication: group membership; the media, especially television; and opinion polls.

It is evident that parties have lost some degree of control over their internal affairs by choosing to democratise their decision-making processes. UK party conferences and US national party conventions have gone the same way — less about substance, more about style. Parties have less control now than they used to have in candidate selection. In the UK, both Labour and the Conservatives have democratised their party leadership election processes. The growth of presidential primaries during the past three decades has done the same to the selection of US presidential candidates. Election campaigns in the UK have become more candidate-centred than they used to be. Indeed, some would argue that the cult of personality permeates UK politics in a way that it did not 30 years ago — witness the election of Ken Livingstone as mayor of London and witness, too, the rise of the 'non-politician' in the USA (Ross Perot, Colin Powell, Jesse Ventura, Arnold Schwarzenegger, Wesley Clark) or of Silvio Berlusconi in Italy. In both the UK and the USA, political parties have to fight what seem to be increasing levels of distrust, cynicism and apathy directed at their politicians.

Colin Powell's distinguished army career brought him to the forefront of US politics

There is, however, another side to the coin. Parties still dominate the political scene in both the UK and the USA. Westminster and Whitehall march largely to the beat of political parties, as does regional, state and local government. Indeed, the number of independents in UK local government has declined over recent decades. The parties in both countries have fought back against the idea that 'the party's over'. Parties have undergone significant modernisation and there is much use of electronic systems of communication, making direct contact with voters more efficient. Scandal and 'sleaze' in society in general, and among politicians in particular, did not begin with Richard Nixon and David Mellor. Parties use the media to their own ends just as much as the media may be thought to detract from parties. Ask any spin doctor or media consultant — or Arnold Schwarzenegger. Partisanship in the UK Parliament is still alive and well. It may even be increasing in the US Congress. To have a significant chance of election or even appointed office in either country, people need to be associated with one of the major parties.

Thus, both sides of the argument have merit. Political parties on both sides of the Atlantic continue to dominate political life despite a number of recent challenges to their supremacy and new hurdles that have been placed in their paths. To talk of the demise of political parties in either country is something of an exaggeration. Nonetheless, Jean

Blondel concluded that: 'the representation of interests and views is increasingly provided by groups which are closer to the people than parties.'

Summary

Theories of party decline and renewal

➤ Political parties in both the USA and the UK have suffered in recent decades from declining membership.

➤ Parties in both countries have lost some of their traditional function of communication, which has been increasingly taken by the media and opinion polls.

➤ Parties in both countries have lost some of their control over internal decision making as parties have been democratised.

➤ Election campaigns, even in the UK, have become less party-centred and more centred on issues and personalities.

➤ In both countries, two major parties still dominate the political scene, whether at national, regional/state or local level.

B Pressure groups

Questions to be answered in this section

➤ What are pressure groups?
➤ How can they be classified?
➤ What functions do pressure groups perform?
➤ What methods do pressure groups use?
➤ How do pressure groups work within the three branches of government?
➤ What are the merits and demerits of pressure groups?

Definitions and classifications

Pressure groups — or interest groups, as they are referred to in the USA — are organised groups in which members share and actively pursue common views and objectives in order to influence government. Unlike political parties, therefore, pressure groups seek to influence those who determine policy, not to win office.

Almost all political scientists and textbook authors have their own means of classifying pressure groups. In comparing groups across different nation-states, it may be helpful to use a relatively simple classification: pressure groups can be classified as defensive or service groups on the one hand, or promotional or cause groups on the other.

Defensive or service groups are concerned with defending the interests of and providing a service to their members. In this category would fall the Trades Union

Congress and the Confederation of British Industry within the UK and the AFL–CIO (American Federation of Labor–Congress of Industrial Organizations) and United States Chamber of Commerce in the USA. Professional associations, too, come under this classification: the British Medical Association and the American Medical Association, for example. Membership of these groups — whether potential or actual — is quite straightforward, as it derives from particular skills or qualifications, a trade or profession.

On the other hand, promotional, or cause, groups seek to promote a cause in which their members are interested. Such groups include the League Against Cruel Sports and the National Council for Civil Liberties in the UK, and the National Rifle Association and the Sierra Club in the USA. Membership of these types of group is much less easily defined. In the end, it is best defined by self-interest and/or a willingness to participate in the democratic process. Potential membership of these groups is significantly larger than for defensive or service groups.

Summary

Definitions and classifications

➤ Pressure groups are organised groups in which members share and actively pursue common views and objectives in order to influence government.

➤ Pressure groups may be classified as defensive/service groups or promotional/cause groups.

Functions

Pressure groups perform five important functions. First, they perform a representative function. There may, of course, be a clash between representing the interests of their members in particular and the interests of society as a whole. Second, they provide opportunities for participation, especially between elections. Third, they can be said to have an educative function, seeking to educate both their specific membership and society in general, as well as those who hold public offices with decision-making powers. Fourth, pressure groups perform the function of agenda building, seeking to influence the agendas of political parties as well as of the holders of specific posts in government — whether legislative, executive or judicial. Finally, pressure groups monitor and scrutinise government. In this sense, they are one of the organs of society that seek to advance accountability in government.

Although there is a clear distinction between political parties and pressure groups, their functions do overlap. Key stated that pressure groups 'fill the gaps in the political system'. Furthermore, in a two-party system such as the UK or the USA, where the parties have broad and quite moderate programmes designed to appeal to a majority of voters, pressure groups see it as their function to put forward narrower, focused programmes of interest to their specialised clientele.

Many pressure groups are wary of becoming too closely associated with one particular party. They see themselves as exerting pressure on and working with politicians of any party. However, there are some groups which do ally themselves closely with one particular party. The trade unions ally themselves with the UK Labour Party and the US Democratic Party but cannot ignore the fact that, when the Conservatives and Republicans are in power, they need to work with them, too.

Summary

Functions of pressure groups

➤ Pressure groups perform five important functions: representation, participation, education, agenda building and advancing accountability.

Methods

While the methods used by pressure groups in both countries may be broadly similar in many respects, there are some notable and subtle differences.

Political action committees

The most significant difference is the rise in the USA of political action committees (PACs). Over the past three decades, PACs have come to play a significant part in US elections, spending vast sums of money to support candidates whom they judge to be in agreement with their views and to oppose those whom they judge to be out of line with their views. The growth in PACs came about as a way of getting around some of the restrictions on campaign fundraising and spending introduced by the Federal Election Campaign Acts of the early 1970s. While limits are placed on the amount that a PAC can actually give to a candidate, there are no limits on the amounts that a PAC may itself spend in support of, or in opposition to, any candidate. Such support and opposition is, of course, decided by the views held and also possibly the votes cast by a candidate for public office and the extent to which they do, or do not, coincide with those espoused by the group itself.

Advertising

Extensive use is made of political advertising in US elections. In a UK general election, most political advertising is organised by the political parties. This is not the case in US elections, where pressure groups in general and PACs in particular spend vast amounts of money on what are called 'issue ads'. Attempts to limit this activity were included in the McCain–Feingold campaign finance law passed in 2002.

New technology

In addition to the traditional methods of lobbying, the impact of pressure groups on both sides of the Atlantic — and especially in the USA — has grown as a direct consequence

Protestors at the 'Million Mom March' in Washington DC, May 2000

of increased use of new technology. The large demonstration against the World Trade Organization that took place in Seattle in November 1999 used electronics to organise and execute the event. The same was true of the so-called 'Million Mom March' in favour of gun control in Washington DC in May 2000.

Using the system

Pressure groups in the USA benefit from a friendlier constitutional and legislative framework in which to operate than that enjoyed by their UK counterparts. US pressure groups operate under the auspices of 1st Amendment rights, safeguarding rights of speech, expression and association. They also have the advantage of 'sunshine laws' (rules that allow inquiry into government affairs) and the Freedom of Information Act, while their UK counterparts must often do battle with the Official Secrets Act. The UK introduced a Freedom of Information Act only in 2000.

Finally, US pressure groups benefit from a greater number of 'access points' in their political system than exist in the UK. Pressure groups in the USA benefit, for example, from a federal system, the enhanced importance of congressional committees and the willingness of the courts to hear cases that are of political significance.

Summary

Methods

➤ There are a number of significant differences in the methods used by pressure groups in the USA and the UK.

➤ These differences concern the existence in US politics of political action committees, political advertising, the use of technology, a friendlier constitutional and legislative framework, and more access points.

Pressure groups and the legislature

The UK Parliament, while not exactly a truly 'legislating' body, is undoubtedly the body that formally ratifies legislation. Pressure groups find that Parliament is not a very amenable institution. Members of Parliament, operating, as they do, under fairly strict party discipline, are more likely to be open to the overtures and arguments of the party leadership, backed up by the whips, than those of pressure groups. Pressure groups may be able to persuade MPs to raise points with ministers, ask questions in the House or pursue a matter in committee, but when it comes to votes, it is the party — not the pressure group — that speaks with a voice that demands obedience in all but a few instances. As Malcolm Walles (1988) stated: '[MPs'] hearts may be won, but rarely their votes.' Even if some backbench MPs are induced to cast their votes against the party's wishes, they are unlikely to do so in great enough numbers even to worry the government, let alone defeat it. It is necessary to go back to 1986 to find a government defeated on a significant vote in the House of Commons as a result of a vigorous pressure group campaign: the defeat at the second reading of the government's Shops Bill to liberalise Sunday trading laws. The defeat was brought about largely by an alliance between a left-wing trade union (USDAW), the Lord's Day Observance Society and an ad hoc pressure group called Keep Sunday Special.

Policy issues that are not the subject of party political division or which result in 'free votes' on matters of conscience may provide pressure groups with opportunities for greater influence. Thus, debates and votes on 'matters of life and death' — abortion, cloning and the death penalty — are likely to see higher levels of pressure group activity.

There is a longstanding tradition within the Labour Party of trade union sponsorship of MPs, while, on the Conservative Party benches, MPs speak up for defensive or service groups such as the Police Association.

In recent decades, the House of Lords, too, has become the target of increased levels of pressure group activity. Peers are less obliged — and willing — to toe the party line and are generally seen as being of a more independent mind. The cross-bench and independent peers make up a growing and influential proportion of the House, especially since the removal of all but a few hereditary peers.

It is quite a different matter in the US Congress, where the role of political parties, although still important, is not the determining factor in voting that it tends to be in the UK House of Commons. The party leadership is generally less powerful. It possesses nothing like the sticks or carrots that its UK counterparts use with such ruthlessness and success in the House of Commons. House and Senate members are not even dependent on their parties for renomination, which, through the use of direct primaries, is in the gift of 'the folks back home'. Their election campaigns, although graced with a party label of convenience, are more candidate-centred affairs than the elections in the 659 parliamentary constituencies in the UK.

If politics were thought of in terms of climate and pressure groups as greenhouse plants, the UK parliament would be the Arctic compared with the sub-tropics of the US Congress. In these more favourable conditions, it is hardly surprising that US pressure groups are seen trailing through the corridors and committee rooms of Congress, looking strong and healthy compared with their UK counterparts. The ever-present lobbyists on Capitol Hill bear testimony to their importance. In any part of Congress — members' offices, committee rooms, the corridors, the dining rooms or even on the many walkways along which members of Congress regularly traipse to or from a vote — a lobbyist will not be far away.

Lobbyists have much to offer House and Senate members: information, proposals for legislation, persuasion, literature, threats, election-time endorsement or opposition and, of course, money. All are used when and where appropriate and often to devastating effect. When their congressional careers are at an end for whatever reason, former members may seek to use the 'revolving door' and re-enter government as lobbyists themselves.

Summary

Pressure groups and the legislature

➤ The UK Parliament is subject to high levels of party discipline and not very amenable to successful pressure group lobbying.

➤ The US Congress is less dominated by party discipline, making members of Congress more open to pressure group lobbying.

➤ Powerful congressional committees provide more 'access points' for US pressure groups.

➤ US pressure groups can contribute significantly to congressional election campaigns.

Pressure groups and the executive

Pressure groups in the UK may not feel that Parliament is fertile soil for them, but it is quite a different matter when it comes to the administrative branch of government. This is where most of the activity of defensive groups is aimed, for the administrative branch of government has responsibility not only for interpreting and administering laws passed by Parliament, but for innovation through proposals made by its political masters.

Many pressure groups build up 'insider' status with relevant government departments and agencies. A two-way street of information develops, which is of equal importance to both. Blondel (1963) observed that 'if firms and other interests were to starve the Civil Service of information the administration of the country would come to a halt.' That the government recognises the importance and value of this relationship with pressure groups is shown by the vast array of advisory committees and quangos that have been established, as well as by the legal obligations put on government departments to consult with such bodies. This gives rise to what Finer called 'the vast anonymous empire' of Whitehall that is largely unknown to the public, but which has a semi-institutionalised role at the heart of UK government.

Not that all is sweetness and light: pressure groups are often disappointed with what government has to offer. Behind-the-scenes consultation gives way to more public forms of lobbying — marches, demonstrations, media briefings and advertising campaigns. When these occur, the public knows that the usual, more hidden, forms of consultation and negotiation have temporarily broken down.

Promotional or cause groups do not generally enjoy — or seek — such 'insider status', lest they be seen to have too cosy a relationship with the government. That is not to say that they are not happy to be consulted by policy-makers, but their success depends more on their level of support in the country than on their behind-the-scenes activity in Whitehall offices. Thus, where defensive or service groups often seek a degree of anonymity, promotional or cause groups court publicity. Their campaigns to stop a road-building project or a nuclear waste dump, to promote the interests of environmentalists or to safeguard certain rights and liberties of minorities within society all require as much involvement of the public as possible. They thrive on what Margaret Thatcher called 'the oxygen of publicity'.

While the US president does not have the legislative power of the UK prime minister, he and his executive branch officials — both in the White House and in the government departments, agencies and regulatory commissions — are popular targets for pressure group activity. The president does, after all, play a major role in establishing policy priorities and in attempting to set the agenda of political debate and activity. There is considerable potential for pressure groups to exert some influence on the countless nominations that the president makes in both the executive and judicial branches of the federal government. Consider, for example, the status that the American Bar Association (ABA) long enjoyed in rating judicial nominees, which President George W. Bush has sought to limit. Many agencies of the federal government enjoy independence from other parts of the government, and so offer further access points for pressure groups. Pressure groups may be involved in so-called 'iron triangles' — the cosy relationships between pressure groups, relevant congressional committees and executive branch agencies.

Summary

Pressure groups and the executive

➤ Pressure groups in the UK seek 'insider status' with government.

➤ Pressure groups in the USA seek to form 'iron triangles' involving relevant executive branch agencies as well as congressional committees.

Pressure groups and the judiciary

In the USA there is one further major channel open to pressure groups seeking to change or obstruct change in the law: the courts. This is a channel largely denied to their UK counterparts because the doctrine of parliamentary sovereignty puts strict limits on the powers of the courts. In the UK, any law passed by Parliament is constitutional. The UK courts can declare ministers to have acted *ultra vires* — beyond the powers bestowed upon them by legislation — but that is a much lesser power than the US courts' power of judicial review.

Pressure groups in the USA often sponsor cases, thereby hoping to bring them all the way to the Supreme Court for final constitutional arbitration. The landmark 1954 case of *Brown v. Board of Education of Topeka* concerning segregation of schools was sponsored by the National Association for the Advancement of Colored People (NAACP). The American Civil Liberties Union (ACLU) has brought some high-profile cases to the Supreme Court in recent years — *Allegheny County v. ACLU* (1989) and *Reno v. ACLU* (1997). In 2002, the Free Speech Coalition brought a case to the Supreme Court against Attorney General John Ashcroft concerning the 1996 Child Pornography Protection Act.

US pressure groups have become increasingly active in their efforts to block court nominations of which they disapprove. Liberal groups worked hard — and successfully — to defeat the nomination of Robert Bork to the Supreme Court in 1987 and equally hard — but unsuccessfully — to defeat the Clarence Thomas nomination in 1991.

Summary

Pressure groups and the judiciary

> US pressure groups enjoy considerable access to both federal and state courts, access which is largely denied to their UK counterparts.

Merits and demerits of pressure groups

The merits of pressure groups are often discussed alongside the useful functions that they perform within a democracy. If democratic government is about participation, representation, openness, accountability and an educated and active citizenry, then pressure groups have some obvious merits.

The demerits of pressure groups in both countries mostly concern at least one of the following:

> the over-importance of money and the correlation between money and success
> groups' undue access to government
> the undemocratic nature of some groups
> 'national interest' versus 'special interest'
> the revolving-door syndrome

➤ the use of illegitimate and sometimes illegal methods

➤ the inequality of power between different groups in the same policy area

A number of the arguments put forward in reply to some of these demerits do not, however, apply equally in both the UK and the USA. Supporters of pressure group activity in the UK may argue that the very nature of the party system offers some degree of protection against the worst excesses of pressure group activity sometimes witnessed in the USA. As parties run for re-election on their record, any overt pandering to special interests at the expense of the national interest would, it is argued, provide easy ammunition for their political opponents. In the USA, on the other hand, the absence of responsible and disciplined parties provides an ideal environment for pressure groups to gain too much political clout. Nonetheless, politicians still have to guard against the appearance of overly favouring a particular group. George Bush's joke at the expense of Michael Dukakis in the 1988 election, stating that 'my opponent can't even visit the bathroom without first asking the Plumbers' Union', was a telling political jibe.

The whole process of governmental control of the legislative process in the UK means that, generally speaking, pressure groups do not have the same opportunity to get their way in terms of legislation passed or defeated as is likely to be the case in the US Congress. Even the multiplicity of subcommittees in Congress compared with the number in the UK Parliament provides countless more access points for US pressure groups than for their UK counterparts. However, with more access points come more opportunities for the misuse of pressure group influence.

Similarly, while the UK civil service is very much part of the structure of responsible government, the US civil service is a patchwork quilt of competing fiefdoms over which even the president struggles to have control. Thus, the US civil service is more at the mercy of pressure groups than is its UK counterpart. Concerns are therefore rightly greater.

These demerits of and concerns about pressure groups in both countries, but especially in the USA, are not matched by effective measures to restrain or control them. Thus, the passage in the USA of the Federal Regulation Lobbying Act (1946) did not herald an era of more responsible and restrained pressure groups. Similarly, in the UK, the establishment of a register of members' interests in the House of Commons in 1976 shed little light on the relationship between members and groups.

Summary

Merits and demerits of pressure groups

➤ The merits of pressure groups in both countries centre on the useful functions they perform.

➤ Their demerits centre on such concerns as: the over-importance of money; undue access; the undemocratic nature of some groups; 'national interest' v. 'special interest'; the revolving door syndrome; the use of illegitimate or illegal methods; the inequality of power among groups.

➤ These merits and demerits do not apply equally in both the USA and the UK.

Exercises

Political parties

1 (a) Define a political party. (b) Explain the four different ways in which political parties can be classified.
2 What are the principal functions of political parties?
3 Explain the main differences between party organisation in the USA and the UK.
4 Explain why the term 'party leader' has a different meaning in the USA and the UK.
5 Compare the ideology of US and UK political parties.
6 Explain the terms (a) two-party system and (b) dominant-party system. Which best describes the US and the UK party system?
7 What differences exist between the two-party systems in the USA and the UK?
8 Explain why third parties seem to flourish more in the UK than in the USA.
9 Explain how the UK constitution encourages 'party government'.
10 Explain how the US Constitution makes 'party government' difficult to achieve.
11 Why is 'responsibility' in government easier to identify in the UK than in the USA?
12 What arguments are put forward in the USA and the UK to suggest that 'party decline' has occurred in recent decades?
13 What arguments are put forward in both countries to suggest the opposite view?

Pressure groups

14 What is a pressure group?
15 Explain the terms (a) defensive or service groups and (b) promotional or cause groups.
16 Explain the functions of pressure groups.
17 What different methods are used by pressure groups in the USA and the UK?
18 What differences exist between pressure groups' relationships with Congress as opposed to Parliament?
19 Explain the term 'insider status'.
20 Why do US pressure groups focus more on lobbying the courts than do their UK counterparts?
21 What are the main merits and demerits of pressure groups?

Exam focus

1 Examine the claim that political parties in both the USA and the UK have become less ideological.
2 'The UK and the US party systems are both dominated by two parties, but thereafter the similarity ends.' Discuss.

3 How significant are differences in the ways in which major 'party leaders' are selected in the UK and the USA?

4 Analyse the link between electoral systems and party systems.

5 Why do third parties always struggle to win anything in both US and UK elections?

6 Analyse ways in which US pressure groups are more significant than their UK counterparts.

7 How does the structure of government affect pressure groups in both the USA and the UK?

8 Discuss the view that pressure groups make US and UK government more, rather than less, democratic.

References

Blondel, J., *Comparative Government* (Macmillan, 1963).

McKenzie, R. T., *British Political Parties* (Mercury, 1964).

Michels, R., *Political Parties* (The Free Press, 1962).

Shaw, M., *Anglo-American Democracy* (Routledge and Kegan Paul, 1968).

Walles, M., *British and American Systems of Government* (Philip Allan/Barnes and Noble, 1988).

Further reading

Batchelor, A., 'UK and US interest groups: similarities and differences', *Politics Review*, vol. 12, no. 1 (September 2002).

Chapter 13

Congress and Parliament

The best way to understand the differences between these two legislatures is to start with the geography of London and Washington. The Palace of Westminster — a grand term if ever there was one — which houses both parliamentary chambers, dominates the Westminster scenery. The prime minister's residence at 10 Downing Street is, in comparison, unimpressive. But in Washington, the Capitol — the building that houses the Senate and the House of Representatives — is rivalled by the White House. Both stand on the same street — Pennsylvania Avenue. Commentators often refer to the president and Congress as being at 'both ends of the Avenue'. From the foot of the Washington Monument — ground zero of the nation's capital — there is a grand view due east to the Capitol and due north to the White House.

Parliament dominates UK government, while Congress is an equal partner in a system of 'separated institutions sharing powers', in Richard Neustadt's excellent phrase. What differences exist between the UK Parliament and the US Congress, why do these differences exist and what are the consequences of these differences?

Questions to be answered in this chapter

- ➤ What are legislatures, parliaments and assemblies?
- ➤ How can legislatures be classified?
- ➤ What are the merits and demerits of bicameral legislatures?
- ➤ How are Congress and Parliament composed?
- ➤ What terms of office do their members have?
- ➤ What are the legislative functions of Congress and Parliament?
- ➤ How do Congress and Parliament have oversight of the executive branch?

> How well do Congress and Parliament fulfil their representative functions?
> What role do committees play in Congress and Parliament?
> What role do political parties play in Congress and Parliament?
> What is the relationship between the upper and lower chambers?

Terminology

Different terms are used in reference to legislatures. 'Parliament' comes from the French *parler*, to speak. It seems to draw attention to its consultative, deliberative and debating functions. Andrew Turner (2002) defined Parliament as: 'an institution of government, comprising representatives elected by voters, whose functions are to debate, scrutinise and pass legislation.' The term 'assembly' is used within the UK — as in Wales and Northern Ireland — to refer to a legislative body with some lesser delegated powers of legislation and scrutiny. The term literally means 'a gathering together of people'.

The USA uses a similar word, 'Congress'. This harks back to British colonial days when delegates representing the east coast colonies first met to protest at their treatment by the government of Great Britain. They met as 'the Continental Congress'. It was the second Continental Congress in 1775 that adopted the Declaration of Independence, conducted the War of Independence and served as the national government until the Articles of Confederation were put into effect in 1781. Jay Shafritz (1993) defined the word 'Congress' simply as 'any large representative assembly'.

The Houses of Parliament, where both UK parliamentary chambers assemble

Types of legislature

Legislatures can be differentiated in three ways: by their method of recruitment; their size; and the number of chambers they possess.

Recruiting legislators

There are essentially two different ways of recruiting legislators: by election and by appointment. Until recently, a third way would have had to be included: by heredity. Although 92 members of the current UK House of Lords are hereditary members, they are awaiting their banishment in the next round of reforms of that chamber.

The majority of legislatures are these days recruited by direct election. The lower houses — the UK House of Commons and the US House of Representatives — have always been recruited in this way. What has changed over the centuries is how widely the electorate has been drawn. So, for example, the right of women to vote in elections to the UK House of Commons was granted by the Representation of the People Act (1918), while the right of women to vote in elections to both houses of the US Congress was granted by the 19th Amendment (1920). In itself, it is an interesting comparison that the reform was brought about in one country through a piece of legislation and in the other by a constitutional amendment. The same situation occurred in lowering the voting age. In 1969, the UK Parliament passed a law lowering the voting age to 18. In the USA, 2 years later, the 26th Amendment did the same for elections to Congress.

An earlier change had occurred in the USA with the passage of the 17th Amendment in 1913, which provided for *direct* elections to the US Senate, replacing the *indirect* elections that had existed since 1788. For the first 126 years of its history, the Senate had been indirectly elected — chosen by members of the state legislatures who themselves were directly elected. Thus, the 1914 mid-term elections were the first in which both houses of Congress were directly elected.

When the Labour government of Tony Blair was first elected in 1997, the House of Lords was still made up principally of members who were there by virtue of the hereditary principle. Others — life peers, Law Lords and Church of England archbishops and bishops — were there by appointment. During its first administration (1997–2001), the Labour government under Blair enacted reform of the House of Lords, which resulted in a chamber made up mainly of appointed life peers, with 92 hereditary peers being allowed to continue as members only until a further raft of reforms could be agreed. During the second administration, Blair was still unable to build a consensus as to the composition of a fully reformed second chamber, with options ranging from a wholly appointed chamber to one that would be wholly elected.

Size of legislature

Legislatures can be differentiated by their size. The UK Parliament is larger than the US Congress. The House of Commons consists of 659 members, and even the slimmed down, partly reformed House of Lords has 687 peers. In the USA, the House of

Representatives has 435 members and the Senate just 100. Two factors determine the size of legislatures: the size of the nation-state concerned and the form of government. Put simply, large countries tend to have larger legislatures than small countries. The National People's Congress of China has over 2,000 members while the west central Pacific island state of Nauru has a national assembly of just 18 people. Unitary systems tend to have larger national legislatures than federal systems. This is the principal reason for the size of Congress being significantly smaller than the Westminster Parliament, for Americans have not only the US Congress but also their state legislatures. With the creation of the Scottish Parliament, there is agreement that Scotland now requires fewer MPs in the UK House of Commons. Thus, the overall size of the House of Commons may well decline in the near future.

Number of chambers

Most legislatures are bicameral rather than unicameral. In the UK and the USA, both national legislatures are bicameral. In the UK, the regional legislatures — the Scottish Parliament and the assemblies in Wales and Northern Ireland — are unicameral. The European Parliament in Strasbourg is unicameral. In the USA, 49 of the 50 states have bicameral legislatures — only Nebraska has a unicameral arrangement. In western democracies generally, bicameralism holds sway. However, Israel established a unicameral legislature — the Knesset — in 1948, and during the second half of the twentieth century second chambers were abolished in New Zealand (1950), Denmark (1954) and Sweden (1970).

The Florida Senate chamber

Bicameral legislatures, first, enhance the system of democratic checks and balances. In the USA, there is an intricate system of checks and balances not only between the three branches of the federal government, but also between the House of Representatives and the Senate. Under the original arrangement, the indirectly elected Senate was meant to cool the passions of the directly elected House. The analogy of the Senate as the saucer to cool what came out of the House was often used. In May 2003, after the House of Representatives had passed a $550 billion tax cut, the Senate refused to pass anything more than a $350 billion tax cut. In the end, President Bush signed a $350 billion tax cut. Second, in federal systems, a second chamber can be used specifically to represent the interests of the individual states. This can be seen in the US Senate where each state, regardless of population, has two Senators. Third, in non-federal systems, regional differences can be given consideration in the second chamber, as in the French Senate, where members are elected indirectly via local government.

There are demerits too, however. First, bicameralism can too often be associated with inefficiency and duplication. If different political parties control the two chambers, the problem can be exacerbated. This has often been seen in the UK when the Labour Party has controlled the House of Commons. In the current Parliament 213 peers take the Conservative whip while only 186 take the Labour whip. It was also the case in the US Congress between June 2001 and January 2003 when the Democrats controlled the Senate but the Republicans controlled the House of Representatives. Each chamber seemed to be working to a different agenda. In addition, most second chambers are politically subservient to the first chamber, as is the case in the UK. The US Senate is an exception in this regard.

Summary

Types of legislature

➤ Legislatures can be classified by method of recruitment, size and number of chambers.
➤ Bicameral legislatures, such as Congress and Parliament, have both merits and demerits.

Composition and terms of office

There are a number of significant differences between Parliament and Congress in their composition and terms of office, and these have some important consequences.

The most important difference in composition is the presence of members of the executive branch in the UK parliament and their complete absence from the US Congress.

In the USA, Article I of the Constitution specifically forbids members of Congress from holding office in other branches of the federal government. When Senator John F. Kennedy was elected president in 1960, he had to resign from the Senate before becoming president in January 1961. The same was true of Senator Al Gore when he was elected vice-president in 1992. When incoming President Clinton appointed Senator

Table 13.1 Differences in composition and terms of office in the US House of Representatives and the UK House of Commons

The US House of Representatives has:	The UK House of Commons has:
fixed elections every 2 years	elections at least every 5 years
a minimum age of 25	a minimum age of 21
a residency qualification and a locality rule in some states	no residency qualification
no executive branch members	executive branch members

Lloyd Bentsen of Texas to be secretary of the treasury in January 1993, Senator Bentsen had to resign his Senate seat immediately.

The only slight break in this 'separation of personnel' in the US Congress is that the vice-president's job includes his being President of the Senate. But the vice-president is not — and cannot be — a *member* of the Senate, although the vice-president may chair debates and, in the event of a tied vote, can make a casting vote. Vice-President Dick Cheney made a casting vote in May 2003 on the final passage of President Bush's $350 billion tax cut, after the Senate vote had ended 50–50.

In the UK, the executive branch — the prime minister, cabinet and other members of the government — is drawn from Parliament, and mostly from the House of Commons. There have been no examples of members of the government being drawn from outside Parliament since Harold Wilson appointed Transport and General Workers' Union leader Frank Cousins to his cabinet in 1964.

At any one time, more than 100 members of the government side of the House of Commons are members of the government. The 'payroll vote', as they are often called, can always be counted on to vote in favour of the government. The only way out — as with Foreign Secretary Robin Cook in 2003 over the war in Iraq — is resignation from the government. This has implications for the prime minister because he or she is elected only by a parliamentary constituency. Tony Blair was elected by the voters of Sedgefield, whereas George W. Bush was elected by the voters of the United States of America. Furthermore, the prime minister and all other members of the government must represent their constituents as well as perform their executive duties.

A significant difference in the composition of these two legislatures is the unelected nature of the House of Lords. Stage 1 of the reform of the House of Lords saw the ousting of all but 92 of the hereditary peers, who were to remain only for the 'transitional' phase until Stage 2 could be agreed upon and implemented. A commission chaired by Lord Wakeham then recommended that Stage 2 should see the House of Lords become a part-elected, part-appointed chamber as well as the setting up of an appointments commission to review the appointment process to the reformed second chamber. The difficulty was trying to find some agreement on what proportion should be elected. By 2004, Stage 2 had foundered on that particular rock. US observers must have found rather quaint a debate about 'modernising' a legislative chamber by introducing appointed members. Americans had left behind in 1913 the idea of Senators being appointed by state legislatures. The UK was in danger of looking as if it were desperately trying to drag itself into the twentieth century just as everyone else was leaving it for the twenty-first.

All other members of Parliament and Congress are directly elected, but for differing terms. Members of Congress serve fixed terms while members of the House of Commons do not. Members of the House of Commons serve terms of up to 5 years, the maximum period permitted between the beginning of one Parliament and the next general election. UK general elections are usually held somewhere between 4 and 5 years apart: 1979, 1983, 1987, 1992, 1997 and 2001. In 1974, however, there were general elections in both February and October.

In the USA, members of the House of Representatives serve fixed 2-year terms while Senators serve fixed 6-year terms. Congressional elections are held in November of the even-numbered years. Every 4 years (1996, 2000 and 2004, for example) they coincide with the presidential election. Congressional elections in the intermediate years (1998 and 2002, for example) are referred to as 'mid-term' elections, coming, as they do, midway through a president's 4-year term of office. Not only is the year fixed, but so is the date — fixed by federal law as the Tuesday after the first Monday in November. Thus a member of the US Congress knows exactly when he or she is next up for re-election. Take, for example, those last elected on 5 November 2002. Any member of the House of Representatives elected on that date knew they faced re-election on 2 November 2004, while any Senator elected on that day will face re-election on 4 November 2008. On the other hand, UK MPs elected on 7 June 2001 knew only that they would face the electorate sometime before June 2006.

In the USA, members of Congress are likely to have long-standing, often life-long, links with the state or district that they represent. Indeed, the Constitution requires members to be resident of the state that they represent. Locality rules in many states go even further by requiring House members to be resident in the *congressional districts* that they represent. True, there are members, like Senator Hillary Clinton of New York, whose links with their state are tenuous, but they are the exception; in the House of Commons, they are much more the rule. The attachment to 'the folks back home' of members of Congress is an important factor when votes are cast.

What are the consequences of these differences? First, it is often said in the USA that, once election year comes around, opportunities for making significant political decisions decrease, implying that every other year Congress suffers from indecision brought on by imminent elections. Second, the fact that members of the US House of Representatives must face their electorate every 2 years makes them wary of actions that might offend a significant minority — let alone, a majority — of their voters. It makes US House members more attentive to their constituents than are members of the UK House of Commons.

How do Parliament and Congress compare in terms of the people who make up their number? Women are better represented in Parliament than in Congress. One of the principal reasons for this is the move in the UK Labour Party towards positive discrim-ination in favour of selecting women candidates for winnable seats. A pressure group called EMILY's List (UK), based on the group known by the same name in the USA, was formed in 1993 to raise money to help women candidates within the Labour Party. At the same time, the party was pursing a policy of 'women-only shortlists'. As a result, the number of Labour women MPs jumped from 37 in the 1992–97 Parliament to 101 in the 1997–2001 Parliament. The total of 120 women MPs at the beginning of that Parliament — the largest number ever elected, as the figure fell back to 118 in 2001 — represented 18% of the membership of the House of Commons. In June 2003, the House of Lords included 113 women in its total membership of 687, which represents 16%. Following the 2002 mid-term elections, women accounted for 14% of both the House of Representatives and the Senate.

In terms of ethnic minorities, the US House of Representatives is the most represent-ative of the four US and UK chambers. Blacks and Hispanics made up 12% of the House membership following the 2002 elections, while only 2% of the House of Commons were either black or Asian. There are three reasons for this. First, and most obviously, blacks and Hispanics form a larger proportion of the population as a whole in the USA (25%) than in the UK (6%). Second, there are congressional districts in the USA that are populated by a majority of black or Hispanic voters. Third, ethnic minorities have been advantaged by the creation of majority-minority districts — congressional districts whose boundaries have been drawn in such a way as to maximise the number of ethnic minority voters within them, thus increasing the likelihood of the election of an ethnic minority member.

In other ways, Parliament and Congress are very similar in their make-up. A typical member of both is middle-aged, highly educated and from a professional background. The average age of a UK MP is just over 50, while the average age of US House members is 54 and of Senators, 59. A person can be elected to the UK House of Commons at the age of 21, but not until 25 and 30 respectively to the House of Representatives and the Senate.

Summary

Composition and terms of office

➤ There are a number of significant differences between Congress and Parliament in composi-tion and terms of office.

➤ The most significant concern: length of terms of office; links with constituency; the presence or absence of executive branch members; and methods of recruitment.

Legislative function

The most significant function of both Parliament and Congress is legislation. To some extent, the legislative processes in Parliament and Congress are similar: essentially, a series of debates and votes on the floor of both chambers, with some work being done

Table 13.2 The legislative function in the US Congress and UK Parliament

US Congress	UK Parliament
No government programme of legislation exists	A government programme of legislation exists
The level of party discipline is low	High levels of party discipline exist
Thousands of bills are introduced in any one session	A limited number of bills are introduced in any session
Few of these bills are passed into law	Most bills are passed into law
The committee stage comes before the second reading	The committee stage comes after the second reading
Standing committees are permanent and policy specialist	Standing committees are non-permanent and non-specialist
Bills are usually considered by both houses concurrently	Bills are considered by each house consecutively
The two chambers have equal powers	The lower chamber dominates
The president has a significant power of veto	The royal assent is no longer withheld

by committees. Amendments can be tabled, and simple majorities are usually required when voting takes place.

Programmes of government legislation

There are a number of important differences in the legislative process in these two institutions. First and foremost, in Parliament there is a readily recognisable government programme of legislation, which is announced to the electorate in the governing party's general election manifesto. The government announces its intention to bring forward specific legislative proposals in the Queen's Speech, with which each session of Parliament begins. As a consequence, most legislation considered in Parliament can best be described as 'government legislation'. There are very few opportunities for individual backbench MPs to introduce their own bills, called 'private members' bills'. Such bills are limited and rarely successful. In Congress, all legislation is sponsored by individual House and Senate members — even bills that have clearly originated within the executive branch. The president's State of the Union Address is not usually as consequential as the Queen's Speech in the UK Parliament.

Party discipline

In the House of Commons, the government programme of legislation is supported — almost without exception — by every member of the governing party and opposed by most members of the opposition parties. Despite the rise of backbench independence during the last three decades, most votes in the House of Commons show exceedingly high levels of party discipline. Dissent is rare and limited, and when it does occur, it is still headline news. In Congress, however, party discipline is more limited. A typical vote in both the House and the Senate is one group of Democrats and Republicans voting against another group of Democrats and Republicans. Despite a seeming rise in partisanship in Congress during the 1990s, party discipline never rose to anything approaching the levels seen in the UK House of Commons.

Numbers of bills

The fact that the legislative agenda in Parliament is so closely controlled by the government affects the number of bills passing through the legislature during any particular session. In Parliament, the government controls the process carefully and introduces only those bills that it believes it has time to get through all their stages within a parliamentary session of about a year — up to 50 government bills during a typical session. With the addition of private members' bills, private bills and the odd hybrid bill, maybe around 125 bills are introduced and perhaps 100 are given the royal assent and become law. There are no such controls in Congress. As a result, in a typical congressional session of about a year, upwards of 4,000 bills will be introduced. Of that number, only around 200 might expect to become law. So a bill's chance of success in Congress is minimal compared with Parliament.

The legislative process

The legislative process in Congress is more exacting than the one that exists in Parliament. First, the committee stage in Congress comes *before* the second reading, and therefore before either chamber has debated the bill. What is more, the committees that conduct this committee stage are permanent, policy-specialist committees with names reflecting the policy areas — the House Agriculture Committee or the Senate Energy and Natural Resources Committee, for example. Members of these committees become policy specialists in their respective areas. In the House of Commons, the committees are generalist and named by a letter: A, B, C and so on. In the USA, the permanent, specialist congressional committees have full power of amendment. In the House of Commons, the standing committees can amend bills only within the principles already agreed at the second reading. These congressional standing committees have the power to 'pigeonhole' bills — giving them no consideration at all. This power causes them to act as a legislative sieve, only passing those bills of which they approve.

There are many other important differences between the parliamentary and congressional legislative processes. In Parliament, each house considers bills consecutively — usually the House of Commons first, then the House of Lords. In Congress, on the other hand, both houses usually consider bills concurrently. There are, therefore, at any one time, two versions of the same bill — a House version and a Senate version. The differences must then be resolved, often through the use of a conference committee, because, to pass through the legislative process in Congress, a bill must be approved by majority votes in *both* chambers. In legislation, the House and the Senate are co-equal, whereas, in Parliament, the House of Lords has only the power to delay legislation. Since the passage of the 1911 and 1949 Parliament Acts, the House of Commons has had the power to override the objections of the Lords.

At the end of the legislative process, in the UK, once Parliament has passed a bill through its agreed procedure, the bill is sent for the royal assent and thus becomes law. Not since Queen Anne in 1707 — 80 years before the meeting of the Founding Fathers in Philadelphia — has the monarch refused to give the royal assent to parliamentary legislation. In the USA, however, the president's signing of a bill into law is not guaranteed. President Clinton vetoed 36 bills during his 8-year presidency. (Presidents have a pocket veto power at the end of a congressional session too.) Congress may then, by a two-thirds majority in both houses, override a president's veto. Two of President Clinton's 36 vetoes were overridden by Congress.

As a result, Congress is a *real* legislature; Parliament is not. Congress legislates; Parliament merely 'legitimises legislation' (Norton, 1985). To paraphrase Andrew Heywood (1998): legislation is passed *through* Parliament; it is passed *by* Congress. In the view of House of Commons clerk Robert Rogers, bills in Parliament 'are not "draft legislation", they are what the government wants — the government's shopping list'. In Congress, the administration can afford no shopping lists, just wish lists. In Parliament, the Queen's speech — written for her by her government — states that 'My government will...'. In Congress, the president's State of the Union Address *asks* Congress if it would be good enough to *consider* ideas.

Summary

Legislative function

➤ There are many significant differences between Congress and Parliament in terms of their legislative function.

➤ In Congress, the legislative process is more exacting, the committees are more powerful and the two chambers are equal in power.

➤ Congress legislates; Parliament legitimises legislation.

Oversight of the executive branch

The differences between Parliament and Congress in their oversight of the executive branch are largely a consequence of the fact that in the UK the legislature and the executive are intertwined while in the USA they are entirely separate. In the UK, the survival of the government depends on maintaining the support of the House of Commons. In the USA, the administration survives regardless of anything that does — or does not — occur in the legislature.

The methods of oversight in Congress may be less numerous but are more effective than those in the UK Parliament. They include: standing committees; select committees; confirmation of appointments and ratification of treaties in the Senate; and impeachment, trial and removal from office of individual members of the executive branch, including the president. However, whereas Parliament can, in effect, remove the entire government,

Table 13.3 Methods of oversight of the executive branch in the US Congress and UK Parliament

US Congress	UK Parliament
Standing committees	Question Time
Select committees	Correspondence with ministers
Confirmation of appointments (Senate)	Tabling of Early Day Motions
Ratification of treaties (Senate)	Policy debates
Impeachment, trial and removal from office	The ombudsman
	Select committees
	Votes of no confidence

Congress can remove only individual members of the administration — and no president has ever been thus removed, although Nixon's resignation occurred against the threat of near certain removal by Congress. In his resignation speech, Nixon stated:

> Throughout the long and difficult period of Watergate, I have felt it was my duty to persevere, to make every possible effort to complete the term of office to which you [the people] elected me. In the past few days, however, it has become evident to me that *I no longer have a strong enough political base in the Congress* to justify continuing that effort.

Congress has oversight over far more matters than Parliament. Congress has more control over the budget than does Parliament. In 1995–96, a Republican-controlled Congress was able to block passage of President Clinton's budget. In 1990, a Democrat-controlled Congress forced President George Bush to break his campaign pledge and raise taxes as part of a deal to pass that year's budget.

It might be argued that Congress has greater power to check the executive's war-making powers. The US Constitution grants Congress the sole power to declare war, whereas Parliament has no similar power. In effect, though, this power has proved illusory: Congress has not declared war since 1941, yet there have been a significant number of 'wars' in which US forces have been directly involved. It could be argued that Parliament played a more significant oversight role during the war in Iraq in 2003 than did Congress.

The US Senate has the power to 'advise and consent' to numerous executive branch appointments and all federal judicial appointments made by the president and it has not been slow to use this power. The UK Parliament has no such power over the prime minister, who has almost unchecked power of patronage. The Senate has the formal power to ratify treaties negotiated by the president, but Parliament has no comparable power.

The methods of oversight in Parliament include: Question Time, including Prime Minister's Question Time each Wednesday; correspondence between backbenchers and ministers; the tabling of Early Day Motions; policy debates; the ombudsman; and select committees. The ultimate check is the debating of votes of no confidence in the government, which, if a government lost, would precipitate a general election. Oversight, therefore, occurs on the floor of both chambers and in the committee rooms. Opportunities for oversight abound, but activity does not always equal effectiveness. Most observers conclude that Parliament is controlled by the government more than the government is controlled by Parliament. The relatively new system of department-related select committees could be described in the same way as French Prime Minister Clemenceau described the League of Nations: 'When it roared it was seen to have no teeth.'

Summary

Oversight of the executive branch

➢ In the USA, the executive and the legislature are separate; in the UK, they are fused.

➢ There is debate over the effectiveness of legislative checks on the executive branch in both political systems.

Representation

There are said to be four principal models of representation.

Trustee model

In the trustee model, as advocated by Edmund Burke and John Stuart Mill, the representative acts as the person who is vested with formal responsibility for the affairs of others. Such representation is based upon 'mature' judgment. This fits well with the way members of Congress may see their representative function. 'I believe in the Burkean model of representation and agree with the Founding Fathers that "the passions of the day should be dampened",' commented David Skaggs, a Democratic member of the House of Representatives from Colorado. Critics see this model as having strongly elitist connotations.

Delegate model

A delegate is a person who is chosen to act for others on the basis of clear guidance or instructions, and who therefore exercises very little private judgment. This model is linked to the idea of popular sovereignty and the holding of referendums.

Mandate model

A mandate is an instruction or command from a higher body — in this case, the electorate — that demands obedience. The mandate model of representation has strong links with party discipline, manifesto promises and responsible government, as found in the UK Parliament.

Resemblance model

The resemblance model is concerned with the 'who', rather than the 'how', of representation. The legislature is seen as a microcosm of society in terms of social class, gender, race, age and religion. In this sense, neither Congress nor Parliament is truly 'representative'. In both institutions, women and ethnic minorities, for example, are underrepresented, especially in the US Senate.

In Parliament, the accusation is often made that backbenchers' knee-jerk loyalty to party leaders turns them into mere 'lobby fodder'. This, however, ignores the important representative functions played by MPs. They are the target for a wealth of requests — by letter, phone, e-mail, petition, demonstration or personal request, through constituency surgeries, public meetings or Westminster lobbying. Addressing the everyday grievances of constituents is the bread and butter of every MP and should not be forgotten. Nonetheless, these acts of representation in the end often take second place to the MP's obligation to support the party line.

In Congress, support for any party line invariably takes second place to constituency pressures. The parties in America are simply vehicles for election. Once members have been elected, the pressures for re-election determine members' activity. According to David Mayhew (1974), activity in pursuit of re-election comes in three forms: advertising or self-promotion; credit claiming; and position taking. All three are usually conducted solely with constituents in mind, not the political party whose name a member happens to bear. Constituents control the nomination process, not the parties. Elections are candidate- and issue-based affairs rather than party-based ones. Split-ticket voting is widespread. The Westminster MP needs to be a team player; the Washington Senator or member of Congress needs to be an entrepreneur.

Summary

Representation

➢ There are four principal models of representation: trustee, delegate, mandate and resemblance.

➢ Congress may be thought of as being nearest to the trustee model; Parliament, on the other hand, fits more into the mandate model.

➢ Neither institution closely fits the resemblance model.

Committees

A committee is a small work group composed of members drawn from a large body and charged with specific responsibilities. All legislatures use committees, and the growth in their importance has been a trend throughout the twentieth century. They are variously described as 'the power houses', 'the work horses' and the 'legislative workshops' of their parent bodies. The stronger the legislature, the stronger are the committees. There is thought to be a correlation between party systems and committees: the stronger the party system, the *weaker* the committees; the weaker the party system, the *stronger* the committees. On both counts, we can expect Congress to have stronger committees than does Parliament. Committees tend to fulfil two main functions: they relieve the full chamber of the burden of considering legislation in detail; they are often where the most effective scrutiny and oversight of the executive branch is conducted. Committees are of two basic types: permanent (usually referred to as standing committees) and temporary (often termed ad hoc).

Committees in Parliament

Both Parliament and Congress make use of standing committees. House of Commons standing committees are not really 'standing' committees at all, for they have no permanent membership. The seven Commons standing committees are lettered A–G. When a committee has considered a bill, it is disbanded and a committee of the same name (that is, letter) is constituted to consider another bill that has no policy connection with its predecessor. For example, during the 2003 session, Standing Committee G moved from consideration of the Planning and Compulsory Purchase Bill to consideration of the Anti-Social Behaviour Bill. European Standing Committees A–C operate in much the same way. Standing committees in Parliament deal only with legislation.

Select committees scrutinise the executive branch. These department-related select committees are a relatively recent innovation, first created in 1979. They have specific policy areas: Health, Defence, and Home Affairs, for example. It is here that ministers are called to account to answer questions of backbench MPs, who, by sitting on the committees, develop a policy expertise. But these select committees are said to have certain limitations. They lack staffing and financial resources. They lack political clout. Their reports, when published, are rarely debated in the full chamber. Governments of both parties have been accused of trying to influence their membership, thereby limiting their effectiveness. Chairmanships of select committees are seen as a second best to a government appointment. Prime ministers from Thatcher to Blair have demurred from appearing before them. They must compete with the scrutiny of the executive that goes on in the chamber itself, at Question Time, and most notably at Prime Minister's Question Time.

Many commentators question whether select committees can operate truly effectively in a system of adversarial politics and high levels of party discipline. Commented House of Commons clerk Robert Rogers: 'Government backbench MPs on select committees have the moral dilemma of a Christian Scientist with appendicitis.'

Committees in Congress

The Commons committees — both standing and select — must look with envy across the Atlantic to their counterparts on Capitol Hill. Here, the standing committees are really an amalgamation of the Commons standing and select committees, in that they both scrutinise legislation and call the executive to account. They are permanent, specialist, well-staffed, well-funded, highly respected, powerful bodies. Committees are where the action is in Congress. They have life and death power over legislation. They have full power of amendment. Their members often influence the votes of others on the floor of their respective chambers as well as making up the membership of conference committees.

When it comes to scrutiny of the executive branch, US standing committees are really the only show in town. In a legislature whose executive branch members are excluded from its chamber, there can be no equivalent to Parliament's Question Time. Only in the committee rooms can members of the executive branch be called to account. Even a president — Gerald Ford in 1974 — is known to have appeared before a congressional committee. President Clinton got to know the power of congressional committees on various occasions. It was in the standing committees of both houses that his flagship Healthcare Reform Bill was thwarted. It was the Senate Foreign Relations Committee that refused even to hold a hearing on his nomination of Governor William Weld to be ambassador to Mexico. It was the House Judiciary Committee that drew up four articles of impeachment against him. As Professor Vile (1999) remarks: 'It is difficult to exaggerate the importance of these committees.' The special standing committee, the House Rules Committee, plays a crucial role in timetabling bills in the House.

Ad hoc select committees can be very influential. A joint select committee on the Iran–Contra Affair in 1987 embarrassed President Reagan. Conference committees can play a critical role in the final stages of the legislative process.

Summary

Committees

➤ Congressional standing committees are far more powerful than their parliamentary counter-parts.

➤ In Congress, oversight of the executive branch is performed mainly in the committee rooms, as executive branch members are not present in the legislative chambers.

➤ In parliament, committees often lack permanence, expertise, staff and resources.

Role of political parties

The relative importance of the role of committees in Parliament and Congress is reversed with regard to the role of political parties: it is a question of strong parties in Parliament and weak parties in Congress, although both these truisms are in need of modification.

First, what of the number of parties that exist in these two legislatures? Despite the fact that all three chambers are elected by a first-past-the-post electoral system, the party systems in the two institutions are quite different (see Table 13.4). Congress clearly has a two-party system. In 2004, there was only one member in each chamber who was not a member of one of the two major parties, and even one of them — Senator James Jeffords of Vermont — was elected as a Republican when he ran for office in 2000, although he now sits as an Independent. The other — Bernie Sanders, also from Vermont — always votes with the Democrats, who usually do not oppose him for re-election.

In the House of Commons, in contrast, ten different political parties are represented, plus independent Dr Richard Taylor representing Wyre Forest. Following the 2001 election

Table 13.4 Party make-up of chambers in Parliament and Congress, 2003

House of Commons (after 2001 election)	House of Lords	House of Representatives	Senate
Labour (412)	Labour (182)	Republican (229)	Republican (51)
Conservative (166)	Conservative (163)	Democrat (205)	Democrat (48)
Liberal Democrat (52)	Liberal Democrat (60)	Independent (1)	Independent (1)
Ulster Unionist (6)	Crossbenchers (146)	–	–
SNP (5)	Others (33)	–	–
DUP (5)	–	–	–
Plaid Cymru (4)	–	–	–
Sinn Fein (4)	–	–	–
SDLP (3)	–	–	–
Independent (1)	–	–	–
Speaker (1)	–	–	–

there were 52 Liberal Democrats; it is unheard of for a third party to gain that level of support in Congress — Ross Perot's Reform Party, which gained 19% and 9% respectively in the presidential elections of 1992 and 1996, could not win so much as one seat in Congress. In the House of Lords, as well as there being 60 peers who take the Liberal Democrat whip, there are 146 'crossbenchers', plus two archbishops and 24 bishops who have no party affiliation at all.

Why the difference? First, six of the ten parties represented in the House of Commons — the three unionist parties, Plaid Cymru, Sinn Fein and the SDLP — are the product of national and regional issues in British politics. Second, the Liberal Democrats — and their various predecessors — have often flourished when one of the two major parties has undergone something of a crisis. The SDP–Liberal Alliance gained 23 seats in the 1983 general election when the Labour Party, led by left-winger Michael Foot, was in turmoil. In 2001, it benefited from the travails in the Conservative Party. In the USA, the major parties are state-based rather than national parties and can therefore reflect different ideological positions from region to region. Republicans can be 'moderate' in Massachusetts but conservative in the Carolinas. The existence of primaries makes the parties more responsive to the voters. In a political system where the voters — not the parties — choose the candidates, voters are more likely to end up with a candidate to their liking, which makes protest voting — which tends to benefit third parties — less attractive.

In Parliament, and especially in the House of Commons, parties play a crucial role. The government is made up of the party with the largest number of seats in the House of Commons. For much of the past three decades, government has had a comfortable — or huge — overall majority of seats in the Commons. All government posts are given to members of the majority party, and the party leader becomes prime minister. The survival of the government depends upon winning major votes in the House of Commons, most critically votes of confidence. Governments can fall, elections can be called and prime ministers change as a result of a vote in the House of Commons — witness what happened after Jim Callaghan's Labour government lost a confidence vote in the Commons in March 1979. High levels of party discipline are the norm. Backbenchers are sometimes regarded as little more than 'lobby fodder'. Party whips are often regarded with some trepidation. They have been known to reduce unconsenting adults to tears.

Bernard Weatherill, now Lord Weatherill and formerly Speaker of the House of Commons, tells a story of when he was a Conservative backbencher in Margaret Thatcher's government. The House was voting on whether to allow television cameras into the chamber. The prime minister was against the proposal but had allowed a 'free vote' — so there was no party whipping and MPs were free to vote as they wished. Weatherill favoured the admission of the cameras, but as he emerged from the 'aye' lobby, he was confronted by the prime minister emerging from the 'no' lobby. 'What do you mean by voting 'yes'?' demanded the prime minister. 'Well, it was a free vote, Prime Minister', replied Weatherill. 'Yes, but not *that* free!' retorted the prime minister.

Party discipline in Parliament is backed up by an effective series of 'sticks and carrots'. The sticks include disciplinary measures, from withdrawal of the party whip to deselection as the party's candidate at the next election. If the government is facing a significant revolt — or even a minor one with a slender majority — the whips may wave the spectre of a government defeat in front of recalcitrant backbenchers. The carrots come in the shape of government jobs — or the promise of them some time in the future. Almost every self-respecting backbench MP hopes some day to become a member of the government, even if only a parliamentary private secretary (PPS).

However, it would be wrong to think of MPs being always dragooned into the division lobbies to support their parties. Most of them vote the party line because they support the party line. They were, after all, elected to office on a policy-specific manifesto. They feel ideologically committed to their party; UK political parties are, on the whole, ideologically cohesive.

In Congress, parties are perhaps more important than they appear, but all in all, the parties are relatively weak, especially when compared with their parliamentary counterparts in the UK. The clout of party leaders, even of party whips, is nothing like that of their namesakes in the House of Commons. In 1995, Republican Senator Mark Hatfield annoyed his party colleagues by voting against a constitutional amendment to require a balanced budget — his 'no' vote meant the vote was lost. Republicans threatened to remove him from his chairmanship of the powerful Senate Appropriations Committee. He was summoned to appear before a meeting of Republican Senators, who would vote on whether to unseat him from the chair. As the meeting broke up, an unrepentant Senator Hatfield emerged, went straight to the waiting press corps and announced with a broad smile: 'Hello, I'm Chairman Hatfield.'

Few, if any, of the 'sticks and carrots' that are so powerful in the UK Parliament apply in Congress. In a system in which nominations are decided not by the party, but by the voters in primaries, the party has few threats it can make. Administrations do not stand or fall as a result of votes in Congress. That is not to say that success for the president in Congress is not important, but presidents can pass off defeats in Congress more easily than a prime minister can in the House of Commons. There is no congressional equivalent of a parliamentary vote of no confidence, although there is the impeachment process. The frequency of elections for the House of Representatives tends to turn members' minds more to the wishes of their constituents than of their parties, especially in competitive districts. There are few, if any, executive branch jobs that would tempt members of Congress. House and Senate members are not aiming to become members of the president's cabinet. They would have to leave Congress to take up the post.

There is some evidence to suggest that parties have become less dominant in Parliament and rather more important in Congress. Philip Norton, among others, has traced the rise of backbench independence in the House of Commons. The relatively new departmental select committees may have encouraged a rather more independent-minded breed of MP. Members today are more aware of constituents' views as a result of opinion polls, pressure groups, the media or e-mail. Dissent within the two major parties has become more marked. Margaret Thatcher, John Major and Tony Blair have all faced significant rebellions from their own backbenchers. Because of the way prime ministers must look over their shoulder to address members of their own party while speaking from the dispatch box in the Commons, Professor Anthony King remarked that: 'British politics is increasingly over-the-shoulder politics.'

There is evidence of increased levels of party unity in Congress. The two major parties may have become more ideologically distinct in the last decade. Levels of party voting have reached historically high proportions during this period. The Republicans' Contract with America, which they tried to push through Congress in 1995–96, looked more like a UK party manifesto than anything normally associated with US politics.

Summary

Role of political parties

➢ More political parties are represented in the UK Parliament than in the US Congress.
➢ This is largely the product of national and regional issues.
➢ Political parties play a more critical role in the UK Parliament than in the US Congress.
➢ Party discipline is more strict in the UK Parliament than in the US Congress.
➢ There is some recent evidence of a weakening of party control in the UK Parliament and a strengthening of party cohesion in the US Congress.

The relationship between upper and lower chambers

Parliament and Congress are poles apart in the relationship between their upper and lower chambers. Essentially, Parliament is dominated by the House of Commons, while Congress is made up of what might be regarded as two co-equal houses — especially in terms of legislation — or as a legislature in which the upper house is more powerful and prestigious than the lower house.

The evolution of the House of Commons — through the extension of the franchise — has led the Commons to a position of pre-eminence in Parliament. The other side of the equation was failure to address the state of the House of Lords. Once the Commons was a house elected by a universal suffrage — in other words, early in the twentieth century — an unreformed House of Lords quickly became an irrelevance. This was at issue in the battle between the two chambers over the 1909 budget. Rather than reform the upper chamber, Asquith's Liberal government decided merely to strip it of its powers through the 1911 Parliament Act. Three decades later, Attlee's Labour government pursued the same policy by passing the 1949 Parliament Act. The introduction of life peers in 1958 was an attempt by the Conservatives to bring some relevance to the Lords. The dawn of the twentieth century saw the House of Lords as a prime-ministerial incubator. By its final decade it was, in most cases, significantly weakened. When the Blair government attempted to resurrect the idea of second chamber reform, it had to settle for tinkering, being unable to find any consensus regarding the personnel or powers of a reformed upper house.

The USA dealt with the situation of an unelected second chamber in quite the opposite way. Rather than having its powers stripped away, it was given a directly elected mandate. The 17th Amendment (1913) turned the Senate into the political powerhouse that it is today, although the Founding Fathers had given it a helpful start by granting it significant powers. While co-equal with the House in legislation, the Senate was given exclusive powers over the confirmation of numerous presidential appointments and the ratification of treaties. During the twentieth century, the Senate produced presidents Harry Truman, John Kennedy, Lyndon Johnson and Richard Nixon as well as vice-presidents Walter Mondale and Al Gore.

The House of Lords and the Senate have at least one element in common: each includes a significant number of former members of the lower house (although the House of Commons and the House of Representatives contain no former members of their respective upper chambers). The reasons for this movement from the lower to the upper chambers are quite different, however. In Parliament, movement to the upper chamber indicates retirement and is usually avoided for as long as possible. In Congress, movement to the upper chamber indicates promotion and is sought after by numerous House members at each election cycle.

The Senate in 2004 contained a record 49 former House members. They sought this move to take advantage of the greater powers, the longer terms of office, the more generous expense allowances, the state-wide name recognition, the greater national media exposure and maybe the hopes of even higher office — the presidency itself. In the last two election cycles, Senators McCain of Arizona, Lieberman of Connecticut, Kerry of Massachusetts, Graham of Florida and Edwards of North Carolina all threw their hats into the presidential contest. Only two House members — Dick Gephardt and Dennis Kucinich — followed suit. Only once, in 1880, did the USA elect a serving House member as president. That's even longer ago than the last peer to serve as UK prime minister.

Summary

The relationship between upper and lower chambers

➢ In Congress, the upper chamber is regarded as more powerful and prestigious than the lower chamber, although they enjoy equal power in legislation.

➢ In Parliament, the lower chamber is more powerful than the upper chamber.

➢ In Congress, both chambers are directly elected; in Parliament, only the lower chamber is directly elected.

Exercises

1 Define 'Parliament' and 'Congress'.

2 Explain the different ways of recruiting legislators.

3 How do Parliament and Congress compare in terms of size?

4 What are the merits and demerits of bicameral legislatures?

5 What are the main differences between Parliament and Congress in terms of (a) links with the executive; (b) the membership of second chambers; (c) terms of office; (d) links with constituents?

6 What are the two most important consequences of these differences?

7 Compare the membership of Parliament and Congress in terms of (a) gender; (b) race; (c) age and social background.

8 What are the most important differences in the legislative process between Parliament and Congress?

9 Explain what Norton means when he states that Parliament merely 'legitimises legislation' and how this differs from the legislative role of Congress.

10 What methods of oversight of the executive branch are available to (a) Parliament and (b) Congress?

11 Explain the four models of representation.

12 Explain how members of Parliament and Congress perform their representative function.

13 Give a definition of a committee.

14 What factor makes committees 'strong' or 'weak' in different systems?

15 What two important functions do committees fulfil?

16 Compare the standing and select committees of Parliament with the standing committees of Congress in their function and importance.

17 Compare the number of parties represented in Parliament and Congress.

18 Why are there so many more parties in Parliament than in Congress?

19 Why are parties so important in the UK Parliament?

20 How important are parties in the US Congress?

21 Explain why some commentators think that parties are becoming less important in Parliament but more important in Congress.

22 Explain the different relationships between the upper and lower chambers in both Parliament and Congress.

Exam focus

1 Examine the importance of the Senate and the House of Lords in the legislative process of Congress and Parliament.

2 Compare and contrast the ways in which Congress and Parliament control the work of the executive.

3 Examine the merits and demerits of bicameral legislatures.

4 How representative are Congress and Parliament?

5 Compare and contrast the standing committees of Congress and Parliament.

6 Examine the role of political parties in Congress and Parliament.

References

Heywood, A., *Politics* (Macmillan, 1998).

Mayhew, D. R., *Congress: The Electoral Connection* (Yale University Press, 1974).

Norton, P., *Parliament in the 1980s* (Blackwell, 1985).

Shafritz, J. M., *American Government and Politics Dictionary* (HarperCollins, 1993).

Turner, A. J., *UK Government and Politics Essential Word Dictionary* (Philip Allan Updates, 2002).

Vile, M. J. C., *Politics in the USA* (Routledge, 1999).

Further reading

Batchelor, A., 'US Congress and UK Parliament: is there really much difference?' *Politics Review*, vol. 13, no. 1, September 2003.

Chapter 14

President and prime minister

In London, the prime minister's official residence is an unimposing terraced house in a side street off Whitehall. An early twentieth-century prime minister's wife groused that the problem with her husband being prime minister was that no taxi drivers knew where Downing Street was. In Washington DC, the White House may not be on the grand scale of Buckingham Palace, but it is certainly more imposing than 10 Downing Street. The White House — or 1600 Pennsylvania Avenue, NW to give it its full address — takes pride of place in the middle of the city. From its south windows, the residents have a glorious view straight over to the Washington Monument and beyond that to the Jefferson Memorial.

Casual observers of British and US politics might think that the architecture — 10 Downing Street versus the White House — mirrors political power. They might see the office of UK prime minister as one that is modest in comparison to the grander office of the US presidency. Whereas the US president works in the Oval Office, itself just one room within a building entirely devoted to the president's staff — namely, the West Wing — there is no UK equivalent of the Oval Office. The UK prime minister is usually pictured in the cabinet room — a room that speaks as much about collegiality as the Oval Office speaks about individuality.

However, impressions can be misleading. While these two great offices — the UK prime minister and the US president — are very different, the former may be more powerful than is generally imagined while the latter may be significantly weaker. Both offices have evolved over a period of more than two centuries. Whereas Americans often refer to their president by number — George W. Bush, for example, is the 43rd president of the US — it would be difficult to do the same in the UK, because no one is entirely sure who *was* the first prime minister.

> ## Questions to be answered in this chapter
> - What are the differences between presidential and prime-ministerial systems of government?
> - How do the ways of electing the US president and UK prime minister compare?
> - How do the formal powers of the US president and the UK prime minister compare?
> - How do the relations between the president and Congress compare with those between the prime minister and Parliament?
> - How do the US and UK cabinets compare?
> - How do the national bureaucracies of the USA and the UK compare?

Presidential and prime-ministerial systems

A presidential system such as that which exists in the USA can be said to have seven basic characteristics. First, the executive and legislature are separately elected, each having independent powers. Second, the roles of head of state and head of the government ('chief executive') are combined. Third, executive power is concentrated in the hands of one person. The cabinet, where it exists, is merely advisory and is responsible only to the president. Fourth, there is a formal separation of personnel between the legislature and the executive. Fifth, the president cannot dismiss the legislature — there are fixed terms of elections. Sixth, the legislature cannot dismiss the president except by impeachment and even this does not precipitate a general election. Finally, presidents might have impressive lists of constitutional powers but are often severely limited in their use.

A prime-ministerial system such as that which exists in the UK, as well as in such nation states as Australia, Canada and Ireland, has five basic characteristics. First, there is a fusion between the legislature and the executive, with the latter relying upon the support of the former. Second, the roles of head of state and head of the government are separated and occupied by different people, the former having a purely symbolic role. Third, the prime minister is part of a collective executive. Fourth, executive branch personnel are almost always drawn from the legislature, and usually only from the majority party within the legislature. Fifth, the executive has the power to dissolve the legislature, thereby precipitating a general election. There are therefore no fixed terms for elections, only maximum terms. Finally, the legislature can dismiss the executive through a vote of no confidence, thereby precipitating a general election.

10 Downing Street — a mirror of political power?

Table 14.1 Features of presidential and prime-ministerial systems

Features of a presidential system	Features of a prime-ministerial system
Legislature and executive separately elected	Fusion between legislature and executive
Roles of chief executive and head of state are combined in one person	Roles of chief executive and head of state are performed by different persons
Singular executive	Collective executive
Separation of personnel between legislature and executive	Executive branch personnel drawn from the legislature
President cannot dismiss the legislature	Prime minister can dissolve the legislature
Fixed-term elections	No fixed-term elections
Significant checks exist on presidential powers	Legislature can dismiss the executive through a 'no confidence vote'

Election

The UK prime minister is not elected to office by a national election. He or she is prime minister by virtue of being the elected leader of the largest single party in the House of Commons. There are, therefore, no national rules for electing prime ministers, only leadership election rules of the UK's major political parties. Tony Blair is prime minister because he is the leader of the Labour Party, which is the largest party in the House of Commons. He was elected according to internal rules set down by the Labour Party. When, in November 1990, the Conservative Party removed Margaret Thatcher as its leader, she ceased to be prime minister. John Major, the newly elected leader of the party, immediately became prime minister. There was no national campaign, no national election.

Both the Labour and Conservative parties have significantly democratised their leadership election procedures over the past 40 years. In the 1960s, Labour Party leaders — and hence prime ministers such as Harold Wilson and Jim Callaghan — were chosen by a ballot in which only Labour MPs could participate. If it resembled anything in the USA, then it resembled the old smoke-filled rooms of the presidential nomination politics that characterised the first half of the twentieth century. Conservative Party leaders of the same period, such as Harold Macmillan and Alec Douglas-Home, were not elected at all. They were said to 'emerge'. This sounded even less democratic than the 'election' of the earliest US presidents from within the Electoral College. Nowadays, however, both parties have thrown open their leadership election contests to party members. The party in the country is now usually more important than the party at Westminster.

The US president is elected to office by a form of national election that has undergone considerable democratisation. It has moved from a strongly party-based system to a voter-based system. Presidential candidates up to and including the 1960s were chosen principally because of their standing amongst professional politicians — the so-called 'party bosses'. Following the McGovern–Fraser reforms within the Democratic Party in the early 1970s, both parties embarked on more open, participatory systems of presidential candidate selection with widespread use of the direct primary, open not just to paid-up party *members*, but to any registered *voter*. The US president *is* elected as president. He is party leader only so long as he remains president. When Bill Clinton ceased to be president on 20 January 2001, he ceased to be the leader of the Democratic Party. It is the very opposite of the situation in the UK.

Table 14.2 The US president and the UK prime minister

The US president:	The UK prime minister:
is elected as president by the people in a national election	is elected by the party as leader — no direct prime-ministerial election
is not a member of the legislature	is leader of the majority party in the legislature
cannot choose the election date	may choose the election date
fights a principally candidate-centred election	fights a principally party-centred election
is held personally responsible for electoral defeat	is held only partly responsible for electoral defeat
is subject to a two-term limit	is not subject to term limits

This crucial difference in the election of these offices underpins important differences that should be borne in mind when comparing and contrasting their respective jobs. The UK prime minister owes his or her job to the *party*. The US president owes his job to the *people*. The UK prime minister is first and foremost a *party* leader. The US president is first and foremost a *national* leader. The prime minister's future is largely bound up with that of the party. In 1979, Prime Minister Jim Callaghan lost office because the electorate turned against his party, not against him personally. Indeed, he was personally more popular than the Conservative Party leader of the time, Margaret Thatcher. The same was true in 1945 of Winston Churchill.

The US president's future is largely bound up with himself, not necessarily with his party. In 1996, the US voters re-elected Democrat Bill Clinton, but his party remained in the minority in both houses of Congress. The UK prime minister is directly elected only as a member of the lower house of the legislature. The US president is directly elected (courtesy of the Electoral College) as chief executive and is excluded from the legislature. The prime minister's future is largely dependent on what occurs in the legislature: witness Jim Callaghan's

US president, George W. Bush and UK prime minister, Tony Blair

defeat in 1979 and John Major's difficulties in the mid-1990s. The president's future is not significantly determined by what does, or does not, occur in the legislature, although President Nixon's resignation remains a salutary lesson.

Given that the UK general election is a party-dominated one, while the US presidential election is a candidate-dominated one, it should not be surprising to find that UK party leaders are held rather less responsible for losses at the polls than are US presidential candidates. Conservative Party leader Ted Heath lost three general elections — 1966, February 1974 and October 1974 — before being ousted as party leader. A US presidential candidate would not lead his party to the polls after two losses. Nixon was allowed a second chance in 1968 but only after waiting 8 years following his 1960 defeat. In the USA one defeat is usually terminal to a presidential candidate's career — witness Jimmy Carter (1980), Walter Mondale (1984) and Michael Dukakis (1988).

The UK prime minister can choose the date of the general election; US presidents cannot. UK prime ministers are not subject to any limits on their term of office. Margaret Thatcher was elected in 1979, re-elected in 1983 and again in 1987. Only her party — not national law — stopped her from running for a fourth term in 1992. US presidents from Dwight Eisenhower to the present day have been subject to the two-term limit imposed by the 22nd Amendment.

Summary

Election

➤ There are significant differences between the election of the US president and the UK prime minister.
➤ The president is directly elected to office by the people; the prime minister is elected as party leader by party members.

Formal powers

A list of formal powers of the US president usually includes:

- head of state
- chief executive
- 'chief legislator'
- granting pardons
- commander-in-chief of the armed forces
- negotiating treaties
- making appointments to the executive and judicial branches

A list of the formal powers and functions of the UK prime minister usually includes:

- party leader
- debating policy
- patronage
- calling general elections
- choosing, chairing and changing the cabinet
- answering questions in the House of Commons

These two lists immediately suggest two quite different offices.

The prime minister's role as party leader is, as we have already seen, vital. Prime ministers hold office only so long as they maintain the position of party leader and their party maintains its majority status in the House of Commons. As Richard Rose commented: 'A prime minister manages a party as one manages a horse: by giving sufficient rein to avoid a straight test of will between horse and rider in which the latter might be overthrown.'

Although a US president is not an elected party leader, he nonetheless needs to fulfil the function of party manager because the party's support can be critical. President Nixon lost the support of his Republican Party in Congress over Watergate and had to resign. President Clinton, on the other hand, maintained the support of his Democratic Party in Congress over the Monica Lewinsky scandal — despite being impeached by the Republican-controlled House of Representatives — and saw out his term of office. Equally, Clinton's failure to sell his healthcare reforms to a significant section of his own party in 1993–94 was one of the reasons for this policy being lost in a Congress dominated by his own party.

President's powers

The president is head of state. He is, in the words of President Theodore Roosevelt: 'both king and prime minister.' No formal anthems to match 'Hail to the Chief' greet the UK prime minister.

According to Article II of the Constitution: 'All executive power shall be vested in a president of the United States of America.' No 'first amongst equals' here. As chief executive, the president is solely responsible for the running of the federal bureaucracy. The prime minister's private office is in no way comparable to the Executive Office of the US president.

Article II further states that the president shall be 'commander in chief' of the armed forces. In the UK, the military are *Her Majesty's* armed forces. They serve *Queen* and country, and only the monarch, not the prime minister, takes the salute of *her* troops. The president, through his treaty-negotiating power, is also seen as 'chief diplomat'.

The president is further described as 'chief legislator', although the term is misleading. What Article II states is that the president may 'give to the Congress information of the state of the Union and shall recommend to their consideration such measures as he shall judge necessary and expedient'. Modern presidents — beginning with Woodrow Wilson — have delivered their State of the Union Address to Congress in person, but it is no more than a list of *requests*. Unlike the so-called 'Queen's Speech' to Parliament — written by the prime minister — it is not a list of near certainties.

Finally, the president enjoys the power of pardon. However, considering the trouble that some recent presidents have got into through this power — notably Ford (1974), Bush (1992) and Clinton (2001) — this, like the prime minister's power to choose election dates, appears to be something of a two-edged sword. Prime ministers are mercifully free from such opportunities and dangers.

Prime minister's powers

A prime minister's power to decide the timing of a general election — within the 5-year maximum life of a Parliament — can be a significant power. US presidents have neither the opportunity to try to tip the scales in their favour by choosing the date, nor the possibility of being blamed for getting it wrong.

UK prime ministers have important powers relating to the cabinet, of which the first power is to choose their cabinet. However, this choice is not as significant as it might appear. There is a shadow cabinet in place, and there will be expectations — indeed, in the Labour Party there are requirements — that the new cabinet will be drawn from the shadow cabinet. Incoming prime ministers are limited in their pool of recruitment, which is essentially senior members of their own party in the House of Commons. They have no formal checks upon their cabinet appointments, although there are doubtless many hidden and informal ones. In chairing the cabinet, the prime minister is said to operate as 'first among equals' and is expected to operate in a collegial fashion. Cabinet changes are a regular feature of British political life and involve removing 'dead wood' and bringing in 'new faces' as well as reshuffling the pack. The career of Labour cabinet member John Reid as Scottish secretary, Northern Ireland secretary, leader of the House of Commons and health secretary all within the life of the second Blair administration shows what can happen.

A brief comparison between US presidents and UK prime ministers in relation to their cabinets reveals some essential differences. An incoming president has no shadow cabinet. There are few, if any expectations. His pool of recruitment is vast. He faces the formal check upon his cabinet appointments of a majority vote in the Senate. In the US president's cabinet, 'reshuffles' in the British sense are unheard of.

Prime ministers play an important role in Parliament and none more so than in answering questions at their weekly half-hour Question Time. A prime minister's ability to be able to 'stand and deliver' at Prime Minister's Question Time is vital to his or her survival, although, as Margaret Thatcher discovered, that ability may not be enough to guarantee survival as prime minister. Presidents face no such ordeal — or opportunity.

Prime ministers debate policy, more often outside Parliament rather than within — at Downing Street press conferences, party rallies or conferences, in set-piece media interviews, on nationwide or foreign tours, or as part of an election campaign. Here, at least, prime ministers and presidents have much in common. White House press conferences and Downing Street press conferences are similar.

Prime ministers and presidents enjoy significant powers of patronage. For the prime minister appointments range from chairman of the BBC to Anglican bishops and archbishops. A president will be able to make appointments from the director of the CIA to justices of the Supreme Court. The prime minister faces only informal checks to this power; the president faces the formal check of the Senate.

The two offices, therefore, have a different list of powers and functions. If Tony Blair and George W. Bush were to swap jobs for a week, they would find things that were unfamiliar and surprising. An office is a lot more than a job description. The job descriptions of the UK prime minister and the US president are like the two countries' respective highway codes, but *being* prime minister or president is like driving on London's M25 or Washington's Beltway on a busy Friday evening. The formal rules may be different, but, apart from than the fact that everyone is driving on the wrong side of the road, the tactics for getting from A to B successfully may be much the same. Both prime ministers and presidents require certain political skills and circumstances to help them turn a list of formal powers into a list of political achievements.

Summary

Formal powers

➤ The formal powers of the US president appear to be greater than those of the UK prime minister.

➤ This may be misleading when it comes to exercising those powers.

Relations with the legislature

President's relations with Congress

The US president is not and cannot be a member of the legislature. Neither are any members of his administration. Any in Congress at the time of their appointment must resign their seats in the legislature. Thus, the president has no formal links with Congress. The opposition party may control one or both houses. The president's continuance in office does not rely on votes in Congress, in the sense that there are no votes of confidence that can abruptly bring his administration to an end and precipitate new elections. The president lacks both the sticks and the carrots that the prime minister enjoys in controlling the legislature. The sticks of party discipline are often ineffective; the carrots of appointments to his administration are almost always unwanted. The president can try to set the agenda of Congress through the State of the Union Address, and he can appeal for party unity with varying degrees of success. Whereas the prime minister can crack the whip, the president must cajole, persuade, wine and dine members of both parties, hoping that by so doing they will support him in crucial votes. When President Clinton was trying to get the North American Free Trade Agreement (NAFTA) ratified through a Congress controlled by his own party, he was having to give away so many goodies that members of Congress joked that there were so many 'shopping days left before NAFTA'.

Congress possesses some significant checks upon the president's powers. These include the powers of: amending, blocking or rejecting the legislation and the budgets he proposes; overriding the presidential veto; confirming most executive branch and all judicial branch appointments (Senate only); ratification of treaties (Senate only); declaration of war; investigation; impeachment, trial and removal from office. Admittedly,

not all these checks are entirely effective. As a whole, though, they are judged more impressive both in title and in effect than those possessed by the UK Parliament over the prime minister.

Prime minister's relation with Parliament

The UK prime minister is leader of the largest single party — usually with an overall majority — in the House of Commons. Prime ministers' survival depends on both their maintaining their leadership position and their party maintaining its majority, at least on confidence votes. Not only is the prime minister a member of the legislature, but so are all the other members of the administration. The prime minister controls the legislature through various means, notably: the Queen's Speech; the parliamentary timetable; a party majority in the House of Commons; party discipline; patronage; the calling of general elections; and the built-in majority for the government in all parliamentary committees.

For its part, the legislature has certain methods of scrutinising the actions of the government and for calling it to account. These include: Question Time; select committees; policy debates; Early Day Motions; and votes of no confidence. The effectiveness of these methods of scrutiny, however, can be questioned. In the battle between the executive and the legislature, the executive holds most of the trump cards. The prime minister has better jobs to offer on the government side of the House of Commons than does the leader of the opposition. The government has all the weight and expertise of the civil service to provide ministers with clever answers to awkward opposition questions at Question Time. The government usually has an easier job keeping its side together in the division lobby, if only because it can guarantee the 'payroll vote'. In the end, it has more people — considerably more in some recent parliaments. Indeed, in the period since 1979, for only 5 years has the government had an overall majority of fewer than 40, and for only 9 years an overall majority of fewer than 100. Lord Hailsham

Table 14.3 The relations of the president with Congress and of the prime minister with Parliament

President's relations with Congress	Prime minister's relations with Parliament
The president is not a member of Congress	The prime minister is leader of the majority party in the House of Commons
The president's party may be in a minority in one or both houses	The prime minister has effective 'sticks' and 'carrots'
The president has few 'sticks' or 'carrots'	There are high levels of party discipline in Parliament
There are low levels of party discipline in Congress	Parliamentary checks on the prime minister are often ineffective
Congress possesses significant checks on the president, including impeachment and removal from office	The government may be removed by a 'no confidence' vote

bemoaned this domination of the executive in his 1976 lecture entitled 'Elective Dictatorship', in which he stated:

> Until recently, the powers of the government within Parliament were largely controlled either by the opposition or by its own backbenchers. It is now largely in the hands of the government machine, so that government controls Parliament and not Parliament the government.

Others, however, would argue that this picture is somewhat bleak and unrealistic. Margaret Thatcher, whose premiership is usually regarded as one that exhibited strong powers of leadership and control, was asked by an interviewer in January 1982 why she had not been tougher on cutting public spending. The prime minister replied: 'I would have liked to have been tougher, but I have to do what I think we can get through Parliament.'

In short, the prime minister is usually in an enviable position in relation to Parliament compared with the position of the president in relation to Congress. When Tony Blair and Bill Clinton met up during what were President Clinton's last 3 years in office, the president must have turned green with envy when the prime minister talked about how easy he found it to get Parliament to do his bidding. Blessed with a well-disciplined parliamentary majority of over 160, Tony Blair could say 'Do this! Do that!' and it happened. Dogged by opposition party majorities in both houses of Congress, Bill Clinton had learned the truth of President Truman's wisdom on the presidency: 'He'll say, "Do this! Do that!" and nothing will happen. He'll find it very frustrating.'

Summary

Relations with the legislature

➤ The UK prime minister has a closer relationship with and generally more control over Parliament than the US president usually enjoys.

➤ The UK prime minister can 'lead' Parliament while the president must often 'persuade' Congress.

Cabinets

The cabinet in the US system of government exists as part of a singular executive. All executive power is vested in the president, none in the cabinet, which is why its members are correctly referred to as cabinet *officers*, not cabinet *ministers*. They are drawn from many different pools of recruitment, but are not permitted to be serving members of the legislature. While most cabinet officers are associated with the same political party as the president, some may be non-political, and it is possible that at least one will be a member of the 'opposition party'. Cabinet officers are appointed by the president but with the advice and consent of the Senate. They will not have served together in any shadow cabinet before taking up office; indeed, cabinet members may not have met some of their colleagues prior to the first cabinet meeting. In terms of election, they are quite clearly not the president's equals. While the president gains office through a national election, cabinet members have no elective base at all. Politically, they are certainly not the president's potential rivals. The cabinet officers are almost always policy specialists of the particular department to which they are appointed.

The cabinet in the UK system of government is part of a plural executive and all its members are bound by the doctrine of collective responsibility. They are drawn exclusively from the legislature. They all belong to one political party — the largest single party in the House of Commons. They are appointed by the prime minister and serve at his or her pleasure — the prime minister has the exclusive powers of 'hire and fire'. They will often have served together in a shadow cabinet before taking up office. In terms of election, they are the prime minister's equals — all of them (except those drawn from the House of Lords) are, like the prime minister, merely elected to represent a constituency somewhere in the UK. Politically, they are the prime minister's potential rivals in that the cabinet is virtually the only pool of recruitment of prime ministers. The departmental ministers who make up the cabinet are usually not policy specialists of their particular portfolio. Cabinet ministers are therefore often moved from one department to another during the lifetime of a government.

It might appear at first glance that the name of 'cabinet' is all that US and UK cabinets have in common. The picture hardly changes when looking at cabinet meetings. Cabinet meetings in the UK tend to be held on a regular basis — Thursday mornings at 10 o'clock while Parliament is in session. Some decades ago, twice-weekly meetings were the rule.

Table 14.4 US and UK cabinets

US cabinet	UK cabinet
Operates within a singular executive	Operates within a plural executive
No 'collective responsibility'	Bound by doctrine of collective responsibility
Members drawn from diverse pools of recruitment: not permitted to be serving members of the legislature	Drawn exclusively from the legislature
May contain people from the 'opposition' party	All belong to one political party
No 'shadow cabinet'	Have usually served together before in 'shadow cabinet'
Members have no elective base	Prime minister seen as 'first among equals'
Members are not political rivals of the president	Members are potential political rivals of the prime minister
Not a common route to the presidency	The usual route to becoming prime minister
Tend to be policy specialists	Tend to be policy generalists — hence frequent 'reshuffles'
Irregular meetings	Regular meetings

Frequency has declined, but the predictability has not. Of course, there may from time to time be emergency meetings of the cabinet, called at short notice by the prime minister in order to discuss some crisis. At a cabinet meeting, discussion takes place and decisions are agreed, with the prime minister often summing up before 'going round the table', asking each cabinet minister for their 'yes' or 'no'. No formal votes are taken, but cabinet members informally count the 'yes' and 'no' votes just to make sure the prime minister gets it right. John Major, for example, went round the cabinet table in such a fashion in order to arrive at a decision about the first Gulf War in 1991.

Cabinet meetings in the USA tend to be held irregularly — and infrequently, depending on the president and often varying during a presidency, with cabinet meetings becoming less frequent as the administration progresses into its second, third and fourth years. There is no particular day of the week or time of day for meetings to be held. Reagan's defense secretary, Caspar Weinberger, observed that 'there was no regular scheduling' for cabinet meetings and 'sometimes they were announced only the day before'. This could lead to problems. Weinberger told of how Reagan called a cabinet meeting suddenly on the day when Prime Minister Margaret Thatcher was to visit the Pentagon. Weinberger had to attend the cabinet meeting and was therefore a moment or two late to greet the prime minister on the steps of the Pentagon. Weinberger continued the narrative:

> I dashed back to the Pentagon with the car sirens blaring and got there at the back of her motorcade. I apologised for being late, but explained I'd had to go to a cabinet meeting that had been suddenly called. The prime minister asked whether the government was in some crisis!

Quite simply, to a prime minister, a sudden cabinet meeting means a government crisis. In Washington, however, it does not: it just means that the president called a cabinet meeting.

At a US cabinet meeting, discussion takes place and presentations are made, but it is not a decision-making forum. There are certainly no votes, and there is no summing up by the president before 'going round the table'. As Anthony King commented: 'The president doesn't sum up at the end of the meeting: he *is* the meeting.' Cabinet officers in many US administrations tell stories of pointless, boring meetings.

This all sounds very different from cabinet meetings in the UK, but here the differences may be less sharp than first appears. The UK cabinet meeting may be less important and the US cabinet meeting more important than some of the conventional wisdom has led us to believe. In the UK, as government has grown in both scope and complexity, the full cabinet is seen less and less as an appropriate forum for detailed policy debate. Cabinet meetings have become fewer and shorter. One Thatcher cabinet member, challenged by a backbencher as to why he was back at the Houses of Parliament so soon after the start of the meeting, remarked caustically: 'Cabinet meetings? Oh no, we don't have those any more. We just have a lecture from Madam!'

Much government business is now conducted in cabinet committees and ad hoc groups. Even as long ago as 1968, *The Times* commented that full cabinet meetings are now 'occasions for coordination and for keeping busy departmental ministers in touch'. But 'coordination' and 'keeping busy [people] in touch' sounds like cabinet meetings in Washington under George W. Bush, who uses the cabinet as an informative, consultative and discursive forum for 'big picture items'.

Summary

Cabinets

➤ The UK cabinet is more important than its US counterpart.

➤ This can be mainly attributed to the doctrine of collective responsibility in the UK system of government and the existence of a 'singular executive' in the US system.

➤ Nonetheless, the US president's cabinet can perform some useful functions.

Prime-ministerial and presidential government

In both systems, allegations have arisen in recent decades concerning what some see as the unjustifiable increase in the power of the chief executive. According to some respected commentators and practitioners of politics, in both Whitehall and Washington, individuality has increased at the expense of collegiality. In the UK this argument appears under the 'elective dictatorship' and 'prime-ministerial power' school of thought. Tony Benn stated that, for example: 'the present centralisation of power in the hands of one person has gone too far and amounts to a system of personal rule in the very heart of our democracy.' He, along with such highly respected observers as Hailsham and Crossman, argued that the prime minister's control of Parliament, party and cabinet, the increased media focus on the prime minister and the subsequent personalisation of UK politics all amounted to a rejection of traditional collective cabinet government and replacing it with what Hailsham called an 'elective dictatorship' and others a 'British presidency'.

At much the same time, political historian Arthur Schlesinger was popularising the idea of the 'imperial presidency' in the USA. His allegation was that modern presidents — especially Johnson and Nixon — had not only usurped power within the executive branch, but also damaged the traditional checks and balances provided by Congress.

Both arguments contain some truth, but both may have been presented in an overly one-sided manner by their most ardent supporters. Some of the means by which prime ministers were supposed to have increased their personal power and control over UK government were not exactly new. Harold Wilson and Margaret Thatcher were not the first prime ministers to enjoy strict party discipline in the House of Commons, the ability to decide dates of the general election, domination over some cabinet members and the attention of the media. If Margaret Thatcher was supposed to be the epitome of rampant 'prime-ministerial power', then the circumstances surrounding her departure are instructive. Furthermore, what would the prime-ministerial power school of thought make of John Major's premiership? Likewise, talk in Washington of 'the imperial presidency' soon gave way to talk of 'the imperilled presidency'. Each argument appears in hindsight to be debatable. Prime-ministerial and presidential power ebbs and flows according to circumstances and personalities. Just as 'the golden age of the legislature' may never have existed, so the age of 'presidents' in Downing Street and 'emperors' in the White House may have been something of a mirage.

To describe the office of the prime minister as having become 'presidential' betrays a certain misunderstanding of the innate differences between parliamentary and presidential systems. For example, we have already seen that in terms of what they can get done in the legislature, prime ministers are in a far more powerful position than are presidents. On the other hand, to call prime ministers 'presidential' in terms of their staff and support looks odd if the comparison is made with the president's office. Even allowing for the annexing of Numbers 11 and 12 Downing Street, the modern Prime Minister's Office looks nothing like the Executive Office of the President in Washington. Tony Blair has maybe 250 people working directly for him, but that is nowhere near the number working in the contemporary Executive Office of the President.

That having been said, just as UK society has changed during the last four decades, so has UK government. This should not be a surprise, as it is a system of government that almost prides itself on its evolutionary nature. Just as in Washington, in London the scope of government has grown — as have people's expectations of what it should deliver. The media have brought the Prime Minister's Office into sharp focus. Both Parliament and the cabinet have declined as forums of political debate and decision making. None of these changes is likely to be reversed. All this affects the way prime ministers must act and organise. To some extent, the Prime Minister's Office is playing 'catch-up'. The words written about the US presidency in the late 1930s — 'The president needs help' — could easily have been adapted to the prime minister in the 1970s. For Wilson, Callaghan and Thatcher read: 'The prime minister needs help.' Tony Blair has gone some way to ensuring that he has that 'help'.

Summary

Prime-ministerial and presidential government

➤ Some commentators suggest that the office of the US presidency has become 'imperial' while the office of the UK prime minister has become 'presidentialised'.

➤ Both arguments contain some elements of truth, but there are counterarguments to both theories.

➤ Presidential and prime-ministerial powers are variables, not constants.

The bureaucracies

The Whitehall and Washington bureaucracies are essentially the creations of three nineteenth-century figures: Stafford Northcote and Charles Trevelyan in the UK and George Pendleton in the USA. Each was responsible for the development of a modern civil service through the Northcote–Trevelyan reforms in the UK and the Pendleton Act in the USA.

In the USA, presidents cannot reorganise the federal bureaucracy at will. Congressional approval must be gained — hence President George W. Bush's initial difficulties in creating a Department of Homeland Security in 2002. Congress has created new departments throughout the nation's history — and especially in the last 50 years — to reflect the increased role of the federal government and the complexity of modern US society. The heads of those departments — as well as those of various agencies and commissions — are political appointees. Political appointments reach some way down the organisational structure of all these bureaucracies. These political appointments are made by the president but with the advice and consent of the Senate. Those appointed cannot be serving members of the legislature, or of any other branch of federal or state government. They therefore have only executive functions to perform. Appointees are usually policy specialists. The doctrines of individual and collective ministerial responsibility are not ones with which they are familiar. They are responsible only to the president for the running of their respective departments. Senior civil servants are largely political appointees, appointed by the political heads of their departments. The civil service operates under a Freedom of Information Act and 'sunshine laws'. Certain reforms — most notably those associated with the 'Reinventing Government' programme introduced during the Clinton–Gore administration — have taken place in recent years.

The way the US bureaucracy works appears to run contrary to the principles of representative and responsible government. As Malcolm Walles (1988) argued:

> The bureaucracy in the United States stands, not as a tool of the executive or even, as some would argue, as an arm of Congress, but as an active and largely independent participant in the political process, negotiating and bargaining with Congress, interest groups and the presidency alike.... Coherent policy making in America, already hampered by the absence of disciplined political parties and by the separation of the legislative and executive branches, is further impeded, then, by the existence of some 2,000 federal agencies with rule-making authority which are not directly amenable to presidential command or congressional directive.

In the UK, prime ministers can reorganise Whitehall departments at will. New departments were created throughout the twentieth century to reflect the increased role of government and the complexity of modern society. Indeed, no modern-day prime minister has failed to reshuffle the departmental responsibilites of Whitehall.

Departments such as 'Technology' (1964–1970) and 'Prices and Consumer Protection' (1974–1979) have come and gone. The heads of these departments are political appointees, appointed by the prime minister with only informal checks upon the choices made. They are in most cases elected Members of Parliament, therefore having executive, legislative and — for their constituents — representative functions to perform. They are usually policy generalists. They are bound by the twin doctrines of individual and collective ministerial responsibility. Ministers are advised by senior civil servants, most notably by permanent secretaries — career civil servants who are seen to possess considerable power and prestige. Almost all civil servants are permanent employees, who are expected to serve governments of any political persuasion. A premium is therefore set on civil service neutrality, and civil servants are bound by an Official Secrets Act. According to Duncan Watts (2002), UK civil servants have traditionally been noted for their permanence, neutrality and anonymity. Certain reforms — most notably those associated with the Next Steps programme introduced by the Conservatives in the late 1980s — have taken place in recent years. Increased — though still quite limited — use is made of political advisers in Whitehall departments.

In the UK, the bureaucracy operates in the climate of parliamentary accountability as well as disciplined and responsible political parties. Bureaucrats are ultimately responsible through their ministers to Parliament, and thereby to the electorate. Bureaucrats do not have their own political power bases.

Once again, differences abound but similarities remain. In both countries, the bureaucracy has struggled to cope with the increased demands of the citizenry. Concerns regarding politicisation, size, inefficiency, waste, red tape, accountability and resistance to change exist in both the UK and the USA. All modern prime ministers and presidents — especially those with reformist agendas — have to some extent felt stymied by their bureaucracies. In both London and Washington, reforms concerning privatisation, contracting out, decentralisation and downsizing have all disappointed their supporters in the more efficient delivery of government services. Concerns exist on both sides of the Atlantic regarding the effectiveness of government watchdogs and the growing influence of special interest groups within the bureaucracy. 'Iron triangles' and 'revolving door syndromes', which began as Washington concerns, are showing their face in UK government too.

Summary

The bureaucracies

➢ The bureaucracy is under greater control by the legislature in the USA than in the UK.

➢ The bureaucracies in both countries are beset with problems concerning politicisation, size, inefficiency, waste, red tape, accountability and resistance to change.

Exercises

1 Explain the principal differences between presidential and prime-ministerial systems of government.
2 In what ways does the election of a US president differ from that of a UK prime minister?
3 Compare and contrast the formal powers of the US president and the UK prime minister.
4 What important differences are there in the relationship of the US president and the UK prime minister with their respective legislatures?
5 In what significant ways do the US and UK cabinets differ?
6 Explain why in both the USA and the UK some think that the office of the chief executive has become more powerful in recent decades.
7 In what significant ways do the bureaucracies of the two countries differ?

Exam focus

1 Examine the effectiveness of the constitutional checks on the US president and the UK prime minister.
2 Compare and contrast the powers of US presidents and UK prime ministers.
3 Compare and contrast the relationships of the US president and the UK prime minister with their respective legislatures.
4 Examine the essential differences between presidential and prime-ministerial systems.
5 Critically analyse the theories of the 'imperial presidency' and of 'elective dictatorship' as they apply, respectively, to the USA and the UK.
6 Compare and contrast the cabinets in the US and UK systems of government.

References

Walles, M., *British and American Systems of Government* (Philip Allan/Barnes and Noble, 1988).
Watts, D., *Understanding American Government and Politics* (Manchester University Press, 2002).

Further reading

Ashbee, E., 'Parliamentary and presidential systems of government', *Politics Review*, vol. 11, no. 3, February 2002.

Appendix I

Presidents of the USA

1	George Washington	1789–97	(F)		23	Benjamin Harrison	1889–93	(R)
2	John Adams	1797–1801	(F)		24	Grover Cleveland	1893–97	(D)
3	Thomas Jefferson	1801–09	(D-R)		25	William McKinley	1897–1901	(R)
4	James Madison	1809–17	(D-R)		26	Theodore Roosevelt	1901–09	(R)
5	James Monroe	1817–25	(D-R)		27	William Taft	1909–13	(R)
6	John Quincy Adams	1825–29	(D-R)		28	Woodrow Wilson	1913–21	(D)
7	Andrew Jackson	1829–37	(D)		29	Warren Harding	1921–23	(R)
8	Martin Van Buren	1837–41	(D)		30	Calvin Coolidge	1923–29	(R)
9	William Harrison	1841	(W)		31	Herbert Hoover	1929–33	(R)
10	John Tyler	1841–45	(W)		32	Franklin Roosevelt	1933–45	(D)
11	James Polk	1845–49	(D)		33	Harry Truman	1945–53	(D)
12	Zachary Taylor	1849–50	(W)		34	Dwight Eisenhower	1953–61	(R)
13	Millard Fillmore	1850–53	(W)		35	John Kennedy	1961–63	(D)
14	Franklin Pierce	1853–57	(D)		36	Lyndon Johnson	1963–69	(D)
15	James Buchanan	1857–61	(D)		37	Richard Nixon	1969–74	(R)
16	Abraham Lincoln	1861–65	(R)		38	Gerald Ford	1974–77	(R)
17	Andrew Johnson	1865–69	(D)		39	Jimmy Carter	1977–81	(D)
18	Ulysses Grant	1869–77	(R)		40	Ronald Reagan	1981–89	(R)
19	Rutherford Hayes	1877–81	(R)		41	George Bush	1989–93	(R)
20	James Garfield	1881	(R)		42	Bill Clinton	1993–2001	(D)
21	Chester Arthur	1881–85	(R)		43	George W. Bush	2001–	(R)
22	Grover Cleveland	1885–89	(D)					

F = Federalist; D-R = Democratic-Republican; W = Whig; D = Democrat; R = Republican

Appendix II

The Constitution of the USA

We the People of the United States, in Order to form a more perfect Union, establish Justice, insure domestic Tranquility, provide for the common defence, promote the general Welfare, and secure the Blessings of Liberty to ourselves and our Posterity, do ordain and establish this Constitution for the United States of America.

Article I

Section 1

All legislative Powers herein granted shall be vested in a Congress of the United States, which shall consist of a Senate and House of Representatives.

Section 2

The House of Representatives shall be composed of Members chosen every second Year by the People of the several States, and the Electors in each State shall have the Qualifications requisite for Electors of the most numerous Branch of the State Legislature.

No Person shall be a Representative who shall not have attained to the Age of twenty five Years, and been seven Years a Citizen of the United States, and who shall not, when elected, be an Inhabitant of that State in which he shall be chosen.

Representatives and direct Taxes shall be apportioned among the several States which may be included within this Union, according to their respective Numbers, which shall be determined by adding to the whole Number of free Persons, including those bound to Service for a Term of Years, and excluding Indians not taxed, three fifths of all other Persons.

The actual Enumeration shall be made within three Years after the first Meeting of the Congress of the United States, and within every subsequent Term of ten Years, in such Manner as they shall by Law direct. The Number of Representatives shall not exceed one for every thirty Thousand, but each State shall have at Least one Representative; and until such enumeration shall be made, the State of New Hampshire shall be entitled to chuse three, Massachusetts eight, Rhode Island and Providence Plantations one, Connecticut five, New York six, New Jersey four, Pennsylvania eight, Delaware one, Maryland six, Virginia ten, North Carolina five, South Carolina five and Georgia three.

When vacancies happen in the Representation from any State, the Executive Authority thereof shall issue Writs of Election to fill such Vacancies.

The House of Representatives shall chuse their Speaker and other Officers; and shall have the sole Power of Impeachment.

Section 3

The Senate of the United States shall be composed of two Senators from each State, chosen by the Legislature thereof, for six Years; and each Senator shall have one Vote.

Immediately after they shall be assembled in Consequence of the first Election, they shall be divided as equally as may be into three Classes. The Seats of the Senators of the first Class shall be vacated at the Expiration of the second Year, of the second Class at the Expiration of the fourth Year, and of the third Class at the Expiration of the sixth Year, so that one third may be chosen every second Year; and if Vacancies happen by Resignation, or otherwise, during the Recess of the Legislature of any State, the Executive thereof may make temporary Appointments until the next Meeting of the Legislature, which shall then fill such Vacancies.

No person shall be a Senator who shall not have attained to the Age of thirty Years, and been nine Years a Citizen of the United States, and who shall not, when elected, be an Inhabitant of that State for which he shall be chosen.

The Vice President of the United States shall be President of the Senate, but shall have no Vote, unless they be equally divided.

The Senate shall chuse their other Officers, and also a President pro tempore, in the absence of the Vice President, or when he shall exercise the Office of President of the United States.

The Senate shall have the sole Power to try all Impeachments. When sitting for that Purpose, they shall be on Oath or Affirmation. When the President of the United States is tried, the Chief Justice shall preside: And no Person shall be convicted without the Concurrence of two thirds of the Members present.

Judgment in Cases of Impeachment shall not extend further than to removal from Office, and disqualification to hold and enjoy any Office of honor, Trust or Profit under the United States: but the Party convicted shall nevertheless be liable and subject to Indictment, Trial, Judgment and Punishment, according to Law.

Section 4

The Times, Places and Manner of holding Elections for Senators and Representatives, shall be prescribed in each State by the Legislature thereof; but the Congress may at any time by Law make or alter such Regulations, except as to the Place of Chusing Senators.

The Congress shall assemble at least once in every Year, and such Meeting shall be on the first Monday in December, unless they shall by Law appoint a different Day.

Section 5

Each House shall be the Judge of the Elections, Returns and Qualifications of its own Members, and a Majority of each shall constitute a Quorum to do Business; but a smaller number may adjourn from day to day, and may be authorized to compel the Attendance of absent Members, in such Manner, and under such Penalties as each House may provide.

Each House may determine the Rules of its Proceedings, punish its Members for disorderly Behavior, and, with the Concurrence of two thirds, expel a Member.

Each House shall keep a Journal of its Proceedings, and from time to time publish the same, excepting such Parts as may in their Judgment require Secrecy; and the Yeas and Nays of the Members of either House on any question shall, at the Desire of one fifth of those Present, be entered on the Journal.

Neither House, during the Session of Congress, shall, without the Consent of the other, adjourn for more than three days, nor to any other Place than that in which the two Houses shall be sitting.

Section 6

The Senators and Representatives shall receive a Compensation for their Services, to be ascertained by Law, and paid out of the Treasury of the United States. They shall in all Cases, except Treason, Felony and Breach of the Peace, be privileged from Arrest during their Attendance at the Session of their respective Houses, and in going to and returning from the same; and for any Speech or Debate in either House, they shall not be questioned in any other Place.

No Senator or Representative shall, during the Time for which he was elected, be appointed to any civil Office under the Authority of the United States which shall have been created, or the Emoluments whereof shall have been increased during such time; and no Person holding any Office under the United States, shall be a Member of either House during his Continuance in Office.

Section 7

All bills for raising Revenue shall originate in the House of Representatives; but the Senate may propose or concur with Amendments as on other Bills.

Every Bill which shall have passed the House of Representatives and the Senate, shall, before it become a Law, be presented to the President of the United States; If he approve he shall sign it, but if not he shall return it, with his Objections to that House in which it shall have originated, who shall enter the Objections at large on their Journal, and proceed to reconsider it. If after such Reconsideration two thirds of that House shall agree to pass the Bill, it shall be sent, together with the Objections, to the other House, by which it shall likewise be reconsidered, and if approved by two thirds of that House, it shall become a Law. But in all such Cases the Votes of both Houses shall be determined by Yeas and Nays, and the Names of the Persons voting for and against the Bill shall be entered on the Journal of each House respectively. If any Bill shall not be returned by the President within ten Days (Sundays excepted) after it shall have been presented to him, the Same shall be a Law, in like Manner as if he had signed it, unless the Congress by their Adjournment prevent its Return, in which Case it shall not be a Law.

Every Order, Resolution, or Vote to which the Concurrence of the Senate and House of Representatives may be necessary (except on a question of Adjournment) shall be presented to the President of the United States; and before the Same shall take Effect, shall be approved by him, or being disapproved by him, shall be repassed by two thirds of the Senate and House of Representatives, according to the Rules and Limitations prescribed in the Case of a Bill.

Section 8

The Congress shall have Power To lay and collect Taxes, Duties, Imposts and Excises, to pay the Debts and provide for the common Defence and general Welfare of the United States; but all Duties, Imposts and Excises shall be uniform throughout the United States;

- To borrow money on the credit of the United States;
- To regulate Commerce with foreign Nations, and among the several States, and with the Indian Tribes;
- To establish an uniform Rule of Naturalization, and uniform Laws on the subject of Bankruptcies throughout the United States;
- To coin Money, regulate the Value thereof, and of foreign Coin, and fix the Standard of Weights and Measures;
- To provide for the Punishment of counterfeiting the Securities and current Coin of the United States;
- To establish Post Offices and Post Roads;
- To promote the Progress of Science and useful Arts, by securing for limited Times to Authors and Inventors the exclusive Right to their respective Writings and Discoveries;
- To constitute Tribunals inferior to the supreme Court;
- To define and punish Piracies and Felonies committed on the high Seas, and Offenses against the Law of Nations;
- To declare War, grant Letters of Marque and Reprisal, and make Rules concerning Captures on Land and Water;
- To raise and support Armies, but no Appropriation of Money to that Use shall be for a longer Term than two Years;
- To provide and maintain a Navy;
- To make Rules for the Government and Regulation of the land and naval Forces;
- To provide for calling forth the Militia to execute the Laws of the Union, suppress Insurrections and repel Invasions;
- To provide for organizing, arming, and disciplining the Militia, and for governing such Part of them as may be employed in the Service of the United States, reserving to the States respectively, the Appointment of the Officers, and the Authority of training the Militia according to the discipline prescribed by Congress;

> To exercise exclusive Legislation in all Cases whatsoever, over such District (not exceeding ten Miles square) as may, by Cession of particular States, and the acceptance of Congress, become the Seat of the Government of the United States, and to exercise like Authority over all Places purchased by the Consent of the Legislature of the State in which the Same shall be, for the Erection of Forts, Magazines, Arsenals, dock-Yards, and other needful Buildings; And

> To make all Laws which shall be necessary and proper for carrying into Execution the foregoing Powers, and all other Powers vested by this Constitution in the Government of the United States, or in any Department or Officer thereof.

Section 9

The Migration or Importation of such Persons as any of the States now existing shall think proper to admit, shall not be prohibited by the Congress prior to the Year one thousand eight hundred and eight, but a tax or duty may be imposed on such Importation, not exceeding ten dollars for each Person.

The privilege of the Writ of Habeas Corpus shall not be suspended, unless when in Cases of Rebellion or Invasion the public Safety may require it.

No Bill of Attainder or ex post facto Law shall be passed.

No capitation, or other direct, Tax shall be laid, unless in Proportion to the Census or Enumeration herein before directed to be taken.

No Tax or Duty shall be laid on Articles exported from any State.

No Preference shall be given by any Regulation of Commerce or Revenue to the Ports of one State over those of another: nor shall Vessels bound to, or from, one State, be obliged to enter, clear, or pay Duties in another.

No Money shall be drawn from the Treasury, but in Consequence of Appropriations made by Law; and a regular Statement and Account of the Receipts and Expenditures of all public Money shall be published from time to time.

No Title of Nobility shall be granted by the United States: And no Person holding any Office of Profit or Trust under them, shall, without the Consent of the Congress, accept of any present, Emolument, Office, or Title, of any kind whatever, from any King, Prince or foreign State.

Section 10

No State shall enter into any Treaty, Alliance, or Confederation; grant Letters of Marque and Reprisal; coin Money; emit Bills of Credit; make any Thing but gold and silver Coin a Tender in Payment of Debts; pass any Bill of Attainder, ex post facto Law, or Law impairing the Obligation of Contracts, or grant any Title of Nobility.

No State shall, without the Consent of the Congress, lay any Imposts or Duties on Imports or Exports, except what may be absolutely necessary for executing it's inspection Laws: and the net Produce of all Duties and Imposts, laid by any State on Imports or Exports, shall be for the Use of the Treasury of the United States; and all such Laws shall be subject to the Revision and Controul of the Congress.

No State shall, without the Consent of Congress, lay any duty of Tonnage, keep Troops, or Ships of War in time of Peace, enter into any Agreement or Compact with another State, or with a foreign Power, or engage in War, unless actually invaded, or in such imminent Danger as will not admit of delay.

Article II

Section 1

The executive Power shall be vested in a President of the United States of America. He shall hold his Office during the Term of four Years, and, together with the Vice-President chosen for the same Term, be elected, as follows: Each State shall appoint, in such Manner as the Legislature thereof may direct, a Number of Electors, equal to the whole Number of Senators and Representatives to which the State may be entitled in the Congress: but no Senator or Representative, or Person holding an Office of Trust or Profit under the United States, shall be appointed an Elector.

The Electors shall meet in their respective States, and vote by Ballot for two persons, of whom one at least shall not lie an Inhabitant of the same State with themselves. And they shall make a List of all the Persons voted for, and of the Number of Votes for each; which List they shall sign and certify, and transmit sealed to the Seat of the Government of the United States, directed to the President of the Senate. The President of the Senate shall, in the Presence of the Senate and House of Representatives, open all the Certificates, and the Votes shall then be counted. The Person having the greatest Number of Votes shall be the President, if such Number be a Majority of the whole Number of Electors appointed; and if there be more than one who have such Majority, and have an equal Number of Votes, then the House of Representatives shall immediately chuse by Ballot one of them for President; and if no Person have a Majority, then from the five highest on the List the said House shall in like Manner chuse the President. But in chusing the President, the Votes shall be taken by States, the Representation from each State having one Vote; a quorum for this Purpose shall consist of a Member or Members from two thirds of the States, and a Majority of all the States shall be necessary to a Choice. In every Case, after the Choice of the President, the Person having the greatest Number of Votes of the Electors shall be the Vice President. But if there should remain two or more who have equal Votes, the Senate shall chuse from them by Ballot the Vice-President.

The Congress may determine the Time of chusing the Electors, and the Day on which they shall give their Votes; which Day shall be the same throughout the United States.

No person except a natural born Citizen, or a Citizen of the United States, at the time of the Adoption of this Constitution, shall be eligible to the Office of President; neither shall any Person be eligible to that Office who shall not have attained to the Age of thirty-five Years, and been fourteen Years a Resident within the United States.

In Case of the Removal of the President from Office, or of his Death, Resignation, or Inability to discharge the Powers and Duties of the said Office, the same shall devolve on the Vice President, and the Congress may by Law provide for the Case of Removal, Death, Resignation or Inability, both of the President and Vice President, declaring what Officer shall then act as President, and such Officer shall act accordingly, until the Disability be removed, or a President shall be elected.

The President shall, at stated Times, receive for his Services, a Compensation, which shall neither be increased nor diminished during the Period for which he shall have been elected, and he shall not receive within that Period any other Emolument from the United States, or any of them.

Before he enter on the Execution of his Office, he shall take the following Oath or Affirmation:

"I do solemnly swear (or affirm) that I will faithfully execute the Office of President of the United States, and will to the best of my Ability, preserve, protect and defend the Constitution of the United States."

Section 2

The President shall be Commander in Chief of the Army and Navy of the United States, and of the Militia of the several States, when called into the actual Service of the United States; he may require the Opinion, in writing, of the principal Officer in each of the executive Departments, upon any subject relating to the Duties of their respective Offices, and he shall have Power to Grant Reprieves and Pardons for Offenses against the United States, except in Cases of Impeachment.

He shall have Power, by and with the Advice and Consent of the Senate, to make Treaties, provided two thirds of the Senators present concur; and he shall nominate, and by and with the Advice and Consent of the Senate, shall appoint Ambassadors, other public Ministers and Consuls, Judges of the supreme Court, and all other Officers of the United States, whose Appointments are not herein otherwise provided for, and which shall be established by Law: but the Congress may by Law vest the Appointment of such inferior Officers, as they think proper, in the President alone, in the Courts of Law, or in the Heads of Departments.

The President shall have Power to fill up all Vacancies that may happen during the Recess of the Senate, by granting Commissions which shall expire at the End of their next Session.

Section 3

He shall from time to time give to the Congress Information of the State of the Union, and recommend to their Consideration such Measures as he shall judge necessary and expedient; he may, on extraordinary Occasions, convene both Houses, or either of them, and in Case of Disagreement between them, with Respect to the Time of Adjournment, he may adjourn them to such Time as he shall think proper; he shall receive Ambassadors and other public Ministers; he shall take Care that the Laws be faithfully executed, and shall Commission all the Officers of the United States.

Section 4

The President, Vice President and all civil Officers of the United States, shall be removed from Office on Impeachment for, and Conviction of, Treason, Bribery, or other high Crimes and Misdemeanors.

Article III

Section 1

The judicial Power of the United States, shall be vested in one supreme Court, and in such inferior Courts as the Congress may from time to time ordain and establish. The Judges, both of the supreme and inferior Courts, shall hold their Offices during good Behavior, and shall, at stated Times, receive for their Services a Compensation which shall not be diminished during their Continuance in Office.

Section 2

The judicial Power shall extend to all Cases, in Law and Equity, arising under this Constitution, the Laws of the United States, and Treaties made, or which shall be made, under their Authority; to all Cases affecting Ambassadors, other public Ministers and Consuls; to all Cases of admiralty and maritime Jurisdiction; to Controversies to which the United States shall be a Party; to Controversies between two or more States; between a State and Citizens of another State; between Citizens of different States; between Citizens of the same State claiming Lands under Grants of different States, and between a State, or the Citizens thereof, and foreign States, Citizens or Subjects.

In all Cases affecting Ambassadors, other public Ministers and Consuls, and those in which a State shall be Party, the supreme Court shall have original Jurisdiction. In all the other Cases before mentioned, the supreme Court shall have appellate Jurisdiction, both as to Law and Fact, with such Exceptions, and under such Regulations as the Congress shall make.

The Trial of all Crimes, except in Cases of Impeachment, shall be by Jury; and such Trial shall be held in the State where the said Crimes shall have been committed; but when not committed within any State, the Trial shall be at such Place or Places as the Congress may by Law have directed.

Section 3

Treason against the United States, shall consist only in levying War against them, or in adhering to their Enemies, giving them Aid and Comfort. No Person shall be convicted of Treason unless on the Testimony of two Witnesses to the same overt Act, or on Confession in open Court.

The Congress shall have power to declare the Punishment of Treason, but no Attainder of Treason shall work Corruption of Blood, or Forfeiture except during the Life of the Person attainted.

Article IV

Section 1

Full Faith and Credit shall be given in each State to the public Acts, Records, and judicial Proceedings of every other State. And the Congress may by general Laws prescribe the Manner in which such Acts, Records and Proceedings shall be proved, and the Effect thereof.

Section 2

The Citizens of each State shall be entitled to all Privileges and Immunities of Citizens in the several States.

A Person charged in any State with Treason, Felony, or other Crime, who shall flee from Justice, and be found in another State, shall on demand of the executive Authority of the State from which he fled, be delivered up, to be removed to the State having Jurisdiction of the Crime.

No Person held to Service or Labour in one State, under the Laws thereof, escaping into another, shall, in Consequence of any Law or Regulation therein, be discharged from such Service or Labour, But shall be delivered up on Claim of the Party to whom such Service or Labour may be due.

Section 3

New States may be admitted by the Congress into this Union; but no new States shall be formed or erected within the Jurisdiction of any other State; nor any State be formed by the Junction of two or more States, or parts of States, without the Consent of the Legislatures of the States concerned as well as of the Congress.

The Congress shall have Power to dispose of and make all needful Rules and Regulations respecting the Territory or other Property belonging to the United States; and nothing in this Constitution shall be so construed as to Prejudice any Claims of the United States, or of any particular State.

Section 4

The United States shall guarantee to every State in this Union a Republican Form of Government, and shall protect each of them against Invasion; and on Application of the Legislature, or of the Executive (when the Legislature cannot be convened) against domestic Violence.

Article V

The Congress, whenever two thirds of both Houses shall deem it necessary, shall propose Amendments to this Constitution, or, on the Application of the Legislatures of two thirds of the several States, shall call a Convention for proposing Amendments, which, in either Case, shall be valid to all Intents and Purposes, as part of this Constitution, when ratified by the Legislatures of three fourths of the several States, or by Conventions in three fourths thereof, as the one or the other Mode of Ratification may be proposed by the

Congress; Provided that no Amendment which may be made prior to the Year One thousand eight hundred and eight shall in any Manner affect the first and fourth Clauses in the Ninth Section of the first Article; and that no State, without its Consent, shall be deprived of its equal Suffrage in the Senate.

Article VI

All Debts contracted and Engagements entered into, before the Adoption of this Constitution, shall be as valid against the United States under this Constitution, as under the Confederation.

This Constitution, and the Laws of the United States which shall be made in Pursuance thereof; and all Treaties made, or which shall be made, under the Authority of the United States, shall be the supreme Law of the Land; and the Judges in every State shall be bound thereby, any Thing in the Constitution or Laws of any State to the Contrary notwithstanding.

The Senators and Representatives before mentioned, and the Members of the several State Legislatures, and all executive and judicial Officers, both of the United States and of the several States, shall be bound by Oath or Affirmation, to support this Constitution; but no religious Test shall ever be required as a Qualification to any Office or public Trust under the United States.

Article VII

The Ratification of the Conventions of nine States, shall be sufficient for the Establishment of this Constitution between the States so ratifying the Same.

Done in Convention by the Unanimous Consent of the States present the Seventeenth Day of September in the Year of our Lord one thousand seven hundred and Eighty seven and of the Independence of the United States of America the Twelfth.

Amendment I (1791)

Congress shall make no law respecting an establishment of religion, or prohibiting the free exercise thereof; or abridging the freedom of speech, or of the press; or the right of the people peaceably to assemble, and to petition the Government for a redress of grievances.

Amendment II (1791)

A well regulated Militia, being necessary to the security of a free State, the right of the people to keep and bear Arms, shall not be infringed.

Amendment III (1791)

No Soldier shall, in time of peace be quartered in any house, without the consent of the Owner, nor in time of war, but in a manner to be prescribed by law.

Amendment IV (1791)

The right of the people to be secure in their persons, houses, papers, and effects, against unreasonable searches and seizures, shall not be violated, and no Warrants shall issue, but upon probable cause, supported by Oath or affirmation, and particularly describing the place to be searched, and the persons or things to be seized.

Amendment V (1791)

No person shall be held to answer for a capital, or otherwise infamous crime, unless on a presentment or indictment of a Grand Jury, except in cases arising in the land or naval forces, or in the Militia, when in actual service in time of War or public danger; nor shall any person be subject for the same offense to be twice put in jeopardy of life or limb; nor shall be compelled in any criminal case to be a witness against himself, nor be deprived of life, liberty, or property, without due process of law; nor shall private property be taken for public use, without just compensation.

Amendment VI (1791)

In all criminal prosecutions, the accused shall enjoy the right to a speedy and public trial, by an impartial jury of the State and district wherein the crime shall have been committed, which district shall have been previously ascertained by law, and to be informed of the nature and cause of the accusation; to be confronted with the witnesses against him; to have compulsory process for obtaining witnesses in his favor, and to have the Assistance of Counsel for his defence.

Amendment VII (1791)

In Suits at common law, where the value in controversy shall exceed twenty dollars, the right of trial by jury shall be preserved, and no fact tried by a jury, shall be otherwise re-examined in any Court of the United States, than according to the rules of the common law.

Amendment VIII (1791)

Excessive bail shall not be required, nor excessive fines imposed, nor cruel and unusual punishments inflicted.

Amendment IX (1791)

The enumeration in the Constitution, of certain rights, shall not be construed to deny or disparage others retained by the people.

Amendment X (1791)

The powers not delegated to the United States by the Constitution, nor prohibited by it to the States, are reserved to the States respectively, or to the people.

Amendment XI (1798)

The Judicial power of the United States shall not be construed to extend to any suit in law or equity, commenced or prosecuted against one of the United States by Citizens of another State, or by Citizens or Subjects of any Foreign State.

Amendment XII (1804)

The Electors shall meet in their respective states, and vote by ballot for President and Vice-President, one of whom, at least, shall not be an inhabitant of the same state with themselves; they shall name in their ballots the person voted for as President, and in distinct ballots the person voted for as Vice-President, and they shall make distinct lists of all persons voted for as President, and of all persons voted for as Vice-President and of the number of votes for each, which lists they shall sign and certify, and transmit sealed to the seat of the government of the United States, directed to the President of the Senate.

- ➤ The President of the Senate shall, in the presence of the Senate and House of Representatives, open all the certificates and the votes shall then be counted.
- ➤ The person having the greatest Number of votes for President, shall be the President, if such number be a majority of the whole number of Electors appointed; and if no person have such majority, then from the persons having the highest numbers not exceeding three on the list of those voted for as President, the House of Representatives shall choose immediately, by ballot, the President. But in choosing the President, the votes shall be taken by states, the representation from each state having one vote; a quorum for this purpose shall consist of a member or members from two-thirds of the states, and a majority of all the states shall be necessary to a choice. And if the House of Representatives shall not choose a President whenever the right of choice shall devolve upon them, before the fourth day of March next following, then the Vice-President shall act as President, as in the case of the death or other constitutional disability of the President.
- ➤ The person having the greatest number of votes as Vice-President, shall be the Vice-President, if such number be a majority of the whole number of Electors appointed, and if no person have a majority, then from the two highest numbers on the list, the Senate shall choose the Vice-President; a quorum for the purpose shall consist of two-thirds of the whole number of Senators, and a majority of the whole number shall be necessary to a choice. But no person constitutionally ineligible to the office of President shall be eligible to that of Vice-President of the United States.

Amendment XIII (1865)

1 Neither slavery nor involuntary servitude, except as a punishment for crime whereof the party shall have been duly convicted, shall exist within the United States, or any place subject to their jurisdiction.

2 Congress shall have power to enforce this article by appropriate legislation.

Amendment XIV (1865)

1 All persons born or naturalized in the United States, and subject to the jurisdiction thereof, are citizens of the United States and of the State wherein they reside. No State shall make or enforce any law which shall abridge the privileges or immunities of citizens of the United States; nor shall any State deprive any person of life, liberty, or property, without due process of law; nor deny to any person within its jurisdiction the equal protection of the laws.

2 Representatives shall be apportioned among the several States according to their respective numbers, counting the whole number of persons in each State, excluding Indians not taxed. But when the right to vote at any election for the choice of electors for President and Vice-President of the United States, Representatives in Congress, the Executive and Judicial officers of a State, or the members of the Legislature thereof, is denied to any of the male inhabitants of such State, being twenty-one years of age, and citizens of the United States, or in any way abridged, except for participation in rebellion, or other crime, the basis of representation therein shall be reduced in the proportion which the number of such male citizens shall bear to the whole number of male citizens twenty-one years of age in such State.

3 No person shall be a Senator or Representative in Congress, or elector of President and Vice-President, or hold any office, civil or military, under the United States, or under any State, who, having previously taken an oath, as a member of Congress, or as an officer of the United States, or as a member of any State legislature, or as an executive or judicial officer of any State, to support the Constitution of the United States, shall have engaged in insurrection or rebellion against the same, or given aid or comfort to the enemies thereof. But Congress may by a vote of two-thirds of each House, remove such disability.

4 The validity of the public debt of the United States, authorized by law, including debts incurred for payment of pensions and bounties for services in suppressing insurrection or rebellion, shall not be questioned. But neither the United States nor any State shall assume or pay any debt or obligation incurred in aid of insurrection or rebellion against the United States, or any claim for the loss or emancipation of any slave; but all such debts, obligations and claims shall be held illegal and void.

5 The Congress shall have power to enforce, by appropriate legislation, the provisions of this article.

Amendment XV (1870)

1 The right of citizens of the United States to vote shall not be denied or abridged by the United States or by any State on account of race, color, or previous condition of servitude.

2 The Congress shall have power to enforce this article by appropriate legislation.

Amendment XVI (1913)

The Congress shall have power to lay and collect taxes on incomes, from whatever source derived, without apportionment among the several States, and without regard to any census or enumeration.

Amendment XVII (1913)

1 The Senate of the United States shall be composed of two Senators from each State, elected by the people thereof, for six years; and each Senator shall have one vote. The electors in each State shall have the qualifications requisite for electors of the most numerous branch of the State legislatures.

2 When vacancies happen in the representation of any State in the Senate, the executive authority of such State shall issue writs of election to fill such vacancies: Provided, That the legislature of any State may empower the executive thereof to make temporary appointments until the people fill the vacancies by election as the legislature may direct.

3 This amendment shall not be so construed as to affect the election or term of any Senator chosen before it becomes valid as part of the Constitution.

Amendment XVIII (1919: Repealed by Amendment XXI, 1933)

1 After one year from the ratification of this article the manufacture, sale, or transportation of intoxicating liquors within, the importation thereof into, or the exportation thereof from the United States and all territory subject to the jurisdiction thereof for beverage purposes is hereby prohibited.

2 The Congress and the several States shall have concurrent power to enforce this article by appropriate legislation.

3 This article shall be inoperative unless it shall have been ratified as an amendment to the Constitution by the legislatures of the several States, as provided in the Constitution, within seven years from the date of the submission hereof to the States by the Congress.

Amendment XIX (1920)

1 The right of citizens of the United States to vote shall not be denied or abridged by the United States or by any State on account of sex.

2 Congress shall have power to enforce this article by appropriate legislation.

Amendment XX (1933)

1 The terms of the President and Vice President shall end at noon on the 20th day of January, and the terms of Senators and Representatives at noon on the 3d day of January, of the years in which such terms would have ended if this article had not been ratified; and the terms of their successors shall then begin.

2 The Congress shall assemble at least once in every year, and such meeting shall begin at noon on the 3d day of January, unless they shall by law appoint a different day.

3 If, at the time fixed for the beginning of the term of the President, the President elect shall have died, the Vice President elect shall become President. If a President shall not have been chosen before the time fixed for the beginning of his term, or if the President elect shall have failed to qualify, then the Vice President elect shall act as President until a President shall have qualified; and the Congress may by law provide for the case wherein neither a President elect nor a Vice President elect shall have qualified, declaring who shall then act as President, or the manner in which one who is to act shall be selected, and such person shall act accordingly until a President or Vice President shall have qualified.

4 The Congress may by law provide for the case of the death of any of the persons from whom the House of Representatives may choose a President whenever the right of choice shall have devolved upon them, and for the case of the death of any of the persons from whom the Senate may choose a Vice President whenever the right of choice shall have devolved upon them.

5 Sections 1 and 2 shall take effect on the 15th day of October following the ratification of this article.

6 This article shall be inoperative unless it shall have been ratified as an amendment to the Constitution by the legislatures of three-fourths of the several States within seven years from the date of its submission.

Amendment XXI (1933)

1 The eighteenth article of amendment to the Constitution of the United States is hereby repealed.

2 The transportation or importation into any State, Territory, or possession of the United States for delivery or use therein of intoxicating liquors, in violation of the laws thereof, is hereby prohibited.

3 The article shall be inoperative unless it shall have been ratified as an amendment to

the Constitution by conventions in the several States, as provided in the Constitution, within seven years from the date of the submission hereof to the States by the Congress.

Amendment XXII (1951)

1 No person shall be elected to the office of the President more than twice, and no person who has held the office of President, or acted as President, for more than two years of a term to which some other person was elected President shall be elected to the office of the President more than once. But this Article shall not apply to any person holding the office of President, when this Article was proposed by the Congress, and shall not prevent any person who may be holding the office of President, or acting as President, during the term within which this Article becomes operative from holding the office of President or acting as President during the remainder of such term.

2 This article shall be inoperative unless it shall have been ratified as an amendment to the Constitution by the legislatures of three-fourths of the several States within seven years from the date of its submission to the States by the Congress.

Amendment XXIII (1961)

1 The District constituting the seat of Government of the United States shall appoint in such manner as the Congress may direct: A number of electors of President and Vice President equal to the whole number of Senators and Representatives in Congress to which the District would be entitled if it were a State, but in no event more than the least populous State; they shall be in addition to those appointed by the States, but they shall be considered, for the purposes of the election of President and Vice President, to be electors appointed by a State; and they shall meet in the District and perform such duties as provided by the twelfth article of amendment.

2 The Congress shall have power to enforce this article by appropriate legislation.

Amendment XXIV (1964)

1 The right of citizens of the United States to vote in any primary or other election for President or Vice President, for electors for President or Vice President, or for Senator or Representative in Congress, shall not be denied or abridged by the United States or any State by reason of failure to pay any poll tax or other tax.

2 The Congress shall have power to enforce this article by appropriate legislation.

Amendment XXV (1967)

1 In case of the removal of the President from office or of his death or resignation, the Vice President shall become President.

2 Whenever there is a vacancy in the office of the Vice President, the President shall nominate a Vice President who shall take office upon confirmation by a majority vote of both Houses of Congress.

3 Whenever the President transmits to the President pro tempore of the Senate and the Speaker of the House of Representatives his written declaration that he is unable to discharge the powers and duties of his office, and until he transmits to them a written declaration to the contrary, such powers and duties shall be discharged by the Vice President as Acting President.

4 Whenever the Vice President and a majority of either the principal officers of the executive departments or of such other body as Congress may by law provide, transmit to the President pro tempore of the Senate and the Speaker of the House of Representatives their written declaration that the President is unable to discharge the powers and duties of his office, the Vice President shall immediately assume the powers and duties of the office as Acting President.

Thereafter, when the President transmits to the President pro tempore of the Senate and the Speaker of the House of Representatives his written declaration that no inability exists, he shall resume the powers and duties of his office unless the Vice President and a majority of either the principal officers of the executive department or of such other body as Congress may by law provide, transmit within four days to the President pro tempore of the Senate and the Speaker of the House of Representatives their written declaration that the President is unable to discharge the powers and duties of his office. Thereupon Congress shall decide the issue, assembling within forty eight hours for that purpose if not in session. If the Congress, within twenty one days after receipt of the latter written declaration, or, if Congress is not in session, within twenty one days after Congress is required to assemble, determines by two thirds vote of both Houses that the President is unable to discharge the powers and duties of his office, the Vice President shall continue to discharge the same as Acting President; otherwise, the President shall resume the powers and duties of his office.

Amendment XXVI (1971)

1 The right of citizens of the United States, who are eighteen years of age or older, to vote shall not be denied or abridged by the United States or by any State on account of age.

2 The Congress shall have power to enforce this article by appropriate legislation.

Amendment XXVII (1992)

No law, varying the compensation for the services of the Senators and Representatives, shall take effect, until an election of Representatives shall have intervened.

Index

Note: Index references to US items in Section B of the textbook are given only where the Section B material is either new or substantial.